The Power and the Writing

The Early Scribes of Mesopotamia

ED - Sargonic

lots of prof. titles

Giuseppe Visicato

CDL Press

Library of Congress Cataloging-in-Publication Data

Visicato, Giuseppe.
The power and the writing : the early scribes of Mesopotamia /Giuseppe Visicato.
p. cm.
Includes index.
ISBN 1-88305-34-71
1. Scribes—Iraq—Babylonia—History. 2. Babylonia—Politics and government. 3. Akkadian language—Writing. 4. Sumerian language—Writing. I. Title.

DS69.9.V58 2000
935–dc21 99-053811

The design on the cover is based upon the Sargonic seal of the scribe Kalki, which is housed in the British Museum.

ISBN 1-883053-471

TABLE OF CONTENTS

INTRODUCTION

CHAPTER I

Scribes from the Early Dynastic to the Early Sargonic Periods

Chapter II

Scribes in the Classical Sargonic Period

Conclusions

PREFACE

In my previous work, *The Bureaucracy of Šuruppak* (Münster, 1995), pages 141–44, I compared the number of scribes mentioned in the administrative documents from Fara to the number of scribes in pre-Ur III Mesopotamian administrative archives. The present work, through a systematic contextual analysis, lists all the scribes—as complete a list as possible at this time—mentioned in the administrative documentation from the Pre-Sargonic through the Sargonic periods. Further, I discuss the roles and functions of these scribes within the institutions in which they worked.

In addition, I have tried to identify, using the limited information available to us from these texts, the continuity and transformation of the role of the scribe in the 350- to 400-year time span covered by the documentation of their institutional structures, that is, from early ED Ur to the end of the Sargonic period.

This study reveals that the earliest scribes were not mere compilers of administrative records. Rather, they were major figures in the management of economic and political power in Mesopotamian society. In reality, the scribe, more than anyone else, seems to have been, from the beginning of the urban revolution, the official who headed administrative organizations and continued in this capacity for centuries in a society undergoing social and economic change. The scribe was, in a phrase, the embodiment of the managerial and technical skills needed to effectively oversee the bureaucratic machinery of political power.

ACKNOWLEDGMENTS

I am greatly indebted to, and thank, Profs. Josef Bauer, Benjamin R. Foster, and Aage Westenholz for their detailed revision of this book and for their corrections and most useful suggestions. My warm thanks to Profs. Jean-Jacques Glassner, Pietro Mander, and Francesco Pomponio, who, besides reading this work, made important corrections and offered many suggestions. All these colleagues have been of constant encouragement and scholarly stimulation during my research.

Access to much unpublished material was generously shared with me by colleagues, whose generosity I acknowledge here. Unpublished documents from Fara and Sargonic Nippur housed in the University Museum of the University of Pennsylvania were placed at my disposal by Prof. Aage Westenholz. Prof. Benjamin R. Foster shared with me unpublished documents from Sargonic Girsu and Fara in the Yale Babylonian Collection. Prof. Jean-Jacques Glassner placed at my disposal unpublished documents from Sargonic Girsu in the Louvre Museum. A small group of unpublished Sargonic documents from Umma at the Museo Egizio in Turin were made available to me by Prof. Francesco Pomponio. For permission to study the unpublished Schmidt tablets from Fara and the late ED tablets from Ur housed in the University Museum, I thank Prof. Erle Leichty, Curator of the Babylonian Section. I state my appreciation to Prof. John Brinkman, who made available a Fara contract housed in the Oriental Institute of the University of Chicago.

For collations of the published Telloh tablets in the Istanbul Archaeological Museum, I am indebted to Benjamin R. Foster, and I thank the Antiquities Authorities of the Republic of Turkey, the Director of the Istanbul Archaeological Museum and his colleagues Veysel Donbaz and Fatma Yildiz.

I am also indebted to Prof. Manfred Sommerfeld, who generously placed at my disposal the transliterations of tablets of MAD 1 from the Oriental Institute of Chicago University, collated again, and still unpublished.

Finally, I thank Dr. Aiden Feerick, who once more undertook the translation of my manuscript into English.

ABBREVIATIONS

The abbreviations used are those of the *Assyrian Dictionary of the Oriental Institute of the University of Chicago*, with the following additions.

A.	Tablets in the Collections of the Oriental Institute. The University of Chicago
A	Tablets from Himrin Area in the Iraq Museum
AAICAB I 1	J.-P. Grégoire, *Contribution à l'Histoire Sociale, économique, Politique et culturelle du Proche-Orient Ancien* (Paris, 1996)
AAS	J.-P. Grégoire, *Archives Administrative Sumeriennes* (Paris, 1970)
Ad	Tablets in the Adab Collection of the Archaeological Museum of Istanbul
AfO 22	D. O. Edzard, "Die Inschriften der altakkadischen Rollsiegel," *AfO* 22 (1968–69): 12–20
AIA	Texts in the Collection of the Australian Institute of Archeology
Akkad	M. Liverani, ed., *Akkad. The First World Empire* (HANE V; Padua, 1993)
AOTb	Tablets from Telloh in the Collections of the Musée du Louvre
Archaic Bookkeeping	H. Nissen - P. Damerow - R. K. Englund, *Archaic Bookkeeping. Early Writing and Techniques of Economic Administration in the Ancient Near East* (English translation from *Frühe Schrift und Techniken der Wirtschaftsverwaltung im alten Vorderen Orient* [Berlin 1990]; Chicago, 1993)
ARRIM, *Annual Review*	*The Annual Report of the Royal Inscriptions of Mesopotamia Project* Toronto 1983–

ASJ	*Acta Sumerologica* (Hiroshima)
AVG I	J. Marzahn, *Altsumerische Verwaltungstexte aus Girsu/Lagaš* (Vorderasiatische Schriftdenkmäler der staatlichen Museen zu Berlin, Neue Folge, Heft IX; Berlin, 1991)
AVG II	J. Marzahn, *Altsumerische Verwaltungstexte aus Girsu/Lagaš* (Vorderasiatische Schriftdenkmäler der staatlichen Museen zu Berlin, Neue Folge, Heft XI; Berlin, 1996)
AWAS	J. G. Selz, *Altsumerische Wirtschaftsurkunden aus amerikanischen Sammlungen* (FAOS 15, 2; Stuttgart, 1993)
AWEL	J. G. Selz, *Altsumerische Verwaltungstexte aus Lagaš* (FAOS 15, 1; Stuttgart, 1989)
AWL	J. Bauer, *Altsumerische Wirtschaftstexte aus Lagaš*, (Rome, 1972)
BAOM	Bulletin of the Ancient Orient Museum (Tokyo)
BIN 8	G. G. Hackman, *Sumerian and Akkadian Administrative Texts from Predynastic Times to the End of the Akkad Dynasty* (New Haven, 1958)
Böhl Coll.	Tablets in F. M. T. de L. Böhl Collections, Rijksmuseum van Oudheden (Leiden)
BSA	*Bulletin of Sumerian Agriculture* (Cambridge, United Kingdom)
Buch. 1966	B. Buchanan, *Catalogue of Ancient Near Eastern Seals in the Ashmolean Museum*, vol. I, (Oxford, 1966)
Buch. 1981	B. Buchanan, *Early Near Eastern Seals in the Yale Babylonian Collection* (New Haven, 1981)
Bureau	G. Visicato, *The Bureaucracy of Šuruppak* (Münster, 1995)
CHÉU	G. Contenau, *Contribution à l'histoire économique d'Umma* (Paris, 1915)
CIRPL	E. Sollberger, *Corpus des Inscriptions royales présargoniques de Lagaš* (Geneva, 1956)
Collon	D. Collon, *Catalogue of the Western Asiatic Seals of British Museum, Cylinder Seals II* (Dorchester, 1982)

J. Cooper, *Inscriptions*	J. Cooper, *Pre-Sargonic Inscriptions* (SARI 1; New Haven, 1986)
CST	Th. Fish, *Catalogue of the Sumerian Tablets in the John Rylands Library* (Manchester, 1932)
CT 50	E. Sollberger, *Cuneiform Texts from Babylonian Tablets in the British Museum*, Part L (London, 1972)
CTNMC	Th. Jacobsen, *Cuneiform Texts in the National Museum, Copenhagen* (Leiden, 1939)
DCS	D. Charpin - J. M. Durand, *Documents cunéiformes de Strasbourg* (Paris, 1981)
DP	M. Allotte de la Fuÿe, *Documents Présargoniques* (Paris, 1908–1920)
ECTJ	A. Westenholz, *Early Cuneiform Texts in Jena* (Copenhagen, 1975)
EDATŠ	F. Pomponio - G. Visicato, *Early Dynastic Administrative Tablets of Šuruppak* (IUON *Series Maior* VI; Naples, 1994)
ELTS	I. J. Gelb - P. Steinkeller - R. M. Whiting, *Earliest Land Tenure Systems in the Near East: Ancient Kudurrus* (OIP 104; Chicago, 1992)
Englund, *Fischerei*	R. Englund, *Organisation und Verwaltung der Ur III Fischerei* (BBVO 10; Berlin, 1990)
F	Field number of Schmidt's tablets from Fara kept in the University Museum of the University of Pennsylvania
FAOS	*Freiburger Altorientalische Studien* (Stuttgart, 1975–)
FAOS 7	I. J. Gelb - B. Kienast, *Die altakkadischen Königsinschriften des dritten Jahrtausends v. Chr.* (FAOS 7; Stuttgart, 1990)
FAOS 19	B. Kienast - K. Volk, *Die sumerischen und akkadischen Briefe des III. Jahrtausends aus der Zeit vor der III. Dynastie von Ur* (FAOS 19; Stuttgart, 1995)
Foster, *Agriculture*	B. R. Foster, "Agriculture and Accountability in Ancient Mesopotamia," in H. Weiss, ed., *The Origins of Cities in Dry-Farming Syria and Mesopotamia in the Third Millennium B.C.* (Guilford, Conn., 1986), pp. 109–28

Foster, *Archives*	B. R. Foster, "Archives and Empire in Sargonic Mesopotamia," *CRRAI* 30 (1983): 46–52
Foster, *Ethnicity*	B. R. Foster, "Ethnicity and Onomastics in Sargonic Mesopotamia," *Or*NS 51 (1982): 297–354
Foster, *Inst. Land*	B. R. Foster, *Administration and Use of Institutional Land in Sargonic Sumer* (Mesopotamia 9; Copenhagen, 1982)
Foster, *JANES* 12	B. R. Foster, "Notes on Sargonic Royal Progress," *JANES* 12 (1980): 29–42
Foster, *Management*	B. R. Foster, "Management and Administration in the Sargonic Period," *Akkad* (1993): 25–39
Foster, *People*	B. R. Foster, "People, Land, and Produce at Sargonic Gasur," in M. A. Morrison and D. I. Owen, eds., *Studies on the Civilization and Culture of Nuzi and the Hurrians* 2 (Winona Lake, Ind., 1987)
Foster, *ZA* 72	B. R. Foster, "Archives and Record-Keeping in Sargonic Mesopotamia," *ZA* 72 (1982): 1–27
Genava 26	E. Sollberger, *Documents cunéiformes au Musée d'Art et Histoire* (Genava 26; 1948), pp. 48–71
Gibson-Biggs, *Seal*	MacGuire Gibson - R. Biggs, eds., *Seal and Sealing in Ancient Near East* (Malibu, Calif., 1977)
IAS	R. Biggs, *Inscriptions from Tell Abū Ṣalābīkh* (OIP 99; Chicago, 1974)
IM	Tablets in the Collection of the Iraq Museum, Baghdad
JAC	*Journal of Ancient Civilizations* (Changchun)
JANES	*Journal of the Ancient Near Eastern Society of Columbia University* (New York)
JEOL	Jaarbericht (van het Vooraziatisch-Egyptish genootschop) "Ex Oriente Lux" (Leiden)
L	Tablets in the Telloh Collection of the Archaeological Museum of Istanbul
Labor	M. A. Powell, ed., *Labor in the Ancient Near East* (AOS 68; New Haven, 1987)

LAK	A. Deimel, *Die Inschriften von Fara I. Liste der archaischen Keilschriftzeichen* (WVDOG 40; Leipzig, 1922)
LdE	L. Cagni, ed., *La lingua di Ebla* (Naples, 1981)
LEM	P. Michalowski, *Letters from Early Mesopotamia* (Atlanta, 1993)
Liverani, *Oriente*	M. Liverani, *Antico Oriente. Storia Società Economia* (Bari, 1988)
MacGuire Gibson, *Kiš*	MacGuire Gibson, *The City and Area of Kiš* (Miami, 1972)
Maekawa, Mes. 8/9	K. Maekawa, "The Development of the É-MÍ in Lagaš during Early Dynastic III," *Mesopotamia* 8/9 (1973–1974): 77–144
Margueron, *recherches*	J. Margueron, *Recherches sur les Palais mésopotamiens de l'Age du bronze* (Paris, 1982)
Martin, *Fara*	H. P. Martin, *Fara: A Reconstruction of the Ancient Mesopotamian City of Shuruppak* (Birmingham, 1988)
MEE	Materiali Epigrafici di Ebla (Naples-Rome, 1979–)
MEE 3	G. Pettinato, *Testi lessicali monolingui della biblioteca L. 2769* (Naples, 1981)
Michail Coll.	G. Pettinato, *L'uomo cominciò a scrivere. Iscrizioni cuneiformi della collezione Michail* (Milan, 1997)
NFT	G. Cros, *Nouvelles fouilles de Telloh* (Paris, 1910)
Nik I	M. V. Nikol'skij, *Dokumenty chozjajstvennoj otčetnosti drevnejšej epochi chaldei iz sobranija N. P. Lichačeva* I (St. Petersburg, 1908)
Nik II	M. V. Nikol'skij, *Dokumenty chozjajstvennoj otčetnosti drevnejšej epochi chaldei is sobranija N. P. Lichačeva* II (Moscow, 1915)
Nissen, *Protostoria*	H. Nissen, *Protostoria del Vicino Oriente* (Italian translation of *Gründzüge einer Geschichte der Frühzeit des Vorderen Orients* [Darmstadt, 1983]; Bari, 1990)
NSRJ	J. Krecher, "Neue sumerische Rechtsurkunden der 3. Jahrtausends," *ZA* 63 (1974): 145–271

NTSŠ	R. Jestin, *Nouvelles tablettes sumériennes de Šuruppak au Musée d'Istanbul* (Paris, 1957)
OAIC	I. J. Gelb, *Old Akkadian Inscriptions in Chicago Natural History Museum* (Fieldiana, Anthropology 4/2; Chicago, 1955)
Orient	Orient, Report of the Society for Near Eastern Studies in Japan (Tokyo)
OSP 1	A. Westenholz, *Old Sumerian and Old Akkadian Texts in Philadelphia Chiefly from Nippur* (Malibu, Calif., 1975)
OSP 2	A. Westenholz, *Old Sumerian and Old Akkadian Texts in Philadelphia* (Copenhagen, 1987)
Powell, *HUCA* 49	M. Powell, "Texts from the Time of Lugalzagesi. Problems and Perspectives in Their Interpretation," *HUCA* 49 (1978): 1–58
PPAC 1	Yang Zhi, *Sargonic Inscriptions from Adab* (PPAC 1; Chanchun, 1989)
PUL	H. Limet, *Étude de documents de la période d'Agadé appartenant à l'Université de Liège* (Paris, 1973)
Rasheed, Himrin 4	F. Rasheed, *The Ancient Inscriptions in Himrin Area* (Himrin 4; Baghdad, 1981)
Rép. géogr.	*Répertoire Géographique des textes Cunéiformes* (Wiesbaden, 1977–)
RIAA	L. Speleers, *Recueil des inscriptions de l'Asie antérieure des Musées Royaux du Cinquantenaire à Bruxelles* (Brussels, 1925)
RIM 2	D. Frayne, *The Royal Inscriptions of Mesopotamia, Early Periods 2, Sargonic and Gutian Periods* (RIM 2; Toronto, 1993)
Salonen, *Fischerei*	A. Salonen, *Die Fischerei in alten Mesopotamien* (Helsinki, 1970)
SEL	*Studi epigrafici e linguistici sul vicino oriente Antico* (Verona)
SRJ	D. O. Edzard, *Sumerische Rechtsurkunden des III. Jahrtausends aus der Zeit vor der III. Dynastie von Ur* (Munich, 1968)
StEb	Studi Eblaiti (Rome, 1979–)

Struve, *Onomastika*	V. V. Struke, *Onomastika rannedinasticeskogo Lagaša* (Moscow, 1984)
STTI	V. Donbaz-B. R. Foster, *Sargonic Texts from Telloh in the Istanbul Archaeological Museums* (Philadelphia, 1982)
Studies Hallo	M. E. Cohen - D. C. Snell- D. B. Weisberg, eds., *The Tablet and the Scroll, Studies in Honor of W. W. Hallo* (Bethesda, Md., 1993)
TLAT	P. Steinkeller - J. N. Postgate, *Third-Millennium Legal and Administrative Texts in the Iraq Museum, Baghdad* (Winona Lake, Ind., 1992)
TSŠ	R. Jestin, *Tablettes sumériennes de Šuruppak conservèes au Musée de Stamboul* (Paris, 1937)
UET 2	E. Burrows, *Ur Excavations, Texts 2* (London, 1935)
Ung	M. Lambert, "Quatre nouveaux contrats de l'époque de Shuruppak," in M. Lurker, ed., *In Memoriam Eckhard Unger. Beiträge zu Geschichte, Kultur und Religion des Alten Orients* (Baden-Baden, 1971)
UNT	H. Waetzoldt, *Untersuchungen zur neusumerischen textilindustrie* (Rome, 1972)
UGASL	G. Selz, *Untersurchungen zur Götterwelt des altsumerischen Stadtstaates von Lagaš* (Philadelphia, 1995)
USP	B. R. Foster, *Umma in the Sargonic Period* (Hamden, Conn., 1982)
VDI	Vestnik drevnej istorii (Moscow)
Westenholz, *Circulation*	A. Westenholz, "The Sargonic Period," in A. Archi, ed., *Circulation of Goods in Non-Palatial Context in the Ancient Near East* (Rome, 1984), pp. 17–30.
WF	A. Deimel, *Die Inschriften von Fara III. Wirtschaftstexte aus Fara* (WVDOG 45; Leipzig, 1924)
ZATU	M. W. Green - H. J. Nissen, *Zeichenliste der archaischen Texte aus Uruk* (Berlin, 1987)

CHRONOLOGY

Reference to the following time periods and reigns occur throughout the book. The dates provided below, particularly those before the reign of Sargon of Akkad, are approximate.

Uruk V :	3700	to	3300 B.C.
Uruk IV :	3300	to	3100
Uruk III/Jemdet Nasr :	3100	to	2900
ED (=Early Dynastic) :	2900	to	2350
Early ED :	2900	to	2700
Late ED :	2450	to	2350
ED II :	2750	to	2600
ED III :	2600	to	2350
ED IIIa :	2600	to	2450
ED IIIb/Pre-Sargonic :	2450	to	2350
Archaic Ur :	2700	to	2600
Fara Period :	2600	to	2550
Abū Ṣalābīkh :	2550	to	2500
Entemena :	2400	to	2370
Enanatum :	2370		
Enentarzi :	2369	to	2365
Lugalanda :	2364	to	2357
Lugalzagesi :	2360	to	2335
Urukagina :	2357	to	2350
Sargonic :	2350	to	2150
Early Sargonic :	2350	to	2250
Classical Sargonic :	2250	to	2200
Late Sargonic :	2200	to	2150
Sargon :	2334	to	2279
Rimuš :	2278	to	2270
Maništusu :	2269	to	2255
Narām-Sîn :	2254	to	2218
Šar-kali-šarrī :	2217	to	2193
Šu-Dural :	2168	to	2154
Post-Sargonic :	2150	to	2100
Gudea :	2120	to	2100
Ur III :	2112	to	2004 B.C.

INTRODUCTION

The Earliest Scribal Activity

Studies of Mesopotamian scribes have focused on the education and development of these officials.[1] An exception is the work of H. Waetzoldt,[2] who, through his detailed analysis of the Ur III documentation, identifies scribes as having a specialized role of the highest importance within the institutional administration.

---

1. For a general discussion on this subject, cf. B. Landsberger, *Scribal Concepts of Education,* in C. H. Kraeling – R. M. Adams, eds., *City Invincible* (Chicago, 1960), pp. 94–102; A. Leo Oppenheim, "A Note on the Scribes in Mesopotamia," in T. H. Gütebork – Th. Jacobsen, eds., *Studies in Honor of Benno Landsberger,* AS 16 (Chicago, 1965), pp. 253–56; A. Leo Oppenheim, *Ancient Mesopotamia* (Chicago, 1977), pp. 235–49. For the most recent works on this topic with a relevant bibliography, cf. D. W. Baker, "Scribes as Transmitters of Tradition," in A. R. Millard – J. N. Hoffmeier – D. K. Baker, eds., *Faith, Tradition and History. Old Testament Historiography in Its Near East Context* (Winona Lake, Ind. 1994), pp. 65–77; L. E. Pierce, "The Scribes and Scholars of Ancient Mesopotamia," in J. M. Sasson, ed., *Civilizations of the Ancient Near East* (New York, 1995), pp. 2265–78; H. L. J. Vanstiphout, "On the Old Eduba Education," in J. W. Drjvers – A. A. Mac Donald, eds., *Centres of Learning. Learning and Location in Pre-Modern Europe and the Near East* (Leiden/New York/Köln, 1995), pp. 3–16; K. R. Nemet-Nejat, "Systems for Learning Mathematics in Mesopotamian Scribal Schools," *JNES* 54 (1995): 241–60.

   For a more detailed analysis of the education of the scribes in the documentation of the third millennium, see A. Westenholz, "Old Akkadian School Texts," *AfO* 25 (1974): 95–110; B. R. Foster, "Education of a Bureaucrat in Sargonic Sumer," *ArOr* 50 (1982): 238–41; H. Waetzoldt, "Keilschrift und Schulen in Mesopotamien und Ebla," in L. Kriss-Rettenbeck – M. Liedtke, eds., *Erziehungs und Unterrichtsmethoden im historischen Wandel* (Heilbrunn, 1986), pp. 36–50; *idem,* "Der Schreiber als Lehrer in Mesopotamien," in J. G. Prinz von Hohenzollern – M. Liedtke, eds., *Schreiber, Magister, Lehrer* (Heilbrunn, 1989), pp. 33–50; and G. Pettinato, *I Sumeri* (Milan, 1992), pp. 347–58.

2. *Das Schreiberwesen in Mesopotamien nach Texten aus neusumerisches Zeit,* an unpublished Habilitationschrift (Heidelberg, 1974).

A similar but shorter study, based on non-Mesopotamian texts from a later period, was conducted by L. M. Muntingh.[3] Although his data is removed both in time and place from the Ur III period, he agrees, in general terms, with Waetzoldt's conclusions concerning the importance of the scribe in all aspects of public life.[4]

The conclusions reached in this study on the role of Pre-Sargonic and Sargonic scribes in Mesopotamia agree with those of Waetzoldt and Muntingh. The most important institutional officials, whether they be of the palace or of the temple, come from the "corporation" of the scribes.[5]

The term dub-sar, "scribe," first appears in the archaic texts of Ur. Although the term dub-sar occurs only once or twice at Ur, it occurs frequently in ED III Šuruppak (=Fara). The terms agrig and um-mi-a first appear in the Fara texts. In texts of the Jemdet Nasr-Uruk III period apparently there is no term to designate this official.

While in ED Lú E, the professions list, which appears for the first time at Fara, the profession of dub-sar (probably an abbreviation for dub-sar-maḫ) occurs in first position.[6] There is no equivalent term in the earliest lexical lists of Uruk, ED Lú A–D,[7] copies of which have been

---

3. "The Role of the Scribe according to the Mari Texts: A Study of Terminology," *Journal of Semitics* 2 (1991): 21–51.

4. A previous study of the scribes of the middle of the second millennium in Ugarit was conducted by A. F. Rainey, "The Scribe at Ugarit. His Position and Influence," *Proceedings of the Israel Academy of Sciences and Humanities* 3 (1968): 126–47

5. Expressions of the type PN_1 dub-sar PN_2, PN_1 dumu PN_2 dub-sar, or PN_1 dub-sar dumu PN_2 dub-sar occur at Fara, ED IIIb, and Sargonic Girsu. This suggests the practice of transmitting the office of scribe from father to son, which appears to be documented from the time of Ur III (cf. AAS, p. 103; H. Waetzoldt, "Zur Weiterverwendung mesopotamischer Siegel im Karum Kaniš," *NABU* [1990]: 48) was already widespread in the Pre-Sargonic and Sargonic periods. However, these expressions do not always mean that PN_1 is the son of PN_2. In Fara and Ur III documents it can sometimes indicate that PN_1 is a subordinate of PN_2 (cf. EDATŠ, p. 63 and F. Pomponio, "Lukalla of Umma," *ZA* 82 [1992]: 169, n. 1, with bibliography).

6. MSL XII, pp. 16–21; MEE 3, pp. 7–46.

7. MSL XII pp. 4–16; MEE 3 pp. 3–25; R. K. Englund – H. Nissen, *Die lexikalischen Listen der archaischen Texte aus Uruk* (Berlin, 1993), pp. 16–18, 69–86.

found in Ur, Fara, Abū Ṣalābīkh, and Nippur. In one of these lists, ED Lú B from Fara,[8] the sanga (or perhaps the sanga-GAR) is in the first position; but it follows dub-sar in ED Lú E. The first 17 lines of this latter list mention high-ranking officials, but the sequence appears to be more random than hierarchical. A different situation occurs at the beginning of the long Names and Professions lists, in which each official is listed with his name, title (e.g., énsi, sanga, sa$_{12}$-du$_{5}$, dub-sar-<maḫ>, šagina), and/or name of city.[9] My analysis of the economic documents from Fara has identified the existence of a clearly defined hierarchy among the dignitaries and officials of the institution that governed and administered Šuruppak in the ED period. At the head of this hierarchy was the énsi, followed by the sanga-GAR, sa$_{12}$-du$_{5}$, dub-sar-maḫ, and then other officials of high rank.[10] This hierarchy fits very well with the beginning sequence of the Names and Professions lists.

R. D. Biggs[11] observes that the profession indicated by the sign SANGA should be understood as šid, "the accounting official," or as umbisag, "administrator," contrary to A. Deimel, ŠL 314, 28: "sanga-priest." Biggs notes that even if the profession of sanga appears to be distinct from that of dub-sar in the Fara period, the same anthroponyms that carry the title sanga in the colophon of lexical texts assume the title dub-sar in certain administrative texts.[12] In particular, the profession sanga-dub, which appears with a certain frequency in some lexical and

8. For ED Lú B from Fara, see A. Cavigneaux, "Lexikalische Listen," *RlA* 6 (L), p. 614.

9. The copies of this list come from Abū Ṣalābīkh (R. D. Biggs, IAS, pp. 62–71), Ebla (MEE 3, 125–34; A. Archi, "La 'lista di nomi e professioni' ad Ebla," *StEb* 4 [1981]: 177–204), and an unknown site dating to the Ur III period (F. M. Fales – Th. J. H. Krispijn, "An Early Ur III Copy of the Abū-Ṣalābīkh 'Names and Professions' List," *JEOL* 26 [1980]: 39–46).

10. Cf. *Bureau,* p. 138.

11. R. D. Biggs, "Semitic Names in the Fara Period," *Or*NS 36 (1967): 59, n. 1; *idem,* IAS, p. 33.

12. R. D. Biggs, IAS, p. 34 and D. O. Edzard, "Die Archive von Šuruppag (Fāra): Umgang und Grenzen der Auswertbarkeit," *OLA* 5 (1979): 154–55.

administrative texts in Uruk III,[13] may indicate the profession of scribe in this period. [14]

There is other evidence to support the proposed equivalence in function of the sanga in the Uruk III period and of the dub-sar in subsequent periods. In fact, when one compares the specialized types of sanga that occur both in lexical texts from Uruk III[15] and administrative texts from Uruk III and Jemdet Nasr[16] with the specialized dub-sar occurring in later documentation from Fara to the Sargonic period one could suppose that these profession names indicate the same function.[17]

The presence, for the first time, of the term dub-sar in the documents of Early ED Ur does not appear to be by chance. If the texts from

---

13. R. K. Englund – H. Nissen, *Die Lexikalischen Listen*, p. 279, sub sanga-dub; R. K. Englund, *Archaic Administrative Texts from Uruk. The Early Campaigns* (Berlin, 1994), p. 152, *sub voce*. See also ZATU, p. 268, *sub* 244. This professional name is absent in the Jemdet Nasr texts.

14. R. B. Englund – H. Nissen, *Archaic Bookkeeping*, p. 147. H. Waetzoldt, "Die Entwicklung der Naturwissenschaften und des naturwissenschaftlichen Unterrichts in Mesopotamien," in J. G. Prinz – M. Liedtke, eds., *Naturwissenschaftlicher Unterricht und Wissenskumulation* (Heilbronn, 1988), p. 46, n. 56, presents an idea already put forth in *Archaic Bookkeeping*, p. 180, "Da die Berufsbezeichnung SANGA=umbisag (?) mit dem Zeichen ŠID, das 'zahlen, rechnen' bedeutet, geschrieben wurde, sehe ich darin den alten Begriff fur 'Rechner'. Dub-sar 'Schreiber' scheint jünger (kommt erst in der offenbar jüngeren ED lu E vor, vgl. MSL 12, S. 8–17; Pettinato [1981], p. XXVIII mit Anm. 91, S. 23 zu Zeile 46, S. 41 zu Zeile 2). Der Begriff SANGA = umbisag (?) wurde offenbar nur bis in die Fara-Zeit benutzt (vgl. Biggs [1974], S. 33 mit Anm. 29). Die Funktionen der 'Rechner' gingen danach offenbar auf die Schreiber (dub-sar) über."

15. R. K. Englund – H. Nissen, *Die Lexikalischen Listen*, pp. 278–80.

16. R. K. Englund, *Archaic Administrative Texts from Uruk*, p. 152, *sub voce* sanga$_a$ and sanga$_b$; R. K. Englund – J. P. Grégoire, *The Proto-Cuneiform Texts from Jemdet Nasr* (Berlin, 1991), p. 138, *sub voce* sanga. See also ZATU, p. 268, *sub voce* 444.

The types of sanga attested are: sanga-aša$_5$, sanga-abgal, sanga-kisal, sanga-kurušda, sanga-ib, sanga-SUḪUR, sanga-sukkal, sanga-UMUN$_2$(simug$^?$), and others of obscure meaning: sanga-ZATU 729, sanga-ZATU 737+DI, sanga-ZATU 737+U$_4$, sanga-ZATU 737+SAL, sanga-ZATU 737+GAR, sanga-ZATU 739, sanga-ZATU 741, sanga-ZATU 743, sanga-ZATU 747.

17. dub-sar-anše, dub-sar-aša$_5$, dub-sar-kurušda, dub-sar-na-gada, dub-sar-sagi, dub-sar-kuš$_7$, dub-sar-tigi$_x$(BALAG)-di, dub-sar-udu; cf. *infra*, TABLES 2, 12, 13, 18, 20.

Uruk and Jemdet Nasr represent the first phase of what will become Mesopotamia's greatest tradition, namely, recording and accounting, then the archaic texts from Ur—a few centuries later than the texts from Uruk—are certainly at a more advanced stage. The writing technique remained, in many ways, close to that of Uruk, but the document recording methodology is clearly much closer to that of Fara than to the more primitive and cumbersome technique employed at Uruk.[18] From the texts from Ur one can observe how the need for simplification in the recording of data caused the abandonment of the complex measurement systems adopted in Uruk, which are connected with production methods and conservation techniques, in favor of more standardized systems of units of measurement. The tablet is clearly divided into lines and columns in which each line records a single entry. The first item carries an indication of the type of goods (if more than one type of goods is indicated, subsequent lines indicate the other goods) and the unit of measurement used. This is not repeated again except in the summary. Each line contains a numerical indicator (the amount of goods), an anthroponym, and sometimes the professional name of the official involved in the transaction. At the end of the list of transactions, which generally is of goods received, the sum—indicated in some cases by the term an-šè-gú—is recorded. The innovation is that explanatory phrases concerning the transactions are clearly written in Sumerian[19]; in the oldest texts they were expressed by symbolic or ideographic indicators that "could have been read in any of a number of languages."[20] It is clear from such innovations that there must have been a category of officials that performed the role of scribes and that this group was not limited to a few people.

---

18. Cf. *Archaic Bookkeeping*, p. 76.

19. UET 2, 102, aša$_5$ apin šà ma-gíd. There are analogous phrases in 168 and 185. In 184 occurs aša$_5$-en gíd-a apin; in 162 še sanga-lugal; in 183 še sanga-èš.

20. R. K. Englund – H. Nissen, *Archaic Bookkeeping*, pp. 116–17. *Idem* p. 117, "in the earliest phase of writing, the signs usually designated concepts or nominal and perhaps also verbal roots, although lacking any apparent syntactic relation within the texts"; cf. also P. Michalowski, "Early Mesopotamian Communicative System: Art, Literature and Writing," in A. C. Gunter, ed., *Investigating Artistic Environments in the Ancient Near East* (Washington D.C., 1990), p. 58.

It seems clear that the absence at Uruk and Jemdet Nasr and the infrequent mention in Early ED Ur of a specific term to indicate scribes, compared to the frequent use of a term in the immediately subsequent documentation from Fara, indicate a developmental issue whose roots must lie in historical processes connected with profound economic and structural changes in society and its system of organization.[21] But in regard to these processes, which are scantily documented by archaeology, we do not possess any written documentation. It is probable that this historical process, which may have begun in the archaic period at Ur, had its greatest rate of change during the hegemony of Kiš, which archaeological evidence places in ED II–III.[22] The documentation at ED IIIa Šuruppak, along with the violent destruction of that site, may be testimony of the end of that historic phase.

Features of Pre-Sargonic and Sargonic Documentation

The documents analyzed in this work span several periods. In the Pre-Sargonic period there are just a few sites that have yielded tablets. In the Sargonic period there are many sites and closely linked historical periods. While archaeology attests to continual occupation at sites such as Adab, Girsu, and Nippur, there is no evidence of scribal continuity, although assuredly it must have existed. Girsu, the site that has yielded the most tablets, has no administrative documents from the period of Urukagina[23] to Lugal-ušum-gal. The same can be said of other sites. Perhaps their archives were periodically destroyed once they were deemed

---

21. Similar conclusions have been expressed recently by P. Mander, "I testi amministrativi e la sigillatura: gli archivi del III millennio," in M. Perna, ed., *Administrative Documents in Aegean and Their Near Eastern Counterparts* (Naples, 1996), p. 12, "il termine dub-sar apre la lista ED lu E. Dal momento che la lista appare per la prima volta ad Abu-Salabikh ed a Abu-Salabikh appare per l'ultima volta il termina umbisag (in testi UD.GAL.NUN) si deve ritenere che nella metà del III millennio fosse in atto una profonda trasformazione della terminologia scribale."

22. McGuire Gibson, *The City and Area of Kish* (Miami, 1972), pp. 48, 52, 268; G. Visicato, *Il ruolo della città di Kiš in epoca Pre-Sargonica,* unpublished dissertation (Rome, 1989), pp. 42–60; EDATŠ, pp. 14–17.

23. For the reading Urukagina or Irikagina, instead of UruKAgina or Uruinimgina, cf. P. Steinkeller, *JAOS* 115 (1995): 541–42.

no longer useful, a practice that seems to have occurred at Fara. The preservation of archives that have reached us is frequently the fortunate result of the violent destruction of a site, as at Šuruppak and the Syrian town of Ebla; the abandonment of a site by its inhabitants, as at Jemdet Nasr and perhaps Tell el-Suleimah; or of tablets being used for other purposes, such as fill material for construction, as at Uruk III and, in the Sargonic period, at Gasur and probably Girsu. Nonetheless, enormous lacunae in the documentation remain, which must render our study incomplete.

We have divided our study into two major sections. This separation reflects changes in administrative procedures within the Sargonic state.

The first section deals with the documentation that preceded this procedural change, namely, from Early ED Ur to the Early Sargonic period. The Pre-Sargonic and Early Sargonic documents have been examined as a unit, despite enormous political changes, because no sharp deviations occurred in the administrative organization or significant transformations in the method of accounting. Only gradual changes in the form of the documents and in the actual orthography can be detected. Large tablets, so common during the Fara period, gradually diminish in number although they continue to be compiled; the form of the signs is generally preserved although it tends to become more stylized. Even the type of texts and their use do not vary greatly. The anthroponyms are normally followed by a characterizing element: the title, the administrative center to which the official belongs, or either his patronymic or direct supervisor. At Fara, the vast majority of documents were ration lists and the allocation of goods—consumable or real estate—and records concerning the conscription of workers. In the subsequent period at Girsu and at Umma at the time of Lugalzagesi, the texts are generally of the same typology, although the contents are more varied.[24] The documents examined in this section are from Ur, Fara

24. During this period few changes occurred despite the long time span. Two radical transformations occurred during the reigns of Narām-Sîn and Šulgi, each the result of a major reform of the bureaucratic system that centralized the management of a state that had become too unwieldy, each occurring within a brief period of time. These are examples of how changes in organizational and bureaucratic systems reflect great historic events.

(=Šuruppak), Abū Ṣalābīkh, Girsu, Umma, and Nippur, the two most significant and substantial archives being those of Fara and ED IIIb Girsu. These latter archives, although they record transactions in which citizens or officials from other cities are involved, have a definite city horizon, although, in some instances, especially in the archive of Fara, a supra-city dimension can be observed.[25]

---

25. Although outside the scope of our study, we cannot ignore the Pre-Sargonic Syrian archives at Mari and Ebla. The archive of Mari consists of only 36 administrative tablets, published by D. Charpin, "Tablettes présargoniques de Mari," *Mari* 5 (1987): 65–127. This lot is dated between ED IIIa and ED IIIb (*id.*, pp. 95–96). In my opinion, the archive certainly cannot be later than the time of Ur-Nanše of Lagaš, and more likely prior. The archive of Ebla is of a completely different nature and is certainly the largest from the ED period. It consists of approximately 5,000 documents (the size of the inventory is about 15,000, but this includes fragments), some still unpublished, which include lexical texts of Mesopotamian and local origin (for an updated list of the published documentation and the inventory of the texts found, cf. M. Baldacci – F. Pomponio, "Bibliografia Eblaita," in L. Cagni, ed., *Ebla 1975–1985* [Naples, 1987], pp. 429–56; F. Baffi Guardata – M. Baldacci – F. Pomponio, "Bibliografia Eblaita II," *SEL* 6 [1989]: 145–48; "Eblaite Bibliography III," *SEL* 10 [1993]: 93–110; "Eblaite Bibliography IV," *SEL* 14 [1997]: 93–110). Although these archives come from a region outside Mesopotamia, they are characterized by archive techniques in the compilation of documents of clear Mesopotamian origin. This implies a close cultural connection between the two areas, which must have had very old roots, probably dating from the late-Uruk period. These cultural relations were probably still in existence at the time of the royal archives of Ebla as is shown, in particular, by a school tablet that records a mathematical exercise signed by a scribe from Kiš (cf. MEE 3, pp. 269–70). For relations between Ebla and the Sumerian city of Kiš, see P. Steinkeller, "Observations on the Sumerian Personal Names in Ebla. Sources and the Onomasticon of Mari and Kish," in M. E. Cohen – D. C. Snell – D. B. Weisberg, eds., *The Tablet and the Scroll* (Bethesda, Md., 1993), pp. 242–44, and for those with the site of Abū Ṣalābīkh, P. Mander, "Sumerian Personal Names in Ebla," *JAOS* 108 (1988): 481–83. The period of the compilation of the royal archives of Ebla has been the subject of great controversy. A dating to the Classical Sargonic period seems to have been abandoned in favor of a dating to the period between the tablets of Fara and the inscriptions of Ur-Nanše.

No scribes are mentioned in the Mari archive, and surprisingly, given the size of the archive, less than ten scribes occur in the Ebla archive (cf. M. G. Biga – F. Pomponio, "Critères de rédaction comptable et chronologie des textes d'Ebla," *MARI* 7 [1993]: 128).

An archive of about one hundred tablets from Tell Beydar in the upper Khabur valley, near Tell Brak, was published by F. Ismail – W. Sallaberger – Ph.

The second section examines documents from the Classical Sargonic period, that is the period from Narām-Sîn to Šar-kali-šarrī. Tablets have been found in about a dozen sites throughout Mesopotamia, from Girsu to Gasur. At some sites, such as Umma, Nippur, and Adab, the documents can be divided into two or more sub-archives. When compared to the preceding period, the break is clear. The reform of the bureaucracy imposed by Narām-Sîn, the meeting of two recording systems with differing characteristics, namely, the Sumerian and the Akkadian, the need for accounting in types of archives that had not previously existed, brought about decisive changes in the recording systems. The tablets assume the elongated classical format, usually having only one column on the obverse and one on the reverse. Large tablets are rare.[26] The script is now more elegant, especially in official documents with seal impressions and in letters—a type of document more numerous than in the preceding period. The technique of document compilation is highly uniform throughout all the sites, even distant ones. Standard systems of units of measurement tend to prevail throughout the entire area as a result of the need for a centralized control system exercised by the Sargonic state. In the documents, phrases either in Akkadian or in Sumerian that refer quite precisely to the contents of the tablets, purpose of the transactions, destination of goods, etc., appear more and more frequently. But what changes most

---

Talon – K. Van Lerberghe, eds., *Administrative Documents from Tell Beydar*, Subartu 2 (Brepols, 1996). The similarity of the *ductus* of these tablets with those from Fara, the occurrence of anthroponyms perhaps of Old Akkadian origin, and finally the use of Mesopotamian scribal techniques (see *idem*, pp. 69–80) is further confirmation of very early trade and cultural relations between Mesopotamia and other areas of the Near East.

26. A large ration tablet found at Ešnunna and some large ration tablets from Nippur go back to the time of Narām-Sîn. Other multi-columned tablets are present in several Sargonic archives (Girsu: L1065, 4703; Me-ság archive: BIN 8 148, 152; Adab: A 637; Mugdan: MAD 5 66; Kiš: MAD 5 45, 56, 57; Gasur: HSS IV 36, 139, 152–55, 159, 185, 187, 188; Tell el-Suleimah archive: A.1, A.7). But the percentage of extant records to what must have existed in all Sargonic documentation is probably lower when compared to the ED and Pre-Sargonic periods. But a mitigating factor is that we have only ration tablets from Nippur and Ešnunna, while no such tablets have been found in archives from Girsu and other Sargonic cities.

of all is the horizon of the single archive. Although they record transactions relative to goods produced locally, the tablets are not confined to this level. Provisions are recorded for journeys by the king and his retinue or by local officials to Akkad or other sites. The presence of dignitaries and royal officials in Umma, Nippur, Girsu, Gasur, and Tutub are mentioned or attested to by their seal impressions.

Although recording techniques utilized in the tablets are now clearer concerning the relationships between production centers and the local or central government, they are more elusive than those of the previous period regarding the identification of the officials mentioned.[27] Officials are generally identified only by their anthroponym. Often, only the contents and the particular role of that official in the transaction offer any clues as to his identity, and with a wide margin of error.[28]

A general study of the typology of the Sargonic archives has been conducted by B. R. Foster. Foster discusses the recording techniques in the Sargonic archives and identifies two systems of accounting of regional origin, one Sumerian and the other Akkadian.[29] The fusion of the two systems probably led to a new system of accounting, namely, that used after the reform of Šulgi during the Third Dynasty of Ur.[30]

Linked to these two accounting systems are different types of archives. The family or private archives, such as those of Ur-Šara in the region of Umma, of Enlile-maba at Nippur, and of Qurādum at Sippar, are not voluminous. The household archives, such as those at Kiš, Mugdan, Ešnunna, Gasur, Tell el Suleimah, and probably of the Me-ság estate—

27. It is possible that this was an "Akkadian" innovation. In fact, many high-level Akkadians disdained titles (suggestion by B. R. Foster).

28. This technique has often been the only way to identify scribes in this documentation.

29. B. R. Foster, "Archives and Record-Keeping in Sargonic Mesopotamia," *ZA* 72 (1982): 3–4; 7–25. Cf., also, P. Steinkeller, "Land-Tenure Conditions in Third Millennium Babylonia: The Problem of Regional Variation," in M. Hudson and B. A. Levine, eds., *Urbanization and Land Ownership in the Ancient Near East* (Cambridge, Mass., 1999), pp. 289–329, who discusses the origin and development of these different accounting systems, with significant variations in the political and socioeconomic systems in southern and northern Babylonia, relating to different ecologies.

30. B. R. Foster, "Archives and Empire in Sargonic Mesopotamia," *RAI* 30 (1983): 48.

whose documentation consists of few hundred texts—follow the Akkadian system of accounting. A third type of archive is that of the great households, which consist of hundreds or even thousands of tablets. These follow the Sumerian accounting system—the archives of the énsi's of Adab, Umma, Girsu, and of the Ekur temple at Nippur are of this type.

Alongside the evolution of tablet form and accounting methodology, the use of seals is important for our understanding of the developing role of the scribe. The seal was an instrument of control and safeguard, already appearing in the remotest of times, certainly prior to the written document—seal impressions containing a written legend appear in the Sargonic period.[31] In fact, the use of cylinder seals can be traced back to Uruk V.[32] Sealing probably confers the authority of a particular institution or official. Thus, we must recognize a difference between tablets with seal impressions and those without (such as ration lists, lists of employees, and cattle accounts).[33]

Our analysis is limited to those scribes mentioned in an archival context. We have excluded scribes who are mentioned out of context, whether in documents or in seal impressions, whose provenance is unknown and, therefore, cannot be linked to an identifiable administrative center. However, for completeness, TABLE 21 lists from administrative texts all anthroponyms bearing the title of scribe that are not in our analysis.

---

31. Cf. *infra*, e.g., pp. 155, 163, 168, 170, 188, 206 and TABLE 21.

32. See Nissen, *Protostoria*, pp. 84–90.

33. Cf. R. J. Matthews, *Cities, Seals and Writing: Archaic Seal Impressions from Jemdet Nasr and Ur*, MSVO 2 (Berlin, 1993), pp. 25, 28–32.

For a general discussion of the relationship between written documents and sealings in the third millennium, with particular reference to the texts of Ur III, with recent bibliography, see P. Mander, "I testi amministrativi e la sigillatura," in M. Perna, ed., *Atti del Convegno sulla Sfragistica-Napoli Archivi di Stato 1996*, Naples (forthcoming).

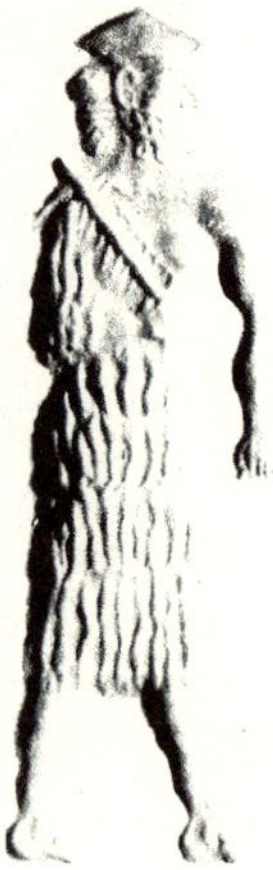

CHAPTER 1

SCRIBES FROM THE EARLY DYNASTIC TO THE EARLY SARGONIC PERIODS

1. The Scribes in the Archives of ED II–IIIa

1.1 *The Early ED Archive of Ur*

The excavation of Ur was carried out between 1920 and 1933 by the Joint Expedition of the British Museum and the University of Pennsylvania under the direction of Sir Leonard Woolley. The excavation uncovered a temple (the *giparu*) from the Ur III period situated in the northwest area of the site and, in the extreme southeast, an ED III royal cemetery, whose tombs revealed extremely lavish funerary furnishings. In the upper layers of the cemetery, the tombs of the kings of the First Dynasty of Ur were found.[1] From the Early ED period, the ruins of the temple of Nanna and the foundations of some small buildings remain. Tablets and seal impressions, as well as other archaeological finds from the Early ED period, were found beneath the cemetery, revealing the existence of an urban structure related to an essentially agricultural economy of significant size with a centralized administration, which managed persons and goods.[2] The tablets were published by E. Burrows in UET 2. The well-defined succession in which the seal impressions were found in the excavation enabled the archaeologists to determine eight strata labelled SIS I–VIII.[3] The vast majority of the tablets were found in SIS IV

1. The inscriptions of the kings of the first dynasty were found in the nearby settlement of Obeid.

2. H. T. Wright, *The Administration of Rural Production in an Early Mesopotamian Town* (Ann Arbor, 1969), presents an archaeological study of settlement from the Obeid to the ED periods. In particular, he concentrates his research on the Early ED period and textual aspects. Wright believes (*ibidem*, pp. 25–27) that the ED settlement of Ur was about 30 hectares in extent with a population of 6,000 persons.

3. Cf. UET 2, pp. 1–2.

(UET 2, 15–273). Some tablets (UET 2, 1, 2, 308, 310) were found in the trial trenches before the stratification was determined. Tablets 305 and 306 are from SIS VII, 307 from SIS VIII, and 232 and 233 from pit G, which was dug at the northern corner of the site and cut transversely across three layers, SIS VI–VIII.

On the basis of paleographical evidence and the findspot, UET 2, p. 3 divides the entire documentation into three chronological groups:

(a) 1, 63, 64, 232, 233 date to the Jemdet Nasr period;
(b) 2, 308, 310 date to the Fara period;
(c) the remaining documentation dates between the Jemdet Nasr and Fara periods.

Burrows considers the documentation of Group (c) to be a homogeneous corpus. However, it should be noted that the majority of the tablets have a very similar *ductus.* Within the group some tablets (6, 9, 166, 277) have a more archaic *ductus* while others (116, 127) a more recent one. But, for prosopographic reasons, which will be explained later, it is probable that these paleographical differences essentially are due to the scribe who compiled the tablet.[4]

With the exception of about 30 school exercise tablets and about 40 tablets that contain only seal impressions, the remaining texts are administrative summaries of various typologies. But the typologies most frequently represented are those connected with land management and

4. Although archaeological, paleographical, and prosopographic evidence indicates the contemporaneity of the tablets from SIS IV, it is difficult to establish a precise chronology beyond that suggested in UET 2. However, the fact that tablets from almost the same period have different paleographic aspects may indicate that the archive recording technique was in a phase of rapid change. Unfortunately, we are not in a position to document a phenomenon of this size. In fact, the scanty data at our disposal do not allow us to establish whether the transformation of the *ductus,* which was to be transformed in time to the more familiar one of Fara, was already under way and whether this was directly connected with a transformation of administrative and recording techniques. If so, perhaps the period of time that separated the tablets of Archaic Ur from those of Fara is much shorter than normally supposed—possibly no more than a hundred years. This hypothesis is supported by results obtained by F. Pomponio, "The Fara Lists of Proper Names," *JAOS* 104 (1984): 554–56, which establishes a definite correspondence between the anthroponyms in the administrative documentation of Archaic Ur and those in Fara lexical texts.

its products, as can be seen from the 290 administrative documents found in SIS IV:

(a)	Texts concerning cereals (še, zíz, gíg)[5]	11%
(b)	Texts concerning lands[6]	23%
(c)	Texts concerning the allocation of grain products (bread, flour, beer) for šuku	27%
(d)	Texts concerning personnel	6%
(e)	Texts concerning sheep	6%
(f)	Texts of other typologies (wood, metal, hides, reeds, etc.)	3%
(g)	Texts whose typology cannot be determined	23%

On the basis of archaeological evidence, H. T. Wright suggests that most of these tablets were written in the span of a few years.[7]

A prosopographic analysis of the 25 anthroponyms that occur most frequently in the texts shows that there are at least 80 documents in which three or more of the persons mentioned occur.[8] This indicates that these 80 texts, consisting of all the large and medium-sized tablets,[9] are contemporary. Conversely, the remaining 60 documents, in which one or two of the names occur, also can be contemporary.[10] These 140

---

5. Some texts in group (a) have a few entries that record large quantities of goods, while others from the same group have many entries that record allocations of barley and other types of grain for seed and for the sustenance of people and animals. In some cases, the documents also record the measurements of the land in addition to the barley allocated for seeding and animal fodder. For example, 20 records: 19 (bùr) and 30 gur še-numun 20 gur še-kú gu_4; and 117: 13+[x] (bùr) 30 zíz 30 gúg 20 še-kú gu_4.

6. The majority of the texts in Group (b) are field allotments. Some tablets (27, 127, 128, 163, 168, 226) are probably *Sammeltafeln*, which must have collected smaller documents. On the other hand, one group of tablets contains brief notes that record the amount of land by means of an explicative clause. For example, 102 records: 20 (bur) 4 (iku) šà ma-gíd—122 and 365 are similar documents as are, perhaps, the fragments 101 and 141.

7. *Ibidem*, p. 40.

8. G.Visicato, *The Internal Chronology of the Documentation of UET 2*, (forthcoming).

9. Among the 80 isolated documents, the larger ones are: 27, 66, 87, 93, 98, 112, 127, 128, 162, 163, 168, 226, 252, 371; the medium-sized ones are: 12, 24, 30, 62, 99, 107–109, 177, 183, 186, 201, 212, 225, 253, 255, 259, 354, 356, 364, 367.

10. Considering that there are at least 60 non-definable fragments that often do not

documents probably were from an archive of a single institution, most likely the temple household of the moon-god Nanna.[11] The mention of the PA.SI Urí^{ki} and the é-gal in the texts suggests that this household might have been connected to the palace administration.[12]

Several of the 25 officials examined sometimes occur with a title: some with sanga, others with nu-bànda, and two with dub-sar—this is the first attestation of dub-sar.

Ma-za-LA dub-sar in 297 II 5' is the recipient of an undefined item. Because of the tablet's unusual numerical indicators, Burrows considers this document to be a school exercise.[13] However the *ductus* of the tablet, which is similar to other administrative texts, indicates that the compiler was an expert scribe, not a novice. It is unclear whether the sign LA is a part of the anthroponym or a professional name, but an official named Ma-za occurs several times in the documentation.[14]

---

record any name, it appears likely that the 290 administrative texts, the 40 seal impressions, and the 30 school texts from SIS IV are all part of the same archive, which must have spanned a brief period of time.

11. This institution must be the same one mentioned in the clauses of certain texts by the term èš(AB), : èš DU in UET 2, 10; géme èš in UET 2, 50; še-kú èš in UET 2, 95; and še sanga èš in UET 2, 183. Lands belonging to the moon-god Nanna are recorded in UET 2, 127 and 147; lands belonging to the en are listed in UET 2, 143, 147, 160, 184. An institution called èš-ŠEŠ.AB occurs in UET 2, 95 o. I 2–3. In UET 2, 93 o. II 4–7 the institution èš occurs with an institution called ŠEŠ.AB AN-é, perhaps indicating the temple of Nanna. For this topic, see P. Charvát, "Early Ur," *ArOr* 47 (1979): 16–17.

12. W. W. Hallo, *Early Mesopotamian Royal Titles* (New Haven, 1957), p. 34 identifies PA.SI Urí^{ki} as the highest political authority of the city. H. T. Wright (*op. cit.*, p. 107) disagrees.

13. UET 2, p. 16, *sub* lú-dub: "It is remarkable that dub-sar, very frequent in Fara, never occurs in these documents."

14. In 70 III 6, Ma-za is in charge of two groups of persons (the other two persons in charge are AK-^{d}Inanna and Lu-lu, elsewhere identified as sanga and nu-bànda respectively); in 109 IV 2 and 226 o. II 1 he is the recipient of a plot of land; in 212 he is mentioned concerning 20 gur of gíg (the text may be parallel to 70. In fact, the three officials in charge of personnel in 70, AK-^{d}Inanna, Lu-lu, and Ma-za, are mentioned together in 212, a text concerning grain, perhaps for the sustenance of their subordinates); in 252 o. I 6 he is mentioned concerning four sheep; and in 353 I 4' he is perhaps the recipient of grain. The name Ma-za

Mes-ma-S137-zi in UET 2, 93 o. III 8 and r. I 4, whose name can be read in UET 2, p. 35 as Mes-ma-S137-zi (PN 528), occurs as recipient of two allocations of different quality breads. Burrows notes that this name also occurs in the fragment UET 2, 148 (Mes-[m]a-S137-[z]i?) and in the incomplete passage UET 2, 187 o. 1 4 (Mes-ma-S137-[zi]).[15]

The presence of many school exercise tablets among the documents of SIS IV indicates that this administrative institution had its own school to train scribes.[16] The existence of a scribal school and the contemporaneous mention in the archive of dub-sar indicates that it was in Archaic Ur that the category "scribe" was used for the first time.

---

occurs in 259 o. I 2, a list of 35 persons described in the summary (r. 1–2) as ìr or géme.

15. The signs S137 and S136 are variations of LAK 218(ZU:ZU.SAR), as demonstrated by F. Pomponio, "Notes in Fara Texts," *Or*NS 53 (1984): 11. This sign appears only in the administrative texts from Archaic Ur and Fara—often in proper names—and in lexical lists from Fara and Ebla. LAK 218 is absent from earlier documents from Uruk III and Jemdet Nasr, as well as from the later texts (cf. Pomponio, *Or*NS 53 [1984]: 10–12).

M. Civil, MEE 3, p. 277, in his comment to line 119, proposes the readings *gulu and *lu, while Pomponio, *Or*NS 53 [1984]:12, 16, suggests a reading lum_x, thus reading PN 528 of UET 2, p. 35 as Lum_x-ma-mes-zi. However, we cannot reject the possibility that PN 528 should, in fact, be interpreted as the anthroponym Ma-zi, which occurs on other occasions in the archive of ED II Ur followed by the professional indicator dub-zu:zu-sar (LAK 218), not mentioned elsewhere. An official named Ma-zi occurs in 87 o. II 1 as recipient of cereals and farming land in 226 o. 1 6. The contemporaneous occurrence of Ma-za and Ma-zi in the same text, respectively 226 o. II 1 and o. I 6, excludes the possibility that these two officials were the same person.

Note that in some anthroponyms the sign SAR (S138) and the sign S136/137 alternate (Ma-SAR in UET 2, 33 and Ma-S136/137 in UET 2, 30 *et passim*; Utu-SAR in UET 2, 17 and 168; and Utu-S137 in UET 2, 354 [both Utu-SAR and Utu-S136 are hypocoristic forms of Amar-Utu-mú, an anthroponym in UET 2, 5, 24, 226 and 371]), while in colophons of lexical texts from Abū Ṣalābīkh and Ebla the professional name dub-zu-zu occurs, which G. Pettinato, MEE 3, p. XXVIII, translates as "il conoscitore di tavolette, il docente." G. Cooper, *RA* 76 (1982): 191, on the other hand, considers the terms su-gal and zu-zu to correspond to the *barû* of the preceding colophons. These elements suggest a hypothesis, not provable at present, that the term dub-LAK 218 in ED II Ur constitutes a form of writing that indicates a scribe "who knows and writes the tablet."

16. Similar training practices for scribes are documented in the Sargonic archive of Girsu.

Although a category of officials—presumably identified as sanga (or better umbisag)— who wrote tablets must have existed during Uruk III / Jemdet Nasr, we are unable to establish with accuracy the relationship between sanga and dub-sar in the archive of Archaic Ur. However, Ma-za may well be the scribe of UET 2, 297, and in UET 2, 70, Ma-za occurs with AK-^{d}Inanna and Lu-lu, mentioned elsewhere as sanga and sanga-GAR.[17] They are the three officials responsible for the workers listed in the text. AK-^{d}Inanna and Ma-za occur together also in UET 2, 212, which concerns cereals destined perhaps for the workers conscripted in UET 2, 70. This relationship suggests that the dub-sar was a very high-ranking official who had responsibilities similar to those of the sanga, and was associated with the sanga and sanga-GAR in the management of the institution that governed the city. It also demonstrates that there existed a category of "scribes," which, with its organization and hierarchy, was one of the most important administrative classes in Mesopotamia.

1.2 *The Fara Archive*

The site of Fara, ancient Šuruppak, was excavated by the Deutsche Orient-Gesellschaft from 1902–3 and, many years later in the spring of 1931, by an expedition from the University Museum of the University of Pennsylvania. These excavations yielded so many tablets and seals that the term "Fara Period" was adopted to date contemporary finds from other sites. Unfortunately, the pioneering excavation techniques and the inadequate methods for recording finds have made it difficult to incorporate and correlate the archaeological and epigraphical finds. The long and patient work carried out recently by H. P. Martin has enabled us to reconstruct the site more accurately.

The site of ancient Šuruppak (modern Fara) was first occupied during the Jemdet Nasr period, developing rapidly during ED I and II—the separation of the two periods is not clearly distinguishable in the excavations. The ED III settlement is about 100 hectares; it is clearly

17. In the documentation of UET 2 at least five sanga and one sanga-GAR are mentioned: Lu-lu is sanga-GAR in 112; AK, probably hypocoristic for AK-^{d}Inanna, is sanga in 360; A-geštin in 135 on; é-IGI+BUR in 363; GIŠ.ŠEŠ.IB-kalam-ti in 343; and Lu-làl in 349. An unnamed sanga-èš and sanga-lugal occur respectively in 29 and 162; an unnamed sanga occurs in 59, 93, and 190.

defined and delimited due to destruction by fire.[18] The Deutsche Orient-Gesellschaft excavations brought to light areas with spacious buildings, especially in the southern part of the site.[19] In the central inhabited area, site IXaa, a large building was excavated, which Martin suggests may be a temple. The approximately 650 ED III published tablets[20] were found by the Deutsche Orient-Gesellschaft in 24 different sites, although the majority came from three sites. In site XVh, situated near the areas with spacious buildings and called the Tablet House by the excavators, about 320 tablets were found; in the adjacent site XIIIf,g about 80 tablets were discovered, and in site XVIIc,d, in the extreme north of the settlement, 96 were found. Other groups of tablets were found adjacent to the Tablet House, sites XVb, XVh, and IIii. Thus, about 70% of the tablets were found in the area of the large buildings in the southern part of the city.

The number of sites where tablets were found gave rise to the hypothesis of the existence of various households.[21] Recently it has been suggested that the tablets were drawn up, in the majority, by a single central administration, which, through a complex capillary organization, managed all aspects of economic and political life and connected hierarchically a series of organizations.[22] At the head of this administration was the énsi-GAR-gal. Utilizing the high officials of the é-géme (e.g., sanga-GAR, sa$_{12}$-du$_5$, dub-sar-maḫ), the énsi coordinated the two principal administrative centers, the palace administration (é-gal) and the city administration (é-uru). About 40 im-ru reported to the palace administration; they were professional, perhaps district structures or clans,[23] which included the a-zu$_5$, agrig, kínda, lú-ad, maškim, muḫaldim, munu$_4$, nar, sukkal, zadim, and others. Also, organizations

---

18. Cf. Martin, *Fara,* p. 115.

19. Cf. Martin, *Fara,* pp. 126–128, sites XIIIf, g; XVaa.

20. Several hundred tablets appear to be missing from the final publications of A. Deimel and R. Jestin. A trawl of the D.O.G. excavation record indicates that they found at least 844 tablets and 128 fragments.

21. Cf. Martin, *Fara,* p. 89.

22. EDATŠ, pp. 4–9, 34.

23. See P. Steinkeller *apud Bureau,* p. 17.

of dam-gàr, gala, and nimgir reported to the é-gal.[24] According to the documentation, the palace administration provided for several thousand workers, including workers in such areas as agriculture, fishing, and husbandry.[25] For the economy of Šuruppak transport was particularly important, and was administered, in part, by the office of KISAL—headed by the nu-bànda—and, in part, by the énsi through high-ranking officials of the é-géme.[26]

The documents, because of contents or usage, were probably divided into various archives. The Tablet House was considered to be the principal archive of the institution, where lists of barley rations, records of land allotments, and records of animals and carts for agricultural work were kept. Site XVIIc,d probably was a military administrative center, dealing with such activities as the recruitment of soldiers.[27] Site IXaa was probably a scribal center[28]; the documents include administrative texts, lexical texts, schools texts, and literary texts.[29] The administra-

---

24. *Bureau*, pp. 25–26; 91–112.

25. *Bureau*, pp. 115–33.

26. Based on new studies of the Fara tablets housed in the University Museum in Philadelphia, it seems that important temple households existed in ED IIIa Šuruppak. They might have been large structures that grouped households—both family and institutional—of different size, kind, and activity, as a hierarchical organization. This system of households represents the capillary organization that managed the economic activities of the city. In turn, all the temple households were controlled by the household of the goddess Sud and supervised by the énsi through the é-géme. The é-gal was controlled directly by the énsi.

27. Cf. *Bureau*, p. 88.

28. We do not know the provenance of 450 of the texts found. We know only the number of tablets were found at each site. This is due to the recording practices adopted by the Deutsche Orient-Gesellschaft, in which only the number of tablets found daily was noted, without any further indication that would enable us to identify the find site. Martin's work on field records has enabled us to identify 70 of the 305 tablets found in the Tablet House; 22 of the 96 tablets found in the site XVIIc, d; and 16 of the remaining tablets found in various other sites. All these tablets were published in WF (cf. Martin, *Fara*, p. 8). Correlations between texts and contexts have enabled us to identify 76 other tablets from the Tablet House (cf. EDATŠ, pp. XVI–XVII; 28) and 58 from the site XVIIc, d (cf. *Bureau*, p. 87).

29. For a complete list of the school and literary texts from Fara, cf. IAS, pp. 35–42.

tive documentation of Fara is comprised of about 450 texts,[30] to which about 40 sale contracts for plots of land and real estate should be added.[31] These 450 texts contain a great variety of document types, although about half concern four typologies (barley, fields, asses, and recruitment of personnel). This documentation spans a relatively brief period, perhaps one year, and probably coincided with the last period of ED IIIa occupation of the settlement.[32]

A special characteristic of the Fara administrative texts is the scribal technique of compiling, for each typology, primary, intermediate, and general summary documents.[33] Possibly once the annual summary texts had been compiled, the primary texts were destroyed or used for other purposes. Contracts, on the other hand, which needed to be kept, must represent a longer period of time, which, however, could not be more than seven years.[34] Because of these recording and maintenance tech-

---

30. Cf. EDATŠ, p. 4. To these texts another 96 archaic tablets (the Schmidt tablets) excavated by the Babylonian Expedition and which are still unpublished should be added. The tablets were found in two different find-spots. S. N. Kramer, "New Tablets from Fara," *JAOS* 55 (1935): 110–31 provides a preliminary description of them and I had an opportunity to collate them. The documents, different from the main corpus of Deutsche Orient-Gesellschaft archives, are small and record single transactions, and appear to be contemporaneous with Deutsche Orient-Gesellschaft documents. Some scribes are mentioned in this documentation: Unken dub-sar (F 41); Lugal-u$_4$-su$_{13}$-šè um-mi-a (F 376); Ur-^{d}nin-UŠ (F 602); and Ur-AB.DÙN (F 89). Lugal-u$_4$-su$_{13}$-šè um-mi-a and, perhaps, Unken-a appear in other Fara documents as scribes. F. Pomponio, A. Westenholz, and I, together with the archaeological collaboration of H. P. Martin, have recently finished preparing an edition of all the Schmidt tablets together with another 15 Fara tablets purchased in the field from local Arabs at the end of the nineteenth century. The volume will be published soon.

31. Cf. ELTS, p. 189. Five other sale contracts should be added to the list of ELTS: W 18581 in M. W. Green, *ZA* 72 (1982): 166, 175; T.Gomi, *Orient* 19 (1983): 1–6; CBS 8830; CBS 7273; and NBC 6842. NBC 6842 will be published by A. Westenholz and me in a volume in memory of Prof. L. Cagni. CBS 8830 and CBS 7273 will be published in the volume on Fara texts in the University Museum.

32. Cf. EDATŠ, p. 9.

33. Cf. EDATŠ, pp. 21–24.

34. Cf. G. Visicato, "An Unusual Sale Contract and a List of Witnesses from Fara," *ASJ* 17 (1995): 171–72.

niques, it is impossible to reconstruct the careers of officials; only in a few instances is it possible to establish the administrative sector in which an official operated.

Throughout all the administrative documentation, including contracts, about one hundred scribes are mentioned, with the titles dub-sar, agrig, and um-mi-a, as well as one dub-sar-aša$_5$, one dub-sar-kuš$_7$ (whose name is lost), an unnamed dub-sar-zì, and an unnamed dub-sar-maḫ (cf. TABLE 2).[35] If one takes into account that these one hundred scribes occur in texts from only one site and that in most cases they are linked to annual accounts, the total number is comparable only with the large number of scribes mentioned in the Ur III documentation.[36]

Of these one hundred anthroponyms identified as scribes in the administrative texts and contracts, 27 occur as umbisag in the lexical texts. Such a large percentage seemingly excludes the likelihood of mere homonymy.[37] On the other hand, the large number of scribes—about 55, at least 34 of whom are mentioned only in this type of text—mentioned in the contracts, does not seem warranted, at least on the basis of the small number of extant contracts. However, it is likely that many of these scribes may also have been engaged as dub-sar-aša$_5$, um-mi-a lú-é-éš-gar, or simply as lú-ki-inim by the administrative center in charge of drawing up contracts or as umbisag by the scribal schools. The limits of the administrative documentation of Fara, which in the vast majority of cases consists of laconic lists of recipients of goods, make it

---

35. Since our study is limited to administrative documentation, the approximately 80 scribes (umbisag and dub-mu-sar) who are mentioned only in lexical texts are not discussed. However, the third column of TABLE 2 lists the lexical texts in which scribes mentioned in the administrative documentation as umbisag or dub-mu-sar occur.

36. H. Waetzoldt *Das Schreiberwesen,* p. 5, has shown that the Ur III documents, which span 50 years, name 1,541 scribes from 17 different sites. The vast majority of these, however, occur in only five sites: Lagaš (620), Umma (384), Ur (202), Drehem (168), and Nippur (103).

37. For a discussion of the relationship between the anthroponyms mentioned as umbisag in the lexical texts and as dub-sar in the administrative texts of Fara, cf. most recently P. Mander, "I colofoni di Fara, Abū-Ṣalābīkh ed Ebla: approccio prosopografico," in L. Cagni, ed., *Il Bilinguismo ad Ebla* (Naples, 1984), pp. 339–44.

difficult, in most cases, to determine clearly and unambiguously the role and task of the scribes mentioned.[38]

This study examines the scribes in three groups: (a) scribes mentioned only in contracts; (b) scribes mentioned only in administrative texts; and (c) scribes mentioned in various document types, including lexical texts.[39]

(a) Scribes Mentioned Only in Contracts:

Thirty-three scribes occur only in contracts. Of these, 12 occur only once, as lú-ki-inim or dub-sar-aša$_5$: A-me-te; A-na-da-ak[40]; AN-da-zu$_5$[41]; AN.DU$_6$.GU-na; EN.PI; Gú-ni-MUŠENxBURU$_5$; Lugal-ir!-nun[42]; Lugal-u$_4$-su$_{13}$-šè[43]; Mu-ni-ùri; ^{d}Nin-Unug-anzu[44]; Sag-a-DU-⸢ba⸣-sum[45]; Šeš-kur-ra[46] (for these 12 scribes, see TABLE 2). Following is a discussion of the remaining 21 scribes:

---

38. Cf. *Bureau*, p. 2.

39. Part of the administrative documentation of Fara has been republished in EDATŠ (Naples, 1994) and *Bureau* (Münster, 1995)—216 texts in all including the four most numerous typologies. For these texts a new numeration has been adopted here (for a table of concordances, see *Bureau*, pp. XV–XIX), while for the other texts we shall continue to use WF, TSŠ, NTSŠ, DP, RTC, and CT 50 numbering.

40. This scribe occurs only in *Ung.* 4 o. V 6–7 (as lú-ki-inim) and without title in CBS 6842 o. III 5'.

41. This scribe occurs only in WF 35 o. III 4–5, an unusual text, which records a list of witnesses on the obverse, among whom is our dub-sar, while a short contract for the sale of a house is recorded on the reverse (cf. G. Visicato, "An Unusual Sale Contract and a List of Witnesses from Fara," *ASJ* 17 [1995]: 284–88).

42. This scribe occurs only once, as a lú-ki-inim in *Ung.* 1 r. I 9–10. A namesake sipa-anše is mentioned in 146 r. I 3–4. If they are the same individual, the title could be an abbreviated form of dub-sar-<sipa>-anše, a profession attested at Fara.

43. This scribe occurs in F 376.

44. A certain ^{d}Nin-unug-anzu dam-gàr occurs as a witness in *RA* 32 (1935): 126 o. IV 2.

45. He occurs, without title, in F 975.

46. He is mentioned as a dub-sar-aša$_5$ in RTC 15 r. III 7–8. Although he is mentioned several times in the Fara texts, this anthroponym is never identified elsewhere as a scribe.

A-ḫar-ši dub-sar is mentioned in several contracts (WF 32 o. IV 2; MVN 10, 84 r. I 1; BAOM 5, p. 28 r. I 9) as a lú-ki-inim, whereas in Ung. 1 r. II 6 he is mentioned as dub-sar-aša$_5$. Probably the namesake official mentioned in *Orient* 19 (1983): 2 o. V 8, without any characterizing element, is this dub-sar.

AK-girin$_x$ dub-sar is mentioned as a lú-ki-inim in WF 36 o. III 4. A namesake official without a characterizing element but always as a lú-ki-inim occurs in WF 33 o. III 4; IV 6.

Amar-^{d}Gú-lá dub-sar is mentioned as a lú-ki-inim in WF 33 r. I 6–7 and in WF 37 r. I 2–3. This anthroponym, relatively widespread in the onomasticon of Fara, is not mentioned elsewhere as a dub-sar.

Amar-ḪA.A um-mi-a is mentioned as a lú-é-éš-gar in MVN 10, 82 r. II 4–6; 83 r. I 9-II 1; and PBS 9, 3 o. V 4–6. He is an official in property sale contracts, his name occurring always before the nimgir-sila or the gal-nimgir.[47] The three contracts are all real estate sale contracts from the time when Maš-^{d}Sùd was bala. A namesake, but untitled, dub-sar appears as a witness in A. 33676 o. IV 2.[48]

E-ta-e$_{11}$ dub-sar is mentioned in CBS 8830 r. I 8–9[49] as a dub-sar-aša$_5$. He occurs as a lú-ki-inim, untitled in A. 33676 o. IV 3, in TSŠ 66 r. I 1 and SRJ p. 31, no. 6, o. IV 9.

É-pa-è dub-sar is a lú-ki-inim in Ung. 2 r. I 2. An untitled namesake official occurs in TSŠ X r. II 9, after the list of witnesses where the dub-sar-aša$_5$ is normally mentioned. He may be our scribe. Perhaps É-pa-è, in some cases, is an abbreviated form of É-zi-pa-è, a dub-sar mentioned in both administrative documents and sale contracts.[50]

Ig-ge-nu-gi$_4$ dub-sar occurs as a dub-sar-aša$_5$ in Ung. 2, o. IV 7; 3 r. I 7; *ArOr* 39 (1971): 14 r. I 4.

---

47. For the interchange between nimgir-sìla and gal-nimgir in the Fara texts, cf. ELTS, p. 204, n. 36.

48. Unpublished contract, courtesy R. Biggs.

49. Unpublished contract, courtesy A. Westenholz.

50. Cf. *infra*, p. 42.

Íl dub-sar is mentioned as a lú-ki-inim in WF 33 r. I 3 and TMH 5, 75 o. III 4; as a lú-šám-kú in Ung. 2, o. III 2; and as a lú-aša$_5$-šám in *ArOr* 39 (1971): 14 o. III 8 and *Orient* 19 (1983): 3 r. II 1.

KA-^{d}Sùd-da–zi dub-sar is mentioned as a dub-sar-aša$_5$ in WF 34 r. II 1 and as lú-ki-inim in A. 33676 o. III 5–6. He occurs without title as a lú-šám-kú in TMH 5, 78 o. III 4.[51]

KA-tar-ni-ga dub-sar occurs as a lú-ki-inim in WF 30 o. III 1–2. A namesake lú-ki-inim, who is dumu UR.UR, is mentioned in *WO* 8 (1975): 18, o. IV 6–8. It is unclear whether UR.UR, to whom KA-tar-ni-ga is either subordinate or a son is the namesake official who occurs as a dub-sar in administrative texts, as a dub-sar-aša$_5$ in contracts, and as an umbisag in lexical texts.[52] If so, perhaps KA-tar-ni-ga dumu UR.UR is the dub-sar mentioned in WF 30.

Lú-na-nam dub-sar occurs as a lú-ki-inim in TLAT 1 o. IV 7–8. A certain Lú-na-nam šeš Nam-maḫ occurs as the single witness in a sale contract in WF 38 o. II 5–III 1. Nam-maḫ, the brother of Lú-na-nam, seems to have also been the seller. A namesake, who purchased a plot of land (lú-aša$_5$-šám), is mentioned in WF 37 r. V 1–2.

Lugal-e-si dub-sar is the dub-sar-aša$_5$ mentioned in WF 33 r. II 1–2. In the same text, his subordinate, indicated only by his professional name ḫar-tu Lugal-e-si, is mentioned in the list of witnesses. He is mentioned in TSŠ X o. VI 4–6 as a lú-ki-inim in which he is described as a dub-sar maškim.[53]

---

51. Evidence seems to exclude that the namesake dam-gàr and the ugula-simug mentioned as lú-ki-inim in RTC 13 o. IV 5 and TSŠ X o. III 4 respectively, should be identified with our dub-sar. Thus, the identity of the KA-^{d}Sùd-da-zi mentioned as a lú-ki-inim in *Or*NS 44 (1975): 435 r. II 1 and WF 35 o. I 3 is uncertain.

52. Cf. *infra*, p. 45.

53. Edzard, SRJ, p. 18 translates this term as "der Schreiber, der Kommissar," indicating that this scribe acted as a supervisor. In general, when the term maškim follows an anthroponym already characterized by a professional name, as in this case, it is an indication that the latter is acting in a supervisory capacity. But it is possible that in this instance the term maškim is an abbreviated form indicating the official at the head of the hierarchy, namely, the maškim of the énsi (cf. *Bureau*, p. 134, n. 104).

Lugal-ezen dub-sar occurs as a lú-ki-inim in TMH 5, 71 o. V 1 and without a characterizing element in *Or*NS 44 (1975): 436 r. II 3. A namesake official involved with the é-géme is mentioned in 147 o. IV 4–5 as the superior of Nam-maḫ.[54] This Lugal-ezen é-géme has been identified as the namesake lùmgi mentioned in 187 o. IV 6–7.[55] The officials, mostly dub-sar, who work for the é-géme are all high- or very high-ranking officials. Therefore it is probable that the lùmgi mentioned in 187 is, in fact, a dub-sar lùmgi and is our scribe.

Lugal-UŠ.ŠIM dub-sar aša$_5$ appears in A. 33676 r. II 1–2. He occurs without title as the seller in WF 40 o. I 3 and in *SEL* 3 (1986): 11 o. III 7.

Munus-ki-nu-zu dub-sar is mentioned in WF 42 o. I 1–2, a list of 13 lú-ki-inim's, similar to WF 35, which we have previously discussed. In this list two other dub-sar's are mentioned: Lugal-ki-dúr-du$_{10}$ and Abzu-ki-du$_{10}$. None of these three scribes occurs again in the contracts. Munus-ki-nu-zu, without any characterizing element, occurs in a copper text, WF 151 o. III 2.

Nin-ig-gal dub-sar is mentioned as a lú-ki-inim in SRJ, p. 31, no. 6, o. V 2.[56]

Ur-abzu dub-sar is mentioned as a lú-ki-inim in Ung. 2 o. V 8; 3 o. IV 1. Based upon parallel passages,[57] we know that abzu(ZU.AB) is often abbreviated to AB in the administrative texts of Fara; thus AB in some cases should be read abzu$_x$. Ur-abzu$_x$ is mentioned in 37 o. IV 7–9' as the official whose subordinate is Šubur ašgab and as a lú-šám-kú in RTC 15 o. III 2. In addition, he is mentioned in TSŠ 775 o. II 2 and in WF 116 o. 2, texts dealing with grain.

Ur-^{d}En-ki dub-sar is mentioned as a lú-ki-inim in PBS 9, 3 o. IV 3–4. With the same function but without the title, he is mentioned in

---

54. Nam-maḫ Lugal-ezen is also mentioned in 116 r. III 12–13 and 121 r. IV 13'–14'.

55. Cf. *Bureau*, pp. 55–56.

56. A namesake ugula is mentioned in 29 r. VII 3–4 as the recipient of a barley ration in the section concerning the engar A-du$_6$-la. He appears again, but without title, in TSŠ 422 I' 2' as the recipient of an allocation of ^{giš}ḫašḫur, which probably came from aša$_5$ A-du$_6$-la. But we cannot identify the namesake ugula with our dub-sar.

57. Cf. EDATŠ, p. 309: 115 o. II 10–11 and 117 o. III 4–5.

MVN 10, 82 o. IV 4; 83 o. V 7. In *RA* 32 (1935): 165 o. III 5, a namesake lú-ki-inim is mentioned with the characterizing element GA.LU, whose meaning is obscure.

Ur-^{d}Gú-lá dub-sar is mentioned as a lú-ki-inim in Ung. 3 o. V 3–4 and MVN 10, 86 o. III 4–5. He is also mentioned in *Or*NS 44 (1975): 436 o. V 2' as a lú-ki-inim but without any characterizing element.

Ur-kin-nir dub-sar is mentioned as a dub-sar-aša$_5$ in SRJ, p. 31 r. I 2–3. He is mentioned without a characterizing element as a lú-ki-inim in *RA* 32 (1935): 126 o. IV 6 and in the list in WF 35 o. I 7 and as a lú-šám-kú in MVN 10, 82 o. III 1. This scribe is never mentioned in administrative texts, but possibly he is to be identified with the namesake official who is in charge of the records in a recruitment text or who puts his seal to the document.[58]

Ur-^{d}Nin-Unug^{ki} dub-sar is mentioned as a dub-sar-aša$_5$ in WF 32 o. III 5. We do not know whether he is the namesake GU.NUN.SUR mentioned in TSŠ X o. VI 7. Officials of the same name but differently titled (a-ru; ašgab; sagi[59]; sipa-u$_8$-gi$_6$-gi$_6$, zadim) appear as lú-ki-inim in different contracts. Without title he appears in texts from Schmidt's excavations (F 89, 377; 380).

(b) Scribes Mentioned Only in the Administrative Documentation:

A-du$_6$ dub-sar is mentioned only in the texts concerning the allocations of asses for agricultural work (EDATŠ 121 o. V 14–15; 127 o. V 3–4; 128 o. IV 5–6; 134 r. III 10–11). The untitled official who is mentioned as the recipient of plots of land in 80 o. IV 6; 81 o. III 2; 89 o. II 4; and 104 o. III 2 may be our dub-sar, considering the relationship between the field allotment texts and those concerning asses and carts for agricultural use.[60] The same anthroponym is mentioned in a list of people in TSŠ 622 o. II 4. Possibly A-du$_6$ is an abbreviated form for A-du$_6$-la, an official who occurs in both a field allotment text (94 o. II 8) and one concerning carts (172 o. IV 9).

58. Cf. *Bureau*, p. 78, 212 r. III 2–4: dub Ur-kin-nir En-ki-zi-da.

59. Ur-^{d}Nin-Unug^{ki} sagi, who occurs as a lú-ki-inim in *Or*NS 44 (1975): 436 o. VI 6' and TMH 5, 75 o. V 3, is mentioned in three administrative texts: 116 o. V 13–14; 147 o. IV 1–2; and 165 r. I 2–3 as the recipient of asses for agricultural use.

60. Cf. EDATŠ, pp. 217, 306–8.

A-ḫu/RI-ti dub-sar is mentioned in field allotment texts (68 o. I 6–7; 69 o. I 6–II 1), in texts concerning asses (121 o. I 3–4; 132 o. V 5–6) and in guruš conscription texts (183 o. III 2–3; 195 o. V 1–2). He is also mentioned in two lists of persons in TSŠ 936 o. I 3 (only the obverse of which has survived) and WF 121 o. I 1–2. Five of the officials mentioned in TSŠ 936, among whom is our dub-sar, apparently travelled to Kiš, for reasons unknown to us (Eden-su Ḫur-sag-šè-maḫ A-ḫu-ti dub-sar Ḫur-sag-šè-maḫ Mu[nus-bá]ra-si Kiš^{ki} DU.DU). Five of the officials mentioned in WF 121 (except for Šeš-tur kuš$_7$, who occurs only in this text) occur almost exclusively in field allotment texts and in texts concerning asses and carts for agricultural use. A namesake official without title occurs as a lú-ki-inim in a contract (Ung. 2 o. IV 2), but identification is very uncertain. This official is one of the scribes in charge of personnel (dumu-dumu) belonging to the palace administration (é-gal) in 183 o. III 2–3 and who are subordinates to different ugula's.[61]

⌜A$^?$⌝-NI dub-sar is mentioned in a barley text (26 o. III 4–5) as the recipient of ½ gur. The reading of this anthroponym is uncertain. Moreover, this official does not appear elsewhere with this characterizing element, so that it is difficult to establish correspondences with other texts of this group.[62] Since text 26 has several correspondences with 23–25 and 27, all of which are texts regarding sailors (lú-má), it appears that this scribe may have worked for the KISAL, the administrative center connected to the lú-má and headed by the nu-bànda ^{d}En-líl-pà, the superior of other dub-sar's and class B engar's.[63]

A-pa-è dub-sar is mentioned in WF 138 r. III 2–3 as the official to whom Me-GÌR is subordinate. The text is a record of various goods, i.e., silver, clothing, copper, sheep, barley, emmer, grease, and a cart. Besides A-pa-è, other scribes are mentioned in the text: ^{d}Sùd-

---

61. Cf. *Bureau*, p. 13.

62. Group II consists of texts 14–37. On the relationship among the barley texts, which have been divided into different groups, cf. EDATŠ, pp. 27, 94, 177, 183, 203.

63. Cf. *Bureau*, pp. 110, 113–14.

anzu, Ul-la, and Amar-[ ]. The findspot of this tablet is unknown, but because of the large variety of goods mentioned, the document should be linked to those that come from site XVIIc,d, such as WF 118; 150; 152; and TSŠ 782.[64] This is confirmed by the mention in WF 138 of ^{d}Sùd-anzu dub-sar, who is one of the scribes mentioned in 40—a text that, with 38 and 39, records large quantities of barley, comes from the site in question, and is concerned with warlike activities.[65]

Amar-é-^{d}Gibil$_{6}$ dub-sar is mentioned in two texts concerning asses (116 o. VIII 18–19 and 139 o. VI 8–9). Occurrences of this anthroponym are rare.[66]

Amar-kù dub-sar sanga-GAR is one of the four scribes who seem to have been direct subordinates of the sanga-GAR. Like direct subordinates of the sa$_{12}$-du$_{5}$, they worked for the small group of dub-sar of the é-géme, the office directly under the énsi-GAR-gal, which controlled both the whole administration and the entire organizational system that managed the production and distribution of goods.[67] This scribe is mentioned in 10 r. II 6–8 as the recipient of 1 gur of barley. An official of the same name, but without a characterizing element, is the recipient of the same amount of barley in 7 r. I 8 and 8 o. I 6 and is certainly our dub-sar.[68] This official probably should be distinguished from the namesake SAL.UŠ sanga-GAR who is mentioned in a barley text of Group II and in some texts concerning asses.

Amar-[ ] dub-sar is mentioned in WF 138 r. I 6–II 1.

Bil$_{x}$-anzu dub-sar is mentioned in 12 r. IV 11–12 as the recipient of 2 gur of barley and in a text concerning asses (141 o. II 3–4). His mention in a barley text in Group I indicates that he worked for the

64. Cf. *Bureau*, pp. 84–88.

65. Cf. *Bureau*, p. 85.

66. A namesake Lú-dag is mentioned in 11 r. III 12–14 as the recipient of 1 gur of barley.

67. Cf. *Bureau*, pp. 109–12.

68. Cf. EDATŠ, pp. 30, 65–68.

palace administration. In all likelihood he should be distinguished both from the ugula-KISAL of the same name who appears in the barley texts of Group II and from the namesake dam-gàr mentioned in a text concerning field allotments (82 o. V 9–10) and in some texts concerning asses (116 o. III 7–8; 117 r. III 5'–6'[69]; 121 r. III 11–12; 140 o. IV 6).

Da-du-lul dub-sar is mentioned as the recipient of ½ gur of barley in 19 o. VIII 10–11, one of the three large *Sammeltafeln* that collect most of the items in the texts of Group II.[70] Although he is not mentioned in any other text of this type, an official of the same name, without any characterizing element, is mentioned in WF 149 r. III 4, a text recording allocations of from 1 to 6 mina of copper. Note that in this text the scribes Á-nu-kúš (r. II 8–9), Šeš-ki-na (r. IV 11–r. I 1), and Šita (r. II 10–11) are mentioned.

Dumu-nun-šita dub-sar is mentioned in WF 135 r. II 3–4 as the scribe who compiled the tablet or as the person in charge of the this transaction. The same official is mentioned in the same text in r. I 5–6 as the supervisor of Da-dum lú-^{giš}gigir-u$_5$. He is also mentioned in TSŠ 649 o. I 3–II 1, a small text concerning reeds, which lists only one recipient, É-AŠ.SAG, who receives 480 gi. Our scribe is mentioned immediately after this recipient; thus, he could be either the compiler of the tablet or É-AŠ.SAG's superior. Possibly É-AŠ.SAG is also a scribe, on the basis of 207 r. I 1.[71] There are no other references to Dumu-nun-šita dub-sar and there are no cogent reasons for identifying him with namesake officials often mentioned in the documents. But since WF 135 and TSŠ 649 concern the allocation of fibers/textiles, for which our scribe seems to have been responsible, it is possible that he is an official in charge of the management of this commodity. If so, perhaps our dub-sar is the Dumu-nun-šita ^{d}Nisaba mentioned in two parallel texts concerning fibers/textiles (TSŠ 303 o. I 4'–5' and NTSŠ 92 o. I 4–7). Dumu-nun-šita ba-ba, an official frequently mentioned in the field allotment texts, which

69. In this text he is titled *na-di-nu*, the Akkadian word for dam-gàr.

70. Cf. EDATŠ, pp. 94–96.

71. Cf. *Bureau*, p. 71.

concern asses and carts for agricultural work, and two grain texts (TSŠ 160; 960) is also mentioned in a text concerning fibers/ textiles (TSŠ 368 r. II 5–6).

É-du$_6$ dub-sar tigi$_x$-di is mentioned in a text from Group I (10 o. VI 6–8) as the recipient of 1 gur of barley. Judging by his title and by the text type, he worked for the palace administration (é-gal) and possibly for the é-géme.[72]

É-gù-nun is mentioned in 38 o. II 2–3 and 40 o. I 3 as the person in charge of large quantities of grain (102 gur in 38; 108 gur in 40; and in 39 o. II 1–2 [2 še gur šu-bad Pa$_4$-á-nu-kúš É-gù-nun]). All the officials mentioned in these three texts, with the exception of É-gù-nun, occur as dub-sar's or agrig's in the administrative documentation. Our official probably had the same title. The fact that no title is listed should probably be attributed to the limits of the tablet. In TSŠ 64 r. I 1'–2', É-gù-[ ] dam-kas$_4$, the official in charge of tributes,[73] is mentioned, who perhaps is the official mentioned in 38–40.

É-ḫur-sag dub-sar is mentioned in some texts concerning asses (116 r. II 14–15; 121 r. V 9–10; 122 r. V 9; and 123 r. IV 5–6). We cannot determine to which administrative center this scribe belonged or his responsibilities.

É-kur-pa-è dub-sar (see Pa$_4$-é-kur-pa-è, TABLE 2) is mentioned in a text concerning asses (127 o. IV 2–3) and in a list of persons (TSŠ 936 o. II 6–r. I 2). Undoubtedly this anthroponym is an abbreviation for Pa$_4$-é-kur-pa-è, a dub-sar mentioned in 143 o. III 13–14. A namesake agrig also occurs in the list of the subordinates of the ugula-agrig Dub-ḫul-tar in 3 r. I 5'. But it is uncertain that this is the same official.

---

72. An official of the same name is mentioned in the barley texts of Group II (14 o. V 7–8; 15 o. V 7; 30 r. II 7'; 31 r. I 5'), where he is followed by the characterizing element kin-nir, one of the cattle-breeding centers (cf. *Bureau*, p. 123). But there is insufficient evidence to link him to our dub-sar. An official with the same name, mentioned without a characterizing element, is the recipient of two anše-kunga (or suḫub$_x$ suggestion by Bauer) in 171 r. I 3–II 1 and of grain products in TSŠ 775 o. I 3.

73. Cf. G. Visicato, *OrNS* 61 (1992): 97, n. 8.

É-na-lu-lu dub-sar is mentioned in two texts concerning asses (115 r. V 18–VI 1 and 144 r. I 2–3). He is not mentioned elsewhere with this characterizing element. He is mentioned untitled in texts concerning fields (88 o. III 5; 92 o. I 3; 97 o. III 1), in texts concerning asses (136 r. I 9'; 147 o. III 4; 151 o. I 1–2; 162 o. I 3; II 2), and in a text concerning carts (172 o. IV 10). Because of the well-known relationship among these kinds of texts it is probable that the individuals in question are the same person. Given the frequency with which this anthroponym is mentioned, it is extremely difficult to identify this dub-sar with namesake officials. The É-na-lu-lu, whose subordinates Abzu-ki-du$_{10}$ and AN-sag-tuku are mentioned elsewhere as dub-sar and umbisag, may be our dub-sar.[74]

É-saḫar-ta/ra dub-sar is mentioned as the official whose subordinate is Uš-<du$_{10}$> (14 o. V 19–20; 15 o. VI 8). Since in the same section of 14 (that of the engar En-ki-šè) several subordinates of Bil$_x$-kalam-du$_{10}$, ugula of the KISAL (an office to which lú-má, engar, and several dub-sar's belonged) occur among the recipients, as well as Uš-du$_{10}$, it is possible that our dub-sar was involved in shipping activities.[75]

Eden-si dub-sar occurs in two parallel texts dealing with asses (127 o. V 6–7 and 128 o. V 1–2).

En-nagar-šà dub-sar is mentioned in a barley text in Group I (7 r. II 9–10) as the official whose subordinate is ^{d}Sùd-anzu. Because of the characteristics of the text and other occurrences, he is probably a dub-sar. In addition, he is mentioned with ^{d}Sùd-anzu in two texts concerning asses (116 o. II 9–10 and 121 r. III 3–4). Probably he was a very high-ranking official and the fact that he is rarely mentioned may be because generally he is mentioned only by his title. In fact, ^{d}Sùd-anzu, a subordinate of En-nagar-šà, may be the namesake dub-sar sanga-GAR who occurs in a barley text in Group I (10 o. VI 3–5), and therefore En-nagar-šà may be the sanga-GAR himself or one of the high-ranking, direct subordinates of the sanga-GAR.

---

74. Abzu-ki-du$_{10}$ É-na-lu-lu 116 o. VII 1–2; 165 o. I 2–3; AN-sag-tuku É-na-lu-lu 68 o. IV 16; 70 o. III 1; 104 r. II 3–5; 124 o. VIII 4–5; 135 r. I 2'–3'; 142 o. V 1–2; 173 o. V 1–2.

75. É-saḫar-ta/ra is a shortened form of É-saḫar-ta-è, a personal name, which occurs often in the Fara documents. Cf. Visicato, *Indices*, p. 35.

GAR-du-la dub-sar is the recipient of 1½ gur of barley in 29 r. II 15–16 and of asses for agricultural work in 116 o. VIII 10–11. In the section of 29 that concerns engar mu$_6$-sùb[76] and where GAR-du-la is mentioned, lú-má, addir$_x$, and personnel who are subordinates of the lú-má-gal-gal occur. Therefore, most likely, GAR-du-la, like É-saḫar-ta, may have been involved in shipping. The fact that GAR-du-la is not mentioned in the dub-lú-má, text 23, the tablet which collects the allocations for the lú-má personnel, need not surprise us. This *Sammeltafel* collects the allocations only for middle-to-low-ranking personnel and not middle-to-high-ranking personnel, who, for the most part, are gathered in text 29. The mention in this section of text 29 of the lú-má-gal-gal, the official in charge of the lú-má, precludes the possibility that GAR-du-la worked for the KISAL. Based on the text, it appears that the lú-má-gal-gal are direct subordinates of the ugula-énsi Amar-nam-nir.[77] An official of the same name, but without a characterizing element, is mentioned in WF 151* o. III 1–r. I 1 as the recipient of oil, wool, copper, textiles, silver, and pigs. The other recipients mentioned in the text are indicated by profession only, gala and sukkal. According to Fara scribal practice, this indicates the highest-ranking official of the corporation, namely the gala-maḫ and the gal-sukkal.[78] Consequently, the GAR-du-la mentioned in WF 151* should be an official of very high rank and probably is our dub-sar. One cannot, however, exclude the possibility that GAR-du-la is just one of the scribes or the scribe in charge of the office of the lú-má-gal-gal.

KA-ni-zi dub-sar sa$_{12}$-du$_5$ is mentioned in 10 o. VI 9–11 as the recipient of 2 gur of barley.[79] He is also mentioned as a recipient of barley in a text of Group II (19 r. V 8–9). It is likely that the KA-ni-zi mentioned

---

76. The engars in the Fara ration texts of the people of group 2 are responsible for the barley delivered; cf. EDATŠ, pp. 98–102.

77. Cf. *Bureau*, pp. 51–53.

78. Cf. EDATŠ, pp. 63, 138.

79. Line 10 o. VI 11 has been lost. A comparison with 36 o. VI 6–7 and 187 r. II 2–3 (KA-ni-zi sa$_{12}$-du$_5$) leads us to suggest that this official may be one of the sa$_{12}$-du$_5$ scribes.

in 7 r. I 6–7 and 8 o. I 1–2 (two texts concerning the allocation of barley to the scribes and to the subordinates of a dub-sar-maḫ) is our dub-sar. Only very few officials are mentioned contemporaneously as recipients in Groups I and II of barley texts. These are the highest-ranking officials, who exercise a supervisory and coordinating function among the various administrative centers on behalf of the é-géme and, therefore, on behalf of the énsi himself. Consequently, it is not surprising that KA-ni-zi is one of the scribes in the barley texts, 38–40.

Lu-lu agrig is mentioned in 10 o. V 5–7 in which he is the recipient of ⅓ gur of barley. He is, however, to be regarded as a middle-to-low-ranking scribe, like all the agrig subordinates of Dub-ḫul-tar who are mentioned in the third section of 3 (r. I 7–II 7). The mention in CT 50, 20 o. II 1' of a namesake dub-sar indicates that this official, although his remuneration is equal to that of middle-to-low-ranking subordinates, is a real scribe, even if he is at the lowest level of the hierarchy.

Lugal-á-maḫ dub-sar is the scribe who signed 212, a list of personnel at work in one or more im-ru.[80] Like KA-ni-zi, this scribe is responsible for large quantities of barley in 38–40.

Mes-nu-šè dub-sar is mentioned as the recipient of 1 gur of barley in two parallel texts (14 o. III 16'–17' and 15 o. III 10–IV 1). We cannot establish the activity in which this scribe was engaged.

Mu-ni-da dub-sar is mentioned in 115 o. V 15–16 as the recipient of asses for agricultural work. Perhaps he is the namesake official, without a characterizing element, who is mentioned as the recipient of 3 gur of barley in 29 r. I 5.

Si-dù agrig is mentioned in 152 o. III 3–4. Like KA-ni-zi and Lugal-á-maḫ, he is one of the scribes mentioned in 38–40. Perhaps the namesake subordinate of Abzu-ki-du$_{10}$, elsewhere a dub-sar and sanga, mentioned in 14 o. X 4–6, is this agrig.

^{d}Sùd-šer$_{7}$-zi dub-sar is mentioned exclusively like the scribe Eden-si in 127 o. V 5–6 and 128 o. IV 3–4. This anthroponym is not mentioned elsewhere.

---

80. Cf. *Bureau*, pp. 76–78.

Šà-ge-TAR dub-sar is mentioned in the dub-lú-má, 23 o. VI 11–r. I 1 and in the parallel passages in 24 and 25 as the official whose subordinate is ^{d}En-líl-unken-a, probably a lú-má. It seems clear that our dub-sar worked for the administration that deals with shipping matters.

Šeš-ama-na dub-sar is the scribe who has recorded or was in charge of one of the SI.NUxŠUŠ transactions in TSŠ 627 o. I 1–6, delivered to an unnamed maškim of Da-da, a subordinate of the sanga-GAR of the household of the god Enlil. He is one of the scribes mentioned in 38 and 39.

Šeš-ki-na dub-sar is mentioned in WF 149 o. IV 11–V 1 as the official whose subordinate, KA-ni, is the recipient of two minas of copper. The document seems to be a *Sammeltafel* that collects other texts concerning copper.[81] This anthroponym is very common in the onomasticon of Fara, and, therefore, it is difficult to identify our dub-sar. Perhaps he is the namesake official responsible for a *ganun*, "granary," who occurs in a barley text (37 o. VI' 10'–11'), in texts concerning asses (132 r. VIII 5–6 and perhaps 135 r. V 5–6), and in a list of names (WF 108 o. III 3–4). Finally, Šeš-ki-na with the characterizing element é-al-la, the name of a district or household, occurs[82] in 117 o. V 3–4 and 124 r. III 4–5.

Ul$_4$-la dub-sar is mentioned in WF 138 o. III 4–6. From the text it would seem that Ul$_4$-la is the official whose "cantor" (tigi$_x$-di),[83] is the recipient of barley, grease, and textiles (tigi$_x$-di Ul$_4$-la). It appears to be more probable that Ul$_4$-la is the person in charge of these goods that are destined for the tigi$_x$-di, a high-ranking official among whose subordinates is the dub-sar É-du$_6$.[84] This anthroponym is not mentioned elsewhere.

---

81. Cf. EDATŠ, p. 23.

82. For a more extensive discussion of the é-al-la, see *Bureau*, pp. 94–95.

83. The professional name tigi$_x$(BALAG)-di occurs many times in the Fara texts (see Visicato, *Indices*, p. 118). For the meaning of tigi$_x$-di as "musician," "lyre player," see SD B p. 79, sub BALAG B. PSD: balag-di

84. Cf. above, p. 31.

Ur-${}^{\langle d\rangle}$Dumu-zi dub-sar is mentioned in 14 o. V 14–15 and in 35 r. IV 4–5 as the official whose subordinate is the dub-sar ^{d}Sùd-anzu. In addition, he occurs as a recipient in 14 o. VII 16–17; 15 r. III 3–4; and 19 r. I 3–4. In 14 o. VII 16–17 and 15 r. III 3–4 he is listed as a scribe, the subordinate of Pa$_{4}$-^{d}anzu, probably one of the higher-ranking dub-sar's. He is also mentioned in field allotment texts (68 o. VI 15–16; 71 o. III 6–7; 73 o. V 4–5; 93 o. III 2–3), in texts concerning asses (124 r. VI 5–6; 140 o. II 3–4; 143 o. V 9–10), and in texts concerning carts for agricultural use (173 o. VI 6–7; 174 o. II 6–7). He may be a scribe subordinate to the nu-bànda ^{d}En-líl-pà and he may be the namesake Ur-Dumu-zi nu-bànda, mentioned in texts concerning asses (different from those where the namesake dub-sar is mentioned) and Ur-Dumu-zi ^{d}En-líl-pà, mentioned in the dub-lú-má 23.[85] Thus, this official may have worked for the KISAL.

Ur-^{d}Šer$_{7}$-da dub-sar is mentioned as a recipient in texts concerning fields (68 o. VII 10–11; 72 o. I 7–11; 74 o. VI 5–6; 77 o. I 5–II 2; 79 o. I 5–II 1) and asses (115 r. II 14–III 1; 147 o. II 10–III1). The namesake lú-ki-inim, mentioned in WF 35 o. II 6 without a characterizing element, and the namesake recipient of 1 udu in TSŠ 385 III' 6' could be our dub-sar.

Utu-á-maḫ dub-sar-maḫ is mentioned in CT 50, 19 o. II 2–3. The title should indicate that he is a subordinate of the dub-sar-maḫ and not the dub-sar-maḫ himself, who is normally unnamed in texts (23 r. I 3–4; 27 o. VI 12; 94 r. I 1–2; TSŠ 420 o. IV 3; 679 o. II 1). An untitled namesake official, mentioned in texts concerning fields (68 r. I 5; 72 o. III 4; 74 o. V 5) and in a text concerning asses (124 r. V 8) may be our dub-sar. In fact, in CT 50, 19, he is the recipient of sheep with ^{d}En-líl-unken-a, Munus-á-nu-kúš, AN-nu-me, Maš-^{d}Sùd and AK.-^{d}<Sùd>.

(c) Scribes Mentioned in Economic Documents and in Lexical Texts[86]

A-geštin dub-sar is mentioned in texts concerning asses (134 r. II 6–7; 135 o. IV 8–9; 146 o. III 6–7). In a barley text in Group II (37 r. I 1–

85. Cf. *Bureau*, pp. 110, 114.

86. The term "economic documentation" is used to refer both to the administrative documentation of the institution and contracts.

4), A-geštin is the recipient of barley and is titled dub-sar na-gada ^{d}Sùd. This characterizing element indicates that A-geštin is the dub-sar or one of the dub-sar's of a cattle-breeding station connected to the household of the goddess ^{d}Sùd.[87] In the contract WF 30 o. V 2 this untitled anthroponym occurs as a lú-ki-inim. In the colophon of NTSŠ 229 V 5', a certain A-dam-geštin occurs as an umbisag; but it is uncertain whether it is the same scribe who appears in the administrative texts.

Abzu-ki-<dúr>-du$_{10}$ dub-sar occurs in 14 o. X 5–6 as the official whose subordinate is Si-dù, the agrig. In addition, he is mentioned as a recipient in field allotment texts (68 o. VI 3–4; 71 o. II 1'–2'; 74 r. I 5–6); in texts concerning asses (121 r. III 14; 135 r. II 5'–6'); and in texts concerning carts (173 o. VI 6–7; 174 o. II 4–5). Abzu-ki-dúr-du$_{10}$ occurs in a list of witnesses (WF 42 o. IV 3–4).

Ad-da-da dub-sar is mentioned in TSŠ 90 o. I 3–4, a text concerning copper, in which recipients are described as lú-simug-<gal> after the summary. Thus, Ad-da-da must have worked for the metal- working center. A namesake official, the recipient of barley in 8 o. I 4 and mentioned without a characterizing element, may be our dub-sar, because of the characteristics of texts 7 and 8. He appears again as a lú-šám-kú in TSŠ X o. II 3. As an umbisag he occurs in SF 77 r. 6. Probably Ad-da umbisag in SF 20 is our Ad-da-da.[88]

Amar-NÁM is mentioned in 7 o. III 9 as the recipient of 1 gur of barley and must therefore be regarded as a scribe or the subordinate of a dub-sar-maḫ. He does not occur elsewhere. A namesake umbisag occurs in the colophons of several lexical texts.[89]

<Amar>-sag-TAR dub-sar occurs in A. 33676 o. III 9 as a witness. Written in the short form Sag-TAR, he is mentioned in 115 o. VI 13–14; 121 r. I 7'–8'; and 122 o. VIII 7'–8'. Perhaps he is the namesake subordinate of the sanga-GAR mentioned in TSŠ 614 o. I 5–6.

87. For breeding stations connected to temple households, cf. *Bureau*, pp. 120–29.

88. Note Ad-da munus Abzu-mud, who occurs in 7 o. I' 4, and Ad-da-da Abzu-mud, who occurs in 124 o. III 6 and TSŠ 90 o. II 3.

89. SF 29; 33; 36; 42; 55; 59; 60; 63; 64; 69; 73; 75; TSS 46R; 80; 124.

Amar-šùba dub-sar is mentioned in 12 r. V 2–3 as the recipient of 1 gur of barley and in 115 o. VI 16–17 as the official whose subordinate is a certain Kun-dù. He is also mentioned as the recipient in WF 138 r. I 6–II 1. A namesake official with the title gal-unken (7 r. II 2–3; 35 o. VII 8–9; and 116 o. II 11–12) and the namesake untitled official mentioned in 8 o. II 1[90] probably are our dub-sar. He occurs in TLAT 1 r. II 9–III 1, a contract for the sale of a house, as lú-ki-inim.[91] Finally, a namesake umbisag is mentioned in SF 37 r. VI 4'.

AN-nu-me is mentioned in 7 r. II 1, without any characterizing element, as the recipient of barley. Like Amar-NÁM he should be regarded as a scribe. But it is extremely difficult to identify him with one of the very many officials mentioned in the documents bearing the same name. A namesake umbisag is mentioned but written differently in SF 13; 16; 39; 44.[92]

AN-sag-tuku dub-sar[93] is mentioned after the summary in two barley texts (20 r. VIII' 4–5; 27 r. VI 12) and in three texts concerning asses (121 r. VI 1'–2'; 122 r. VII 2–4; 138 r. I 1–4), probably as the scribe who compiled these tablets or as the official who supervised the recording of the transactions. It should be noted that administrative tablets, in contrast to literary or lexical ones, are rarely signed by a dub-sar. Besides the tablets where AN-sag-tuku is mentioned, only a

---

90. Amar-šùba, a namesake official mentioned as an ugula-é-géme, occurs in 46 o. II 8–9. This ugula occurs several times in sequence with two other officials in texts concerning carts (172 o. V 11–13) and in two guruš conscription texts (188 o. IV 1–3 and 191 o. II 5'–9'). The two officials who occur with Amar-šùba are Amar-tùr (described in 46 o. III 1–2 following Amar-šùba as ugula-é-géme) and Amar-nam-nir (described in 23 o. VI 9–12 and in the parallel passages in 24 and 25 as ugula-énsi-GAR). This last-mentioned profession is the same as ugula-é-géme (cf. *Bureau*, pp. 109–12). Amar-tùr and Amar-nam-nir are mentioned as umbisag in lexical texts, in SF 57 and NTSŠ 229 r. 6 respectively. This set of coincidences may indicate that not only Amar-šùba but also Amar-tùr and Amar-nim-nir ugula-é-géme/ugula-énsi-GAR may have been scribes.

91. Steinkeller and Postgate, TLAT, p. 14, read this PN as Amar-⌜má⌝, but Bauer (personal communication) has suggested a restoration Amar-⌜šùba⌝.

92. Cf. P. Mander, "I colofoni di Fara, Abū-Ṣalābīkh ed Ebla: approccio prosopografico," in L. Cagni, ed., *Il Bilinguismo ad Ebla* (Naples, 1984), p. 340.

93. Perhaps a reading sag-dingir-tuku is better.

few others contain an indication of a scribe: 19, one of the barley *Sammeltafeln* in Group II, is signed by the dub-sar Šubur; 183, a conscription text regarding personnel of the palace administration (é-gal) is signed by Aḫuti; 195, a guruš conscription text, is signed by Šubur bur-šu-ma (probably the same scribe who had signed 19); 211, a text listing personnel belonging to one or more im-ru's, is signed by Lugal-á-maḫ; and 212, a text concerning personnel involved in agricultural work, is signed by Ur-kin-nir. AN-sag-tuku also occurs as an umbisag in the colophons of several lexical texts.[94]

AN-úr-šè dub-sar is mentioned as the recipient of barley in 37 r. V' 5'–6'; of land in 68 r. II 3–4; 72 o. IV 4–5; 73 o. IV 8–9; and of asses in 115 r. V 16–17; 121 r. VI 7'–8'; 122 r. IV 4–5; and 123 r. V 3–4. An official of the same name has é-al-la as a characterizing element. A namesake untitled official is mentioned in 124 r. IV 13–14; 128 r. IV 2–3; 132 r. III 9–10; 134 r. I 1–2; 135 o. I 6–7; 136 r. IV 9–10, all texts concerning asses. It cannot be excluded that here we are dealing with the same official. An umbisag of the same name is mentioned in the colophons of lexical texts.[95]

Bil$_x$-á-nu-kúš dub-sar should be distinguished from Pa$_4$-á-nu-kúš dub-sar-udu (see below). That this latter anthroponym could be an abbreviated form of the former can be excluded in as much as both dub-sar's occur contemporaneously in the same texts as recipients of asses (Bil$_x$-á-nu-kúš dub-sar in 121 o. VI 13–14; 123 o. IV 6' and Pa$_4$-á-nu-kúš dub-sar in 121 r. I 3'–4'; 123 r. II 1–2). The two scribes could be related; this seems to be suggested by a passage in a contract, *WO* 8 (1975): 180 o. V 5–r. I 1–2; [ ] kù gín Pa$_4$-nu-kúš dub-sar Bil$_x$-nu-kúš dub-sar dumu Pa$_4$-nu-kúš,[96] "x sickles of silver for Pa$_4$-nu-kúš the scribe and for Bil$_x$-nu-kúš the scribe, the son of Pa$_4$-nu-kúš"; both of the officials mentioned after the GU.NUN.SUR

94. SF 18 o. VII 9; 29 r. III 16; 33 r. II 12; 36 o. IX 5; TSŠ 124 r. II 3'; and others.

95. SF 59 o. VII 3'; 64 r. II 17.

96. In both anthroponyms the sign Á is omitted, but there can be no doubt about the identity of the two scribes. Moreover, the term dumu does not necessarily indicate a blood relationship. It could simply mean, as in all the administrative documentation of Fara, that the first-mentioned official was a subordinate of the second (cf. EDATŠ, p. 63).

should be the dub-sar-aša$_5$ of the contract.[97] Our official is mentioned as a recipient in field allotment texts (68 r. III 14–15; 72 r. II 1–2; 74 r. III 9–10; 76 o. II 3–4; 82 r. I 1–2) and in texts concerning asses (121 o. VI 13–14; 123 o. IV 6'; 134 o. VII 1–2; 135 r. V 3–4; 140 o. V 2–3). A namesake umbisag is mentioned in TSŠ 46 *partie gauche* 2'.

Du-du occurs as dub-sar-aša$_5$ in YBC 12305 r. II 56. Probably he is the namesake maškim dub-sar-maḫ dam-kas$_4$ who occurs in a text of SI.NUxŠUŠ (TSŠ 369 t. I 3–5). A namesake agrig occurs in 3 r. II 4'.

Dub-ḫul-tar dub-sar/agrig is the recipient, as a dub-sar, of 1 gur of barley in 14 o. IX 7–8 and 15 r. VI 5. His name means "he who smashes the bad tablet."[98] He is mentioned as an ugula-agrig in 3 c. II 6'–7'. In this latter text he is in charge of a group of agrig's, who receive monthly rations amounting to ⅓ gur while he receives ½ gur. Although he is mentioned as an agrig only in a dumu-dumu conscription text, he is in fact the ugula in charge of an im-ru of agrig's (181 o. IV 2–3). Dub-ḫul-tar agrig is the recipient of a plot of land in 68 r. III 8–9 and 73 o. IV 6–7 and of asses in 134 r. III 12–13. He is also one of the scribes mentioned in 38 and 39. Finally, he is mentioned as an umbisag in NTSŠ 229 r. 3 (collated by R. Biggs).

É-^{d}Nanna dub-sar is mentioned in two texts concerning asses (132 r. II 6–7 and 136 r. I 5–6). A namesake official, without a characterizing element, is the recipient of 1 gur of barley in 8 o. III 6 and certainly is our dub-sar in accordance with what has been said in our discussion of texts 7 and 8. In NBC 6842 r. I 2–3 he is dub-sar-aša$_5$.

É-šùd-du$_{10}$ dub-sar is mentioned in 132 r. V 7–8 as recipient of asses. In 187 r. I 4–5, a text concerning the conscription of soldiers, he is the official who, with ^{d}Sùd-anzu dub-sar and Nam-maḫ sipa, is in charge of a contingent of 60 guruš-mè. He occurs in TSŠ 423 r. I 1–2 as the superior of a recipient of LAḪTANxGU whose name is lost. A namesake official, without a characterizing element but who should definitely be identified with our dub-sar, signed a tablet concerning the allocation of beverages (TSŠ 775 r. II 2). It is likely that the official

97. This would be the only case where two dub-sar-aša$_5$'s were mentioned in a sale contract of a field.

98. Cf. F. Pomponio, "Colui che spezza la tavoletta cattiva," *SEL* 3 (1986): 13–16.

who is the recipient of grain and sheep in TSŠ 928 II 2 is our dub-sar. It is also possible to connect our scribe with the namesake gal-dilmun mentioned as a recipient in a text concerning textiles (WF 136 o. III 1–2). Finally, it should be noted that the name, partially lost, of the umbisag É-[ ]-du$_{10}$ in SF 39 can be read É-[šùd]-du$_{10}$.

É-zi-pa-è dub-sar is mentioned as a recipient in field allotment texts (68 o. V 7–8; 70 o. IV 2–3; 82 o. IV 5; 96 o. I 2), of asses (136 o. V 9–10), and of carts for use in agriculture (172 o. VII 6). He is also mentioned in a personnel recruitment text, 212 o. I 6–II 1, as overseeing a subordinate. A certain É-zi, perhaps an abbreviation of É-zi-pa-è, occurs as an um-mi-a lú-é-éš-gar in TMH 5, 71 r. I 2. The same may be true for the name É-pa-è dub-sar, who occurs as a lú-ki-inim in Ung. 2 r. I 2.

Gissu-šè dub-sar is mentioned as a lú-ki-inim in MVN 10, 83 r. I 1. An umbisag of the same name is mentioned in the colophons of lexical and literary texts.[99]

Ḫar-tu-^{d}Sùd dub-sar occurs in 11 r. III 2–3 as the recipient of 1 [+x] gur of barley. A namesake umbisag is mentioned in SF 1 r. VII 9'. A namesake sa$_{12}$-du$_5$ occurs in A. 33676 o. VI 8–9, but there is insufficient evidence for an identification of this official with our scribe.

KA-lugal-da-zi, without any characterizing element, is mentioned in WF 34 r. IV 1–2 as a lu-aša$_5$-šám, the purchaser of a field. A namesake umbisag is mentioned in TSŠ 46R *partie gauche* 4'; TSŠ 80 r. I 1 and in NTSŠ 294 r. 2.

Lugal-ki-dúr-du$_{10}$ dub-sar occurs in texts concerning asses (121 r. III 9–10; 123 r. II 1–2; 141 o. II 5–6); in a list of persons (NTSŠ 258 o. III 2–3); and in a list of witnesses (WF 42 o. I 3). He is one of the ten dub-sar's mentioned in 38–40.[100] A namesake umbisag is mentioned in NTSŠ 294 r. 5 and SF 62 r. VI 3.

---

99. SF 36; 69 (dub mu-sar). This anthroponym, often mentioned in the administrative documents as a Class A engar (cf. EDATŠ, pp. 98–101, Table 3), never occurs as a dub-sar in the latter.

100. A namesake official described as a dam-gàr and a subordinate of Lugal-dumu-zi is mentioned in 124 o. IV 5–6; 125 o. IV 3–4; 126 o. II 8–9; 139 o. II 5–6; and 145 r. II 5–6. Possibly the two officials are the same individual.

Lum-ma dub-sar is mentioned in texts concerning asses (116 o. VI 10–11; 117 r. V 7'–8'; 128 r. III 4–5; 164 o. I 7–8) and in a list of persons (WF 120 r. I 1–2). He also occurs as the recipient of 4 gur of barley in 7 r. I 2–3 in which he is described as dub-sar-anše sa$_{12}$-du$_{5}$. He is mentioned in 121 r. IV 6–8 and 122 r. IV 1–3 with the title dub-sar-<é>-géme—as has been shown in *Bureau*,[101] both terms denote the same office. He occurs as one of the officials in charge of barley in 39. This official is of very high rank and worked for the office of the é-géme. Lum-ma works for the é-géme on behalf of the sa$_{12}$-du$_{5}$, one of the highest-ranking officials in the administration. He is probably the supervisor of management and breeding stations for asses. A namesake umbisag and dub-mu-sar is mentioned in NTSŠ 294; SF 16; SF 27; and in a literary text, see IAS p. 27.

Nam-maḫ dub-sar occurs several times in TSŠ 881 o. VIII 4–5; IX 13–14; r. I 12'; II 9'–10'; 16'–17'; VII 6'–7'; 11'–12'. This document contains 20 columns and is divided into various sections, each of which is concluded by the name of the official in charge of the allocations (UR.UR maškim-maškim-gi$_{4}$ or Nam-maḫ dub-sar). The sections are divided into subsections with various entries listed in each, one for each type of goods (e.g., barley, flour, oil, beverages), followed by the name of the official who is the recipient of the allocation and often the u$_{4}$+number clause, indicating the day the goods were delivered. After the summary, the numerical part of which is lost, the iti-[ ]-clause is recorded, which provides a monthly summary of a long series of daily allocations.[102] Nam-maḫ is one of the ten scribes mentioned in 38–40. He also occurs as um-mi-a lú-é-éš-gar in RTC 13 r. I 4–6; TLAT 1 r. III 10–IV 2. In an unpublished contract (De Marcellis tablet r. III 2–4) the um-mi-a lú-é-éš-gar is Nam-maḫ-^{d}Sùd-da. Nam-maḫ is surely a hypocoristic form of this

101. *Bureau*, pp. 109–11.

102. Because of the type of goods allocated and the mention of recipients from other cities ([ ]-ma [x]-x-ma^{ki} o. I 7'–8'; GAR.AB-si Sippar^{ki} VI 11–12; Amar-sún šu-ku$_{6}$ NIM r. IV 3'–4'; lú-ú-ku$_{5}$ Kiš^{ki} šu ba-ti IV 14'–17'; lú-u$_{5}$ NIM VIII 5'–6'), it is possible that TSŠ 881 is a summary document of messenger tablets. Unfortunately, only two examples of this text typology are attested, 60 and TSŠ 135 (cf. EDATŠ, p. 206). Among the Schmidt tablets, F 600 belongs to this typology.

name.[103] As a witness, he occurs in A. 33676 o. IV 2 and MVN 10, 85 o. V 5. Nam-maḫ-^{d}Sùd-da occurs as an umbisag in SF 39 and in NTSŠ 294.

<Pa$_4$>-<á>-nu-kúš dub-sar is mentioned in 19 r. I 4–5 as recipient of 1 gur of barley; in 132 o. V 5–6 and 146 o. II 3–4 as a recipient of asses. In WF 121 o. III 3–4 (a list of persons discussed above), he is mentioned as dub-sar-udu, an official seemingly connected with husbandry. The mention in two texts (CT 50, 17 o. I 3–4; 25 r. I 2') of Á-nu-kúš dub-sar as the recipient of wool seems to confirm this connection. A certain Pa$_4$-á-nu-kúš is mentioned with the same title, dub-sar-udu, in 47 r. I 3–4. This latter scribe is also mentioned as a dub-sar in texts concerning asses (115 o. V 8–9; 121 r. I 3'–4'; 123 r. II 1–2), which are different from those in which Á-nu-kúš is mentioned. We must conclude that Á-nu-kúš and Pa$_4$-á-nu-kúš are the same individual. Pa$_4$-á-nu-kúš is one of the officials identified as scribes, who, in 38 o. I 3 and 39 o. I 3, had the authority to control large amounts of barley, possibly destined for guruš conscripted for military purposes.[104] In *WO* 8 (1975): 180 r. I 1.2 he occurs as dub-sar-aša$_5$.

^{d}Sùd-anzu dub-sar is mentioned in 14 o. V 13–14; 15 o. VI 3–4; and 35 r. IV 3–4 as the subordinate of Ur-Dumu-zi, a dub-sar who seems to have been a subordinate of the nu-bànda ^{d}En-líl-pà.[105] Consequently, ^{d}Sùd-anzu ^{d}En-líl-pà mentioned in 120 o. III 4–r. I 2 is the namesake dub-sar. Two officials of the same name are mentioned in 7 and they are both recipients of 1 gur of barley; the first occurs in r. I 9 without any characterizing element and the second in r. II 8–10 is recorded as a subordinate of En-nagar-šà dub-sar, who is also mentioned in texts concerning asses.[106] ^{d}Sùd-anzu is mentioned as a dub-sar-sanga-GAR in 10 o. VI 3–5 and is also one of the ten officials mentioned in the barley texts in Group III, 40 r. II 2.[107] Thus two name-

103. Cf. Visicato, *Indices*, pp. 70–71.

104. Cf. *Bureau*, p. 85.

105. Cf. *Bureau*, pp. 110–11.

106. Cf. above, sub En-nagar-šà.

107. ^{d}Sùd-anzu, the official to whom the largest amount of barley is allocated (408 gur in 40) and who does not occur in the parallel texts 38 and 39, might be the official whose name appears in ED IIIa seal impressions found in site XIII f–i,

sake dub-sar's may have worked in the administration of Fara, one, a subordinate of Ur-Dumu-zi, served in the KISAL, and the other, a subordinate of En-nagar-šà, served in the é-géme. It is unclear as to which of the two is the namesake dub-sar-aša$_5$ mentioned in TSŠ X r. II 4 and the namesake dub-sar who is a witness in de Marcellis tablet r. I 6–7. Probably the namesake umbisag who occurs in SF 39 is our dub-sar sanga-GAR.

Šeš-tur dub-sar occurs in several texts concerning asses: 121 r. IV 1–2; 123 r. III 5–6; 128 r. V 8–9; 129 o. III 5–6. He does not occur in the field allotment texts or in the barley ration texts.[108] A namesake umbisag is mentioned in TSŠ 973 r. IV 5.

Šita dub-sar is mentioned on numerous occasions in texts concerning asses (116 o. IV 6–7; 117 o. IV' 2'–3'; 124 r. I 7–8; 138 o. V 3–4; 154 o. III 3–4) and in a text concerning copper (WF 149 r. II 10–11). This anthroponym should not be regarded as an abbreviated form of the dub-sar Utu-šita, since they both occur in the same texts. Šita may be a short form of Šita-AK, a scribe who occurs as a witness in A. 33676 o. III 10.

Šubur dub-sar is the scribe who compiled *Sammeltafel* 19. He also occurs in WF 153 o. IV 10–11, a text concerning grain offerings to the gods, and in TSŠ 897 o. I 3–4 as the recipient of allocations of bread. As the recipient of asses in 116 o. V 10–11, he is called ugula-dub-sar,[109] while in TSŠ 430 o. III' 4'–6', a SI.NUxŠUŠ text, he is titled

---

and who consequently gives his name to a type of seal representation (cf. Martin, *Fara*, pp. 66, 78–81, and most recently R. J. Matthews, "Fragments of Officialdom from Fara," *Iraq* 53 [1991]: 9–11). The assertion by P. Charvát, "The Name Anzu-^{d}Sùd in the Texts from Fara," in K. Hecker – W. Sommerfeld, eds., *Keilschriftliche Literaturen*, XXXII CRRAI, pp. 45–49, that all the attestations of PN ^{d}Sùd-anzu not characterized by a professional name refer to the same "prominent personage" has not been proved.

108. This anthroponym appears several times in the administrative documentation, both as an official, probably an ugula, whose subordinate was a certain Nam-maḫ, and as a nagar, a nimgir, a sukkal, and a kuš$_7$. But no identification can be posited between our dub-sar and any of these officials.

109. The unnamed ugula-dub-sar mentioned in WF 147 o. III 1 as the recipient of copper vessels probably is Šubur.

dub-sar sanga-GAR. The namesake official described as bur-šu-ma, "the elder," who is in charge of food rations(?) for the 142 guruš mentioned in 192 r. III 2–3, and of large amounts of barley in 41 o I 1–3, may be our dub-sar.[110] He is certainly one of the most important scribes and probably worked for the é-géme. As a lú-inim-til, Šubur dub-sar is mentioned in the contract WF 36 r. III 7. A namesake umbisag is mentioned in SF 33 and 39.

Ur-^{d}Sùd um-mi-a is mentioned as a lú-é-éš-gar in MVN 10, 85 r. I 6 and Ung. 2 r. II 1 and as a lú-ki-inim in MVN 10, 86 o. III 2.[111] A namesake umbisag occurs in TSŠ 46R *partie gauche* 4. This anthroponym is one of the most common in Fara, but none of the officials with this name who are mentioned in the administrative documentation is listed as a scribe.

Ur-túl-sag dub-sar is mentioned only once, in 7 o. III 3–4, where he is described as dub-sar-<é>-geme and is the recipient of 2 gur of barley. A namesake GU.NUN.SUR is mentioned in a contract in *WO* 8 (1975): 180 o. V 3. As an umbisag he occurs in TSŠ 46 *partie gauche* 14. Many officials with different characterizing elements are mentioned in the documents, but the one who is most likely to be our scribe is the official in 11 o. I 7, whose subordinate is the dam-gàr AK-^{d}Sùd.[112] This official and the aforementioned GU.NUN.SUR are the only officials of requisite rank to be identified with our scribe.

UR.UR dub-sar is mentioned in a text concerning asses (116 r. IV 11–12) and in a personnel list (WF 108 o. I 2–3). In addition, he is mentioned in a contract (WF 37 r. II 8–III 1) as a dub-sar-aša$_5$ and in another (WF 33 o. III 1–2) as a lú-ki-inim. He is mentioned as an umbisag in SF 39 and TSŠ 46, *partie gauche* 13'. A namesake without title signed a tablet concerning asses (150 r. I 3)—quite likely he is in charge of the recipients listed in the text.[113] This official has been

110. Cf. EDATŠ, p. 179; *Bureau*, p. 45.

111. The lú-ki-inim homonyms, which occur in other contracts with a different characterizing element (guruš-tab in *Ung.* 1 o. VI 7; ì-du$_8$ in MVN 10, 86 o. III 6; ganun in *Or*NS 44 [1975]: 436 o. VI 4'), should be distinguished from our um-mi-a.

112. For a discussion of the dam-gàr in the Fara texts, cf. *Bureau*, pp. 101–5.

113. The implication of the mention of certain officials (PA.PA; Šubur ú-dul$_4$; AN-sag-

identified with certainty with the namesake maškim-maškim-gi$_4$, an official who occurs with Nam-maḫ dub-sar, who is in charge of the allocation of goods in TSŠ 881. On the basis of this text, UR.UR dub-sar and the namesake maškim-maškim-gi$_4$ may be the same individual.

Utu-šita dub-sar is mentioned in different texts concerning asses (116 o. I 6–7; 117 r. I 7'–8'; 146 o. III 4–5; 157 o. II 3–5) and in a personnel list (TSŠ 70 o. II 2–3). In 157 o. II 5 he is described as a dub-sar lú-dub-sar-zì, i.e., a scribe who is subordinate to the official (a scribe) who supervises the administration's flour transactions. This notation enables us to identify the branch of the administration in which our scribe worked. The namesake official who is a subordinate of Pa$_4$-anzu mentioned in 7 o. II 8–9 and 37 o. II 16'–17' and the namesake recipient of barley mentioned in 8 o. II 6 most likely are to be identified with our scribe. He is mentioned as an umbisag in SF 77 r. I 3.

Zà-ta dub-sar sanga-GAR is mentioned as the recipient of barley in 10 r. V 1–3. The namesake official mentioned in 7 r. II 4 as the recipient of 2 gur of barley probably is our dub-sar. He is mentioned as an umbisag in SF 77 r. I 4. Possibly Zà-ta is hypocoristic for Zà-ta-ḫar-tu, an umbisag mentioned in SF 33 r. III 3[114] or better Zà-^{d}Sùd-ta, an official who occurs as lú-ki-inim in some contracts and as recipient of beer in some of Schmidt's tablets (F 490, 506).

P. Mander,[115] building upon a hypothesis of S. Picchioni,[160] has established a chronological sequence for the lexical texts of Fara, basing his assertions on the findspot identified by H. P. Martin[117] and on the

---

tuku) in the colophons of texts concerning asses has been discussed in EDATŠ, p. 421.

114. Cf. P. Mander, "I colofoni di Fara, Abū-Ṣalābīkh ed Ebla: approccio prosopografico," in L. Cagni, ed., *Il Bilinguismo ad Ebla* (Naples, 1984), p. 340.

115. *Ibidem*, pp. 340–44.

116. S. Picchioni, "Osservazioni sulla paleografia e sulla cronologia dei testi di Ebla," in LdE, pp. 110ff.

117. *Fara*, p. 88.

paleographic and prosopographic evidence. These texts consist of two groups of colophons.

The first group contains three chronological subgroups: (a1), the earliest, includes SF 12; (a2) includes SF 36, 69, 77; and (a3), the latest, consists of the greatest number of documents (SF 18, 29, 55, 59, 60, 63, 64, 75, TSŠ 124+SF 26) to which we must add two documents (SF 33 and SF 42) that are slightly older, but, in any case, later than those in a2.

The second group, Group (b), consists of eight documents (SF 13, 16, 37, 39, 62, TSŠ 46, 80, NTSŠ 294+SF 27+). All the colophons of this second group mention umbisag KA-lugal-da-zi. Paleographic and prosopographic analysis indicates that the compilation of Group (b) chronologically matches the compilation of Group (a3). By comparing the scribes listed in this last section, i.e., scribes who occur both in the lexical and economic documentation, we observe that the majority of them occur in Group (b), several scribes occur in the colophons of Group (a3), and some of the colophons of Group (a2), while none of them occur in Group (a1) (cf. TABLE 2a). Since the vast majority of the administrative documents span a very brief period of time, a year or slightly more, then the scribes mentioned in the administrative documentation all operated at the same time. Consequently Group (b) must be more recent. The mention of scribes in Group (a2) and (a3) seems to confirm the chronological connection that Mander has established.

Lastly, the dub-sar-maḫ always occurs unnamed in the documents. In 23 r. I 4 and in its parallel 27 o. VI 12, he occurs concerning a certain Amar-kù, his SAL.UŠ. In 94 r. I 2 he is the recipient of a plot of land. He is also mentioned in TSŠ 679, a small text which records on its obverse the allocation of sheep to other high-ranking officials, i.e., sagi-maḫ, dub-sar-maḫ and sa$_{12}$-du$_5$.

The large number of scribes in the Fara texts is an indication of the importance of these officials in the administration of ED IIIa Šuruppak(Fara).This is likely to have been true for all Mesopotamian society in the middle of the third millennium. But other important elements clarify the role of the scribes at Fara:

(1) Some scribes are mentioned both in the barley texts of Groups I and II; we know that these documents are general summary documents from two different administrative centers, the é-gal and é-uru.

(2) The mention of ten officials, identified as scribes in the barley texts of Group III 38–40,[118] are responsible for large amounts of barley destined for recruits.[119]

(3) The mention of dub-sar é-géme, dub-sar sanga-GAR, dub-sar sa$_{12}$-du$_5$ indicates that many scribes worked for the office that is considered "the control tower" of the administration of Šuruppak.[120]

(4) Other categories of Fara texts record a monthly allocation of ⅓ or ⅙ gur, but the allocations to the dub-sar vary from ½ to 2 gur, with even allocations of 3 or 4 gur. Two texts, 7 and 8, record only allocations to scribes.[121] Clearly career level and competence accounted for wide variations in remuneration.[122]

These elements suggest that the dub-sar's carried out a supervisory function and a liaison role among the various administrative centers and were in the direct employ of the highest authorities of the state in these centers and that, in this capacity, they formed part of the office directly connected to the énsi, namely the é-géme.

The list of scribes in the Fara texts confirms the difficulty in establishing, in many cases, the role of these officials in the context of the administration. In fact, of the 63 scribes who occur in the administrative texts of that institution, at least 20 occur exclusively as recipients and thus outside contexts that might help us determine their function. For another 20, the data are too scarce to establish anything about them. Only for slightly more than 20 scribes is it possible, albeit with some uncertainty, to establish their roles or specific duties.

---

118. Cf. EDATŠ, p. 178; *Bureau*, p. 101.

119. Cf. *Bureau*, p. 85: "The texts of type 38–40 list considerable amounts of barley. This barley, as was shown was the responsibility of some dub-sar's. Keeping in mind that 182 lists dumu-dumu personnel under the responsibility of the dub-sar a-ḫu-ti as indicated in the colophon, and that 195, 207, 210–12 contain a similar clause in the colophon we can reasonably conclude that the barley in the charge of the dub-sar's in 38–40 was destined for the contingents which had been recruited."

120. Cf. *Bureau*, pp. 109–10.

121. EDATŠ, p. 30.

122. The only officials that have similar allocations are the dam-gàr and engar-énsi/é-géme (cf. EDATŠ, p. 33).

At least three or four scribes seem to be linked to two offices connected with shipping activities, the KISAL of the nu-bànda ᵈEn-líl-pà, that of the ugula-énsi Amar-Nam-nir, and of the lú-má-gal-gal[123]: A?-NI, Ur-Dumu-zi, and perhaps É-sahar-ta-è work for the KISAL and GAR-du-la perhaps to the office of the lú-má-gal-gal. Four scribes seem to be connected with the breeding of cattle. Lum-ma was involved with cattle and was under the supervision of the sa₁₂-du₅ (dub-sar anše sa₁₂-du₅); Pa₄-á-nu-kúš was in charge of sheep (dub-sar-udu); and A-geštin was in charge of personnel employed in sheep breeding for the temple of the goddess ᵈSùd (dub-sar-na-gada ᵈSùd). The fourth scribe, whose name is lost, seems to have been a direct subordinate of the person who clearly was in charge of animal breeding, [ ] dub-sar-kuš₇ (10 r. V 11–VI 2).

ᵈSùd goddess

Two scribes are connected with the administration of metal working, Ad-da-da (dub-sar lú-simug) and probably Da-du-lul. Utu-šita seems to work for the grain administration; he is a subordinate of an unnamed scribe involved with flour (dub-sar lú-dub-sar-zì) and perhaps Šeš-ki-na, the person in charge of the granary. Dumu-nun-šita may have been in charge of textiles and similar goods; É-šùd-du₁₀ may have been in charge of beverages. The scribes É-du₆ and perhaps Ul₄-la may have been connected with the bard's activity.[124] Several scribes worked for the é-géme and were subordinates of the sanga-GAR (Amar-kù, Amar-sag-TAR, ᵈSùd-anzu, Šubur, and perhaps En-nagar-šà), the sa₁₂-du₅ (KA-ni-zi, Lum-ma), and the dub-sar-mah (Utu-á-mah). Four other scribes seem to have had special roles. AN-sag-tuku signed several barley and ass documents; he is the only one, with Šubur, to do so. Nam-mah and UR.UR, judging by TSŠ 881, may have managed several kinds of goods. Besides signing an important document, Šubur appears to be in charge of the scribes subordinate to the sanga-GAR (ugula dub-sar; dub-sar sanga-GAR). In addition, he is described as bur-šu-ma, the elder (among the scribes) and is in charge of the enlisted personnel and their maintenance.

na-gada/ nāqidu "herds- men"

---

123. This activity seems to have been of vital importance for the Fara economy, as noted by the number of lú-má, about 300 in all (cf. *Bureau*, pp. 145–46).

124. For a discussion of the relationships between the corporation of the scribes and that of the bards in the documentation of Early Mesopotamia, cf. A. Westenholz, "Old Akkadian School Texts," *AfO* 25 (1974): 107–10, with bibliography.

Ten scribes were responsible for the barley rations of war recruits and six others were responsible for similar personnel.[125]

read
umbisag
not sanga
a certainly
not sanga
Lastly, among the scribes who occur as umbisag in the lexical documents the most important of those mentioned above were AN-sag-tuku, Lum-ma, Nam-maḫ, ᵈSùd-anzu, Šubur, UR.UR, and Zà-ta. Probably the other scribes who occur as umbisag and whose role within the administration cannot be determined also were high-ranking officials, namely, A-geštin, Amar-nam, Amar-šùba, AN-nu-me, AN-úr-šè, Bil$_x$-á-nu-kúš, Dub-ḫul-tar, Ḫar-tu-ᵈSùd, Lugal-ki-dúr-du$_{10}$, Šeš-tur, and Utu-šita.

confu-
sion
It is quite possible that all high-ranking officials within the administration, e.g., sanga-GAR, sa$_{12}$-du$_5$, enku, nu-bànda, came from the corporation of the scribes. We do not know whether the title dub-sar connotes the specific function of "scribe" or whether, in some cases, it is a generic description for an official. Certainly, however, this title, clearly an indication of importance, seems to have been a prerequisite for entry into the administration and the highest levels of the state bureaucracy.

1.3 *The Scribes of Abū Ṣalābīkh*

Approximately one hundred scribes are mentioned in the colophons of lexical and literary texts from Abū Ṣalābīkh,[126] yet just one scribe is mentioned in the few administrative texts,[127] A-DU dub-sar, who, according to IAS 494 r. II 1, was the compiler of the tablet.[128] This scribe is not mentioned in the list in OIP 99, pp. 34–35. This omission is not surprising, since in cuneiform literature there seems to be a clear distinction between scribes who exercise their profession exclusively within the scribal schools and those who serve within the administration. But at Fara, which was close in time to Abū Ṣalābīkh, the scribes who copied literary and lexical texts also were mentioned in administrative documents. Therefore, perhaps this discrepancy at Abū Ṣalābīkh is

125. Cf. *Bureau*, p. 85.

126. Cf. IAS, pp. 34–35.

127. Cf. IAS 490–515; R. D. Biggs – P. N. Postgate, "The Inscriptions of Abū-Ṣalābīkh, 1975," *Iraq* 40 (1978), IAS 516–19, 528–32.

128. For an analysis of this text, cf. G. Visicato, "Un testo di assegnazioni d'orzo ad Abū-Ṣalābīkh," *NABU* (1994): 97.

merely a result of so few administrative tablets having survived. Moreover, of the approximately 70 anthroponyms, often without any characterizing element, mentioned in these documents several occur in the list of scribes (OIP 99, p. 34).[129]

A-geštin-⸢x⸣ is mentioned in a list of persons, IAS 516 o. II 1.[130] Perhaps this anthroponym is for A-geštin-abzu.[131] A namesake um-mi-a is mentioned, generally in the first position, in the colophons of IAS 34; 39; 46; 59; 91; 117; 131; 142; 268; 476; 480.

A-UZU-gal(?) is mentioned in IAS 495 o. II 1, a text of barley allocations probably related to field work. Perhaps he is the same as A-ul$_4$-gal who occurs only in the colophon of IAS 298.[132]

Bí-bí-um is mentioned in IAS 531 o. II 6 as being in charge of an administrative center. É-bí-bí-um should be identified with the household of Bí-bí-ù, the scribe mentioned as dub mu-sar in the colophons of IAS 254 and 480 or with I-bí-um mentioned in the colophon of IAS 116.

Gu-NI-sum mentioned in IAS 498 o. II' 1 occurs also in the colophon of IAS 126.

I-gi-ì-lum mentioned in IAS 503 r. II 6 as the recipient of allocations of barley is mentioned in the colophons of IAS 18; 20; 59; 124; 163 (dub mu-sar); and 254. With the variant I-gi$_4$-ì-lum, he is mentioned in the colophons of IAS 20 and 126.

129. Cf. P. Mander, *Il Pantheon di Abu Salabikh* (Naples, 1986), pp. 126–27; F. Pomponio, "I nomi personali dei testi amministrativi di Abu Salabikh," *SEL* 8 (1991): 141–46. IAS, p. 34: "some names occurring in the colophons also occur in the other administrative documents from the same building, it is highly probable that they are all contemporary."

130. R. D. Biggs, "The Inscriptions of Abū-Ṣalābīkh, 1975," *Iraq* 40 (1978): 105, regards IAS 516 as a barley distribution text whose entries record the allocation of one bariga to the listed officials.

131. Cf. Pomponio, *SEL* 8 (1991): 142.

132. Pomponio, *SEL* 8 (1991): 142, identifies LAK 350 (UZU) as the archaic writing of ul$_4$.

I-ku-il is mentioned in IAS 503 r. I 5, a barley allocation text. He is also mentioned in the colophons of IAS 61 and 481. With the variant I-ku-gu-il, he is mentioned in IAS 113; 268; 479.

Il-LAK 647[133] mentioned in IAS 515 II' 2 is also mentioned in the colophons of IAS 116 and 283.

Im-ri-i-rúm is mentioned in IAS 518 r. II 5, a text concerning the allocation of plots of land for sustenance (šuku). The anthroponym is followed by the characterizing element EN.KI.GI. In the summary, the officials listed are described as lú-aša$_5$-gíd. This anthroponym should perhaps be compared with [ ]-i-rúm, a scribe mentioned in the colophon of IAS 141.

Puzur$_4$-il, mentioned in IAS 503 r. I 6, is also mentioned in IAS 13 and 268 and as a dub-mu-sar in IAS 142.

Other anthroponyms that are mentioned in the list of scribes in IAS, pp. 34–35 occur in administrative texts, but they are listed with a characterizing element that specifies a professional name different from that which characterizes the scribes. These are DI-Utu engar (IAS 518 o. II 2); En-na-il PA.É (IAS 503 o. VI 2); Iš-lul-il mu$_6$-sùb (IAS 510 o. I 3); and kuš$_7$-áb, "the tanner of cow(hides)," in a text concerning cattle (IAS 513 o. III 2–3); Iš-ṭup-il engar (IAS 528 o. IV 3'; Iš-ṭup-il occurs without a characterizing element in 513 r. III 1' and probably is Iš-ṭup-il engar); Ù-aš-dar nin (IAS 506 o. II' 4'–5').

While the latter are certainly to be distinguished from the namesake scribes, it is not certain that the preceding nine are the namesake officials.

2. The Scribes of ED IIIb Girsu

Girsu was excavated several times between 1887 and 1929 by a French expedition. The most spectacular discoveries were made by E. de Sarzec, especially during the first years, between 1887 and 1900. He excavated four tells from north to south: Tell du Palais (A), Tell de la Maison du Fruit (K), le Gran Tell, and Tell du Tablettes. The two latter tells are

133. For the reading ad/t for LAK 647, see Pomponio, *SEL* 8 (1991): 144.

aligned from west to east and lie to the south of Tell de la Maison du Fruit.[134] The Tell du Tablettes was excavated in 1894 and about 30,000 tablets were found from the Ur III period and the subsequent period.[135] Another 35,000 to 40,000 tablets were excavated clandestinely and sold on the market. In 1895, 3,800 tablets from the Sargonic and Post-Sargonic periods were found in various sites on Tell du Tablettes. Another 11,000 from the time of Gudea and Ur III were excavated in 1900.[136] The oldest settlement area, Tell K or Tell de la Maison du Fruit, was excavated in 1898.

Buildings from the period of Ur-Nanše, Eanatum, and Entemena/Enmetena were uncovered. The mace of Mesilim and the table of Enḫegal were discovered at the same site. Following the death of de Sarzec, excavations were halted.

In 1902, as a consequence of this interruption, clandestine excavations were carried out by the local inhabitants, probably at Tell K, where more than 1,600 administrative tablets from the Pre-Sargonic period were unearthed and illicitly sold.[137] A provenance of Tell K for these tablets has been posited on the basis of a small group of tablets from the same period that were discovered by the French expedition and later published in NFT.[138]

Tell K may have been the headquarters of the administration that compiled these documents, that is, the é-mí.[139] The destruction of the

---

134. Other tells were excavated by De Sarzec and his successors. From *Tell du Palais* statues of Gudea and Ur-Baba were found, and near Tell B, to the northeast of *Tell du Palais,* a stele of Gudea was found (cf. A. Parrot, *Tello* [Paris, 1948], pp. 18–19).

135. Cf. Parrot, *Tello,* p. 20.

136. Cf. *ibidem,* p. 21.

137. 540 were bought by Allotte de la Fuÿe, 400 by the Berlin Museum, 227 by the British Museum, 325 ended up in the Nikolsky collection, 60 in the Louvre, and 20 in the Amherst collection (cf. Parrot, *Tello,* p. 26, nos. 33–35, and UGASL, p. 9). Other small groups of tablets were bought by individuals or institutions.

138. NFT, pp. 45–51.

139. A. Westenholz, *Circulation,* pp. 18, 22, has observed that several tablets from the time of Enentarzi, signed only by the énsi, but not by his wife, come from the northern parts of the *Tell du Tablettes.* It is likely that the archive of the é-gal, as opposed to that of the é-mí, was localized in the latter tell.

site was probably carried out by Lugalzagesi and perhaps by Sargon as well.[140] During the Gudea period, Tell K was probably levelled and rebuilt.

The archive at ED IIIb Girsu is the only one from the Pre-Sargonic and Sargonic periods that has a documented, temporal continuity. The texts were compiled over a period of about 20 years, from the reign of Enentarzi, to Lugalanda, and then to Urukagina Most of the texts are dated to the reign and year of one of these three kings, thus making it possible to establish a secure internal chronological continuity. About 60 dub-sar's, agrig's, and um-mi-a's are mentioned in this archive, as well as four dub-sar-maḫ's. As can be seen in TABLE 4 and TABLE 5,[141] there are about 20 scribes in texts dating to the reign of Enentarzi, about 30 from the reign of Lugalanda, and about 25 from the reign of Urukagina. Therefore, it is reasonable to conjecture that, at minimum, 30 scribes served contemporaneously during the reign of each king in the é-mí and other institutions.

Based on the chronology of the tablets, most of the scribes listed in TABLE 4 can be subdivided:[142]

(1) scribes mentioned in texts from the reigns of all three kings: A-ba-DI-<ì-e/bé>, Amar-Gírid^{ki}, Aš$_{10}$-ne, En-kù, Maš-dà.

(2) scribes mentioned in texts from the reigns of just Enentarzi and Lugalanda: Gú-bé, Ki-ti-<la-ni>, Lugal-nam-gú-sù, Šeš-tur, Šul-me-<šár-ra-DU>, Šubur-<tur>.

---

140. A different point of view is expressed by M. Powell, "The Sin of Lugalzagesi," *Festschrift für H. Hirsch* (Vienna, 1996), pp. 307–11, who hypothesizes that Urukagina was allied with Sargon in his war against Lugalzagesi. In this case, such a destruction, revealed by archaeology, might have been carried out, perhaps, by Rīmuš, during the rebellion of the Sumerian cities.

141. All the published documents from ED IIIb Girsu are listed in UGASL, pp. 9–10. Copies of the 202 texts from the Berlin Museum have been published in AVG I, 1–104 and AVG II, 1–98. UGASL, p. 10, enumerates 1,752 administrative documents, including the tablets excavated at Al Hiba/Lagaš.

142. The following abbreviations are used: Enan for Enanatum; ENT for Entemena; EN for Enentarzi; L for Lugalanda; Ue for Urukagina énsi; U for Urukagina lugal. The number accompanying the name of the ruler indicates the year of his reign. TABLE 4 lists the scribes who occur in documents from the time of Enanatum or Entemena—although not discussed here.

(3) scribes mentioned in texts from the reigns of just Lugalanda and Urukagina: Du-du, En-bi-<šà-ge>, En-da-<mu>-gal-di, En-ig-gal, Igi-mu-<an-šè-gál>, IGI?.ḪUŠ?, Šeš-lú-du$_{10}$, Ur-sag, Ur-túl-sag, Ú.Ú agrig, Ú.Ú dub-sar.

(4) scribes mentioned in texts from the reign of just Urukagina: E-ge-<a-na-ak>, Bára-zi-<šà-gal>, En-DU, En-šu-gi$_4$-gi$_4$, Lugal-èš-du$_{10}$-ga, Lugal-Kèš^{ki}, Lugal-šà-lá-tuku, Puzur$_4$-Ma-ma, Šul-ig-gal; ^{d}Šul-utul$_x$-men; Ur-igi-gál, Úr-mud, [x.x]-[s]ikil$^{?}$.

(5) scribes mentioned in texts only during the reign of Enentarzi: E-gu$_4$-gim-saḫar-ra, E-li-li, E-ta, En-an-na-túm-sipa-zi, En-ki-sár-ra, Gìri-né-ba-tuš, NÌGIN-mud dumu Gu-bé; NÌGIN-mud dumu Na-na, Ur-^{d}Nin-gír-su, Ur-šu.

(6) scribes mentioned in texts only during the reign of Lugalanda: A-li-ì-ba, É-me, Gú-ú, Lugal-a, Lugal-mu, Lugal-pa-è, Lum-ma-šà-tam, Nam-maḫ, (x)-A.NI-du$_{10}$.

(7) scribes mentioned in texts whose dates are lost: É-an-né-mud, En-lú-[ ], Ki-tuš-lú, Lum-ma-mes-ni, Nì-lú-nu-DU.[143]

The officials listed in groups (5) to (7) occur, with rare exception, once only. Consequently, it is often impossible to identify their role in the context of the institution to which they belonged. Therefore, our study will concentrate on the scribes listed in groups (1) to (4) and on the dub-sar-maḫ listed in TABLE 5.

Group (1) consists of five scribes, who worked contemporaneously for many years in various sectors of the administration. The career of En-kù will be discussed in a later section. The activities of the other four—A-ba-DI,[144] Amar-Gírid^{ki}, Aš$_{10}$-né, and Maš-dà—can be subdivided by time period. The earliest period spans the reign of Enentarzi to the second year of Lugalanda. During this time A-ba-DI, Aš$_{10}$-né, and Maš-dà

143. This scribe is mentioned only in Nik I, 30 o. III 7–8, if we exclude a contract in which he is the dub-sar who compiled the document (cf. SRJ 30 V 6–VI 3). G. Selz, AWEL, pp. 187–88, dates Nik, I, 30 to the reign of Urukagina. For a dating to EN or L1, see G. Visicato, "The Dating of Nik I, 30," *NABU* (1996): 116.

144. For the discussion of the variants A-ba-DI-ì-bé and A-ba-DI-í-e, cf. AWAS, pp. 100–1, sub 5:5.

received allocations of emmer, wool, and plots of agricultural land for their sustenance.[145]

Maš-dà is in charge of the allocation of ninda to 12 géme-ḪAR in L1.[146] Amar-Gírid^{ki} is never mentioned in any of the allocation texts from these years. All four are mentioned in texts concerning maintenance of irrigation canals.[147] A-ba-DI, Aš$_{10}$-né, and Maš-dà may well have served in the institution that compiled AWAS 75 and DP 195 during the reign of Enentarzi and RTC 75; DCS 8; Nik I, 30; 44; 125 in L1 and L2. The administration must have been headed first by Dimtur, wife of Enentarzi, and subsequently by Baranamtara, wife of Lugalanda, who must have been the core of that structure, which took the name é-mí in L1. K. Maekawa suggests that these officials initially worked for the palace administration (é-gal), and were then transferred, for a period of some years, with other officials who were employed in production and accounting, to form the é-mí.[148]

The second subdivision extends from L3 to L5, during which none of the four officials received allocations of barley or emmer. A-ba-DI is the recipient of a plot of 9 iku in L3.[149] A-ba-DI, Aš$_{10}$-né, and Maš-dà

145. A-ba-DI and Aš$_{10}$-né receive emmer in AWAS 75 o. I 7; III 8 (EN2); A-ba-DI, Aš$_{10}$-né and Maš-dà in DCS 8 o. II–III 3 (L1) and in DP 231 o. III' 10'–13 (L$^{?}$2); Aš$_{10}$-né and Maš-dà in Nik I 125 r. III 3; IV 3 (L2); A-ba-DI and perhaps Aš$_{10}$-né and Maš-dà receive wool in DP 195 o. IV' 1' (EN); A-ba-DI and Maš-dà receive 1½ iku and 3 iku 40 sar of land respectively in Nik I, 30 r. III 1–2; I 2–4; Maš-dà receives 6 iku in Nik I, 44 o. II 2–3 (EN/L1) and A-ba-DI receives 2½ iku in RTC 75 o. III 3–4 (L1).

146. Cf. AVG I 8 o. V 4–6.

147. Aš$_{10}$-né and Maš-dà in DP 617 r. I 4–II 3 (EN/L1); A-ba-DI, Amar-Gírid^{ki}, Aš$_{10}$-né, and Maš-dà in DP 622 o. VI 7–r. I 2 (L2); DP 641 o. V 6 – r. I 2 (L2). For the relationship between DP 622 and DP 641, cf. T. Maeda, "Work concerning Irrigation Canals in Pre-Sargonic Girsu," *ASJ* 6 (1984): 35. For an analysis of the various stages of work on the canals, see *ibid.*, pp. 33–53.

148. K. Maekawa, "The Development of the É-MÍ in Lagaš during Early Dynastic III," in *Mesopotamia* 8/9 (1973–74), pp. 101–7.
For studies on this topic, now see Y. Wu, "Lugalanda's Economic Reform in Lagash", and G. R. Magid, "Micromanagement in the Queen's Household: Notes on the Organization of the Labor at ED Lagash," in XLVe CRRAI (Harvard, 1998), (forthcoming).

149. AVG I 40 o. III 4–5.

received textiles in L4 and L5.[150] However, in L3 A-ba-DI and Maš-dà were in charge of considerable quantities of nì-en-na barley, the property of Baranamtara,[151] probably for the sustenance of their subordinate personnel working on the canals. Maš-dà received barley and emmer destined for the sustenance of the énsi in L5.[152] In addition, Maš-dà was in charge of the barley rations of 15 géme-ḪAR in the third year (RTC 52 o. III 11–IV 2). Maš-dà occurs also in texts concerning sá-du$_{11}$, "regular offerings," from the twelfth offering of L1 (DP 145 o. IV 1–7), involving the é-muḫaldim, until U2. Amar-Gírid^{ki} continues to be mentioned in these years only in texts concerning canal work, texts in which the three other dub-sar's are mentioned. From their absence in ration texts and from the latter type of attestation, it would seem that our three officials were not, in this second period, supported by the administration of Baranamtara. But they continued to have occasional dealings with that institution as can be seen from the fact that all the texts in which they occur are related to En-ig-gal, the nu-bànda of é-mí and the dam-énsi. Perhaps only Maš-dà continued to have a continuous relationship with it; in fact, from L1 to L5 this official is regularly mentioned in sá-du$_{11}$ texts as being responsible for personnel.

The third period spans L6 to U1. The four scribes, belonging to the category lú-šuku-dab$_5$-ba,[153] are mentioned as recipients of rations of 72

150. AWL 130 o. III 4–6; DP 192 o. III 3–5.

151. Nik I, 79 o. III 9–11.

152. Nik I, 83 o. II 6–8; Nik I, 97 o. III 3–5.

153. A. Deimel, *Sumerische Tempelwirtschaft*, AnOr 2 (1931), p. 21, translates "Leute, denen ein Stück Land vom Tempel als Arbeitslos (šuku) festgesetzt (dab$_5$-ba) wurde" as opposed to the lú-iti-da, "die monatlich ausgel öhnt wurden." This interpretation is followed by G. Selz, AWAS, pp. 38, 74: "Gerstezutellungen für die Leute, die ein Versorgunslos übernommen haben." R. Englund, *Fischerei*, p. 53, n. 181, is, however, of a different opinion: "Es sind Gersterationen der Empganger festern Rationen." Thus Deimel and Selz believe that šuku is an abbreviated form of <aša$_5$->šuku and therefore here concerns personnel who, for their usual work, had the use of parcels of agricultural land and who were recruited for duty, such as canal digging and military service. The interpretation of Englund, on the other hand, should be linked to the meaning of the term lú-šuku(r)-ra, "people of šuku-provisions" in the Ur III texts (cf. H. Waetzoldt, "Compensation of Craft Workers and Officials in the Ur III Period," in *Labor*, p. 120, n. 26).

sìla of barley in the second distribution of L6 (RTC 54 o. IV 7–10). In L6 A-ba-DI, Maš-dà, and Aš$_{10}$-né received clothes and in L7,[154] with Amar-Gírid^{ki}, plots of land. In addition, these three scribes and Šeš-tur dub-sar were responsible for barley coming from different nì-en-na fields in the same year (L6) (AVG I 41 r. V 9–12). On the one hand, Maš-dà continued to be responsible for the barley for the šà-du$_{10}$-nita and šà-du$_{10}$-mí workers (TSA 10 o. VIII 4–5) in the twelfth distribution in L6, and in charge of workers, nita, and géme, in AVG II, 7 r, IV 7–9; on the other, he occurs in the sá-du$_{11}$ texts in the years L6 and L7. In Ue, on the occasion of the second distribution (the first in Ue follows the seventh of L7[155]), A-ba-DI, Amar-Gírid^{ki}, and the dub-sar's Ú.Ú and En-bi received an extraordinary allocation of 1 gur of barley (AWAS 5 o. V 5–7)—all other recipients in the text received normal rations. In fact, Maš-dà, who had become an agrig,[156] received 72 sìla. Most likely then, Maš-dà was already in the employ of the é-mí, whereas these four other dub-sar's may have become employed there on the ascent to the throne of the new king. In the same year Maš-dà agrig and four unnamed dub-sar's, assuredly A-ba-DI, Amar-Gírid^{ki}, Ú.Ú, and En-bi, received an allocation of 4 bán of emmer (AWAS 4 o. IV 5–6; 11–12). Aš$_{10}$-né is no longer mentioned in ration texts; he may have been transferred to another administration.[157]

---

154. DP 193 o. II 5–7; AVG I 39 o. I 5–6; r. II 1–2.

155. L7 and Ue are the same year.

156. It should be noted that from Ue to U1, Maš-dà is identified as an agrig in some texts, while in others he continues to be identified as a dub-sar. Examples are the sá-du$_{11}$ texts (AWL 43 o. 1; DP 152 o. IV 10–11; DP 156 o. IV 9–10; DP 155 o. V 10–11; AWAS 30 o. IV 9–10; AVG I 66 o. V 7'–8'; AWAS 31 o. V 4'–5') and those in which he is responsible for barley for the géme-dumu workers (CT 50, 33 o. VII 8–9; AWAS 19 o. VII 7–8). Again, in U1 in a land allocation text, he is titled dub-sar (AVG I 70 o. VI 6–7), while in a text of the same type from the same year he is titled agrig (AWAS 39 o. II 12–13). In a U1 text regarding canals (DP 637 o. V 8–9) he is still called dub-sar, but this reference is distinct from the four other references to dub-sar in r. I 3–7. This happens in all documents in which he is mentioned as an agrig. Probably the scribe who compiled the tablet continued, out of habit, to refer to him as a dub-sar although he knew that his responsibilities and status had changed.

157. Aš$_{10}$-ne, who is regularly mentioned in texts until L6, appears only once in Ue, as a recipient of textiles (DP 194 o. II 4). He does not occur from U1 on. He reappears as the official in charge of a group of ki-siki who receive barley rations

The fourth period spans U2 to U4. In U2, the three remaining scribes of this group, A-ba-DI, Amar-Gírid^{ki}, and Maš-dà, are regularly mentioned as recipients of monthly rations of barley, emmer,[158] and of plots of land. But they are not mentioned together.[159] Maš-dà is no longer listed with the dub-sar in the ration texts, but rather with two other agrig's, Bára-zi and Úr-mud, while A-ba-DI, Amar-Gírid^{ki}, and En-bi, a dub-sar mentioned from L6, are listed separately.[160] In U2 Amar-Gírid^{ki} and En-bi occur in a text concerning canal work. Maš-dà occurs in sá-du$_{11}$ texts from the ninth offering of U2; the records of the tenth are missing but he is not mentioned in the eleventh. Another agrig appears in his place. From that period on, Maš-dà disappears from the texts with the one exception of a mention in U3, where he is the recipient of 1½ sìla of bread (DP 130 r. I 10). Probably at the end of the second year he retired from active service. In U3 A-ba-DI and Amar-

---

as dumu-di$_4$-di$_4$-la-ne in the fifth year in Nik I, 20 o. III 9'–10' (ki-siki-me aš$_{10}$-né dub-sar ugula-bi, "they are the wool workers of whom Aš$_{10}$-ne, the dub-sar is in charge"). In a text from the fourth year, Aš$_{10}$-ne is titled together with Igi-bar (perhaps an abbreviation of Igi-bar-lú-ti) as a ki-siki (DP 567 o. II 1–3) and should be our dub-sar. In this regard the dumu-di$_4$-di$_4$-la-ne personnel should be regarded as basically extraneous to the é-mí and worked for the é-nam-dumu, the household of the sons of the énsi (cf. AWAS p. 290, 11: 3; K. Maekawa, *Mesopotamia* 8/9, pp. 98, 131–32). The hypothesis that Aš$_{10}$-ne went to this administration in the first year of Urukagina seems to be correct.

158. They are recipients of rations of 72 sìla of barley in AWAS 6 r. I 9–12; IV 5; TSA 20 o. VI 3–4; 5–8; AVG II, 6 o. VII 13; r. III 4; allocations of emmer in Nik I, 13 r. II 2 (4 bán to four unnamed scribes); IV I; and plots of land in AVG I 79 r. II 10–11; IV 1; 4.

159. A-ba-DI occurs in two similar texts, AVG II, 4 v: III 5–6 and AVG II, 71 r. I 1–2, in which he seems to be in charge of barley and emmer during the same month for the estate (bára-guru$_5$-a) of Géme-sila-sír-sír-ra (cf. AWL, p. 139, for Géme-sila-sír-sír-ra as a daughter of Urukagina), še bára-guru$_5$-a Géme-sila-šír-šír-ra dumu A-ba-DI dub-sar šu-na gál-la-am$_6$ iti guru$_7$-im-du$_8$-a. In AVG II, 71 r. II 1–III 1, the grain is delivered by En-ig-gal nu-bànda: En-ig-gal nu-bànda ganun giš-kin-ti-ta e-ne-ta-gar 2 dub-bé 2-am$_6$. AVG II 4 and 71, because of their typology, should be connected to AWL 35 and DP 143. AVG II 4 is undated, whereas AVG II, 71 records only the second regnal year, but not the name of the ruler. On the basis of the occurrence of Géme-sila-šír-šír-ra, AVG II, p. 12 dates AVG II 4 and 71 to U2.

160. In the same year Amar-Gírid^{ki} had use of a rented plot of land measuring 4 iku (AVG I 93 o. II 1–4) and A-ba-DI had one of 6 iku (TSA 8 o. II 7').

Gírid^{ki} were recipients of rations of barley and emmer[161] but they are not mentioned as recipients of plots of land. In U4, on the other hand, they are recipients of plots of land,[162] but they are not mentioned in ration texts. In the period between U2 and U4, A-ba-DI seems to have risen to a position of greater responsibility. In fact, he is mentioned in two texts as the person in charge of grain allocation.[163] There is no other mention of our scribes in the texts of the fifth year, texts which are rather rare. Finally, in the sixth year they are mentioned exclusively in ration texts; A-ba-DI continues to receive 72 sìla, whereas the ration for Amar-Gírid^{ki} decreases to 48 sìla. This clearly shows the difference in rank of the two officials and, moreover, it is a precise index of the difficult political and economic situation in which Girsu found itself from the fourth year of the reign of Urukagina as a consequence of the war with Lugalzagesi.[164]

The fifth scribe of this group, En-kù, is a dub-sar in a contract from the reign of Enentarzi (RTC 17 o. II 7) and in a text from L3 concerning

161. Barley in AWAS 7 r. IV 3–6; 8 r. IV 3; 9 r. IV 5–7; 10 r. III 7–10; and emmer in AWAS 68 r. II 5'–7'.

162. TSA 7 o. IV 11–14; r. V 2–3; DP 603 o. II 5–6.

163. AWL 19 (r. II 4–III 1): gig A-ba-DI dub-sar šu-na gál-la-am$_6$ 2, "(allocated) grain which A-ba-DI, the scribe, has in his hand, (the allocation of the) second year" and AVG I 95 r. III 1–3: kú-a A-ba-DI-ì-e dub-sar 2, "(grain) for eating (under the responsibility of) A-ba-DI, the scribe, (the allocation of the) second year." It should be noted that both texts are dated to the same year; in fact, AVG I 95 records three allocations of gig, the first of which coincides with the only one recorded in AWL 19 r. I 1–II 3: 4 (ban) gig gig-numun aša$_5$-en-né-gù-ba-dè-a-šè á-ni-kur-ra sag-apin-na-ke$_4$ šu-ba-ti. In AVG I 95 r. I 1–4, (4 (bàn) gig gig-numun aša$_5$-en-né-gù-ba-dè-a-šè šu-ba-ti) the name of the king is not mentioned. He should be identified as Urukagina, because the same official is mentioned, with a similar function, as the person responsible for 30 gur of barley destined for both cattle and sheep in DP 545 o. II 4–5, a document dating from the fourth year of his reign. DP 257 and 567 must also date from Urukagina, since A-ba-DI is mentioned similarly (DP 257 r. II 1–4 šu-nígin 98 bàppir-kas-sig$_{15}$ zi-zi-ga A-ba-DI dub-sar-kam 4 and DP 567 r. II 1–III 1: šu-nígin 5 (gur) 2 (bariga) 2 (bàn) zíz-sig$_{15}$ gur-sag-gál zíz šu-a gi$_4$-a-am$_6$ A-ba-DI dub-sar-ré e-ág 4).

164. The first incursion of the king of Umma into the territory of Lagaš should be dated to the fourth year of Urukagina (cf. DP 545 r. I 3–4); the third incursion dates to his sixth year (Cf. Nik I, 227 o. II 4–r. I 4). Consequently, it is probable that the second should be dated to his fifth year.

the allocation of land for the maintenance of the énsi (AVG I 40 o. I 8–II 1).[165] He reoccurs later, probably toward the end of his career, as um-mi-a, the highest position in the scribal profession. He appears exclusively in sá-du$_{11}$ texts from U2 (DP 158 r. II 4–5) until the fourth year (AWAS 32 r. I 5–7). There is no mention of him from L3 until the first distributions of U2. But from L1 to U3, a namesake kurušda is almost always mentioned in sheep texts concerning maš-da-ri-a and feasts. His task is to check and count the sheep entering and leaving (ba-se$_{12}$), to carry out inspections (kurúm-ma e-ak) and to deliver the sheep to the palace and to the é-mí (ba-túm é-gal-la; é-mí-a šu-a-bí-gi$_4$). A passage in DP 246 r. II 2–III 2 from L3, En-ig-gal nu-bànda En-kù kurušda-da dub-bi e-da-bal, "En-ig-gal, the superintendent [of the é-mí] with En-kù, the person in charge of the sheep,[166] the tablet [of the deliveries] transcribed,"[167] suggests that this En-kù might himself be a scribe and the namesake dub-sar from the time of Lugalanda. Note that En-kù is mentioned for the first time as um-mi-a in a text from U2 and the last mention of the namesake kurušda is in DP 130 r. I 1–2, a document from U3. Similarly, at the beginning of U3, Ú.Ú is mentioned as kurušda while the namesake agrig disappears from the texts. Thus, it appears from our texts that term kurušda often could be an abbreviation of dub-sar/agrig kurušda (or at least that a scribe was in charge of checking the organization in charge of husbandry).[168]

---

165. aša$_5$ ki-uzug$_5$ (KAxÚ) šuku Lugal-an-da énsi. For the reading uzug$_5$ for KAxÚ and the interpretation of aša$_5$ ki-uzug$_5$<-ga> as a field name, cf. AWEL, p. 434, sub 8:3 (Nik I, 194 r. IV 3).

166. For this meaning of the term kurušda, cf. AWL p. 296, sub 97 o. V 6.

167. It should be noted that a similar clause, which concludes DP 246 r. III 2: sar-ru-am$_6$ dub-tur-tur-ta e-ta-[sar], "This is the wide tablet from the small tablets he transcribed," concludes also DP 248 o. III 3–r. I 1: kuš-šu-a-gi$_4$-a-am$_6$ En-kù kurušda 5 dub-tur-tur-ta e-ta-sar sar-ru-am$_6$ 5, "the hides (of the animals) brought in, En-kù, the kurušda, (in the) fifth year from the small tablets he transcribed (it); this is the tablet which gathers them." This clause seems to indicate scribal activity for our official. For sar-šub(RU), see *CAD* I p. 138 sub *(im)sar-šubbû*.

168. For the interchange PN kurušda/dub-sar kurušda in documents of the Ur III period, cf. AAS p. 75, 4.

The second group is made up of 6 scribes:

Gú-bé dub-sar is mentioned in L4 as the leaseholder of a plot of land of 3 bur, property of Baranamtara (Nik I, 33 o. I 3–4). Gú-bé is mentioned in Nik I, 177 o. II 2, a letter regarding cattle and sheep,[169] in which he informs Lugal-mu that the animals may be taken away only upon the return of an unnamed dub-sar, perhaps the dub-sar-maḫ of the é-mí (Gú-bé na-e-a Lugal-mu du$_{11}$-ga-na dub-sar mu-gi-a ba-ra).[170] The text is dated to the fourth year of an unnamed ruler. Since a certain Lugal-mu dub-sar also occurs in Nik I, 44 o. I 3, a text quite likely from L1,[171] it appears probable that the year 4 in Nik I, 177 is EN4. Furthermore, Gú-bé untitled occurs in RTC 17 o. III 7, a contract perhaps from the time of Enentarzi or L1, as father or superior of the scribe NÌGIN-mud. The identification of Gú-bé with the namesake sanga ^{d}Nin-mar-ki mentioned during the reign of Enentarzi and Lugalanda is possible.[172]

Ki-ti dub-sar, whose full name is Ki-ti-la-né/na, is a dub-sar already mentioned during the reign of Entemena when Enentarzi was sanga of Ningirsu.[173] He appears subsequently as the supervisor of large amounts of cereals destined for (the house of) the énsi (DP 39 r. I 3–4) and in L1 in a maš-da-ri-a text (Nik I, 158 o. II 2–r. I 2).[174] In addi-

169. Cf. FAOS 19, pp. 30–31.

170. FAOS 19, p. 30, translates lugal-mu, the addressee of the letter, "zu meinem Herrn" but does not exclude the possibility that lugal-mu is a hypocoristic form of the PN Lugal-mu-da-kúš (cf. Struve, *Onomastika,* pp. 106–7: Lugal-mu muḫaldim / Lugal-mu-da-kúš muḫaldim; Lugal-mu sipa-anše / Lugal-mu-da-kúš sipa-anše).

171. This text, which also mentions the scribes Lum-ma-šà-tam, É-me, and Maš-dà, is signed by the nu-bànda Šubur and is dated to the first year, although the king's name is missing. Since Šubur nu-bànda occurs, with few exceptions (DP 352, RTC 58 of L3, and AWL 189 of L5) up through L1, we must conclude that the text refers to this last year.

172. AWAS 79 from EN2; Nik I, 125 from L2; and AWL 175 from L3; AWL 182 undated.

173. DP 31 IV 9–10; RTC 16 o. IV 4–5.

174. G. Selz, AWEL, p. 382, on the basis of the mention of the PN NI-a'a, the religious name of Dìm-tur, wife of Enentarzi, in o. I 3, dates this text to the first year of this king. But against this is the mention of the é-mí, which is never attested prior to

tion, he is mentioned in RTC 17 o. III 6–7. He was probably a scribe at the head of the administration of either the temple of Ningirsu, the palace administration (é-gal), or the temple of Ningirsu in the é-gal.[175]

Lugal-nam-gú-sù agrig is mentioned in DP 59 o. V 15–16, a maš-da-ri-a text from L3. He may be the agrig Lugal-nam mentioned in ITT 5, 9249 o. II 1–2, a text from EN2.

Šeš-tur dub-sar occurs in a contract that can be dated to the last years of Entemena (DP 32 VI 4–5) and in AVG I, 41 r. V 7 as being responsible for barley in L6.

Šubur-<tur> dub-sar is mentioned in the years of Enentarzi. In DP 93 r. I 1–2 (EN5), he is in charge of ten two-year-old oxen. In Shileiko, *RA* 11 (1914): 62 o. II 3–4; r. II 3–4 (EN6), he is responsible for cattle hides for the king's administration (é-gal). Finally, in DP 576 r. II 1'–2', a partially preserved, undated tablet, he is in charge of large plots of land cultivated with grain.

Šul-me-<šár-ra-DU> agrig occurs during EN3 in a maš-da-ri-a text (DP 42 o. II 2) in which two dub-sar-maḫ's, a sanga-GAR, a sanga of the é-gal, the sanga of Nanše, and the nu-bànda of the é-nam-dumu (Ur-^{d}Igi-ama-šè) are mentioned. Šul-me, like Ki-ti, may have been an official of the highest rank during the reign of Enentarzi. Šul-me agrig is mentioned in L1 as an official who makes a payment of silver (DP 516 o. II 2; III 5; r. II 2), in L2 in a sá-du$_{11}$ text (AWL 177 o. II 10–11), in L3 as the official who receives the sheep in the é-mí (Nik I, 182 o. I 1–5), and in L4 as the official who transferred ingredients for the preparation of unguents[176] from the é-gal to the é-mí.

Lugalanda. Selz also cites the mention of the dam Ki-ti in two texts dating to the third year of Lugalanda (DP 352 o. I 4 and DP 354 o. II 1). But in DP 352 o. I 1–2, the wife of Šubur nu-bànda is also mentioned. Because Šubur nu-bànda probably had ceased active service in L5 and Ki-ti is never mentioned after L1, it is probable that Ki-ti had also ended his active service in L1.

175. Cf. *infra*, p. 78.

176. DP 512 r. I 4–II 4: é-mí-<a> šul-me agrig-ge é-gal-ta e-ta-gar. Nik I, 301, from the second year of Lugalanda, is a similar text, in which the receiving official is En-šu-gi$_4$-gi$_4$ ka-šakan. This latter official probably is the namesake agrig from the period of Urukagina. For a discussion of this text, see AWEL, pp. 530–31.

From these few occurrences, Lugal-nam-gú-sù seems to be an old scribe who was in active service during the reign of Enentarzi and who disappeared during the rule of Lugalanda, while Šeš-tur was active until the sixth year of Lugalanda.

The scribes of this second group are never mentioned in the ration texts or in the texts concerning the allocation of plots of land for sustenance. This seems to confirm, particularly in the cases of Šubur-tur and Kiti, that, as opposed to scribes of the first group, they were never directly subordinates of the é-mí and that, beginning in the rule of Entemena, they worked for the é-gal.

The third group comprises ten scribes, six of whom do not occur in ration texts.

Du-du dub-sar occurs, only as the husband of Kù-ge-pà, in a maš-da-ri-a text from L3 (RTC 44 o. III 8–IV 1) and in a text concerning the allocation of plots of apin-lá land in U1 (AWAS 39 r. II 14–16). Thus, it is probable that at the time of these texts Du-du had ceased active service or else worked for a different institution.

En-ig-gal dub-sar is mentioned with A-ba-DI and Ú.Ú in DP 137 r. II 5, an undated list of lú-ki-inim-ma-bi-me[177] and in AWL 138 o. I 3–II 2, a fish text, from the fourth year of an unnamed ruler, where En-ig-gal dub-sar énsi (Enentarzi) is in charge of the delivery of goods. This dub-sar occurs in two seal impressions. The first, from the reign of Lugalanda, has the inscription, En-ig-gal dub-sar-é-mí[178]; the other, from the reign of Urukagina reads, En-ig-gal dub-sar-^{d}Ba-ba$_6$.[179] Consequently En-ig-gal must have been a scribe of the énsi prior to these inscriptions, when he had been transferred to the administration of the é-mí. If our hypothesis about the dating of AWL 138 is correct, En-ig-gal was the scribe of the énsi in the é-gal at the time of Enentarzi, subsequently the scribe of Baranamtara in the é-mí at the time of Lugalanda, and of Sasa in the é-^{d}Ba-ba$_6$ at the time of Urukagina. Bauer does not exclude the possibility that the

177. DP 137, which mentions Ú.Ú dub-sar, may date from L6 onwards.

178. CIRPL p. 47, Lug. 6 (= Nik I, 324).

179. CIRPL p. 47, Lug. 12 (= Nik I, 325). For the dating of these two inscriptions, cf. J. Cooper, *Inscriptions,* pp. 70, 82.

scribe En-ig-gal and the namesake nu-bànda were the same individual.[180] It would be an amazing coincidence were the three scribes Šubur-tur, Šul-me-sár-ra-DU, and En-ig-gal active in institutional administrations contemporary with the namesake nu-bànda's. Moreover, Šubur-tur occurs as nu-bànda from EN3 to L5 whereas the namesake dub-sar occurs in EN5 and EN6. Šul-me-sár-ra-DU nu-bànda occurs only in L1, whereas the namesake agrig occurs from EN3 to L4. En-ig-gal nu-bànda occurs from L1 onwards, whereas the namesake dub-sar occurs from EN4 to perhaps the time of Urukagina. It appears very probable then that the nu-bànda and the namesake scribes are the same persons.[181] This indicates that the scribe in the institutions of ED IIIb Girsu was always a high-ranking official.

Igi-mu dub-sar, a shortened form of Igi-mu-an-šè-gal, is mentioned as the recipient of a large plot of land (17½ iku) for sustenance in L2 (DP 577 r. II 6–7). He occurs in a maš-da-ri-a text in L4 (Nik I, 157 o. II 2–3) and is the recipient of 5 gur of barley and 2½ gur of emmer in U1 (TSA 2 r. II 6–7). The size of these allocation and his mention in TSA 2, where the highest-ranking officials of the administration are listed,[182] in addition to his absence from the ration texts, indicate that Igi-mu was a very high-ranking official. As can be seen from his mention in RTC 75 o. I 3–4, he was in active service from L2 to U1 in an administrative center whose identity we have been unable to establish.

Ur-sag agrig appears only in AWL 122 o. I 1–3, a text from L3, as the recipient of four mina of wool from the é-mí. This official occurs also in a maš-da-ri-a text from the reign of Lugalanda.[183]

---

180. J. Bauer, AWL, p. 387.

181. For a discussion of possible chronological sequences and the institutions to which this nu-bànda belonged, see G. Visicato, "The nu-bànda of ED IIIb Girsu and Their Chronological Sequence" (forthcoming).

182. In the order mentioned they are: the ka-šakan; the mí-us-sá of the énsi; a nu-bànda named Íl; the sukkal-maḫ; the sagi-maḫ; the mu$_6$-sùb; the gal-nimgir; the ga-eš$_8$-maḫ; the gala of Girsu; the sanga-GAR; the énsi-gal; Baranamtara; Nìgin-mud dub-sar-maḫ; the sanga of URUxGÁNA*tenû*^{ki}; the nu-bànda of Ningirsu; and the nu-bànda of the nam-dumu, Ur-Igi<-ama-šè>.

183. H.p. 12 o. VII' 1'-2' (see G. J. Selz, *WO* 20–21 [1990–91]: 35–44).

Ur-túl-sag agrig/dub-sar is probably mentioned in L1 as a dub-sar, with Amar-Gírid^{ki} and Aš$_{10}$-ne (DP 657 o. III 6),[184] in a text regarding work on irrigation canals. But he is never mentioned in the reign of Lugalanda.[185] As agrig, he is mentioned in the first and second years of Urukagina as the recipient of a plot of land and as the person in charge of canal work.[186] It is likely that Ur-túl-sag did not work for the é-mí until U1 and that he was recruited to that center in its period of greatest growth, namely, in the early years of Urukagina.[187] However, his relationship with the latter administration is less direct than that of the scribes of the first group; in fact, he is never mentioned in ration texts.

Ú.Ú agrig, whom we have already discussed concerning En-kù, occurs as agrig from L2 until U1 and as kurušda from U3 until U6. In L2 and L4 he was responsible for sheep "for eating" (nì-kú-dè),[188] and in L5 he received allocations of barley as fodder for oxen (RTC 51 o. VI 7'–10'). In L4 and L5, Ú.Ú was the agrig in charge of counting the tools and faggot bundles in the Ekisala.[189] In L6 and U2 he was in charge of rations for the igi-nu-du$_8$ šà-dub-didli personnel.[190] Along with En-ig-gal nu-bànda, he was responsible for the counting of goods in L7 (DP 435 o. III 2–3). From L6 until U2 he is mentioned often untitled in sá-du$_{11}$ texts.[191] In the texts from U2, En-kù

184. I read Ur-GIGIR as an abbreviation of Ur-túl-sag, rather than reading Ur-pú, an anthroponym never mentioned in the documentation as a scribe.

185. Possibly a namesake official mentioned with Lum-ma-šà-tam (a namesake dub-sar is mentioned in Nik I, 44 o. I 1–2 and RTC 75 o. III 1 relative to L1) in two irrigation canal texts from L5 (DP 626 o. II 7 and DP 627 o. III 1) might be our scribe.

186. AVG I 70 o. VIII 5–6; AVG I 79 r. V 1–2; TSA 23 r. II 5–6; AVG I 74 o. III 3–4.

187. Cf. K. Maekawa, *Mesopotamia* 8/9, pp. 120–35. In fact, this official is among a roster of personnel, lú ú-rum ^{d}Ba-ba$_6$, in AVG II, 13 r. V 11–12 from U2.

188. AWL 108 o. IV 5; DP 338 r. III 1'-2'; DP 218 o. I 1–4.

189. Nik I, 280 r. II 1–3; DP 430 r. I 6–II 2.

190. AVG I 71 r. III 14–15; AVG I 11 r. III 5–9; Nik I, 9 r. II 1–6; AWAS 52 r. IV 15; 119 r. II 2.

191. Cf. RTC 67 o. II 2–3 (L6); AWAS 29 r. I 5–6 (L7/1); AWL 43 r. I 7 (Ue/2); DP 152 o. VI 11 (Ue/3); AWAS 14 r. II 7 (Ue/5); 15 r. III 2 (Ue/6); AVG I 66 r. II

um-mi-a is mentioned for the first time as a recipient. A certain Ú.Ú kurušda appears in this kind of document from U3 until U6.[192]

It seem probable that in U2, the kurušda En-kù left his office to become um-mi-a and the agrig Ú.Ú succeeded him as kurušda,[193] although he continued to maintain some of the responsibilities of his previous office. In fact, he continued to be in charge of the rations of the same subordinates[194] as he had been in L6 and Ue.

The scribes of this third group who are mentioned in the ration texts are: En-bi, En-da-gal-di, Šeš-lú-du$_{10}$, and Ú.Ú dub-sar (to be distinguished from the namesake agrig). On the basis of ration size, En-bi and Ú.Ú seem to have been of higher rank.[195]

1–2 (Ue/6); DP 155 r. I 2–3 (Ue/7); AWAS 30 o. VII 2–3 (Ue/9); AWAS 31 o. VII 9–r. I 1 (U1/3); DP 158 o. VI 10 (U2/4); Nik I, 60 r. I 5 (U2/9); Nik 64 r. I 1 (U2/11).

192. Cf. TSA 34 r. I 7–8 (U3/4); Nik I, 59 r.I 8–9 (U3/5); TSA 36 r. II 1–2 (U3/10); Nik I, 63 r. I 1–2 (U3/11); AWAS 32 r. I 3–4 (U4/2); CT 50, 37 r. I 5–6 (U4/4); AWAS 33 r. I 7–8 (U4/8); AWAS 65 o. V' 9'–10' (U4/?); CTNMC 3 o. VII 9–10 (U5/2); AWAS 34 r. I 1–2 (U5/5); AWAS 35 r. I 8–9 (U5/6); TSA 35 r. I 2–3 (U5/13); Nik I, 57 r. II 8–10 (U6/1).

193. In the sá-du$_{11}$ texts from EN4 until L1, a namesake official is mentioned without a characterizing element; cf. Nik I, 67 o. III 7 (EN4); AWL 41 o. IV 8 (L1/10); DP 145 o. IV 4 (L1/12); Nik I, 62 o. III 6 (L1/12). In the first distribution of L3, a namesake ugula-uru appears in his place (AWL 42 o. V 5–6). In the distributions of the same year and in those of subsequent years, Ú.Ú is mentioned again without any characterizing element; cf. DCS 6 o. V 8 (L3/?); RTC 51 o. VI 7' (L5/8). Finally, Ú.Ú agrig appears in L6. It is difficult to establish if this is always the same official, but we cannot exclude this possibility. As ugula-uru, Ú.Ú is mentioned in texts that span L1 to L4. In Nik I, 157 o. I 4 (L4), a namesake ugula is mentioned in connection with sheep. We have already seen that the namesake agrig mentioned in AWL 108 and DP 218 carries out the same task.

194. Cf. CT 50, 36 r. VI 14–15 (U3/6); AWAS 121 r. VI 18–19 (U3/8); AWAS 16 r. V 18–19 (U3/10); AWAS 120 r. IV 18–19 (U4/2); TSA 14 r. IV 18–19 (U4/4); TSA 15 r. V 14–15 (U4/7); AWAS 36 r. I 8–9; II 4–6 (U4/?); DP 115 r. IV 5–6 (U6/?); DP 114 r. IV 14–15 (U5/3); TSA 16 r. III 15—IV 1 (U6/8); TSA 17 r. V 3-5 (U6/?).

195. With the exception of the sixth year, their dues were 72 sìla of barley, while only 48 sìla went to the other two.

En-bi is mentioned in L6 and in Ue as the recipient of barley rations and plots of land.[196] In U1, however, he is absent from the ration texts while being the recipient of a plot of agricultural land (AVG I 70 o. VI 12). In L6 (AVG II, 7 o. V 3–4) and in Ue (DP 637 r. II 5) he was in charge of barley for six subordinates; and in U1 he was in charge of work on the irrigation canals (AVG I 74 o. III 1). Possibly these texts are related to one another in the sense that the barley allocated in AVG II, 7 was destined for the sustenance of those who worked on the canals. In U2 he was the recipient of regular allocations of barley amounting to 72 sìla and of plots of land for various reasons,[197] all the while continuing to be in charge of work on the canals (AVG II, 96 r. II 4–5). In the same year he occurs in AVG II, 13 r. IV 11–12, a roster of people belonging to ^{d}Ba-ba$_{6}$. In the third year he is mentioned only as the recipient of regular rations of barley and allocations of emmer.[198] It should be noted that in all these texts he is mentioned with A-ba-DI and not with Amar-Gírid^{ki}, while in other texts he occurs with En-da-gal-di, Šeš-lú-du$_{10}$, and Ú.Ú. In addition, he received an allocation of 1½ sìla of bread (DP 130 o. V 11). In U4 he was the sole recipient of plots of land (DP 603 o. II 5), but not barley rations. He is mentioned also in U4, as being in charge of work on the irrigation canals (DP 647 r. II 2). There is no mention of him in U5. In U6 he was the recipient of regular rations of 48 sìla of barley with A-ba-DI and Amar-Gírid^{ki}.

Ú.Ú dub-sar is mentioned in L6, with A-ba-DI, Amar-Gírid^{ki}, Aš$_{10}$-ne, En-bi, and Maš-dà, as the recipient of a ration of 72 sìla of barley (RTC 54 o. IV 12) and of a land plot of 6 iku (AWL 6 o. III 6–7)[199]

196. Barley in RTC 54 o. IV 11 (L6); AWAS 5 o. V 8 (Ue) and plots of land in AVG I 39 r. II 3 (L6); AWAS 37 o. IV 5 (Ue).

197. AWAS 6 r. I 10; TSA 20 o. VI 7; AVG I 79 o. II 1–2; AVG I 93 o. II 3–4; AVG II, 6 r, VII 14.

198. AWAS 7 r. II 9; AWAS 10 r. III 8; AWAS 8 r. IV 4; AWAS 9 r. IV 6; AWAS 68 r. II 7'.

199. The date of this text is uncertain due to a lacuna at r. II 5. After the mention of our official, there is a clause at o. III 8, aša$_{5}$ é-gal-kam "the 6 iku of the field belonging to the palace," while in the colophon after the summary there is an indication that the field belonged to Baranamtara. This may indicate that Ú.Ú was still in the employ of the é-gal, but at that moment he was working for the

role vs. title

and in Ue of an extraordinary ration of one gur with the same scribes (AWAS 5 o. V 7). He appears also with A-ba-DI in two texts of the same typology in U1 and U2.[200] In the ration texts of U2 and U3, Ú.Ú is mentioned together with En-da-gal-di, Šeš-lú-du$_{10}$, and Lugal-šà-lá-tuku, a dub-sar of the fourth group.[201] In U3, together with A-ba-DI, En-bi, Amar-Girid^{ki}, and Ur-igi-gál, he is the recipient of bread (DP 130 o. VI 1). In the ration texts of U4, U5, and U6, he is mentioned only with En-da-gal-di and Lugal-šà-lá-tuku, but, as in AWAS 16, they are ration texts for igi-nu-du$_8$ personnel, whereas the former concern lú-šuku-dab$_5$-ba personnel who were of higher rank. Probably in these latter years their jobs involved this type of personnel. Ú.Ú's rations, which were 72 sìla[202] in U4, 36 in U5,[203] and in U6 sometimes 48[204] and sometimes 36[205] and the smaller number of recipients mentioned in the ration texts suggest that the é-mí/é-^{d}Ba-ba$_6$ may have undergone a drastic reduction in size.

The last two scribes, En-da-gal-di and Šeš-lú-du$_{10}$, are mentioned only in ration texts from Ue to U6; they receive 48 sìla each with the exception of Šeš-lú-du$_{10}$, who receives an extraordinary ration of 108 sìla in the first distribution of U1 (AWAS 123 o. VI 12). Šeš-lú-du$_{10}$ in L4 (DP 226 o. VII 3') and En-da-gal-di in L5 (DP 132 r. II 8) are mentioned in the lú-IGI.NÍGIN lists, probably a list of officials to be transferred to the é-mí.[206]

The scribes of this third group have differing ranks and positions. We have high-ranking officials, such as Igi-mu, who probably were never

---

é-mí, or that our scribe had just joined the latter organization, but was still affiliated with the é-gal. If the first hypothesis is valid, then the text should date before L6, if the second hypothesis, it could date to L6.

200. DP 113 o. VI 1 and TSA 5 r. III' 5.

201. DP 113 o. IX 4; perhaps Nik I, 13 o. II 2; AWAS 16 o. VIII 12; AWAS 121 r. I 3; CT 50, 36 o. VIII 8.

202. TSA 14 o. VIII 12'; TSA 15 o. IX 12'; AWAS 120 o. VIII 13; Nik I, 2 o. VIII 13; AWAS 64 o. IV' 6'.

203. DP 114 o. IX 6.

204. AWAS 17 o. VIII 9 (3 unnamed dub-sar); AWAS 23 o. III 10.

205. AWAS 122 o. IX 13; DP 115 o. IX 9'.

206. Cf. K. Maekawa, *Mesopotamia* 8/9, pp. 114–20 for this reconstruction.

in the employ of the é-mí; mid-ranking officials, such as Ur-túl-sag, who probably were only temporarily employed in the é-mí; and officials who, though they were of differing levels, were permanently employed by the é-mí, some in L6 and others in U1. Many of these, with the exception of En-da-gal-di, Šeš-lú-du$_{10}$, and Ú.Ú, were probably reassigned at the end of U4 to their old organization or to a new one.

The fourth group is made up of 13 scribes of differing rank.

E-ge dub-sar, a shortened form of E-ge-a-na-ak, is mentioned only in TSA 8 o. III 9–10[207] and TSA 7 r. IV 7–8 (U4),[208] respectively. These are two documents concerning the allocation of plots of lands for sustenance and for leaseholding. In the former, E-ge receives 1 bur apin-lá, in the latter, 12 iku. Since TSA 7 lists other officials who were in the employ of the é-mí, E-ge may have worked there; but, given the lack of other references, this must have been only temporary.

Lugal-èš-du$_{10}$-ga and En-DU are mentioned once each. The former appears in AWAS 42 o. II 4–r. I 1 as being in charge of counting in a text dated to U3 concerning personnel who were subordinates of A-en-ra-DU dumu-énsi[209] and was thus probably part of the administrative organization of this high-ranking official. The latter is mentioned in a text concerning wool-bearing sheep from Ue.[210] From the reference to Lagaš in this text, it is probable that this agrig worked in that center.

Lugal-kèš appears in texts with the title of dub-sar in U3, as the official who was the recipient of an allocation of 18 sìla of emmer (AWAS 68 r. III 4–6), and as the person in charge of the barley rations of the

207. The mention of é-^{d}Ba-ba$_6$ in r. IV 3' after the summary suggests a date in the reign of Urukagina.

208. For the attribution to the reign of this ruler, cf. J. La Placa – M. Powell, "The Agricultural Cycle and the Calendar at Pre-Sargonic Girsu," *BSA* 5 (1990): 89.

209. For this dating, cf. AWAS, pp. 398–99.

210. DP 258 o. III 1–2, 22 udu-siki udu-dub-kam En-DU agrig-ge Lagaš^{ki}-a e-tuku, "22 sheep for wool, sheep which are of the tablet/account, En-DU the agrig in Lagaš has in his possession."

géme-ḪAR.[211] He is mentioned in the same year as a scribe who received barley for animal fodder, for seeding, and for the maintenance of the lú-DUN personnel, subordinates of a certain É-me-lám-su[212] allocated by DI-Utu and the nu-bànda En-ig-gal in Nik I, 90 r. I 2–3 (and probably recorded this fact). In U4, he received a ration of 72 sìla of barley (CT 50, 35 o. VII' 11'–12') and is mentioned as the official in charge of barley for the géme-ḪAR and the sag-apin personnel.[213] Finally, in U5 he was the recipient of a barley ration of 72 sìla (Nik I, 20 o. VI 3–4). His sporadic occurrence in the ration texts suggests that his work in the é-mí was temporary. His being in charge of sag-apin in texts from U4 and his description in AWAS 68 r. III 4–6 as dub-sar lú géme-sila-<sír-sír> suggest that he may be the namesake Sag-apin, a subordinate of Géme-sila<-sír-sír>, who distributed barley for the maintenance of personnel and as fodder, and who is mentioned in AWL 22 o. II 4–III 2 dated in U4. Like A-en-ra-gub, Géme-sila-sír-sír is described as dumu-<énsi> in Nik I, 218 r. I 2–3 and was in charge of an administrative center whose employees were paid by the é-mí beginning in U4.

Lugal-šà-lá-tuku also appears as a dub-sar from U3. He is usually mentioned with En-da-gal-di, Šeš-lú-du$_{10}$, and Ú.Ú, in ration texts from U3 until U6.[214] Along with the aforementioned three individuals, this dub-sar should be regarded as a mid-ranking scribe who fully participated in the administration of the é-mí/é-^{d}Ba-ba$_{6}$.[215]

211. AWAS 124 o. V 8–10; AWAS 26 o. VI 2–3; r. IV 5–6.

212. AWEL, pp. 306–7, 2:5, translate lú-DUN "unterstellten Leute or unterstellter Mann."

213. AVG II, 77 r. I 5–6; DP 116 o. VI 10–11; r. II 3–4; DP 117 o. VI 5–6; r. I 6–7; DP 118 o. VI 3–4; r. II 10–III 1; Nik I, 16 r. V 11–12.

214. U3: AWAS 16 o. VIII 14; 121 r. I 5; CT 50, 36 r. I 2. U4: AWAS 120 o. VIII 5'; TSA 14 o. VIII 14'; TSA 15 o. IX 13'; Nik I, 2 o. VIII 14. U5: DP 114 r, IX 7. U6: AWAS 17 o. VII 10; TSA 16 o. VIII 5'; DP 115 o. IX 10'.

215. A namesake Lú-é-éš-gíd occurs in a maš-da-ri-a text from L3 (DP 59 o. IX 13–14), but his identification with our dub-sar is unsure.

Puzur$_4$-Ma-ma agrig occurs in U2+[x] in AWL 156 r. V 4–5, an account of goods delivered to the gods in NINA.[216] He does not appear in ration texts. Perhaps he worked for institutions other than the é-mí.

Šul-ig-gal dub-sar occurs in DP 591 r. IV 12–V 1 as recipient of šuku of a plot of aša$_5$ še-mú-a. A namesake untitled official is rationed in DP 110 o. IV 5 (EN3) and DP 111 o. II 4 (EN4) but we do not have any evidence to identify him as the dub-sar mentioned in DP 591.

^{d}Šul-utul$_x$-men agrig occurs in DP 167 r. I 2–3 from U2 as the official who brought the goods delivered to the gods by Sasa in NINA.[217] His duties seem similar to those of Puzur$_4$-Ma-ma in AWL 156. Possibly these two agrig's both worked in NINA.

Ur-igi-gál occurs in AWAS 52 o. VIII 8, a ration text for igi-nu-du$_8$ šà-dub-didli personnel (Ue). He is mentioned, with En-da-gal-di and Šeš-lú-du$_{10}$, as the recipient of a barley ration of 48 sìla. He is mentioned subsequently only in DP 130 o. VI 2–3 (U3) as the recipient of 1 sìla of ninda in U3. Probably this official was in active service from the time of Lugalanda to the period of AWAS 52 (Ue) and subsequently, in contrast to the two scribes with whom he appears in the latter text, he was transferred to another administrative unit, since he is never again mentioned in the ration texts. Alternatively, he could have ceased active service although he continued to receive ninda.

Úr-mud and Bára-zi-<šà-gal> are two agrig's first mentioned in U2. The former is the recipient of rations of barley and emmer[218] in U2

---

216. Bauer, AWL, p. 387, had suggested NINA=siraran, but Bauer (personal communication) offers a new reading nimin$_x$ or nigin$_x$.

During the reign of Urukagina, a certain untitled Puzur$_4$-Ma-ma is recipient of zíz-numun as sá-du$_{11}$ on a tablet whose date is lost (DP 161 o. II 7), barley in U3 (DP 545 o. II 2), and še-ba in first distribution of U3 (DP 229 r. II' 3). Finally, Puzur$_4$-Ma-ma and En-ig-gal nu-bànda compiled a balanced account of tamarisk in U2 (DP 449 r. III 5). But we do not know if this official is the agrig or the namesake engar.

217. NINA^{ki}-na balag e-ta-ru-a ^{d}Šul-utul$_x$-men agrig-ge mu-túm; cf. AWL, pp. 387 and 448.

218. Barley in AWAS 6 r. IV 6; AVG II, 6 r. I 7–8. Emmer in Nik I, 13 r. IV 2.

and of rations of barley in U3, U4, and U6.[219] In the same years, starting from the ninth distribution of U2 (AWAS 20 r. I 5–6), he was in charge of the barley of the géme-dumu personnel, as well as working on the irrigation canals from U2–U4. As was established previously,[220] from the eleventh offering of sá-du$_{11}$ of U2[221] Úr-mud replaced Maš-dà and is mentioned in these texts until U6 (DP 150 r. II 3–4). Bára-zi is mentioned as the recipient of rations, usually in tandem with Úr-mud in the second, third, and fourth years.[222] From U4 on, Bára-zi is not mentioned. Probably the namesake official, mentioned without a title, whose subordinates are several géme-ḪAR[223] is our agrig. If this identification is correct, then we must identify as an agrig the homonym with one géme-ḪAR subordinate mentioned in RTC 52 o. IV 9 in L 3. It seems clear that the two agrig's were already active, probably in other administrative units, before Urukagina's ascent to the throne, but worked in the é-mí with Úr-mud until U6 and with Bára-zi after U2 through U4.

En-šu-gi$_4$-gi$_4$ agrig appears in U1 (DP 416 o. II 2–r. I 1), with the abbreviation En-šu, as the official who brought to the é-gal timber from the garden of Ur-ki.[224] In U2 in a sá-du$_{11}$ text, he is mentioned, with several sanga's and a sagi-maḫ, sá-du$_{11}$ received in the é-gal (TSA 3 o. I 4–5). He reappears subsequently only in U5 and in U6, as an agrig performing the duties of a nu-bànda with (AVG II, 1 r. III 3–4; 40 o. II 3) or in place of En-ig-gal, thus in charge of allocating rations and

---

219. U3: AWAS 7 r. I 5; AWAS 8 r. I 4; TSA 18 o. III 11–12. U4: AWAS 57 r. I 3. U6: DP 121 r. I 3–4; AWAS 12 r. I 4–5; AWAS 11 r. V 3–4; AWAS 23 r. I 6–7; AWAS 22 r. IV 13–14.

220. Cf. above, p. 59.

221. Nik I, 64 o. V 7–8; he occurs also in U2 in AVG II, 71 o. III 1–2.

222. Úr-mud and Bára-zi usually appear together. However, in TSA 18 o. III 11–12 only Úr-mud occurs while in AWAS 10 r. I 5–6 and Nik I, 52 r. I 5–6 only Bára-zi.

223. DP 112 r. I 18 (U2/11); CTNM 4, XII 18 (U2); DP 171 r. I 20–21 (U2); Nik I, 1 r. II 7–8; AWAS 20 r. II 16.

224. kiri$_6$ Ur-ki-ta En-šu agri-gé na e-ma-ri é-gal-šè e-ma-DU kiri$_6$ ú-rum ^{d}Ba-ba$_6$. Similar texts are DP 427; 428 and AWL 74, but in these latter documents it is En-ig-gal nu-bànda who brought the goods. For the meaning of the verb na-ri, "cut out" and the verbal form na ì-mi-ri, na e-me-ri, na e-ma-ri, cf. AWL p. 636, sub ri(g).

distributing sá-du$_{11}$ (še-ba e-ne-ba; sá-du$_{11}$ e-ta-gar). He is never mentioned as an agrig or as a dub-sar in the texts of Lugalanda. But the namesake official who in the time of Lugalanda occurs as a lú-IGI.NÍGIN immediately after the nu-bànda En-ig-gal in some personnel lists[225] and immediately after the dub-sar's in texts concerning the allocation of textiles[226] perhaps is our agrig. We do not have sufficient evidence to identify him with the namesake ka-šakan ("superintendent of the fat") also mentioned in the time of Lugalanda,[227] although such an identification seems likely. Whatever his position before U1, he was part of the administration of the é-gal. Only in U6 was he in the employ of the é-mí, possibly a position directly below Queen Sasa.

[x.x?]-[s]ikil dub-sar occurs in U1 as recipient of one sheep in DP 82 r. I 12–II 1, a text recording goods delivered by various sanga's and other officials as maš-da-ri-a.

The final group of scribes contains the four dub-sar-maḫ's listed in TABLE 4.

Amar-šùba dub-sar-maḫ is mentioned only in maš-da-ri-a texts from the third year of Enentarzi to the sixth year of Lugalanda.[228]

Íl is mentioned as a dub-sar in DP 32 VI 7–9, a contract from the rule of Entemena, and as a dub-sar-maḫ in AVG I 5 o. I 1–II 4, a document perhaps from L1 that records the delivery of large quantities of barley, one of which came from Íl's own household (é-Íl dub-sar-maḫ-ta e-ta-è). Subsequently, he is mentioned as the husband of Ki-tuš-lú (dam Íl dub-sar-maḫ), who is the recipient of allocations of

---

225. AWL 130 o. I 5 (L4); DP 226 o. I 5 (L4); DP 132 o. I 5 [L5].

226. DP 192 o. III 7 (L4?); DP 193 o. II 8 (L6].

227. Nik I, 125 r. VI 1; 301 r. IV 2 (L2); DP 624 I 2 (L3); DP 268 r. II 3 (L5); AVG I 11 r. II 14; 44 o. III 10; 71 r. III 3; AWL 118 r. I 1; 119 r. I 1; DP 269 I 2 (L6). He also occurs in texts that do not bear the name of the king, although it is probably Lugalanda: DP 264 I 3 (2); 270 I 3 (3); Nik I, 17 r. V 6 (3); DP 514 r. III 3 (4); Nik I, 45 I 2 (6). In AVG II, 12 o. I 3–4 he is recipient of sheep for šuku, in year 1 of some ruler.

228. DP 42 o. I 4–5 (EN3); AWL 177 r. I 1–2 (L2); DP 86 o. II 1–3 (L2); AWL 175 o. IV 9–10 (L3); Geneva 1 o. VI 1–2 (L3); Geneva 3 r. I 8–9 (L4); RTC 39 o. III 7–r. I 1 (L5); DP 131 o. II 8–III 1 (L6); H.P 12 o. IV 2' (L).

plots of šuku and apin-lá land during the reign of Urukagina.[229] Probably at the time of these latter documents, Íl was no longer in active service.

Lugal-šùd-dè dub-sar-maḫ is mentioned in DP 42 o. II 1–III 1, in which Amar-šùba is also mentioned. Lugal-šùd-dè is mentioned in DP 59 r. I 19–II 1, a maš-da-ri-a text from L3, and in DP 578 r. II 6–7, a text that has the year but not name of the king.[230] He is also mentioned in DP 133 r. I 7–8 in connection with Ur-sag, a lú-IGI.NÍGIN, allocated to the wife of this official in U1. He is also mentioned in CT 50, 44 r. III 2–3, a text concerning sheep perhaps from U1, and in DP 591 r. IV 14–15, a text concerning the allocation of plots of šuku and apin-lá land from U5.

NÌGIN-mud is mentioned in TSA 2 r. II 8–9 as the recipient of large quantities of barley in U1. He occurs also in VAT 4845.[231] In RTC 17, a text from the period of Enentarzi, two namesake dub-sar's are mentioned (r. IV 1; IV 3), one a subordinate of a certain Na-na and the other of the dub-sar Gú-bé. We are inclined to identify the latter as the future dub-sar-maḫ from the reign of Urukagina.

It appears that these officials, in many instances, worked contemporaneously: Amar-šùba and Lugal-šùd-dè were dub-sar-maḫ's in the reign of Enentarzi; Amar-šùba, Lugal-šùd-dè, and Íl in the reign of Lugalanda; Lugal-šùd-dè and NÌGIN-mud occupied similar positions in the reign of Urukagina. Since it is probable that an administrative unit had only one head-scribe, our officials must have performed their duties in several centers. The mention of the unnamed dub-sar-maḫ ^{d}Nin-gír-su (DP 226 o. II 1 [L4]; DP 132 o. II 2 [L5]) and dub-sar-maḫ ^{d}Nin-mar-ki (DP 133 r. V 6 [U1]) confirms that every administrative center had its own head-

229. AVG I 70 r. III 14–15 (U1); AWAS 39 o. III 14–15 (U1); AVG I 93 o. I 1–3 (U2); DP 592 r. III 8–10 (U4). For the dating of DP 592, cf. P. J. LaPlace – M. A. Powell, "The Agricultural Cycle and the Calendar at Pre-Sargonic Girsu," *BSA* 5 (1990): 97.

230. In our opinion, DP 578 should be assigned to L1 because of the mention of Šà-TAR sanga-é-gal, who is attested most often in the first year of Lugalanda's reign (DP 134 r. I 12'–13'; Nik 53 o. V 6–7; RTC 61 o. VI 8–9). LaPlaca – Powell, *BSA* 5 (1990): 99 are of a different opinion.

231. Cf. Struve, *Onomastika*, p. 132.

scribe. We do not know which of these dub-sar-maḫ's was the head of the scribes of the é-mí.[232] But we do know that of the approximately 60 scribes mentioned in the ED IIIb Girsu documentation, only 17 were active, in different periods and at different levels, in the administration of the é-mí. The others, although working for different administrative units, had frequent contact with the é-mí.

In ED IIIb Girsu, in contrast to Fara, the function of the sanga is clearly distinguishable from that of the dub-sar and agrig in institutions such as the é-gal or the é-mí. The sanga's in ED IIIb Girsu were the administrators of the temples of the gods (e.g., sanga ^{d}Nanše, ^{d}Nin-mar-ki, ^{d}Nin-dar, é-babbar, ^{d}Dumu-zi, ^{d}En-ki-da-nigin or Abzu-da-nigin). Two exceptions are the sanga-GAR and the sanga-é-gal.[233]

Úr-mud sanga-GAR occurs in maš-da-ri-a texts in EN3 (DP 42 o. II 8–9) and L3 (DP 59 o. VI 18–19) and in L4 and L5 as a recipient of onions for šuku (DP 399 o. I 3–4; AWAS 50 o. II 2–3). The wife of Úr-mud sanga-GAR, in a undated text (AWL 124 o. II 5–6), is a recipient of wool.

An unnamed sanga-GAR occurs in maš-da-ri-a texts perhaps in L1 (AWL 182 o. II 7), in L2 (AWL 176 o. VI 1), perhaps in L3 (H.p. 12 r. V' 6'), and in U2 (Nik I, 146 r. I 10 and TSA 4 r. III 2). He occurs in Nik I, 30 r. I 1 as a recipient of a field allotment.

It is difficult to discern the chronological sequence of the three sanga-é-gal's:

Šà-TAR sanga-é-gal occurs in maš-da-ri-a texts in EN3 (DP 42 o. IV 2–3) and in L1 (DP 134 r. I 17–18; Nik I, 53 o. V 6–7; RTC 61 o. VI 8–9). In undated text (perhaps from the rule of Lugalanda), Šà-TAR received a field for šuku (DP 578 o. II 3–4). His wife occurs, in L3, in a maš-

---

232. The mention of Amar-šùba dub-sar-maḫ in RTC 39, a text concerning sheep delivered for maš-da-ri-a by Géme-^{d}Nanše dumu énsi (Lugalanda), holder of the é-nam-dumu, suggests that he was the head scribe of this organization. Because he is not mentioned in L6 and NÌGIN-mud appears in U1, it is possible that the latter succeeded to his office. Lugal-šùd-dè and Íl could be the dub-sar-maḫ of the é-gal or of the é-^{d}Nin-gír-su and é-mí respectively; but this very hypothetical.

233. For the list, cf. TABLE 5a.

da-ri-a text (AWL 175 o. I 2–3). He occurs, surprisingly, as a recipient of goods in U2 (AVG II, 72 o. I 8).

Ur-é-zi-da sanga-é-gal in L2 is allocated barley for meal (Nik I, 125 o. I 9–10) and in L4 he is allocated sheep (DP 218 v, II 5–6). He occurs also in H.P. 12 r. VI' 4'–5'.

Ú.Ú sanga-é-gal occurs in records of the distribution of barley rations from U3 (AWAS 7 o. IV 17–18; 8 o. V 3–4; 9 o. V 3–4; 10 o. IV 12–13; 16 r. VI 1–2). In U4 and U5 he occurs in texts concerning allocations of barley as sheep fodder (AWAS 33 r. I 15–II 1; 34 r. I 9–10; 35 r. I 16–II 1; TSA 35 o. VII 10–11). In U4 he was in charge of a field allotment (TSA 7 o. II 5–6). Ú.Ú occurs in TSA 28 r. III 1–2 (U?3), a text concerning cattle, harnesses, reins, and covers for cattle that Ú.Ú sanga-é-gal had returned to the palace, and in AWL 76 r. I 4–5, a text concerning plowing implements that Ú.Ú sanga-é-gal received from En-ig-gal nu-bànda from é-zag-uru in the fourth year.[234] Ú.Ú is an administrator and sanga-<^{d}En-ki>-abzu-da-nigin in texts from L2 to U2.[235] Thus, he came from the temple administration.

The texts do not provide any indication of the role of the sanga-GAR in the institutional administration of ED IIIb Girsu. However, information about the roles of the sanga é-gal and his nu-bànda in the palace administration of the énsi is discernible. In his study of these officials, Maekawa[236] suggests that when Enentarzi assumed rulership, he retained the office of sanga of the temple of the god Ningirsu, which he held during the reign of Entemena.[237] This office, with the énsi-ship, was passed on to Lugalanda.[238] Maekawa's hypothesis is supported by the absence of any reference to the sanga of Ningirsu beginning in the reign of Enentarzi; the sanga of Ningirsu never occurs with the sanga of other temples in the sá-du$_{11}$ texts. Moreover, the temple of Ningirsu,

234. For the meaning of é-zag-uru as "Haus an der Stadtgrenze," cf. AWL, p. 262.

235. DP 184 2. III 2–3 (L1); AVG II, 13 r. I 1–2 (L2); AVG I, 33 r. II 6–7 (L6); DP 133 r. VI 9–10 (U1); TSA 5 r. V' 2–4 (U2).

236. *Mesopotamia* 8/9.

237. *Mesopotamia* 8/9, p. 118.

238. *Mesopotamia* 8/9, p. 138.

with few exceptions,[239] is never mentioned in texts concerning offerings to the gods. Although the sanga of Ningirsu is not mentioned in the administrative texts from EN, the sanga é-gal occurs in the maš-da-ri-a texts of EN3; this office was assumed by Šà-TAR.[240] Probably first Šà-TAR and then Ur-é-zi-da were the administrators of the property and personnel of the temple of Ningirsu in the time of Enentarzi and Lugalanda, the temple itself having been absorbed by the é-gal when Enentarzi assumed énsi-ship. As befitting any holder of that office, they received allocations for maš-da-ri-a,[241] allocations that had formerly been given to the sanga of Ningirsu. Maekawa suggests that in L1 some of the é-gal personnel were transferred to the é-mí from the administration of the temple of Ningirsu.[242] However, the administrative structure of the temple continued to exist within the é-gal.[243] According to Maekawa,[244] in the first years of Urukagina lugal, the remainder of the personnel of the temple of Ningirsu, as well as its property, was transferred to the é-^{d}Ba-ba$_6$. Šà-TAR, then, would have been transferred, along with the other workers, from the é-gal to the é-^{d}Ba-ba$_6$. But in U2 sanga é-gal Šà-TAR begins to appear in the texts. In U3 Ú.Ú sanga, who came from another temple administration, assumed the office of sanga é-gal, subordinate to the é-^{d}Ba-ba$_6$ (lú ú-rum ^{d}Ba-ba$_6$), probably as the administrator of the temple of Ningirsu, which, according to Maekawa,[245] had already been incorporated into the é-^{d}Ba-ba$_6$.

---

239. Cf. Nik I, 163 o. I 2.

240. A similar point of view has been expressed by A. Westenholz, *Circulation*, pp. 21–22, no. 18.

241. In chronological order: DP 42; 134; Nik I, 53; RTC 61; AWL 175; Nik I, 125; DP 218.

242. *Mesopotamia* 8/9, p. 120.

243. The mention of Amar-ezen nu-bànda ^{d}Nin-gír-su in DP 466 r. I 7–8 (L$^{?}$4), of an unnamed nu-bànda ^{d}Nin-gír-su in AWL 68 r. II 1 (L4), and of an unnamed dub-sar-maḫ ^{d}Nin-gír-su in some texts from the period of Lugalanda, seems to confirm that the organizational structure of the temple of Ningirsu had been maintained in some manner during the reign of Lugalanda.

244. *Mesopotamia* 8/9, p. 112.

245. *Mesopotamia* 8/9, pp. 120–34.

Under all three rulers, various scribes (A-ba-DI, Aš$_{10}$-ne, Amar-Gírid^{ki}, En-bi, Maš-dà, Ur-^{d}Nin-gír-su, Ur-túl-sag) were responsible for the work on the irrigation canals—a further indication of the importance of these canals for the life of the city. Other scribes (Bára-zi, Lugal-Kèš^{ki}, and Maš-dà) were responsible for the mills and were involved with the royal kitchens (é-muḫaldim). At least one scribe (Aš$_{10}$-ne) was in charge of wool for the weavers; another (Lugal-Kèš^{ki}) for the engar's, and still others (Lugal-èš-du$_{10}$-ga, Úr-mud) for various personnel categories. One scribe (A-ba-DI) was responsible for grain and at least two (En-kù, Ú.Ú) were connected with sheep breeding. In addition, probably the agrig En-šu-gi$_4$-gi$_4$ was responsible for the management of fat products and ingredients necessary for the manufacture of perfume.

This analysis of roles and responsibilities clearly shows that the scribes of Girsu, in this period, managed the goods and personnel necessary for the administration of the é-mí. The identification of some scribes with namesake officials who, in certain periods, were described by professional names other than dub-sar or agrig (e.g., Šubur-tur, Šul-me-šár-ra-DU, En-ig-gal, Aš$_{10}$-ne, En-kù, Ú.Ú, and perhaps En-šu-gi$_4$-gi$_4$) suggests that other officials mentioned in the texts, despite not being listed as dub-sar or agrig, may have been scribes nonetheless.

3. The Scribes of Nippur in the Late ED and Early Sargonic Periods

The Nippur tablets excavated by the Babylonian Expedition are housed in Istanbul, Jena, and Philadelphia. The Jena and Philadelphia tablets, with the exception of those from Fara, were apparently excavated during the Third Expedition in 1893. Tablets housed in Jena come from one site.[246] Probably almost all the tablets come from Mound III or Mound X[247] or, at least, from the area of the é-kur.[248] None of these tablets seem to have come from Mound V, where the Sargonic tablets of the Onion archive were found. A. Westenholz has published 378 admin-

246. Cf. ECTJ, p. 5.

247. Cf. ECTJ, pp. 6–7.

248. Cf. OSP 1, pp. 3–4.

istrative documents from Late ED and Early Sargonic Nippur in ECTJ and OSP 1, as well as others.[249]

A few of these Nippur tablets date earlier, to the Fara period, and another 40 date later, to the reign of Narām-Sîn. However the vast majority of texts have been dated between the Late ED and Early Sargonic periods.[250] Paleography is often the sole means of dating, despite its limitations; usually there is no recorded archaeological context for connecting groups of texts. In contrast to Fara and ED IIIb Girsu, the Nippur material is not homogeneous, making any attempt to reconstruct the administrative organization—and all the more so the role of the scribe—quite problematic. The six scribes mentioned in the texts cannot possibly be the only scribes to have worked in Nippur, a large and important center. For these reasons, this section is limited to listing scribes and offering correlations only in the few instances where possible.

AN-šeš-mu dub-sar is mentioned once only in OSP 1, 101 o. II–r. I 1. The text records the slaughter of bulls in the tenth month of the year in which the man of Uruk (Enšakušana) laid siege to Kiš: mu lú-Unug^{ki} Kiš^{ki}-da ì-da-tuš.[251] AN-šeš-mu dub-sar is the official who skinned the animals (kuš bí-zi-zi). This anthroponym does not occur elsewhere.

^{d}Inanna-ur-sag dub-sar is mentioned in OSP 1, 122 o. III 2–3. A comparison of this tablet with OSP 1, 101—a document that from internal evidence should certainly be dated to the reign of Enšakušana—indicates a considerable paleographic similarity. OSP 1, 122 was a list of about 15 anthroponyms of which only ten have survived. These individuals were recipients of rented plots of land (apin-lá), among whom ^{d}Inanna-ur-sag dub-sar was granted 18 iku

249. ECTJ is a new edition of the texts that A. Pohl had published in 1935 in TMH V. Pohl's edition contains copies of the tablets, an inventory, and indices. A. Westenholz has collated the Jena tablets, proposing changes to some of the copies. The texts have been transliterated, commented on, and, in many cases, translated. Some of the OSP 1 texts (127) were previously published in PBS 1/2 and 4, in PBS 9, 2, and in PBS 13. The remaining texts are unpublished (cf. OSP 1, p. 1).

250. Cf. ECTJ, pp. 9–10; OSP 1, pp. 3–4.

251. Cf. ECTJ 158 r. I 1–4; OSP 1, p. 115.

of land. A namesake official, also the recipient of 18 iku of land, is mentioned without title in OSP 1. 121 o. III 2'. The paleography of this latter text appears to be the same as that of OSP 1, 122, so that this may be the same official. Note that the surviving names of the recipients who benefited from grants of land from 4 to 18 iku is concluded by ^{d}Inanna-ur-sag, the only one followed by a professional name. However, this professional name, which concludes the list, could also refer to the entire list of officials, not only to ^{d}Inanna-ur-sag.[252] Unfortunately, none of the officials is mentioned elsewhere as a scribe. Moreover, the practice of appending a professional name after the last individual in a list to indicate that all the aforementioned individuals were of this profession is unattested at Nippur (albeit the number of texts is comparatively small). This practice does occur, however, in the administrative texts of Fara and ED IIIb Girsu.[253] The extent of the plots of apin-lá land is comparable to the land rented out to the high-ranking officials of the administration of ED IIIb Girsu.

Lugal-al-sa$_{6}$ dub-sar-maḫ is mentioned in ECTJ 166 r. II 2–3, a maš-da-ri-a text. In this document, as in all the other maš-da-ri-a texts, only high-ranking officials are mentioned.[254] An unnamed dub-sar-maḫ is mentioned in OSP 1, 31 r. II 3 as the official to whom four workers were allocated in the month KIN-ku$_{5}$.[255] Another unnamed dub-sar-maḫ, GAR.GU.NUN.SUR, appears in a maš-da-ri-a text, ECTJ 164 o. II

---

252. The officials mentioned are, in order: Ur-^{d}Nin-urta; Lugal-nì-BE-du$_{10}$; UD.UD; Du-du; LUL.KA; A-ba-^{d}En-líl; Ur-^{d}Li$_{9}$-si$_{4}$; Nin-^{d}Utu-mu, and ^{d}Inanna-ur-sag. In some texts that can be linked to OSP 1 121 and 122 on the basis of paleography, officials who have the same anthroponym as those listed in OSP 1, 121 appear to be contemporaneous (ECTJ 3; UD.UD, A-ba-^{d}En-líl, and ^{d}Inanna-ur-sag; ECTJ 9 A-ba-^{d}En-líl and Ur-^{d}Li$_{9}$-si$_{4}$; ECTJ 11 Lugal-nì-BE-du$_{10}$, Ur-^{d}Nin-urta and A-ba-^{d}En-líl; ECTJ 124 ^{d}Inanna-ur-sag, A-ba-^{d}En-líl, and LUL.KA; ECTJ 159 LUL.KA, ^{d}Inanna-ur-sag, UD.UD, and Lugal-nì-BE-du$_{10}$; ECTJ 167 Lugal-nì-BE-du$_{10}$ and ^{d}Inanna-ur-sag.

253. Cf. EDATŠ, p. 138, n. 46.

254. Cf. ECTJ, p. 82.

255. This document partially parallels ECTJ 56, which records the number of workers but not their rations. OSP 1, 31 should be dated to the Early Sargonic period: "Note the occurrence of the royal gur which indicates that this text was written

3. There is no way of determining whether these unnamed officials should be identified with Lugal-al-sa$_6$.

ḪA.N[I] dub-sar is mentioned in ECTJ 53 o. II 7–III 1 as the recipient or the person in charge of 15 workers. Some of the officials mentioned in the text also occur in ECTJ 26, an analogous but badly preserved text.

Lugal-urì dub-sar is mentioned only in a votive inscription to Inanna.[256] But the namesake official, subordinate/son of the dub-sar-maḫ Ù-mu-ni-ni, who occurs in OSP 1, 85, 5, probably is our dub-sar. He should therefore be included among the scribes who were employed in an administrative capacity. Perhaps the Lugal-urì mentioned in OSP 1, 56 o. I 2 and ECTJ 38 o. I 9, two beer texts probably addressed to messengers,[257] is the namesake dub-sar.

Ur-tur dub-sar is mentioned in OSP 1, 12, on the edge of the tablet. He is probably the scribe who recorded or checked the document.

No other likely identifications with namesake officials mentioned in the documentation[258] is possible.

---

during one of the Early Akkadian kings, presumably Sargon" (OSP, 1, p. 29). The gur-lugal is regarded by the author as a primitive form of the later gur of Akkad. The gur-lugal, before Ur III, occurs only in BIN 8, 62 o. I 1 and 116 o. I 1, two texts dating from the time of Lugalzagesi; cf. M. Powell, *HUCA* 49 (1978): 30–31. Consequently, it is possible that this unit of measurement had been introduced by Lugalzagesi and disappeared when Sargon ascended to the throne. According to this hypothesis, OSP 1, 31 and ECTJ 56 should date to the period shortly before Sargon. A different point of view is suggested by M. Powell, *RlA* M, 7, p. 498, "lugal in BIN 8, 62 and 116 is the beginning of names not gur-lugal; uncertain : OSP 1, 31."

256. Cf. OSP 1, p. 92, ama-a-zu$_5$ dam Lugal-urì dub-sar.

257. These two documents are part of a group of 16 texts (ECTJ 32, 35, 38, 40, 168, 206; OSP 1, 53, 54, 55, 56, 57, 58, 59, 60, 153, 154) concerning the allocation of beer. In this group of documents, with the exception of ECTJ 40 and 168, the same officials occur. Among the recipients, persons are mentioned who come from cities identified simply by the expression lú-GN^{ki} (Adab, Ereš, Kazallu, Kiš, Ku'ara, Larsa, Marad, Šuruppak, Umma, Ur, Urusagrig). Westenholz, OSP 1, p. 38, considers these persons "presumably ambassadors in Nippur from the city in question" and dates these texts to the period of Sargon. Similar texts have been found in Archaic Ur and Fara. Two similar texts are BIN 8, 67 and 68.

258. Cf. OSP 1, p. 104.

4. The Scribes of Umma from Lugalzagesi to the Early Sargonic Period

4.1 *Texts from the Time of Lugalzagesi*

The administrative documents of ED IIIb Umma/Zabalam probably come from the temple household of the goddess Inanna at Zabalam and, with few exceptions, date to years 6–8 of Lugalzagesi énsi. M. Powell has examined the texts of this archive[259] and determined their typology and dating.[260] Within the 91 texts, Powell recognized six categories of documents:[261] (1) land and/or grain texts [64]; (2) copper and metal products [12]; (3) silver [2]; (4) giš-gíd-da texts [4]; (5) personnel texts [6]; (6) work assignment texts [3].

This first grouping, which comprises 60% of the documents, can be further subdivided:

(a) land texts [34]
(b) land-grain texts [16]
(c) grain texts [14]

Subgroup (1a) consists of large and small tablets recording allocations of agricultural plots, coming from different domains. Generally the recipients "have some direct connection to the temple in a service capacity."[262]

Subgroup (1b) tablets record in each entry the extent of land and one amount of barley followed by the name of the recipient. Several

259. "Texts from the Time of Lugalzagesi. Problems and Perspectives in Their Interpretation," *HUCA* 49 (1978): 30–33.

260. The documentation of Umma/Zabalam consists of 104 published texts of various typologies. Of these, 71 are published in BIN 8; 3 in MVN 3; 25 in *HUCA* 49 (1978); 2 in M. deJong-Ellis, "Cuneiform Tablets at Bryn Mawr College," *JCS* 31 (1979): 31–32; 1 in E. Sollberger, *BiOr* 16 (1959): plate V; 1 in J. A. Brinkman, AOAT 25 plates III–IV. One, TLAT, 3, is to be added to the texts listed in *HUCA* 49. Like all the documents in BIN 8, these tablets come from clandestine digs and were sold privately to museums and collectors. Thus, it is impossible to determine their findspots.

261. Powell, *HUCA* 49 (1978): 13–18. It is impossible to establish the typology of the remaining texts, since they are severely damaged.

262. Powell, *HUCA* 49 (1978): 27.

texts are concluded by the clauses še è-a and še ág. The meaning of these terms is unclear. Powell[263] regards še è-a and še ág as "being roughly equivalent" and interprets these amounts of barley as payments owed to the temple by the renter or the allotment holders as a fraction of the total crop.[264] "The amount owed appears to have been determined in advance, so that "making the reckoning seems to have con-sisted of determining how much and what kind of land was involved and whether or not the allotment holder had paid the correct amount." The steps in this accounting appear similar to those recorded in Umma C.2,[265] but in the former the place of accounting is the Inanna temple and in the latter the é-gidri (see below). Subgroups (1b) and (1c) are interrelated as can be noted by a comparison between BIN 8, 54, a land-grain text, and *HUCA* 49, 9 (NBC 10720), a grain text. In fact several entries of barley recorded in BIN 8, 54 are also recorded in *HUCA* 49, 9.

In these texts, the names of eight scribes have been preserved. The anthroponyms of three others have been lost.[266]

(a) Scribes Mentioned Only Once:

Lugal-an-né dub-sar is mentioned in *HUCA* 49, 2 o. II 12 as the recipient of agricultural land. In BIN 8, 48 I 4, a še-è-a text, he occurs without title. The barley "which has come out" is measured in the é-UD-gál-kúš.[267]

Lugal-ki dub-sar is mentioned in BIN 8, 104 o. II 2 among other officials (generally identified only by their anthroponym) concerning a

---

263. Powell, *HUCA* 49 (1978): 23.

264. This interpretation is complicated because the ratio between land and grain is, in some cases, very high. For the meaning of še-bi concerning rented fields, cf. P. Steinkeller, "The Renting of Fields in Early Mesopotamia and the Development of the Concept of 'Interest' in Sumerian," *JESHO* 24 (1981): 114, 130.

265. Cf. USP, pp. 89ff.

266. Cf. BIN 8, 76 r. I 1; Powell, *HUCA* 49 (1978): 3 r. I 4; 7 r. I 4.

267. The é-UD-gál-kúš is mentioned also in BIN 8, 48 r. 2; 52 r. 2; 60 II 2; 75 r. 2; *HUCA* 49 (1978): 10 r. 2; 13 r. II 2(?). In BIN 8, 20, a text concerning the allocation of plots of land, Lugal-an-né nu-kiri$_6$ is mentioned. In the same text, Tir-kù um-mi-a and Á-kal-le are among the recipients. Thus, it is possible that Lugal-an-né nu-kiri$_6$ is an abbreviated form of Lugal-an-né dub-sar nu-kiri$_6$. If this hypothesis is correct, perhaps the official mentioned in BIN 8, 48 is our dub-sar.

number of copper objects, ^{urudu}šum, "knives."[268] A namesake official described as a sanga is mentioned in AOAT 25 o. II 14'; Bryn Mawr 6 o. I 2; 10; II 14; III 8; V 5; Bryn Mawr 7 o. IV 14; BIN 8, 86 o. II 13; and *HUCA* 49, 7 o. III 5, as the recipient of plots of land. But a link between the two officials cannot be demonstrated.

Lugal-mas-sú dub-sar is mentioned in BIN 8, 102 o. I 4 as owing 20 gur of barley to the household of the sanga Giš-šà.

Ne-sag dub-sar is mentioned in AOAT 25 o. V 11, a land-grain text. Perhaps Ne-sag, who occurs without title in Bryn Mawr 6 o. II 15; 7 o. II 9; BIN 8, 82 o. IV 1; 3; r. II 8', is our scribe.

(b) Scribes Mentioned Several Times in the Texts:

Má-gur$_8$ dub-sar is mentioned in the colophon of BIN 8, 51 and 52 as the official who wrote the tablets. BIN 8, 51 lists three entries of land-grain measured in the é-giš-šà sanga (še-ág é-giš-<šà> Má-gur$_8$ sar).[269] BIN 8, 52 is very similar to the preceding text and lists four entries with the clause še-ág é-UD-gál-kúš Má-gur$_8$ dub-sar u$_4$ 1. This clause, which contains an additional temporal clause whose meaning is unclear, indicates a different center from that of BIN 8, 51.[270]

Má-gur$_8$ is mentioned in BIN 8, 116 r. I 1. The obverse of this text lists 15 measures of barley (from 1 gur to 26 gur and 2 bariga), each followed by the name of the person who delivered it. On the reverse there is the name of the scribe responsible for the record (Má-gur$_8$), the center where the barley is stored (the granary of Zabalam [AB.INANNA-ama KA-gur$_7$]), and the date (7<mu> 1 <iti> 7 <u$_4$>).[271]

Mes-é dub-sar-maḫ is mentioned in BIN 8, 86 o. II 11–12 and Bryn Mawr 6 o. II 11; III 16. These two texts concern the allocation of land for sustenance (aša$_5$-šuku) and date to the seventh year of Lugalzagesi. Both texts list middle-to-high-ranking officials. In BIN

268. For a discussion of this term, cf. J. Bauer, *AfO* 36/37 (1989–90): 85 sub 88 I 1k.

269. This administrative center is also mentioned in BIN 8, 102 II 2 and 109 r. 2.

270. Other texts contain an analogous temporal indication: BIN 8, 48; 50; 62; 78.

271. The meaning of this indication was discovered by B. R. Foster, "New Light on 'mu-iti' Texts," *Or*NS 48 (1979): 156 and USP, p. 7, and discussed in *HUCA* 49, 10; and more recently B. R. Foster, *JAOS* 114 (1994): 452.

8, 111 o. I 9, Mes-é is the recipient of land as well as delivering barley due. The text consists of seven sections, each of which lists from one to four officials, and a quantity of barley, and concludes with the name of the official who brought/took away the barley (ba-DU). The final clause indicates that the incoming barley was measured by Ur-sa$_6$-ga (še Ur-sa$_6$-ga è).[272] Mes-é dub-sar is the supervisor of a barley transaction (maškim-bi) in BIN 8, 61 o. II 2.[273] BIN 8, 47 is a sealed order by Mes-é, assuredly our dub-sar-maḫ,[274] to pay 140 gur of barley.[275] Perhaps we should link this high-ranking official to the namesake énsi of Umma at the time when Lugalzagesi was lugal.[276]

Tir-kù dub-sar/um-mi-a is mentioned as dub-sar in BIN 8, 51 o. I 4. In this text, Má-gur$_8$ who wrote the tablet, seems to be the official responsible for the balanced account of three entries of barley. With the title um-mi-a, he is the recipient of land for sustenance in Bryn Mawr 7 r. II' 7; BIN 8, 120 o. I 1'; and perhaps BIN 8, 82 r. III 11'. Tir-kù um-mi-a occurs also in BIN 8, 62 o. I 3, a land-grain text, and in BIN 8, 111 o. II 9, a document previously discussed, in which ½ gur and 2 bariga of barley are due. The same amount due by the same official but untitled is recorded in BIN 8, 109 o. I 4.[277] Tir-kù um-mi-

272. A different interpretation is possible. The people listed in each section have delivered the barley and the official who concludes the section has brought/taken it.

273. The text lists three transactions, two of 20 and one of 150 gur, involving KA-Utu-zi nu-bànda and three other officials, Lugal-abzu gudu$_4$-abzu, Ur-^{d}En-líl nu-èš Nibru^{ki}, and Lugal-aša$_5$ ugula. The latter two transactions were supervised by Lugal-x-da and our dub-sar.

274. Cf. *HUCA* 49 (1978): 17.

275. The text concludes with the mention of É-zi kù-dím, perhaps the official supervisor: Mes-é na-⸢e⸣-[a] 140 še gur ḫa-mu-ra-ág-ág É-zi kù-dím, "Mes-e says 140 gur of barley are to be paid to you, É-zi, the silversmith (is the supervisor)" (cf. more recently FAOS 19, p. 36). The same official concludes, perhaps in the same capacity, *HUCA* 49 (1978): 9, a text in which nine measures of barley are listed.

276. According to inscriptions, he was defeated by Sargon. Cf. RIM 2, pp. 11, 59–66; 14, 62–70; caption 2', 31; caption 7.

277. The obverse of BIN 8, 108 has two columns, but only the first is inscribed, recording four allocations of barley. The fourth line, that relating to Tir-kù, is longer than the others; in the upper part the amount of barley and the recipient is indicated; in the bottom there is the sign TIR, whose meaning in this context

a remains active, as does Má-gur$_8$, into the Early Sargonic period with the title dub-sar-maḫ.

Ur-é-zi-da dub-sar is mentioned in two large texts, *HUCA* 49 3 r. 1 and Bryn Mawr 6 r. II 7, as the recipient of plots of land of various quality (še, maḫ). In addition, he is mentioned in BIN 8, 52, a land-grain text previously discussed concerning Má-gur$_8$.

Lugal-gu$_4$ dub-sar, mentioned in BIN 8, 26 r. II 3–5, should perhaps be added to the list of scribes. He is the official of whom Ur-nab dub-sar is a subordinate or son (Ur-nab dumu Lugal-gu$_4$ dub-sar dub-sar-bi). The text appears to be a list of officials who came/went (ba-DU) while É-ki-gal-la was énsi of Adab and Lugalzagesi was lugal.[278]

While little can be said about the scribes of the first group, the four who comprise the second group form part of the administrative core of the Zabalam household at its highest level. They are not simple compilers of tablets, but rather officials in charge of the management of the institution's property.

---

is obscure. The reverse contains the formula [še]-ág [É]-giš-šà sanga [š]e <šu>-a-gi$_4$. Possibly the sign TIR at the bottom on o. 4 is to be connected to the subsequent clause in the reverse (suggestion by Bauer).

278. This text has been considered by F. J Stephens (cf. BIN 8, p. 6) to be subsequent to the group of texts characterized by the clause: Lugalzagesi énsi. M. Powell, *HUCA* 49 (1978): 27–28, does not exclude the possibility that it is contemporaneous with the texts of the archive under discussion. On the other hand, Foster (USP, p. 155) considers this archive to be later than BIN 8, 26 and dates it to the Sargonic period. He supposes that Lugalzagesi, after the defeat, was confirmed as énsi of Umma by the king of Akkad (A. Westenholz, *AfO* 31 [1981]: 77, is of a different opinion). However, Lugal-gu$_4$, like the other anthroponyms in the text (with the exception of Amar-Kuara^{ki} and Aba-^{d}En-líl), is never mentioned in the texts of Umma A, which immediately follows them. Possibly this text does not come from Umma, but from Adab. If the aforementioned hypothesis concerning the identification of the dub-sar Mes-e and the namesake énsi of Umma is correct, it must necessarily follow that the Zabalam texts are older than BIN 8, 26.

The administrative documents of the Early Sargonic period at Umma can be considered as a continuation of the Pre-Sargonic, on the basis of paleography and structure.[279]

The administrative archive of Umma contemporaneous to the earliest Old Akkadian period contains 104 mu-iti texts of varying typology. Another text, published by D. Frame – G. Frayne – G. McEvans[280] should be added, and perhaps another text published by H. Neumann.[281] This archive was identified by B. R. Foster and published in his study in USP.[282] In USP, the texts belonging to this archive, called Umma A, are grouped according to typology. There are texts of grain and foodstuffs made from grain, other foods (oil, aromatics, dates, fish), personnel, livestock, and miscellaneous commodities.[283]

According to Foster's scenario, this archive collected the records of the administration of the énsi of Umma dealing with the great project of Rīmuš at Sabum, a place east of Umma, on the frontiers of modern Iran. For this project, Rīmuš forcibly enlisted prisoners from the defeated Sumerian league, led by Umma, which had rebelled against Akkad.[284] During the period covered by these texts, Umma and its énsi, Ennalum —most likely appointed énsi by Rīmuš after Rīmuš deposed the rebel énsi—were responsible for the logistics of this operation. A. Westenholz disagrees with Foster, maintaining that there is no evidence connecting the Sabum archive to any forced labor camp and he therefore proposes an alternative date for Group A.[285] Because of the close connection

279. Cf. Foster, *Archives*, p. 3.

280. D. Frayne, "Cuneiform Texts in the Collection of the McGill University, Montreal," *ARRIM* 7 (1984): 3–7, n. 1.

281. "Ein neuer mu-iti-Text aus einer Berliner Privatsammlung," *AoF* 24 (1994): 31–34.

282. USP, Chapter II, pp. 2–51.

283. USP pp. 9–10.

284. Cf. USP, pp. 48–50. This is an Old Babylonian copy that describes the victory of Rīmuš over the Sumerian cities (see FAOS 9, pp. 202–5; RIM 2, pp. 43–45); the passage in question, *ana karašim iškun,* is interpreted as "to place prisoners in a forced labor camp."

285. A. Westenholz, *AfO* 31 (1981): 77–78.

between the archive of Umma A and that of Zabalam at the period of Lugalzagesi, he suggests a date in the first part of Sargon's reign. According to Westenholz, this archive might be a collection of summaries relating to the construction of a fortress in Iran, possibly related to Sargon's military campaign against Elam.[286] Workers throughout the kingdom might have taken part in this project. Since Umma was nearest the frontier, it is reasonable that it would have been the city that made the greatest contribution to the project. P. Steinkeller refutes the hypothesis of a forced conscription of workers by the ruler,[287] on the basis of his interpretation of passage in the inscription, and the location of Sabum as proposed by Foster. Steinkeller asserts that Za-búm is not a place-name, but an irrigation canal in the vicinity of Umma. The workers mentioned in the texts of archive A would have been employed to work on this canal.[288]

But whatever the correct interpretation is, this archive, which appears to be coherent and homogeneous, seems to collect a group of records from the énsi of Umma over a brief period. This is the only surviving archive that enables us to study the administrative system of a Sumerian city and the role of the scribe during the reign of the first Sargonic kings.

The 16 scribes mentioned in Umma archive A are listed in TABLE 8. They have been divided into two groups:

(a) Scribes Mentioned Once Only [6]:

Á-kal-le um-mi-a is mentioned as the recipient of bread in Nik II 14 o. II 3. This document, in which the scribe Ú-URUxA is also mentioned, lists all the high-ranking and middle-to-high-ranking officials (dub-

286. Note that in an Old Babylonian copy of the original monument, CBS 13972, caption 14 1–2, Sargon mentions conquering Sabum; see FAOS 9; RIM 2, pp. 22–24.

287. P. Steinkeller, *WZKM* 77 (1987): 185–89.

288. According to this interpretation, it is difficult to explain why so many people died working on canals, why slaves and citizens worked together, and why the énsi journeyed to Sabum.

sar, dub-sar-maḫ). A namesake nu-bànda[289] occurs in Nik II, 64 o. 4, a record of copper objects, urudu nì-gul.[290]

Bára-ga-ni dub-sar is mentioned in Nik II, 51 o. 4, with Tir-kù dub-sar, as the official in charge of weighing the hides of wool-bearing sheep. The text is dated to year 1, month 2, day 13. A namesake official with the title šabra$_x$ (PA.É) occurs in Nik II, 22 o. 6 in which Ad-da and Ili-beli[291] are in charge of the summary of a large quantity of barley (3108 gur-sag-gál) delivered by the sag-apin as the produce of the field SU.A in year 4 month 12. Nik II, 55 r. 3 is an undated document that lists seven measures of silver concerning four nu-bànda (Ildum, [x]-ba, Mes-é, Giš-šà), 1 kišib-lá "archivist" (Ur-é), 1 dub-sar-dingir-ra (Ur-^{d}Al-la), and our šabra$_x$. Note that Mes-é nu-bànda occurs also in a text from the beginning of the sixth year (Nik II, 58); Giš-šà nu-bànda occurs in a text from the fifth year (Nik II, 60); Bára-ga-ni šabra$_x$ is mentioned in a text from the end of the fourth year (Nik II, 22); and Ur-e kišib-lá in CHÉU 53 from the fifth year. Thus, we can conclude that Nik II, 55 was assuredly compiled between the end of the fourth and the beginning of the sixth years of the reign of the same ruler. If Nik II, 22, 51, and 55 refer to the period of the same ruler, perhaps the Bára-ga-ni dub-sar mentioned in the texts of the first year and the Bára-ga-ni šabra$_x$ mentioned in the texts of the fourth year are the same individual. The énsi who succeeded Lugal-zagesi, Ennalum, and who was, in turn, succeeded by Iš$_{11}$-RU.BI, reigned perhaps for only six years.[292] Thus, the date of Nik II, 22

---

289. An untitled namesake official who occurs in Nik II, 63 o. 3 (a record of copper objects) and Nik II, 66 o. 4 (a list of officials mentioned without titles as the recipients of reeds) is the namesake nu-bànda (cf. USP, p. 37). Although possible, there is no compelling reason to identify the nu-bànda with the namesake um-mi-a.

290. This is probably nì-gul dím-ma, which USP, p. 35, translates: "tools that had been newly worked by smiths" as opposed to nì-gul dab$_5$-ba rendered as "tools that had been used and needed reworking." While only the weight is indicated for the tools used (dab$_5$-ba), both the number and weight is indicated for the dím-ma tools.

291. An official mentioned several times but always without title; cf. Foster, *Ethnicity*, p. 308.

292. Cf. USP, p. 154.

and probably 55 refer to the first-mentioned énsi and the date of Nik II, 51 to the second. Finally, a namesake official without title occurs in Nik II, 14 o. 1'–3'.

Giš-šà dub-sar is mentioned in USP 15 o. 2 as the recipient of ^{kuš}UD-ga in connection with ^{giš}gíd-da, perhaps a type of hide used to cover spears (USP, p. 38). The text has only 1 iti as a temporal indicator; the absence of the year number might mean that the text was written in the first year. The namesake nu-bànda who occurs in Nik II, 55 r. 7 is probably the same individual as in Nik I, 60 r. I 5, a document from the fifth year that is similar to Nik II, 61; 62; 64; 65. Finally, in Nik II, 19 different persons described as lú-giš-šà are mentioned (r. II 6; r. II 3'; 6').

Lú-giš dub-sar is mentioned in Nik II, 35 r. I 8' as the recipient of bread. The text is dated year 5 month 2 day 9.

Lugal-gaba dub-sar is mentioned in Nik II, 46 (dated year 5 month 10) r. 1 as the recipient of ninda and sag-ninda. A namesake official is mentioned in CHÉU 53 o. 3 as the maškim supervisor in a copper transaction. Because of the officials mentioned and its date (year 5 month 9 day 14), the text is closely connected to CST 11.[293] The dating to the fifth year in both Nik II, 46 and CHÉU 53, as well as CST 11, makes it probable that Lugal-gaba dub-sar and Lugal-gaba maškim are the same person. A certain Lugal-gaba šabra occurs in a record of hides delivered by the shepherds of the é-mí; Lugal-gaba was the supervisor.[294] The text is dated Ennalum énsi 5 mu 8 iti.

NIM dub-sar is mentioned in Nik II, 61 (year 4 month 9 day 2) o. 3 as the official who, with Má-gur$_8$ dub-sar, was the keeper of wrought copper objects.

Ú-URUxA dub-sar is mentioned as the recipient of bread in Nik II, 14 o. III 14. Since the reverse is not preserved, the date is unknown.

---

293. Cf. USP, pp. 34–35.

294. D. Frayne, "Cuneiform Texts in the Collection of the McGill University, Montreal," *ARRIM* 7 (1984): 3–7, n. 1 r. II 11.

Ur-^{d}Al-la dub-sar dingir-ra is mentioned in Nik II, 55 o. 2.[295] The title of this official indicates that he worked for a temple institution, but there are no other references of this title.[296]

Ur-bi dub-sar is mentioned in Nik II, 54 r. 2 as the official who receives 1 eme kúnga, property of the énsi, purchased from Èš-me-bi nu-bànda. The date of the text is lost in a lacuna.

Ur-é-maḫ dub-sar is mentioned in Nik II, 19 r. II' 8', which dates to the third year of the énsi Iš$_{11}$-RU.BI. There is a major lacuna, so that the final part of the first column of the obverse and the beginning of the second and third columns of the reverse have been lost. The text lists groups of lú and géme, subordinates of various officials.[297] Every group, identified as lú ḫun-gá dam-gàr-ne, "personnel hired by the commercial agents," is placed in charge of a PA.URU and associated with a má-laḫ$_4$, probably the boatman who transports these persons. Ur-é-maḫ, who occurs at the end of the text, seems to have been the scribe who wrote the tablet and was probably in charge of the transport operation. In CHÉU 54 r. II 3–4 a namesake official, to be identified with our dub-sar, is indicated as the ugula in charge of 30 guruš described as ir$_{11}$-dub-sar-ne-me, "they are the servants of the scribes." Finally, in Nik II, 40 o. 4, Ur-é-maḫ, without title, is the official who receives flour from the dub-sar Ur-^{giš}gigir.

Ur-^{giš}gigir dub-sar is mentioned in Nik II, 40 o. 2 in connection with zì-sig$_5$, "flour of good quality," delivered in three installments[298] by Ur-^{giš}gigir and perhaps allocated to Ur-é-maḫ in the third year.

---

295. A namesake nu-bànda is mentioned in Nik II, 17 o. 5 and 65 o. 5. The former is not dated and the latter is dated year 5 month 2 day 30. We should take into account that Nik II, 55; 58–66 probably dates to the time of the same énsi because, with the exception of Nik II, 66, they have a similar typology and the same officials are mentioned several times in the texts. So, it seems difficult to identify Ur-^{d}Al-la dub-sar with the namesake nu-bànda.

296. It seems unlikely that dingir-ra is a personal name.

297. PN$_1$ lú PN$_2$; PN$_1$ lú/géme Prof. N$_2$; PN$_1$ PN$_2$ Prof. N$_2$.

298. For the expression a-rá 3-kam-ma DU-àm as "in three installments," cf. USP, pp. 12–13.

(b) Scribes Mentioned More than Once [4]:

Ad-da dub-sar is mentioned in CHÉU 53 r. 8 and perhaps in CST 11 r. 5,[299] both texts dated to year 5. Both texts record copper pellets (urudu nì-saḫar-ra) allocated to Du-du gal-simug, "the head blacksmith," the official responsible for this copper.

A namesake énsi-gal, a profession of uncertain meaning,[300] is mentioned in Nik II, 56 o. 2 as receiving silver from the scribe Má-gur$_8$. In Nik II, 59 o. 4 and 61 r. 5 he is mentioned in connection with nì-gul dím-ma and nì-gul dab$_5$-ba. These texts, both dated year 4, month 9, day 20, are balanced accounts compiled by Má-gur$_8$ and Ad-da (Ad-da énsi-gal-e Má-gur$_8$ dub-sar-da nì-kas$_7$-bi e-da-ak). Probably the Ad-da without title in BIN 8, 309 o. 2 and Nik II, 63 r. 9' is the namesake énsi-gal.[301] Nik II, 60 and 62 should be related to Nik II, 63.[302] While Nik II, 60 is dated to year 5, month 3, day 10, Nik II, 62 has lost the year number in a lacuna, but has preserved the month (5) and day (6). It is likely that it too should be dated to year 5. Ad-da also occurs in these two texts and may be the namesake

299. CST 11 r. 5: [ ]-da dub-sar-e. USP, p. 35, restores the anthroponym as [Da]-da. But if we consider that this anthroponym never occurs in the archives of the earliest mu-iti texts and its extremely close relationship with CHEU 53, in which the function of [ ]-da is explained by Ad-da (CST 11 r. 5–8: [ ]-da dub-sar-e Du-du gal-simug e-na-lá 5 mu 9 iti 8$^?$ u$_4$ and CHÉU 53 16–19: Ad-da dub-sar-kam [Du-d]u gal-simug e-na-lá 5 mu 9 iti 14 u$_4$), then the restoration [Ad]-da should be preferred.

300. Cf. USP, p. 32. The profession énsi-gal, which occurs both in the ED IIIb and Sargonic texts of Girsu, is probably to be connected with scribal activity (cf. *infra*, p. 138, no. 142).

301. BIN 8, 309 concerns copper owned(?) by Ad-da, in the hands of Má-gur$_8$ lú-è-ùr$^?$-ra, to be used in a job lasting one month and 19 days. A summary in *Sà-búm* was made for this job in year 5, month 3, day 12. Nik II, 63 r. 9' lists urudu nì-gul [ ] delivered by various officials (Á-kal-le nu-bànda; [ ]gal-la; [ ]-SAG; Ad-da <énsi-gal>; Tir-kù nu-bànda; Du-du <nu-bànda>; and Lugal-GAR.NI <nu-bànda>) and of which Ad-da compiled a balanced account, [A]d-da [nì$^?$] urudu kas$_7$ e-[da-ak] kin-aka 1 <iti> 5 mu 1[+x] iti 13 u$_4$ *sà-búm*. Foster, USP, p. 35, proposes that the Ad-da mentioned in BIN 8, 309 is the namesake dub-sar. If so, Ad-da énsi-gal and Ad-da dub-sar are probably the same individual.

302. Nik II, 60 and 62 list amounts of urudu nì-gul dab$_5$-ba that various officials, described in the colophon as nu-bànda, have weighed out/paid to Ad-da: urudu nì-gul dab$_5$-ba ki-la-bi...ma-na nu-bànda-ne ad-da-ra e-na-lá.

énsi-gal. A similar identification should be made for the Ad-da in Nik II, 22 o. 4 in year 4 and month 12; Ili-beli with Bára-ga-ni šabra$_x$ compiled the balanced account of the 3,108 gur-sag-gál of barley delivered, probably as dues, by the sag-apin. In Nik II, 45 o. 6 from year 5 month 5 day 27, he appears as the official whose subordinate is an àga-uš, and who receives 20 loaves and beer. He also appears in BIN 8, 314 o. 6 from year 5 month 3 day 27 as the official whose subordinate was a slave who had died.

Based upon the aforementioned references, it seems likely that the nu-bànda's were subordinates of Ad-da énsi-gal. Thus, the latter appears to have been one of the highest-ranking officials of the énsi's administration. The fact that Ad-da is frequently mentioned without title indicates that there was no doubt about the identity of this official. Since Ad-da énsi-gal and Ad-da dub-sar performed similar duties in the same years (4 and 5), it plausible that they are the same individual.

En-ki-ág dub-sar is mentioned in CST 8 o. II 3 and in BIN 8, 332 o. 3. The former text is dated to year 4 month 2 and the latter to year 3 month 4. In CST 8 En-ki-ág dub-sar and Má-gur$_8$ dub-sar weighed out/paid nine units of copper belonging to the énsi in Sabum, whereas in BIN 8, 332 Má-gur$_8$ dub-sar weighed out/paid 120 nì-gul-dab$_5$-ba objects to En-ki-ág dub-sar and Nam-zi simug[303] in Sabum.

Má-gur$_8$ dub-sar is mentioned in Nik II, 56 o. 3 (2 mu 12 iti) as the official who weighed out the silver for Ad-da énsi-gal in the storehouse as profit of the household.[304] In Nik II, 59 r. 1 he is the official who, with Ad-da énsi-gal, drew up the balanced account of the copper nì-gul dím-ma objects (year 4 month 9 day 20). In Nik II, 61 r. 2; 6, he is mentioned as possessing the copper nì-gul dím-ma and dab$_5$-ba objects and who, with Ad-da énsi-gal, drew up the balanced account (year 4 month 9 day 20). He is mentioned in BIN 8, 332 o. 2 and

303. Nam-zi simug is also mentioned as the official who enrolled 1,619 guruš, 21 šitim, and 11 simug in Nik II, 2 o. 3 dated to year 4, month 8, day 13 and 1,554 guruš 19 šitim and 11 simug in Nik II, 4 o. 4 dated year 4, month 9 for work of varying duration.

304. Ad-da énsi-gal-ra Má-gur$_8$ dub-sar-e é-TUM-[al] é-ka e-na-lá. For TUM-al "profit," see USP, p. 32.

CST 8 r. I 5, which we have discussed in reference to En-ki-ág dub-sar. He is also mentioned in AO 5657 o. 5 as the official who received textiles and wooden objects (^{giš}ḪAR) from Lú-dingir-mu IB (4 mu 4 iti) and in Nik II, 47 r. 5 as the official who, on the occasion of two journeys made by the énsi to Sabum, delivered dates for the ugula and for DI-Utu dam-gàr-gal.[305]

Thus, the long active service of Má-gur$_8$ appears to span, at least, from the sixth year of Lugalzagesi énsi until the fifth year of the following énsi, probably Ennalum.

Tir-kù dub-sar-maḫ occurs in Nik II, 14 o. I 5. With only the title dub-sar (assuredly here an abbreviation for dub-sar-maḫ), he occurs in Nik II, 51 o. 5 as the official who, with Bára-ga-ni dub-sar, weighed out wool in the giš-kin-ti in year 1 month 2 day 13. In USP 2 o. 4–5, from year 1 month 8,[306] Tir-kù is mentioned twice; the first time as the official in charge of stored flour and the second concerning 2 quantities of flour that Ad-da é-kikk[en?] took to (or set on) kar-na$_4$ to be consumed(?) on the boat(s) for Dilmun.[307]

Thus, at least two scribes (Má-gur$_8$ and Tir-kù) mentioned in the early mu-iti texts already were in active service at the time of Lugalzagesi. It should also be noted that at least three other officials occur in both archives, namely, Ad-da ugula (Nik o. II 20 I 8, USP 16 o. 5; BIN 8, 57 o. II 5), Lugal-ka sipa (USP 5 r. 4; BIN 8, 86 o. III 1; BIN 8, 62 o. I 8), and Lugal-ka ugula (Nik II, 10 r. 2; *HUCA* 49, 13 o. II 1).[308] But it is possible that other officials, often mentioned without title, may occur in both archives.[309] This suggests that not only should the administrative documentation of the Early Sargonic period be regarded, on the basis of paleography and textual content, as a continuation of the late Pre-

---

305. Má-gur$_8$ lú-é-ùr-ra, who has copper for which Ad-da is responsible, is mentioned in BIN 8, 309 o. 3 (5 mu 3 iti 12 u$_4$). Perhaps he is our dub-sar.

306. Some scribes and nu-bànda have the same name. This is the case with Á-kal-le, Du-du, Giš-šà, Tir-kù, and Ur-^{d}Al-la.

307. Cf. USP, p. 115. A namesake nu-bànda occurs in Nik II, 64 r. 1. The namesake official who occurs in Nik II, 60 r. I 2; 63 r. 2' is this nu-bànda.

308. Lugal-KA as ugula nu-bànda dingir also occurs in BIN 8, 108 o. II 1 and in *HUCA*, 49 (1978) o. I 6; 21 o. II 4; 22 o. II 1.

309. See USP, p. 43.

Sargonic period, but that some features of the bureaucratic organization, at least in Umma, remained intact when it passed from the administration of Lugalzagesi to that of Sargon and Rīmuš. Only with subsequent kings, in particular Narām-Sîn and Šar-kali-šarrī, did the situation radically change.

5. The Scribes of Ur in the Late ED and the Early Sargonic Periods

In the Supplement to UET 2, a lot of 50 tablets and two seal impressions from the period following that of the Early ED Ur tablets were published. Burrows dates these tablets to between the Fara and the Classical Sargonic periods. Tablets 1–5 come from the upper part of the well southwest of the cemetery. If they are not intrusive here, they are, according to Burrows, contemporaneous with the royal tombs, that is, between the Fara period and the First Dynasty of Ur. Tablets 6–12 come from layer SIS I–II, which delimits the upper part of the royal cemetery and should be dated between the Ur-Nanše period and that of Entemena, that is, to ED IIIb. The majority of tablets (13–50) was found among the detritus and filling material of the site around the cemetery. Burrows dates these texts to between the end of the ED period and the Early Sargonic period, with the exception of some that clearly belong to the Classical Sargonic period (29, 33, 48, 49); in fact, probably 24, 30, 31, 32, and 50 should be dated also to that period.

A. Alberti and F. Pomponio identified two groups of homogeneous texts within this small archive.[310] The first of these consists of texts 7, 11, 12, and 14; these are closely related for prosopographic reasons.[311] The second and more interesting group is comprised of about 20 texts concerning cattle, of which eight (13, 15, 37, 43–47) are characterized by the clause šu-Šubur-kam "(cattle) belonging to (or managed by) Šubur."[312] Paleography, content, and especially prosopography indicate that the other texts concerning cattle should be linked to these eight. Thus texts 25, 35, 38, 40, 42, and perhaps 36 belong to this group.

---

310. A. Alberti – F. Pomponio, *Pre-Sargonic and Sargonic Texts from Ur Published in UET 2 Supplement* (Rome, 1986), pp. 17–18.

311. *Ibidem*, pp. 6, 17.

312. *Ibidem*, p. 87.

Finally, on the basis of prosopography, text 22, which concerns oil, should be added. This group of texts appears to be homogeneous and to belong to a central administration, probably the é-gal[313] and should be dated to the Enšakušana period (suggestion of Westenholz).[314] These texts mention five, non-contemporaneous scribes.

Amar-[sa]nga? dub-sar is mentioned in UET 2, Supp. 2 r. II 1–2, a list of persons from the Fara period. The anthroponyms mentioned in the list are followed, in some cases, by profession or place of provenance.

Ù-[x] dub-sar is mentioned in UET, Supp. 2 r. II 3–4.

Lugal-KA-sì-ga dub-sar is mentioned in UET 2, Supp. 16 r. II 11, a record of allocations of bitumen. He is the official who brought/took away (ba-DU) 3 ban of ÉSIR.A to Lugal-gaba-gál. This text, whose content is unique, should be dated to the period immediately before that of the most numerous group of Šubur texts. None of the anthroponyms mentioned in this text occur elsewhere in the archive.

Lugal-šùd-dè dub-sar is one of two scribes who occur in the archive of Šubur. He is mentioned in UET 2, Supp. 43 o. 3–4 (dated to iti-Amar-sag-kú-ka) as the official (maškim) who supervised an allocation to the é-gal of six head of cattle belonging to Šubur. Perhaps the Lú-šùd-dè who is the recipient of one goat in UET 2, Supp. 36.3 is our scribe, assuming the latter is an abbreviation for Lugal-šùd-dè. He occurs also in U 4382 and U 4393.

Lugal-šu-sukkal-⸢kú⸣-an-na dub-sar in UET 2, Supp. 44, is supervisor of a series of seven allocations of sheep to the énsi of Gir$_x$(ŠID. NUN)^{ki}.[315] He occurs in U 4388.

313. *Ibidem*, p. 7.

314. To these texts we add a group of documents housed in the University Museum. Some of these texts were published with copy by M. Civil, "Tablillas Sargonicas de Ur," *Au Or* 6 (1989): 105–6 (U 4384, 4385, 4386, 4388, 4389, 4390, 4394, 4395, 4396); others are still unpublished (U 4382, 4387, 4391, 4392, 4393, 7844, 8828). All these documents, with the exception of U 4389, 7844, and 8828, seem to be linked to the livestock accounts of Šubur. I have an edition of these texts in preparation.

315. Perhaps this toponym is a writing for Gir$_x$-tab^{ki}, a locality mentioned in UET 2, Supp. 16 r. II 5'. A locality Gir$_{13}$(ŠID)-tab^{ki} occurs in Sargonic texts. Cf. *Rép. géog.* I, p. 19.

CHAPTER 2

SCRIBES IN THE CLASSICAL SARGONIC PERIOD

1. Scribes of the Umma Region

Two archives have been identified in the documentation from the Classical Sargonic period of Umma. The first of these, designated Umma B, seems to be of the type B. R. Foster describes as a "family or private archive."[1] The second archive, designated Umma C, is a type described as a "great household archive." In addition, on the basis of its relationship with Umma, we have identified a third group of texts, which we shall refer to as the Me-ság archive. This archive adopts a recording system that Foster describes as Akkadian; thus it could be classified as a "household archive." However, this third archive, which concerns a vast agricultural estate situated in the region between Umma and Lagaš, land granted directly by the Crown, not by local administrations, has some distinct characteristics.

1.1 *The Ur-^{d}Šara Archive*

Foster identified an archive of 128 texts,[2] (Umma B) and dated it to the time of Narām-Sîn.[3] Nine other texts should be added to this archive, namely, TLAT, 13–21 and perhaps MVN 10, 121. The archive contains documents of different typologies, but the most common documents concern cattle (47), grain (42), and sheepskins (29). Foster considers these documents to be the archive of a family enterprise, managed by a husband and wife, Ur-^{d}Šára and Ama-é, and an associate, Ur-^{d}EN.ZU, who was loosely connected to the state administration.[4] Near Umma,

1. B. R. Foster, "Archives and Record-Keeping in Sargonic Mesopotamia," *ZA* 72 (1982): 7–8.
2. Cf. USP, pp. 52–54.
3. Foster, *ZA* 72 (1982): 22.
4. USP, pp. 77–78.

Ur-^{d}Šára and his subordinates bred cattle that belonged to the palace.[5] His wife, Ama-é, probably as part of the business, managed large tracts of arable land belonging to the institution. A part of this land was subdivided into small plots and rented to other persons,[6] so she should be regarded as "a business woman with a sphere of activity independent of her husband."[7] Only five scribes are mentioned in this documentation.

Gala dub-sar occurs in three grain texts: BIN 8, 287 r. 1–3, in which he receives barley in Apišal[8]; USP 24 o. 4, in which he receives, always in Apišal, emmer and, perhaps, barley from Lugal-KA, one of the subordinates of Ur-^{d}Šára; and in MAD 4, 104 r. 2, a record of the delivery of barley and emmer from Lugal-TAR to Lugal-KA. Our scribe was the compiler of the tablet or the maškim on the transaction, which occurred in the é-gal-edin.[9] This scribe is not mentioned in any other text in which Ama-é occurs. Gala dub-sar occurs, however, in a text in the Me-ság archive (BIN 8, 152 o. I 11) with two other scribes, Ur-^{d}Al-la and Ur-me-ga (Gala Ur-^{d}Al-la Ur-me-ga dub-sar-me) as a recipient of wool.

Me-zu dub-sar is mentioned only in MAD 4, 21 o. 5, a barley text, as the recipient of 46 gur and 2 bariga. Ama-é occurs among the recipients. None of the officials listed in the text occurs in other archive B texts.

---

5. MAD 4, 156: máš é-gal-kam.

6. For a different opinion, see N. V. Kozyreva, *VDI* (1985): 177–78. TLAT, p. 8 expresses reservations that Group B is older than Group C and also is perplexed about the attribution of the B.2 group to Ur-^{d}Šára. For analysis, especially concerning the interpretation of MAD 4, 167, cf. TLAT, p. 41. According to TLAT, the enterprise of Ur-^{d}Šára, rather than a free enterprise, was a peripheral center under the jurisdiction of the central administration.

7. USP, p. 78. It should be noted that of the 30 anthroponyms in the documents in which Ama-é is mentioned, only seven occur in those in which Ur-^{d}Šára is mentioned.

8. For a reading A-ka-sal$_{4}^{ki}$, see K. Maekawa, "The Agricultural Texts of Ur III Lagash of the British Museum (VII)," *ASJ* 13 (1991): 203–4.

9. Similar to MAD 4, 124, in which two officials are mentioned as lú-ki-inim, Foster, USP, p. 62, regards the dub-sar Gala as the witness to the transaction in this text.

Šà-da dub-sar is mentioned as the recipient of a loan of various goods made by Ama-é in MAD 4, 41 r. 3 (Ama-é Šà-da dub-sar-da ì-da-tuku). This anthroponym does not occur elsewhere in the archive.

Ur-gidri dub-sar occurs in MAD 4, 74 o. 10. This text lists four measures of barley for four officials, concluding with the clause še giš-ra-a Ur-gidri dub-sar ašag$_4$ bar-im$_4$. In this clause, the relationship between the scribe and the previously mentioned barley is unclear. A similar clause concludes MAD 4, 72, ašag$_4$ bar-im$_4$ gala šu-i šu-ba-ti. Perhaps then Ur-gidri dub-sar might be the recipient of four measures of barley. So too, he may have sealed the text as supervisor on behalf of the administration. A namesake official is mentioned without title in MAD 4, 167 r. 8, which concerns the recruitment of teams of 10 to 15 people. Perhaps he is our dub-sar.

Ur-^{d}Šára dub-sar dingir-ra should be distinguished from his namesake. He is mentioned as the recipient of one kid in MAD 4, 24 r. 2 and MAD 4, 61 o. 4, both dated to year 5 month 4. The goods are delivered by Utu-mu sipa, an official who occurs in about 20 texts from the Ur-^{d}Šára archive, which should be dated to between years 4 and 8. The title dub-sar dingir-ra suggests that he probably belonged to a temple household.[10]

It is difficult to establish the precise connection between the scribes listed in the Umma B documentation and the household of Ur-^{d}Šára and Ama-é. These officials do not seem to be employed by or have a stake in the management of the enterprise. They occur solely as recipients of goods. Possibly these officials received the goods on behalf of the administration as taxes to be paid by the cattle holders. In the case of Šà-da, the goods in question concern a private transaction. These observations are in agreement with Foster's understanding of the Ur-^{d}Šára archive.

10. The mention of this dub-sar-dingir-ra raises the question whether the household of Ur-^{d}Šára had any connection with this temple household.

1.2 *The Mesag Archive*

The Me-ság archive is comprised of 129 documents, of which 110 are published.[11] Foster has identified this as an archive of an agricultural administrative center established in a region between Umma and Lagaš and administered by an important official, frequently Me-ság.[12] Me-ság describes himself as a dub-sar and sa$_{12}$-du$_5$ in YBC 12139.[13] This agricultural center possessed a total of 1,270 hectares of land (the equivalent of 360,000 sar) given in usufruct by the king. A part of this estate was worked directly and the other section was rented. It seems to have been part of a much larger estate of 6,236 hectares, which was perhaps administered by Ur-tur, the sa$_{12}$-du$_5$.[14] YBC 12139, the text that begins with the mention of Me-ság dub-sar and sa$_{12}$-du$_5$, lists after Me-ság both the personnel who belonged to the estate (172 men, women and children) and its cattle.[15]

Eight scribes are mentioned in this documentation; two others whose names have been lost should perhaps be added. From YBC 12139, it seems that only two dub-sar's, Da-da and Ur-me-ga, belonged to the household, and at least three of them, Dur$_8$-mu-pi$_5$, Ama-bára, and Ìl-mu-da, were not part of the staff.

Dur$_8$-mu-pi$_5$ dub-sar is mentioned in the seal impressions of several tablets (BIN 8, 274; 283; 284; 285: Dur$_8$-mu-pi$_5$ dub-sar árad *ru-ba-*

---

11. Ninety-six in BIN 8 (cf. Foster, "Archives and Empire in Sargonic Mesopotamia," CRRAI 30 [1983], p. 6); BMC 15, published in M. deJong-Ellis, "Cuneiform Tablets at Bryn Mawr College," *JCS* 31 (1979): 51; TLAT, nos. 33–45. The remainder are unpublished. The texts of this archive were studied by S. Bridges, *The Me-ság Archive: A Study of Sargonic Society and Economy* (University Microfilms, Yale University, 1981). YBC 12319, NBC 7022, NBC 6967, and NBC 6969 have been published in B. R. Foster, "Notes on Women in Sargonic Society," in J. M. Durand, ed., *La femme dans le proche-orient antique*, CRRAI 33 (1987), pp. 57–61.

12. Foster, *Inst. Land*, pp. 57–58, sub BIN 8, 291.

13. Cf. Foster, CRRAI 33 (1987), pp. 57–58.

14. Cf. Foster, *Inst. Land*, p. 63, sub BIN 8, 198.

15. Foster suggests that this property was still part of a vast imperial estate created during the reign of Rīmuš in the region of Lagaš. Its area was about 129,000 hectares (cf. Foster, *Archives*, p. 47; Foster, *Inst. Land*, pp. 110–11) and was perhaps under the jurisdiction of the šabra-é.

tim, "Dur$_8$-mu-pi$_5$ the scribe, the servant of the princess.").[16] Foster identified Dur$_8$-mu-pi$_5$ as a royal agent who arrived at Zabalam on a tour of inspection where he received cattle (BIN 8, 273; NBC 6947), sheep (BIN 8, 283–85), dairy products, hides, and animal fat (BIN 8, 118).[17] He carried out an accounting inspection as can be seen from the clause recorded after the summary in BIN 8, 273 and NBC 6947,[18] *in* Zabalam^{ki} Dur$_8$-mu-pi$_5$ *ib-rí*, "In Zabalam Dur$_8$-mu-pi$_5$ carried out an inspection"; in BIN 8, 118, é-gal-la ba-túm Dur$_8$-mu-pi$_5$ *im-ḫur*, "It (the goods) brought in the palace, Dur$_8$-mu-pi$_5$ received"; or from his sealing on the surface of the tablet's reverse (BIN 8, 274; 283–85).

As Foster notes,[19] it comes as no surprise that royal officials like Dur$_8$-mu-pi$_5$ are mentioned. The process of the centralization of the empire, which began in the reign of Narām-Sîn with the standardization of the units of measure, made officials a necessity. Not only did they come from the class of scribes, but they were also able to understand local methods of recording documents and, in addition, they knew how to easily convert local units of measurement into standard units.

Ama-bára dub-sar-maḫ is mentioned in a group of allotment field texts as the official who measured the fields.[20] He is also mentioned in BIN 8, 182 r. II 8', which records monthly expenditures (seed, fodder, and worker rations) for agricultural plots (land grants or rented) by people who frequently are mentioned in the Me-ság archive (I-lu$_5$-lu$_5$; Ur-sipa-da; Gala; Giš-šà). After the summaries of

16. Foster, *Archives*, pp. 49–50, suggests that the princess in question was a daughter of Narām-Sîn.

17. Foster, *Archives*, pp. 49–50.

18. This clause has been restored in BIN 8, 273 in Foster, *Archives*, p. 50, n. 25, from a comparison with the parallel passage in NBC 6947. For the meaning of *ibri* (Akk. *barû*) "he inspected," see Foster, *Archives*, p. 50.

19. Foster, *Archives*, p. 49.

20. Ama-bára-ke$_4$ ì-gíd-da-kam in BIN 8, 184 r. 7; 195 r. 11; a-šà gíd-da Ama-bára-kam in BIN 8, 192 r. 6; 199 o. 5. and NBC 5920; numun-ù Ama-bára-kam in BIN 8, 200 o. 5. For a discussion of these formulae, cf. Foster, *Inst. Land*, p. 56, a–d; p. 61, TABLE C.4.

the barley expended for seed, fodder, and rations, an obscure clause is written: *šu* engar-[engar] Ama-bára *u-na-ki-*⸢*is*⸣ *šu* aša$_5$ gibil, "(it is the barley) of cultivators, Ama-bára compiled a balanced account of the aša$_5$ gibil field."[21]

Ama-bára occurs in BIN 8, 123 o. II 1–2 and in its parallel TLAT, 42 o. II 1, as a recipient of 152 gur of barley. These texts record barley[22] from an agricultural unit measuring 28 bur as a part of the estimated yield due the Crown and royal officials, to be used as seed, fodder for draft animals, and worker rations (in descending order of working capacity), and sheep and pigs.[23] Our official also occurs in BIN 8, 265 o. 7, a text which records the delivery of sheepskins for the city of Sagub; Dingir-sukkal ašgab received them when Ama-bára and Me-ság went there for the barley rations.[24] Finally, Ama-bára dub-sar-maḫ is mentioned in a personnel text, BIN 8, 254 r. 3. In the first four lines, the text lists four anthroponyms with their respective *Personenkeil* and in the fifth and sixth lines the name of the official in charge, Lú-dingir-ra, and the clause [á]-RU, which probably indicates the type of work or payment. Some unclear lines follow, with many lacunae ([È-^{giš}ḫ]a-lu-úb-e [ ] gub-ba [ ] NAGAR [ ] géme TAR.⸢x⸣), "when È-^{giš}ḫa-lu-úb-e concerning female workers...."[25]

These officials are recipients of agricultural plots (BIN 8, 184; 193; 194; 343). In TLAT 33 some of these are sag-apin and in BIN 8, 148, ugula.

21. For *nukkusu* = nì-kas$_7$, see Foster, "Old Akkadian Nukkusu(m) <<Balance an Account>>," *NABU* (1989): 115.

22. BIN 8, 123 and BIN 8, 122; 131 are discussed in Foster, *Agriculture*, pp. 109ff.

23. The amount received by Ama-bára in TLAT 42 is lost in a lacuna. Since all the recipients mentioned in this text receive the same amounts as in BIN 8, 123, it is probable that the amount in this case is the same, namely, 152 gur. The comparison of BIN 8, 123 with TLAT 42 allows us to restore [é]-nam in BIN 8, 123 o. I 15. É-nam sa$_{12}$-du$_5$ is the recipient in both texts of 30 gur (measured in BIN 8, 123 o. I 14 in gur-maḫ and in TLAT 42 o. II 3 in gur si-sá).

24. 1 kuš-udu Sag-ub^{ki}-šè šum-kuš ì-šum dingir-sukkal ašgab šu-ba-ti *ì-nu a-na* še-ba engar-e Me-ság *ù* Ama-bára dub-sar *i-li-kà-ni*. For similar formulae in the Me-ság archive, cf. BIN 8, 146 o. 9–11; r. 1–2: *ì-nu* Me-ság *in A-kà-dè*^{ki} *i-lí-k*[*à-n*] *i*/ *i-li-kam*. For other verbal formulae with *alāku* in the Sargonic period, cf. MAD 3, p. 39.

25. The official È-^{giš}ḫa-lu-úb-e is, perhaps, to be identified with the namesake titled gu-sur who occurs in Nik II 78 o. III 5'.

The text concludes in r. 3–4 with the clause Ama-bára dub-sar-maḫ á-RU.

Ama-bára does not seem to have been part of the staff of the estate administration, although he performed supervisory tasks and activities associated with it.[26]

Ìl-mu-da dub-sar-maḫ seems to have had a similar function to that of Ama-bára as can be seen from the clause recorded on the margin of BIN 8, 196, Ìl-mu-da ì-gíd *šu* 1-mu, "Ìl-mu-da measured the fields, of the current year."[27] In the same text, he is the recipient of a plot of land of 5 bur for sustenance (aša$_5$-šuku) and follows Me-ság in the list of recipients who instead receive a plot of nu-tuku land[28] and 5 bur of aša$_5$-šuku. These two recipients are followed by a list of 11 others of differing rank who receive between 6 and 18 iku. These last-mentioned officials are all from the staff of Me-ság's estate; among them are the officials mentioned in BIN 8, 182. A parallel text concerning allocations of plots of land for sustenance is TLAT 33. Among the recipients mentioned in TLAT 33, in addition to Me-ság and Ìl-mu-da dub-sar-maḫ, there are several officials already mentioned in BIN 8, 196.[29] The recipients in TLAT 33 are grouped according to profession (sag-apin-me, utul-me, sipa-udu-me), while in BIN 8, 196 they are listed without these subdivisions; however, the sequence of the anthroponyms of the group of the sag-apin and sipa-udu is the same. In some cases, the size of the plots of land is the same; in others it is different. The utul group does not appear in BIN 8, 196.

Ìl-mu-da is mentioned in another text concerning fields (BIN 8, 203 o. 5) in which he is the recipient of 5 bur of irrigated land (aša$_5$ ki-duru$_5$ ì-dab$_5$). In this text too, Ìl-mu-da is mentioned after Me-ság,

26. Cf. Foster, *Agriculture,* p. 124.

27. *Šu* 1-mu may be the Akkadian equivalent of the Sumerian mu-a-kam (see Foster, *Inst. Land,* p. 67).

28. For the meaning of this term, cf. Foster, *Inst. Land,* p. 61.

29. Da-da; Ur-sipa-da; Šeš-tur; An-ki-ág; Az. The grantor or the lessor of these agricultural plots was likely Me-ság himself (cf. Foster, *Inst. Land*).

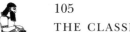

the recipient of 10 bur, and he precedes five other officials.[30] Finally, in BIN 8, 195 r. 9–11, Ìl-mu-da is mentioned as the official who, with Ama-bára, measured the fields (aša$_5$ gíd-da Íl-[mu]-da Ama-bára [d]ub?-[sar?]).

The documentation, as a whole, indicates that Ama-bára and Ìl-mu-da fulfilled similar roles, and BIN 8, 195 proves that they were active at the same time. Since the documentation does not indicate that there was a hierarchical relationship between the two officials, it is possible that they were dub-sar-maḫ's for two different administrative units. In the Umma C archive, (which dates shortly after Umma B), an unnamed dub-sar-maḫ of the énsi and an unnamed dub-sar-maḫ of the šabra-é are mentioned. In USP 57 o. I 8, a text from the Umma C archive, a certain Ama-bára sa$_{12}$-du$_5$ occurs before this unnamed dub-sar-maḫ. He again occurs without title, performing the same function in MAD 4, 43 o. 2. A comparison suggests that the Ama-bára dub-sar-maḫ of the Me-ság archive and the namesake sa$_{12}$-du$_5$ of the Umma C archive are the same individual. In this case, Ama-bára must have belonged to the administration of the énsi of Umma while Ìl-mu-da must have been the dub-sar-maḫ of the šabra-é.[31]

The remaining dub-sar's (Da-da, Ur-me-ga, and perhaps Gala) must have been an integral part of the staff of the household; whereas Ur-^{d}Al-la and Ur-ù were not.

Da-da dub-sar is mentioned in the list YBC 12319 o. I 3 and in BIN 8, 268 o. 6. This latter document records the receipt by Dingir-sukkal

30. Li-bur-ki-^{d}En-líl receives 2 bur; KA-kù gala 9 iku; é-ta! Su-pi-um 6 iku; Ur-ù dub-sar 1 bur.

31. Ìl-mu-da occurs in the Umma C archive (CT 50, 55 o. II 17; MCS 9, 235.15; 246.15), but there is no basis for establishing a connection with the namesake dub-sar-maḫ. The šabra-é, who probably is Eṭib-Mer (cf. USP, p. 88), must have had his own administrative organization completely separate from that of the énsi of Umma and of Girsu. This administrative organization was probably not local, but directly connected to the central power of Akkad and operating in the entire region of Umma and Lagaš (Foster, *Archives*, p. 48). The scribes En-urì, Ur-^{d}Al-la, Ur-ù, and perhaps Gala, as well as Ìl-mu-da, may have belonged to this administration.

ašgab of sheepskins *a-na* a-GAR[32] when Da-da, the scribe, came with the barley ship$^{?}$.[33] This text should be compared to BIN 8, 265, in which Da-da functions in place of Me-ság and Ama-bára.[34] In fact, both in BIN 8, 265 and 268 the person who receives the sheepskins is Dingir-sukkal ašgab.[35] A certain Da-da is mentioned in many texts without any characterizing element. Despite the fact that this anthroponym is widespread in Mesopotamian documentation of the third millennium, it seems possible that the Da-da mentioned in this archive is the namesake scribe who was an integral part of this household.

Da-da is mentioned as the recipient of plots of land in different texts: in BIN 8, 184 o. 3 and in the parallel BIN 8, 343 r. 3 he is the recipient of 43 iku of aša$_{5}$-gu$_{4}$ and 18[+x] iku aša$_{5}$ SU.LÁ[36]; in BIN 8, 193 o. 2 he is the recipient of a plot of aša$_{5}$-SU.A characterized by the formula [K]A-še [mu]-a-kam[37]; in BIN 8, 194 o. 6 he is the leaseholder of the land of a field described as aša$_{5}$ ⸢apin-lá⸣-ne šuku-*sà-tum* Me-ság, "plots of land given in leasehold allocated to Me-ság for sustenance"[38]; in BIN 8, 196 o. 6 and r. 8 he is the recipient of a plot

---

32. a-GAR is "a flower-based watery solution used to the process of tanning hides and skins" (see *PSD* A, pp. 76ff.).

33. Granary ships are already mentioned in the Fara documents (cf. G. Visicato, *Or*NS 61 [1992]: 95, sub TSŠ 627 o. IV 3: 10 [SI.NUxŠUŠ] lú-má-še, "10 [fishing nets or material to make nets (suggestion by Bauer)] for the sailor of the granary ship").

34. Both BIN 8, 265 and 268 seem to be written in Akkadian. The use of the preposition *a-na* can be noted in BIN 8, 268, while in BIN 8, 265 the verbal form is written in Akkadian *i-li-kà-ni*. In BIN 8, 268 it is written in Sumerian, im-da-gín-na. But perhaps it should be read *illikam*.

35. Dingir-sukkal occurs in other texts (BIN 8, 133; 249) and seems to have been in the employ of the household of Me-ság. In fact, in BIN 8, 249 o. 12 the clause *šu* Me-ság concludes a list of barley allocations to different people, among whom are the ašgab Ilum-dan and Dingir-sukkal. The other officials who are mentioned in the text are má-laḫ$_{4}$, sipa anše, sagi, simug.

36. For the meaning of the terms aša$_{5}$-gu$_{4}$, aša$_{5}$-SU.LÁ, and aša$_{5}$-SU.A, cf. Foster, *Inst. Land*, pp. 66–67 and PPAC 1, p. 153.

37. Cf. Foster, *Inst. Land*, p. 68.

38. Cf. Foster, *Inst. Land*, pp. 64–65.

of aša$_5$-še land, a plot of aša$_5$ nu-tuku, and a plot of aša$_5$ šuku-*sà-tum*; and in BIN 8, 199 o. 2, which is signed KA-še agar$_4$[39] aša$_5$-gibil a-⌜šà⌝ gíd-da Ama-bára-kam.[40] He is also mentioned in texts concerning grain and its derivatives: in BIN 8, 136 o. 3 he receives 6 gur of barley *a-na* šáḫ and 2 gur *a-na* dabin; in BIN 8, 143 o. 3, a text concerning rations for one year; in BIN 8, 204 o. 4 concerning emmer (30 gur-sag-gál lá 2 bariga); in BIN 8, 233 concerning a amount of nì-ḫar-ra and dabin, a debt (zi-zi-ga) incurred by Nin-an-zu; and in BIN 8, 236 o. 6 as the recipient of a ration of barley. The text concludes with the clause še-ba *šu* 2 iti. The official mentioned in these texts without title could be identified either with Da-da dub-sar or more probably with the namesake ugula.[41]

Gala dub-sar is mentioned with Ur-^{d}Al-la and Ur-me-ga in BIN 8,152 o. 10 as the recipient of 10 minas of wool (10 gala 8 Ur-^{d}Al-la 6[+2] Ur-

---

39. For the reading agar$_4$ for SIG$_7$, cf. PPAC 1, pp. 145–48. Bauer has suggested the reading úgur.

40. In all these texts he is mentioned with other officials who frequently occur in the archive and whom we have previously discussed (Ur-sipa-da; Giš-šà; I-lu$_5$-lu$_5$; É-^{d}En-líl-e; Gala; E-li-li; Ur-é).

41. Da-da ugula occurs in 2 wool texts, BIN 8, 148 o. 5, in which he is the official in charge of subordinate recipients; and in BIN 8, 152 o. II 7 in which he himself is the recipient of 10 sìla of wool. Da-da ugula also occurs in BIN 8, 243 o. 8 and in a parallel text, TLAT 45 o. 7. These are two personnel rosters of subordinates of some ugula who were not present for work. (The unpublished text NBC 7008 [cf. TLAT, p. 82] appears to be similar.) Certainly, the Da-da who is mentioned only by name or as an ugula in the above-mentioned texts is always the same person. In fact, as has been indicated many times in these texts, he always occurs with the same officials, all of whom belong to the household staff. He is also mentioned without title in texts concerning cattle: in BIN 8, 183 o. 2, he receives two three-year-old oxen in a place whose name is lost—it could be Umma (amar dab$_5$-ba *im-ḫur in* U[mma$^{ki?}$]; in BIN 8, 266 o. 2 he is mentioned concerning two oxhides (kuš-gu$_4$); the text records the number of hides, the names of the officials: Da-da; É-^{d}En-líl-e; Ur-sipa-da; and I-lul-lul), but it specifies neither the purpose of the transaction nor whether it was a question of allocations or contributions; and in BIN 8, 268 o. 4, a text similar to BIN 8, 266, in which a summary of the listed hides is recorded. He is also mentioned in BIN 8, 276 o. I.13, which concerns animal by-products (ì-áb; ì-šáḫ; kuš-áb; sa-áb; si-áb; x gu$_4$-giš). Comparing the activity of the scribe Da-da in BIN 8, 268 with that of the namesake ugula and the official who occurs in BIN 8, 183; 266; 269; 276 and TLAT 45, they may all be the same person.

me-ga dub-sar-me). Whereas Da-da dub-sar occurs in Umma C, Gala dub-sar occurs in the Ur-^{d}Šára archive. A certain Gala without title occurs in the Me-ság archive. He is mentioned, as is Da-da, in the field texts discussed above: in BIN 8, 194 o. 5; 199 r. 1; in a text concerning wool: BIN 8, 148 o. II 15' and in BIN 8, 183 o. 4; 269 o. 2 concerning cattle. In addition, he is mentioned in BIN 8, 182 r. I 5, previously discussed.[42]

Ur-me-ga dub-sar is mentioned in YBC 12319 o. I 4 and BIN 8, 152 o. 12. A namesake dub-sar is also mentioned in the Umma C documentation. He is mentioned without any title in the Me-ság archive in BIN 8, 165 r. 1 as the official "who gave 17 gur of emmer, which Pù-zu-zu (of the) ship A.NE-si took (released) from the granary for Me-ság's journey to Akkad."[43] He is mentioned in BIN 8, 194.4 as the recipient of a plot of land from the Me-ság estate of 6 iku given in leasehold. Given the unusual nature of this anthroponym, which is sometimes mentioned using the variant Ur-um-me-ga, he may be this same official, namely, the namesake dub-sar.

Ur-^{d}Al-la dub-sar is mentioned in BIN 8, 152 o. I 11. A namesake official is mentioned in BIN 8, 251 o. 4 as being in the employ of the šabra-é.[44]

Ur-ù dub-sar is mentioned only once (BIN 8, 203 o. 10), as the recipient of a plot of irrigated land measuring 18 iku.[45] This anthroponym never occurs in the Me-ság archive. Probably he was not part of the household staff.

A group of two and one of three officials should, perhaps, be added from the barley text, BIN 8, 245 I 6–12: [x] Lugal-iti-da [x] Ur-mes [ ]-SAR-me [x+]1 Ur-^{d}Iškur [x] [Sa]g$^{?}$-lum-lum [N]in-ama-na [ ]-SAR-me.

---

42. He is mentioned as an ugula in BIN 8, 243, 4. A namesake utul is mentioned in BIN 8, 276 o. I 8 concerning cattle by-products.

43. 20 lá 3 gur-sag-gál-si-sá Pù-zu-zu má A.NE-si ganun-ta im-ta-è Me-ság *A-kà-dè*^{ki}-šè du-ni Ur-me-ga-ke$_4$ ì-na-sum. For du-ni "trip," cf OSP 2, p. 130, sub 115, 3.

44. He is mentioned in the Umma C archive (BIN 8, 301 o. 4), where Ur-um-me-ga and Puzur$_4$-A-a are subordinates of the šabra-é (lú-šabra-é-me).

45. Mentioned in the same text among the recipients are Me-ság, Ìl-mu-da, KA-kù gala, Li-bur-ki-^{d}En-líl, and two other officials not referred to elsewhere.

BIN 8 regards them as scribes integrating I. 6 and 12 as [dub]-sar-me, although none of these anthroponyms is mentioned elsewhere as scribes.[46]

There was a clear hierarchical stratification among these officials. Dur$_8$-mu-pi$_5$ is a very high-ranking scribe, who might even be a member of the royal family.[47] He is certainly a totally new type of official, directly linked to the central power of Akkad that makes its appearance with Narām-Sîn. This type of official indicates the importance of scribes in the management of resources. In fact, a restructuring of the organizational system of the administration, like that which seems to have been carried out by Narām-Sîn, made it necessary to have officials who could function in the name of the king. It is unclear whether these officials were placed in charge of particular regions or were sent from time to time or on particular occasions to various regions of the empire.

There are at least one or two officials, Ama-bára and Ìl-mu-da, who work for the administration of the šabra-é, which exercises jurisdiction over extensive lands used for agriculture and breeding—lands leased from the king and royal officials such as Eṭib-Mer. The remaining scribes performed the standard administrative tasks previously analyzed in these archives. Da-da and Ur-me-ga were the only scribes belonging to a household.

---

46. With regard to the former group consisting of Lugal-iti-da and Ur-mes, in BIN 8, 152 o. III 7–8 a certain Lugal-iti-da munu$_4$-mú is mentioned. Furthermore, these two officials occur together in BIN 8, 148 o. I' 9'–10' as recipients of wool. The professional name is lost in the lacuna, 5 Lugal-iti-da 3 Ur-mes šeš-ni [ ]-me. In addition, an untitled Lugal-iti-da is mentioned in BIN 8, 137 o. 2 as receiving 10 gur of barley for the production of malt when Me-ság went from Urusag-rig to é-GIŠ.KIN.TI: 10 še gur-sag-gál-si-sá *a-na* munu$_4$ Lugal-[iti]-da šu-ba-ti Me-ság URU.SAG.RIG$_7$(PA.DU.ḪÚB)^{ki}-ta im-ma-gín-na é-GIŠ.KIN.TI (for the toponyms GIŠ.KIN.TI and URU.SAG.RIG$_7$, see *Rep. Geog.* I, pp. 94 and186). Thus, it seems more probable that the sign lost in the first lacuna is MUNU4 and not DUB, even though Ur-mes is never mentioned as a munu$_4$-mú.

With regard to the latter group, Ur-^{d}Iškur is mentioned once as a sagi in BIN 8, 249 o. 8; SIKI-lum-lum, without any title, is mentioned in BIN8, 148 r. II 4, while ⌜x⌝-ama-na is never mentioned. Thus, we cannot ascertain if they were scribes.

47. Nabi-Ulmaš, presumably a son of Narām-Sîn, occurs in a Tutub text, MAD 1, 220, (cf. Foster, *Archives*, p. 50) with the function of royal inspector, like Dur$_8$-mu-pi$_5$.

1.3 *The Umma C Archive*

Foster has identified a group of 257 texts that he considers to be the documentation of a large institutional household, dating between the end of the reign of Narām-Sîn and the beginning of that of Šar-kali-šarrī.[48] This large household was probably that of Me-ság, the énsi of Umma, a contemporary of the šabra-é Eṭib-Mer, a very high-ranking official in charge of large tracts of land between Umma and Lagaš and mentioned several times in the Girsu[49] and Umma C archives.[50] This archive seems to have been later than that of Ur-^{d}Šára but probably contemporary or a little later than the Me-ság archive.[51]

---

48. Foster, USP, pp. 79–148. Among these 257 texts, USP p. 97 includes IM 44021, a small barley record, because a certain Ur-gú is mentioned who was responsible for the three recorded entries. The copy of the text that appears in TLAT (Plate 31 no. 70) clearly shows that the anthroponym in question should be read Ur-gá, which seems to be why TLAT, p. 106 excludes the possibility that this document could be regarded as one of the mu-iti texts of Umma. In fact, a certain Ur-gá occurs in several mu-iti texts (cf. Foster, *Ethnicity*, p. 349). This official is mentioned in BIN 8, 338 r. 2 as the supervisor (maškim) of three allocations of ì-du$_{10}$-ga. Since he appears in this capacity in IM 44021, he may be the same official and the document can be considered as one of the mu-iti texts of Umma.

    Ten texts are published in TLAT (nos. 22–27; 29–32; [TLAT no. 28 also publishes IM 5592/8, a document discussed in USP p. 131 and included in the list of the 257 mu-iti texts]) and two published in DCS 4 nos. 11 and 12 (see, *infra*, p. 126, n. 104) should be added and one from the Erlenmeyer Collection (no. 93, published by R. Englund, "Ur III Sundries," *ASJ* 14 [1992]: 92–93).

    Other texts from Sargonic Umma are being prepared by B. R. Foster and D. I. Owen. Unpublished tablets are housed in the Rosicrucian Museum, California, and in the *Museo Egizio* of Turin. A private collection of 114 texts has been published by G. Pettinato, *L'Uomo comincìo a scrivere. Iscrizioni cuneiformi della collezione Michail* (Milan, 1997). Many of these texts (nos. 10–35) are certainly Sargonic. Possibly some records come from Sargonic Umma, but they do not appear as records belonging to an institutional archive, but rather to a private archive similar to that of Ur-^{d}Šára. This is the case for nos. 15–16, 27–30, transactions of aromatics, cereals, bitumen, etc., in which the trading agent (dam-gàr in 15, ga-eš in the remaining documents) Ur-^{d}Inanna appears.

49. Cf. B. R. Foster, "Notes on Sargonic Royal Progress," *JANES* 12 (1980): 31.

50. Cf. USP, p. 88.

51. Foster, *Inst. Land*, p. 52, believes there is insufficient evidence to identify the énsi Me-ság with the namesake official who was both responsible for and the leaseholder of a very large estate. According to Foster, if account is taken of the

The Umma C archive consists of records concerning barley, emmer, flour, bread, beer, animal and vegetable fats, cattle, and plots of land granted for various reasons, as well as documents linked to the management of personnel. The texts mention 17 dub-sar's, an unnamed dub-sar-maḫ, and an unnamed dub-sar-maḫ-šabra-é (TABLE 12).[52]

É$^{?}$-abzu dub-sar is mentioned in BIN 8, 303 o. 3 as the recipient of 2 Sumerian sìla (eme-gi$_7$) of ì-giš disbursed by Ba-al-lí.[53] This anthro-

---

spread of this name in the region, it is impossible to identify the two officials in question solely on the basis of their anthroponyms (Foster, *Or*NS 62 [1993], p. 444). Steinkeller and Postgate, TLAT p. 8, no. 36, are of a different opinion: "in spite of Foster's objections, there is a very good chance that this dignitary is identical with the Mesag, the governor of Umma. In my opinion, this conclusion is difficult to avoid if one considers the importance of the former Mesag." In fact, the Umma C archive shows some links with that of Me-ság and of Ur-^{d}Šára, for example some officials occur both in the Umma C archive and in the Me-ság or Ur-^{d}Šára archives, even if this does not guarantee the identity of the two officials (cf. *infra*, p. 124). Now, in the Umma C archive besides the énsi Me-ság, both a namesake šabra and a namesake dub-sar occur. The latter official may be the holder of the namesake estate. The šabra Me-ság, as M. Lambert, "Mesag le prince et Mesag le shabra (La vie économique à l'époque d'Agadé)," *RSO* 49 (1975): 166–67, had already observed, occurs in several Umma C texts (BIN 8, 286 r. 8–9; 335 o. 13; 337 o. 3). In particular, in BIN 8, 335, a text concerning allocations of ì-nun, the šabra Me-ság is mentioned immediately after the unnamed énsi and immediately before the dub-sar-maḫ, Ur-gidri. Furthermore, in BIN 8, 286, this šabra appears to be engaged in administrative activity often within the jurisdiction of the énsi: kù túg siki ì bar-ra gál-la nì-kas$_7$-aka Me-ság šabra ì-da-gál, "(The value of the) silver for clothing, wool, and oil was reckoned by the šabra Me-ság and is with him." If the šabra Me-ság and the namesake énsi are the same person, then the texts in which the šabra Me-ság is mentioned must be prior to those in which Me-ság the énsi occurs. While it is fairly probable that the šabra and the énsi Me-ság are the same person, the only vague element for identifying him with the namesake dub-sar and sa$_{12}$-du$_5$ is the fact that Lugal-giš and Lugal-ušum-gal, énsi's of two nearby cities, Girsu and Adab, come from the category of scribes. In that case, we would have an example of an énsi who was also the holder of a vast estate, as Foster has recently affirmed: "If Mesag who was énsi of Umma was the same person who controlled the estate of Mesag, somewhere near Umma, he would be a good example of an énsi as administrator for the Crown and énsi as head of his personal estate" (Foster, *Management*, p. 30).

52. These texts have been discussed at length in USP, pp. 79–148.

53. Ba-al-lí is an important official, who is never mentioned by profession. With Ba-

ponym probably occurs in two personnel texts, Nik II, 70.9' (PN$_1$ dumu É-abzu) and USP 46 o. 3 (PN$_2$ dumu É-ab[$^{?}$]zu).

En-ùri dub-sar is mentioned in MCS 9, 251 r. 2, a letter which the šabra-é, probably Eṭib-Mer,[54] sent to Me-ság, the énsi, concerning goods for delivery to Da-da, the subordinate of Iddin-Erra, for Us-ga (PN?) or for the sanctuary ([*a-n*]*a* US.GA [*l*]*i-di-in*).[55] The official who delivered these goods was En-ùri dub-sar. Probably this official, who does not occur elsewhere in the archive,[56] did not belong to the administration of the énsi of Umma, but rather to that of the šabra-é.

Gu-gu-uz dub-sar-lugal is mentioned in USP 18 r. 5–6, a text closely connected to CST 18.[57] He is the official who, with Me-ság, the énsi,

---

ti and Uru-du$_{10}$-ga, he is in charge of the majority of the deliveries for this type of goods (cf. USP, pp. 118–23).

54. Cf. A.Westenholz, *AfO* 31 (1981): 78.

55. Iddin-Erra is probably the same person who addresses a letter to Me-ság, MCS 4, 13 o. 2; cf. A.Westenholz, *AfO* 31 (1981): 78.
Cf.USP, p. 137, for *a-na* US.GA *li-di-in*.
Foster, USP, p. 105 observes that the term US.GA is usually connected to the fattening of sheep, but this meaning does not fit well within context in the Umma texts. The existence of an é-us-ga, which occurs in Serota 28, would seem to support the interpretation of US.GA as a sanctuary. Michalowski, LEM 52, p. 43 is of the same opinion. For the interpretation of US.GA as "Masthaus," cf. FAOS 19, p. 130.

56. A namesake ugula occurs in a personnel text, CT 50, 188 o. II 8, in which he is the official whose subordinate is Lugal-iti-da.

57. CST 18 (and consequently USP 18) is regarded by Foster, "Sargonic and Pre-Sargonic Tablets in the John Rylands University Library," *Bulletin of the John Rylands University Library* 64 (1982): 459, to be "from Girsu or perhaps Umma." He observes that the sign PAP, which characterizes the land parcels, only occurs in the Girsu text, L.1072 (Foster, *Inst. Land*, p. 50). But it should be noted that none of the fields mentioned in the two texts occurs elsewhere in the Girsu documentation or in a nearby region. But these fields, with the exception of agar$_4$ amar-ú-ga mentioned in USP 18, occur in the Umma texts (eden-ḫu-bu$_7^{bu}$ in Nik II, 78; bar-bar-ra in CST 27; the field da-^{giš}pèš, as well as in USP 18, occurs frequently in the Lugalzagesi archive). CST 18 and USP 18 must be related, given that the recipient, Eṭib-Mer, is the same, also to L.1152 (Foster, *Inst. Land*, pp. 18; 35 and STTI 14). The four parcels mentioned in the latter text, as well as in other Girsu texts, also occur in the Me-ság and Umma archives. The field GÀR.MUD in BIN 8, 161; 191; 192; 201; 291; NBC 5920; 10269; ki-uš in CST 27; du$_6$ PU-ra should be compared to agar$_4$ Ù.PU-ra mentioned in BIN 8, 190. Prob-

measured five plots of land totalling 126,000 sar, granted to Eṭib-Mer in Umma.[58] Gu-gu-uz does not occur elsewhere in the documentation of Umma C. He had probably come to Umma because the allocation of lands to a high-ranking official like Eṭib-Mer required the supervision and ratification not only of the local authority, represented by Me-ság, but also of the king on whose behalf Gu-gu-uz functioned. His duties must have been similar to those of Dur$_8$-mu-pi$_5$ mentioned in the documents of the Me-ság estate, Gal-zu-[x], and perhaps Lugal-GAR-[x], who occur in the Girsu archive.

IŠ dub-sar-sagi is mentioned only once, in CT 50, 58 o. 13 as the recipient of bread and beer.[59] It is not clear whether the title sagi after dub-sar refers to the official to whom the scribe is a subordinate or to the specific function of the latter.[60] Since no official by this name occurs in the Umma C documents, perhaps the title dub-sar-sagi is an abbreviation of dub-sar-sagi-lugal. In other words, it is possible that IŠ does not belong to the administration of the énsi, but to the staff of the king.

Kar-dù dub-sar is mentioned in BIN 8, 306 o. 2 as the recipient of an allocation of ì-giš. The text consists of three items[61]: one records the allocation to Kar-dù, the second the allocation of 16 sìla of ì-giš for soldiers, and the third 8 sìla as the monthly ration of oil, which the NIM soldiers, "Elamites," received.[62] The fact that our scribe is asso-

---

ably the parcels mentioned in the three texts should be located, in agreement with Foster, in a border region between Lagaš and Umma perhaps under the direct control of the šabra-é. This is likely to have been the region that caused so much controversy between the two cities in the Pre-Sargonic period.

58. <a-šà dab$_5$-ba> [*È*]-*ṭib-me-er in* Umma^{ki} Me-ság énsi Gu-gu-uz dub-sar-lugal ì-gíd mu-[1-kam].

59. Cf. USP, pp. 109–16, Group C.3.3.

60. The mention of a dub-sar-sagi in the Umma archive could be compared to the mention of a certain Me-ság in the Adab archive, in which this official sometimes appears with the title sagi and once with the title dub-sar.

61. Cf. USP, p. 119.

62. For the allocation of ì-giš to the soldiers in the Umma A archive, cf. USP, pp. 25ff. For similar allocations at Fara, cf. *Bureau*, p. 66.

ciated with the allocation to the soldiers and that the anthroponym Kar-dù does not occur elsewhere in the archive makes it probable that this official was connected with the military, thus not in the employ of the administration of Umma.

Lugal-^{giš}gigir dub-sar is mentioned in BIN 8, 335 o. 3 and BIN 8, 340 o. 4, two texts of the same typology. In the first text, he is the recipient of 3 Sumerian sìla (eme-gi$_7$) and in the second text of 3 Akkadian sìla of ì-nun.[63] Both texts are signed by Ba-al-lí. A namesake maškim is mentioned in a text concerning the purchase of threshed barley from the field LÁL.TUR in Serota 2.8. He also occurs without title in TLAT 28 o. I 10, a text that lists amounts of wool, one of which concerns Lugal-^{giš}gigir, described after the summary as "arrears of the shepherds of the énsi are forthcoming." In USP 73 o. 9, a text recording cattle arrears from Ur-sa$_6$ sipa-ùz, a certain Lugal-^{giš}gigir compiled the balanced account in Umma and computed the deductions.[64] A namesake official who occurs in the lacuna of RIAA 43 could have had the same role. In CT 50, 53 r. 7 Lugal-^{giš}gigir is the gu-sur official who measured the fields with Tir-kù. In Nik II, 70 o. 7' Lugal-^{giš}gigir is the recipient of a plot of land with its še-bi.[65] A namesake official, dumu É-abzu, the anthroponym of a scribe already discussed, is mentioned in the same text.[66]

Based on their duties, the Lugal-^{giš}gigir mentioned in TLAT 28 and in USP 73 and CT 50, 53 may have been the same individual and this official could be the namesake dub-sar.[67]

---

63. For the two types of sìla, probably of different capacities, used in texts of this type, cf. USP, p. 123.

64. lá-NI Ur-sa$_6$ sipa-ùz Lugal-^{giš}gigir-e Umma^{ki} nì-kas$_7$-bi ì-ak zi-zi-ga-ga ib-ta-zi. For the meaning of the term zi-zi-ga-ga ib-ta-zi, cf. USP, pp. 92–93; 127.

65. For the meaning of še-bi concerning rented fields, cf. *supra*, p. 84, n. 264.

66. Cf. Foster, *Inst. Land*, p. 75.

67. This identification cannot be excluded in the case of the official mentioned in archive C.5b texts (AAS 202; USP 44–48). In fact, a namesake ugula is mentioned in USP 48 r. 4'; v. 10' as the person in charge of a group of workers. This latter text is part of a group of documents (USP 44–48; AAS 202) that contain the formula, Me-ság énsi-ke$_4$ é-gidri Umma^{ki}-ka gúrum-bi ì-ak, "Me-ság the énsi in the é-gidri of Umma carried out the inspection." In USP 47 v.13 a namesake

LUL-gu-ak dub-sar is mentioned as a dub-sar only in BIN 8, 190 r. 7. LUL-gu-ak is the scribe who, with Pu-ḫa-lum, measured the fields. He is mentioned without any title as a recipient in other texts concerning fields.[68] He is also mentioned, but by anthroponym only, in some texts concerning the storage and weighing of barley and belongs to the Group C.2b of USP. In MCS 9, 236, Nik II, 76 o. I 10 and USP 22 o. I 8 he is one of the persons collectively described as sag-apin lugal in debt for barley arrears to the accounting office.[69] Among the officials mentioned in these texts are the dub-sar-maḫ (Nik II, 76 o. I 13; USP 22 o. I 10), Lugal-KA šu-gíd (Nik II, 76 r I.8; USP 22 o. I 6), and Da-da gala (USP 22 o. I 12)—it seems unlikely that they are directly involved in agricultural work. The sag-apin, in this case, must have been landholders and the barley must have been due to the institution from the estimated harvest or as taxes. In all the texts of this group, with the exception of CST 23 and MCS 9, 236, the preceding formula is followed by an indication of the official who compiled the balanced account, the énsi Me-ság, and the place where it was compiled, the é-gidri of Umma (Me-ság énsi-ke$_4$ é-gidri Umma^{ki} nì-kas$_7$-bi ì-ak). Finally, a namesake official in texts

---

nu-bànda is mentioned. Finally, the official, without any description, whose subordinate or son is a certain Ur-[èn/li] is mentioned in USP 45 r. I 4. He also occurs without title in several texts.

68. MCS 9, 237 o. 2, an aša$_5$-gu$_4$ text in which he is the recipient of a plot of 1 bur and 1 eše$^?$; CT 50, 53 o. 2, an aša$_5$-še text, in which he is the recipient of 4 bur and 2½ iku from the fields ki-lugal agar$_4$ aša$_5$-maḫ and a-zag a-šà ^{d}Uttu. In the latter text, two people described by the formula PN$_1$ ugula LUL-gu-ak are mentioned: "PN$_1$, the supervisor is LUL-gu-ak." The meaning of the ugula that precedes the name LUL-gu-ak is not clear. Foster, USP p. 85, comments: "This may mean that the others were subordinates to LUL-gu-ak, or that he actually supervised these parcels though they were designated for others." Since the first possibility is generally expressed by the formula PN$_1$ PN$_2$ ugula, the second hypothesis appears more probable (USP, p. 164, n. 13).

69. In MCS 9, 236 (še lá-NI è-a sag-apin-na lugal), Nik II, 76 (lá-NI sag-apin-na lugal-ke$_4$-ne è-è-dam) the arrears are forthcoming; in USP 22, the seed barley and the fodder for the animals was deducted from the arrears due (še-numun še-gu$_4$-e kú sag-apin lugal-ke$_4$-ne lá-NI-ta ì-ne-zi). For a discussion of the formulae in the texts of group C.2b, cf. USP, pp. 91–92.

concerning bread and beer occurs as a recipient.[70] It appears probable that both in the barley texts and in these latter ones that a high-ranking official is present who could be our dub-sar.

Me-ság dub-sar is mentioned only in USP 23 o. 6. The text lists barley for seven people, one of whom is our dub-sar. The barley, given the similarity this text displays with those of archive C.2b, is probably arrears due the administration.[71] Me-ság dub-sar may be the namesake official in charge of the management of the estate bearing his name.

NA-id-maḫ-ra-áš dub-sar is mentioned in MCS 9, 240 r. 8 as the official who brought barley, dried fish, salt, lard, straw, and small wooden brick molds to/from Umma in month 7 year 2.[72] The anthroponym NA-id-maḫ-ar-šum mentioned in Serota 20.6 and 25.5 could be a phonetic variant for NA-id-maḫ-ra-áš. These two texts date also from month 7 year 2. They list amounts of barley in a range of 10 to 160 sìla, which appear as zi-ga, "expense" or zi-zi-ga, "deduction."[73] NA-id-maḫ-ra-áš is also mentioned in MCS 9, 241 o. 10 as the recipient of bread and beer.

Nam-zi dub-sar is mentioned in USP 53 r. 3, a text concerning cattle allocated to Nam-zi by Nam-maḫ under the supervision of the šabra Lugal-nisag-e. A namesake official without title seems to be mentioned in USP 55 o. I 8 and II 9. The text is a list of draft animals and

70. CST 6.12; 17.12; CT 50, 55.10; and USP 32.12.

71. But this text has a different subscription to other texts of C.2b: [zi-z]i-ga-bi [ib-t]a-zi ì-PI-gál, which Foster, USP p. 94 translates: "Their deductions have been made and are with them." In agreement with Foster, this should mean that the amounts of barley listed are credited and already in the possession of the administration; the deductions, probably for seed and fodder for the draft animals and for rations to the agricultural workers, had already been made and are in the possession of the debtors. It cannot, however, be excluded that the amounts of barley listed were deductions to be made from the total amount of barley to be paid to the administration.

72. Cf USP, p. 101. ^{giš}u$_5$-šub-tur should be regarded as a written variant of ^{giš}ù-šub; cf. P. Steinkeller, review of USP in *WZKM* 77 (1987): 194. The interchange in writing between ù and u$_5$ has been attested since the Fara period, cf. *Ù-ri-ti-lum*$_x$ Šu-a-ba$_4$ maškim-gi$_4$ in TSŠ 732 o. II 2; *U$_5$-ri-ti* maškim-gi$_4$ in CT 50, 15 o. I 3.

73. Cf. USP, p. 97.

is concluded by the formula "arrears of the sag-apin of the énsi about to be delivered, (arrears) present in the regular roster" (lá-NI sag-apin-na énsi-ke$_4$-ne è-è-dam šà im-si-sá-a-ka ì-gál). This means that the animals belonging to the administration of the énsi had been used for work in the fields by the farmers of the énsi; but, as can be seen from the general roster, they still have to be returned.[74] Finally, a certain Nam-zi is mentioned in USP 47 r. I 20 as the official to whom Ur-su is the subordinate or son. Like all the texts of archive C.5b,[75] this text is a general roster (im-si-sá-a) of workers who had been recruited for unspecified activities ([x]+11 guruš, 6 šeš, [x]+3 guruš-kaškal and 4 šeš-kaškal) as subordinates of the ugula Tir-kù, and of the nu-bànda Lugal-^{giš}gigir. The importance of the operations recorded in the texts of archive C.5b (USP 44–48; AAS 202) is indicated by the clause which concludes them, Me-ság énsi-ke$_4$ é-gidri Umma^{ki}-ka gurum-bi ì-ak *pá-nu* 3. This formula is analogous to that which concludes many texts concerning barley arrears in archive C.2b.

Pu-ḫa-lum dub-sar is mentioned in BIN 8, 190 r. 6, which records the lease of six arable land parcels to six persons, four of whom are listed with their professional names.[76] Our scribe is the official who, with LUL-gu-ak dub-sar, measured the lands leased.[77] Pu-ḫa-lum occurs without title only in seven texts, all of the same typology,[78] as the recipient of bread and beer. The texts of this typology are closely connected in content, anthroponyms mentioned, mid-to-high-ranking officials, and for the short period they cover. It seems clear that the Pu-ḫa-lum mentioned in these seven texts is the same person.

---

74. Cf. USP, p. 129.

75. Cf. USP, p. 125.

76. The text is discussed in USP, p. 87 in the context of archive C.1b and Foster, *Inst. Land*, p. 71.

77. agar$_4$ ù-sír-ra apin-lá gur$_7$(ŠE.MÙŠxŠÈ) a-šà gíd-da-àm pu-ḫa-lum dub-sar ù LUL-gu-ak. For the reading gur$_7$ of ŠE.MÙŠxŠÈ in the Sargonic period, see P. Steinkeller, *WZKM* 77 (1987): 190.

78. This is the sub-group C.3.3.I of USP. The texts in question are: Buttrum 1; CST 5; MCS 9, 246; 248; 249; Serota 15; and 16.

He probably is the dub-sar of BIN 8, 190, but that cannot be satisfactorily demonstrated.

Sipa-sa$_6$-ga dub-sar is mentioned only in Serota 2 o. 6, a text concerning the receipt of threshed barley from the field LÁL.TUR.[79]

Šeš-šeš dub-sar is mentioned in USP 54 o. 5 as the official who has (ì-da-LUL, "in safekeeping"$^{?}$) an anše-nita-libir-giš, "draft horse$^{?}$" belonging to the official Ka-ki.[80] A namesake official, who should perhaps be identified with our scribe, is mentioned in S.378 o. 3 without any characterizing element as the recipient of ì-šeš$_4$ (USP, p.121) and in MVN 3, 110 o. 5 of bread and beer. Finally, a certain Šeš-šeš, described as árad dub-sar maḫ, occurs in TLAT 30 o. II 1, a register of conscriptees.[81]

Ur-gidri dub-sar-maḫ is mentioned in CT 50, 52 r. II 6'. Foster considers this text to be the list of gifts presented to the royal family on the occasion of one of the king's visits to Sumer,[82] "these are the gifts for the king, ...the gifts for the queen, ...the gifts for the children of the king, when the king came to Sumer, Ur-gidri, head of the scribes, transported (upstream) to Zabalam."[83] In addition, Ur-gidri is mentioned in BIN 8, 312.8 and 335.12, which record allocations of oil.[84] In the former text, which appears to be undated, Ur-gidri, mentioned only as dub-sar, received 6 sìla eme-gi$_7$ of ì-GÌR, while in the latter text he received 1 sìla of ì-nun. Among the recip-

---

79. USP, p. 89.

80. Cf. USP, p. 126. For the interpretation of ì-da-LUL as "having in safekeeping," cf. USP, pp. 67; 126. For the reading luk$_x$ for LUL and the interpretation of ì-da-luk$_x$ "remains /lives with him," cf. P. Steinkeller, *WZKM* 77 (1987): 193; TLAT p. 35, sub i.8. Finally cf. AWEL p. 447, sub Nik I, 217 r. I 4, e-da lug$_x$, "aufhalten lassen." More exactly LUL is to read lu$_5$(g/k) (suggestion by Bauer).

81. Archive C.5 is discussed in USP, pp. 124–26.
It is tempting to link the Šeš-šeš mentioned in USP 54 to the namesake dub-sar mentioned in the Girsu archive; cf. *infra*, pp. 137ff.

82. Foster, USP, pp. 133–35.

83. nindaba lugal... [nindaba] nin... ninda[ba dumu lugal] Ur-gidri [dub-sar-maḫ-e] lugal ki-en-ki-šè ì-gín-na-a Zabalam^{ki}-a ì-gíd-da-àm. For the interpretation of ì-gíd-da-àm (literally, measured) as "he hauled upstream," cf. USP p. 135, sub 49.

84. Cf. USP C.4.1 pp. 120; 122.

ients in this latter text, he immediately follows the énsi, who received 2⅔ sìla and the šabra Me-ság, who received 1 sìla. Ur-gidri is not mentioned elsewhere by name, but it is probable that he is referred to in other texts by just his professional title. Thus, the unnamed dub-sar-maḫ mentioned frequently in the Umma C archive might be Ur-gidri, given the brief period of time this documentation spans. He is mentioned in Nik II, 76.13; MCS 9, 236; 238 and USP 22.10. In these four documents, all of the same C.2b typology, he is in debt to the administration for barley. This barley is owed by the king's farmers, probably for the leased fields. From this the seed barley and the fodder for the animals used for work in the fields was subtracted, since the latter was at the expense of the leaseholder. The énsi Me-ság compiled a balanced account of this barley in the é-gidri.[85] He is also mentioned in USP 57 o. I 13 as the recipient of animals belonging to the king,[86] probably provided by the administration for agricultural work. Finally an unnamed dub-sar-maḫ is mentioned in TLAT 30 II 2 concerning Šeš-šeš (árad dub-sar-maḫ).[87]

Remembering that Ur-gidri in BIN 8, 335 follows the énsi and the šabra Me-ság, while in USP 57 he follows the sa_{12}-du_5 Ama-bára and precedes Me-ság, who is certainly the namesake šabra, it is possible that he is similar in rank both to the sa_{12}-du_5 and to the šabra.

Ur-giš dub-sar is mentioned in BIN 8, 307 o. 2 e 312 r. 3 as the recipient of ì-erin and ì-anše respectively. A namesake official without title, but who certainly is the namesake dub-sar, is mentioned twice in a text of the same typology. In BIN 8, 320 o. 2–3 he receives 4 sìla of ì-erin-babar and in r. 4 9 10 sìla ì-nun ^{giš}gigir aka-dè, "oil for treating a wagon."[88] As the supervisor maškim of three transactions of ì-du_{10}-ga, he occurs in BIN 8, 338, 7. If the official mentioned in BIN 8, 338 was the namesake scribe, he must have belonged to the office dealing with the administration of the goods listed in Group C.4.

85. For similar formulae that conclude these texts, cf. USP, p. 92.

86. For a discussion of this text and its relationship to USP 22, cf. USP, pp. 128–29.

87. Probably the unnamed dub-sar mentioned in TLAT 24 o. 6 as the recipient of bread and beer should be the dub-sar-maḫ.

88. Cf. USP, p. 118.

Ur-^{d}Lamma dub-sar is mentioned in MCS 9, 266 o. 7, which records the allocation of 6,600 sar of arable land (aša$_5$ numun ì-dab$_5$).[89] A namesake official without title occurs in AAS 1 o. II 5; r. I 10; II 3. The text, discussed by Foster in USP, pp. 96–97, lists amounts of barley to be deducted concerning various officials only some of whom are mentioned with title. The reason for these deductions from what is due is indicated only in a few cases. After a summary of the barley, the text has the clause "expenses (incurred in the name) of Ur-Lamma." Foster concludes that Ur-^{d}Lamma was a farmer who recorded his expenses for work in the fields, deductions and payments to various people. All these expenses are credited to Ur-^{d}Lamma by the administration. In many texts already discussed different officials described as dub-sar, dub-sar-maḫ, gala, etc. are indicated in the subscriptions of the text as sag-apin lugal or sag-apin-énsi. Therefore, it seems probable that Ur-^{d}Lamma was an official who probably is the namesake dub-sar and who was given lands for sustenance. Parcels of this land were given in leasehold and Ur-^{d}Lamma reimbursed the leaseholder for expenses incurred. In turn, the administration calculated the total expenses in favor of the latter.[90] He is also mentioned in CST 21 r. I 5, which concerns animals that had been provided by the administration for agricultural work and which had not been returned. Ur-^{d}Lamma is mentioned in CST 10.10 as the recipient of ⅔ sìla of ì-erin.

Ur-me-ga dub-sar is mentioned in BIN 8, 190 o. 8, in which he is the recipient of a parcel of land of 4 iku and 20 sar from the field ù-pu-ra. Ur-me-ga receives a plot of land, perhaps in leasehold in MCS 9, 266 o. 2. A namesake maškim is mentioned in USP 17 o. 3, a text concerning the allocation of land, described as aša$_5$-gu$_4$, from the royal holdings. For each entry the recipient is followed by another official described as a maškim. The significance of this format is unclear. Perhaps each maškim listed supervised and guaranteed

---

89. Cf. USP, p. 88.

90. It is possible that Ur-^{d}Lamma was the official in charge of collecting that part of the barley due to be paid to the administration by the persons who had leased parcels of land from it. Therefore, these amounts of barley were debited to him, just as the deductions, to be paid by the administration, were credited to him.

that the recipients would be paid his dues by the royal administration. A maškim Ur-um-me-ga is mentioned in Nik II, 78 o. I 3', a text that records barley, silver, and sheep due to the administration for the leasehold of the plots of arable land worked by different gu-sur.[91] The mention of this official in this text appears to be similar to that of the preceding text; in fact, each transaction lists the goods due, the name of the gu-sur, and the name of the maškim. Since Ur-um-me-ga should be regarded as a variant of Ur-me-ga,[92] he may be the maškim mentioned in Nik II, 78. It is quite probable that this official, who supervised the operations recorded in the aforementioned texts, could be the namesake dub-sar. A certain Ur-me-ga, without title, is mentioned in USP 27 r. 1, a text concerning ingredients for brewing beer, as the official who brought the flour and malt from Adab. I_7-pa-è received these goods from Ur-me-ga and deposited them where the summaries were compiled.[93]

Besides the dub-sar-maḫ, an unnamed dub-sar-maḫ šabra<-é> is mentioned only once in the Umma C archive, in Serota 18, as the recipient of bread and beer.

Finally, an unnamed dub-sar-gal is mentioned in Serota 35 o. 6 as the recipient of 24 sìla of zì-gu flour. This title, which Foster translates "senior scribe,"[94] occurs only this once in the archives. The mention of US.GA in line 4 suggests that this official may have been connected with the temple or with the administration in charge of fattening of sheep.

---

91. Cf. USP, p. 93; for the similarity with MCS 9, 244, cf. USP, p. 96.

92. Cf. TLAT, p. 62, 28 o. II 7.

93. zì $munu_4$ $Adab^{ki}$-ta gín-a ki-Ur-me-ga-ta I_7-pa-è šu-ba-ti ki nì-kas_7-ka ì-na-gá-gá. Ur-me-ga and I_7-pa-è mentioned in USP 27 are certainly scribes. In fact, in one unpublished text that probably came from Umma, two dub-sar's with this name occur several times in connection with barley for an unknown destination. The tablet, of which two columns of the obverse and two of the reverse are preserved, is part of a small batch of Sargonic texts kept in the *Museo Egizio* of Turin; they will soon be published by A. Archi and F. Pomponio. A certain Ì-pa-è without title occurs in TLAT, 28 r. I 13, in connection with 20 minas of wool due to the énsi, [l]á-NI ⸢sipa⸣-énsi-ka è-è-dam.

94. USP, p. 105. This term would be equivalent to *bur-šu-ma*, which occurs in connection with Šubur in the Fara texts (cf. *supra*, p. 45).

The texts we have discussed in paragraphs II 1.1–3 are related to three different types of administrative units:

(1) the Ur-^{d}Šára archive contains "the records of business dealings between a family or group of associates and a large institution, presumably the state"[95];

(2) the Me-ság archive contains "the records of an estate of Akkadian type transplanted to Sumer granted by a Sargonic king to a certain Me-ság"[96];

(3) the Umma C archive contains "the records of the énsi's accountability for the operation and assets of the state household at Umma."[97]

Foster observes that a prosopographical comparison between the Ur-^{d}Šára archive and Umma C does not enable us to demonstrate that the persons in both archives, with the same anthroponym but without title, are the same persons.[98] A cross-referenced comparison of the three archives helps to establish the concordances:

Name	*Archive of Ur-^{d}Šára*	*Archive of Me-ság*	*Archive of Umma C*
Gala	dub-sar	dub-sar	
Ur-gidri	dub-sar		dub-sar-maḫ
Ama-bára		dub-sar-maḫ	sa$_{12}$-du$_{5}$
Me-ság		dub-sar; ugula; sa$_{12}$-du$_{5}$	dub-sar; ugula; gu-sur
Ur-me-ga		dub-sar	dub-sar

95. Cf. USP, p. 78.

96. Cf. Foster, *Agriculture*, pp. 113, 123.

97. USP, p. 150.

98. USP, pp. 75–76.

To these scribes should be added other officials: Ama-é and Ur-^{d}Šára who, besides occurring in the namesake archive, can be found in MAD 4, 149 from Umma C (Ama-é dam Ur-^{d}Šára); Gala sipa occurs both in the Me-ság archive and in that of Ur-^{d}Šára (MAD 4, 57 r. 6); Ur-Ab-ba ugula is mentioned in USP 51v. II 13 from the Umma C archive, in MAD 4, 144 r. 2 and in TLAT 13 r. 14 from the Ur-^{d}Šára archive. These correspondences, which cannot be random, suggest links between the households of Ur-^{d}Šára, Me-ság, and the énsi of Umma. This is not unexpected, since the free enterprise of Ur-^{d}Šára and Ama-é and the domain of Me-ság surely had as their counterpart, in many cases, the énsi's administration. But we are not able to establish with certainty the exact nature of the relationship.

2. The Scribes of Girsu

The size of the Girsu archive is a measure of the importance the Girsu region had in the economy and organization of the empire of Akkad and which it continued to have in subsequent periods. The Sargonic Girsu archive consists of about 1,800 texts[99]—the exact number of tablets contained in the archive cannot be established.[100] Almost all of Girsu's Sargonic texts come from De Sarzec's excavations and are housed in the Istanbul Museum.[101]

---

99. Cf. Foster, *ZA* 72 (1982): 6.

100. Cf. STTI, p. VII, n. 1.

101. There are very few Sargonic texts from Girsu that come from clandestine digs unlike texts from other periods (cf. Foster, *Inst. Land*, p. 19).

We shall cite the Istanbul texts by the museum catalogue number. The texts whose copies can be found in ITT are recognizable, because beside the catalogue number they carry an indication of the line or column: for example, L 1042 o. 3 or L 1449 r. I 3. On the other hand, texts whose copies have been published in STTI have the STTI number and the indication of the line in brackets beside the Museum number: for example, L 1095 (S6) o. 4'.

Below is a list of the Istanbul texts attributable to the Sargonic period or immediately following:

L 1039–1476. The contents of these tablets with copies of parts of them have been published in ITT I.

L 2820–3158; 4343–4707; 5670–5907. The contents of these tablets with copies of parts of them have been published in ITT II.

A batch of tablets, both complete and fragments, from the excavations of De Sarzec was transferred to the Louvre with the permission of the Ottoman authorities. The complete tablets from the Sargonic period were published by F. Thureau-Dangin in RTC 77–171 (3rd series),[102] but the fragments are still unpublished.[103] Some Sargonic documents from clandestine digs or stolen from those found in de Sarzec's excavations are scattered in various museums; most of them have been published.[104]

The most representative text typologies in the archive are given below as approximate percentages of the entire legible documentation:

L 6666–6681; 6749–6753; 9251; 9253–9254; 9258–9259; 9264; 9268?–9269?; 9271; 9277; 9281; 9289?; 9299?; 9303–9304; 9313–9314?; 9327; 9336; 9349; 9353; 9361; 9363–9364; 9369; 9374; 9377; 9381; L 9390–9474.

L 9251–9389 is a group of tablets in which Late and Post-Sargonic documents are mixed. Besides those listed above, it is possible that other documents are Sargonic, but this has been impossible to establish on the basis of the prosopography, the only way, in this case, to date them. The documents which have a question mark are of uncertain attribution.

The contents of these tablets with the copies of parts of them have been published in ITT V. Copies of 182 documents whose contents were known from ITT I, II and V were published in STTI with the addition of another document L 11101 (S185).

102. RTC includes documents from the Fara period (1st series), the ED IIIb period (2nd series), the Post-Sargonic period (4th series), and from the Ur III period (5th and 6th series). Not all the tablets of RTC come from De Sarzec's excavations; some from Fara or other sites were purchased on the clandestine market.

The tablets from the 3rd series of RTC and those from ITT I, II, and V were made from unbaked clay and were found at the center of the *tell des tablettes* piled up without any order on the remains of a floor of baked tiles 3.7 m deep (ITT I, p. 1), and had probably been used as filling material. The tablets of the 4th series of RTC and from ITT IV, also of unbaked clay, were found in a deposit on the north side of the same *tell des tablettes*, in an area about 22.5 m in diameter, in separate groups at a depth of between 2.90 and 4.30 m. They span from the Sargonic period to that of Ur III.

103. The fragmentary tablets from the Sargonic and Post-Sargonic periods in the Louvre that come from De Sarzec's excavations, series AOTb, are still unpublished. They are soon to be published by J.-J. Glassner.

104. CT 50, 49–51; 82–187 (the provenance of 82 and 109 is of uncertain); MVN 3, 42–44; 47–48; 50–51; 76; 89; 114; it is possible that MVN 3, 55; 69; 75; 83; and 113 also come from Girsu.

Text Typology	%
personnel recruitment and others concerning persons	22.0
allocation of bread, beer, and sá-du$_{11}$	13.5
sheep	11.5
metals, silver, gold, bronze, copper, and precious objects	7.0
barley	6.2
fish	6.0
plots of agricultural land	5.5
cattle and pigs	4.5
flour	3.5
wool and clothing	3.0

BIN 8, 225 certainly comes from Girsu because of the mention of the nu-bànda's, Amar-su$_4$ and Šeš$_4$-da, frequently mentioned with this title in the Girsu documentation (L 1065; 1148; 1149; 1162; 1193; 1237; 1430; 1431; 1448; 1449; 2859; 3016; 4458; 4502; 4507; 4508; 5884; CT 50, 99; 103; particularly in L 1065; 1148; 1149; 1237; 2859; CT 50, 99; 103 they are mentioned contemporaneously) and Su-bappir-a, an official who generally occurs without title and who has several subordinates (L 1365; 2925; 3149; 4640; 4691; 9448; CT 50,148; RTC 113; 116). Two other officials mentioned, KA-kù (L 4556) and NÌGIN (L 3006), also occur in the documentation as nu-bànda's. To these should be added PUL 23–24; 26; 38; it is possible that other PUL documents come from the region of Girsu.

Some of the tablets are published in DCS. The tablets marked with the numbers 31; 33–36; 38–40 are probably Sargonic. At least two other tablets, the mu-iti texts 1 and 12 from this small archive, are Sargonic and come from Umma. The remaining tablets are from Girsu, some from ED IIIb, others from the Post-Sargonic and Ur III periods. To these texts should probably be added some tablets published by T. C. Pinches, *The Babylonian Tablets of the Berens Collection*, ASM 16 (London, 1915), nos. 7–11; 13. No. 12 should certainly be dated to the Gudea period by reason of its final clause zi-ga ^{d}Šára-ì-sa$_6$. ^{d}Šára-ì-sa$_6$ is an official who appears in the archive of this énsi.

Probably YBC 5107–5124 should be included. These documents were published by Foster, "A Sargonic Archive from the Lagash Region," in H. Behrens *et al.*, eds., *Dumu é-dub-ba-a, Studies in Honor of Åke W. Sjöberg* (Philadelphia, 1989), pp. 155–65, and are regarded by the author as belonging to the Late or Post-Sargonic period (*id.*, p. 159). The provenance of these 18 tablets, like those of the Liege group (PUL), is probably the region of Lagaš (*id.*, p. 158).

Other unpublished documents are at present housed in the Yale Babylonian Collection, the Louvre, the Ashmolean Museum, and the Royal Scottish Museum of Edinburgh.

The other typologies that can be distinguished in smaller percentages concern oil, birds, eggs, spices, fruit, wood, wooden objects, hides, and pottery.[105] In addition, there are numerous contracts and letters and a fairly large number of school exercises,[106] although lexical texts are rare.

These texts should be considered, like the texts of the Umma C archive, to be records of the é-gal,[107] spanning a time period that cannot be delimited precisely, but falls certainly between the reigns of Narām-Sîn and Šar-kali-šarrī and that must have largely coincided with the period when Lugal-ušum-gal was énsi of Girsu. This énsi, as documented by his seal impressions, was certainly a contemporary of both Narām-Sîn (RTC 165–66; 170) and Šar-kali-šarrī (RTC 136; 161–62). Some of the documents probably belong to the period of the énsi Puzur$_4$-Ma-ma, who succeeded Lugal-ušum-gal (RTC 83; 181). But, as Foster demonstrates, most of the documentation should be dated to the reign of Šar-kali-šarrī. In fact, many documents may belong to the last period of his reign.[108]

---

105. The percentages were calculated on the number of texts whose typology it was possible to establish; unintelligible fragments were not counted. These percentages agree well with those of Foster, *ZA* 72 (1982): 11, even if some discrepancies can be noted. These are probably due to the number of texts on which the statistical calculation was made.

106. Identified by B. R. Foster, "The Education of a Bureaucrat in Sargonic Sumer," *ArOr* 50 (1982): 238–42.

107. Cf. Foster, *Inst. Land,* p. 18.

108. It is difficult to establish an internal chronology for the Sargonic documents of Girsu. It is perhaps possible with meticulous prosopographic comparison to find "chronological indicators" that would enable us, on the one hand, to group batches of contemporaneous texts and, on the other, to establish temporal sequences. One could, for example, try:
   (a) to establish which official occurs in the texts where Eṭib-Mer is mentioned and to identify the texts where these officials occur.
   (b) to identify the numerous nu-bànda mentioned in the texts and in groups. For example, in L 1448 a group of six nu-bànda's is mentioned with their ugula; in L 1449 there are three nu-bànda's; in L 1149 two nu-bànda's.
   (c) to establish which officials, dub-sar, gal$_5$-lá, sukkal, sagi, etc. occur together in texts and to see whether it is possible to link these text groups with related ones, for example with L 1448.

The field allotment texts were studied by Foster[109] in the context of his analysis of the land distribution system in the Sumerian cities during the Sargonic period. This study showed that the allotment holders were members of the court, the administration, and the temple hierarchy; in other words, officials with power over the local economy. Énsi's from other cities, such as Susa, Elam, and Ešnunna also enjoyed allotments of agricultural land. This practice was not new in Sumerian cities, being attested from the period of Lugalzagesi (BIN 8, 82; 86). The difference was the role of people such as Eṭib-Mer, a holder of vast tracts of agricultural land in the territory of both Girsu and Umma. Eṭib-Mer must have been the head of the royal Sargonic settlement in the regions of Girsu and Umma and hierarchically superior to the énsi's of both cities, Meság and Lugal-ušum-gal.[110]

Another group of texts analyzed by Foster[111] are the allocations of goods to members of the royal family (lugal, nin, dumu-nita/mí lugal) and to high-ranking officials of the kingdom, both royal and local, on the occasion of journeys made by the king and his followers to the Sumerian cities.[112]

---

109. Foster, *Inst. Land*, pp. 17–45; 45–52.

110. Foster *Inst. Land*, pp. 35–37. Foster and I are preparing a study of the organizational system of production, distribution of goods, industry, etc. of Sargonic Girsu.

111. Foster, *JANES* 12 (1980): 29–42.

112. This group consists of L 1212+4672; 1472; 2940; 4548; 4566; 4686; 4699; 5791; 9374; 9428; RTC 127; 134; 135; CT 50, 172.

Foster, *JANES* 12 (1980): 32–36 links RTC 221–23 to these texts; they are documents with controversial dating, which Foster dates to late in the reign of Šar-kali-šarrī. T. Maeda, "Two Rulers by the Name Ur-Ningirsu in Pre-Ur III Lagash," *ASJ* 10 (1988): 27–31, attributes RTC 221–23 to the period when Ur-^{d}Ningírsu, son of Gudea, was énsi and identifies the unnamed lugal mentioned in these texts as Utu-ḫegal, the king of Uruk. F. Carroué, "La situation Chronologique de Lagaš II," *ASJ* 16 (1994): 67, agrees with Maeda as regards the dating of RTC 221–23, but disagrees with the identification of the lugal in RTC 221–23; he believes that he was one of the Gutian kings. K. Volk, "Puzur-Mama und die Reise des Königs," *ZA* 82 (1992): 23; 27, suggests that RTC 221–23 belong to the period immediately after the reign of Šar-kali-šarrī and identifies the lugal in question as Puzur$_4$-Ma-ma, the énsi who seems to have succeeded Lugal-ušum-gal, on the basis of L 6758 (Puzur$_4$-Ma-ma lugal Lagaš^{ki}) and AO 11353 III' 6'–7' (Puzur$_4$-Ma-ma lugal Lagaš^{ki}-kam). Furthermore, while Maeda

About 80 scribes whose anthroponyms are entirely preserved are mentioned in those texts—the anthroponym is only partially preserved or has been entirely lost in about 20 places.[113] Here we have the most numerous body of scribes in the whole of the Sargonic documentation and it can be likened in number only to that of Fara. This large number of scribes not only agrees with the size of the documentation but testifies to an extremely complex organizational system comprising a very large number of people.[114]

---

seems to have established that the period of time that separates Šar-kali-šarrī from Ur-Nammu is relatively long, J.-J.Glassner, "La Fin d'Akkadé: approche chronologique," *NABU* (1994): 9, believes that the time lapse between the end of the reign of Šar-kali-šarrī and the beginning of that of Ur-Nammu is not more than 30 years. If it seems to complicate the chronological situation considering the number of énsi's who seem to have reigned in this period in Lagaš, it could explain some peculiarities arising from the long chronology, such as officials who were in active service in the Sargonic period still working in the administrations of subsequent énsi's.

To those already listed, it is perhaps possible to add other documents (L 3072; 4548; 4638; RTC 102; 103) that fit the categories analyzed in Foster.

113. For a list of these scribes, cf. TABLE 13.

114. This institution must have been able to enrol a large number of people both as soldiers (as the numerous surviving military ration summaries demonstrate; cf. Foster, *Management*, p. 27, nos. 17; 66) and as workers. This could be demonstrated by the mention of at least 55 nu-bànda's in the documentation. In some cases, their function is clearly military (L 1065; 4507; 5829; 5837; CT 50, 99; 100) in others it is undefined, but it could be either as leaders of military contingents or of teams of workers. Since the documents span about a generation, we can reasonably estimate that the number of nu-bànda's active contemporaneously was not less than 25, although we do not know whether the documentation was uniformly distributed in this time span (there is, indeed, a legitimate suspicion that most of the documentation refers to the late period of Šar-kali-šarrī). L 1448 is a four-column document, which lists the ugula who were the subordinates of six nu-bànda's, in order: Amar-su$_4$ (8 ugula); En-uru-na (9 ugula); Šeš-da (7 ugula); Lú-ba (9 ugula); Ur-GAR (9 ugula); and Ur-šer$_7$-da (7 ugula). These ugula, however, do not exhaust the number of ugula who were subordinate to each nu-bànda. L 1449 lists the number of guruš with their ugula who were the subordinates of three of the nu-bànda's mentioned in L 1448: Amar-su$_4$, En-uru-na, and Lú-ba. A comparison of the anthroponyms mentioned as ugula in the two texts shows that other ugula's, besides those mentioned in L 1448, were subordinates of these nu-bànda. L 1449 also records the number of guruš who comprised the team of each nu-bànda: 172 guruš belong to Amar-su$_4$; 159 belong to En-uru-na, and 149 of Lú-ba. L 1149 must have been a similar list, only

Three, unfortunately fragmentary, texts, L 1095,[115] L 5807, and AOTb 198, are important for ascertaining the importance of the scribe.[116]

L 1095 (S 6)

o. 1)	[x kù-babbar]	[x shekels] of silver,
2)	[107] še gu[r]	[107] gur of barley,
3)	[x anš]e nita libi[r]	[x] male old donkeys,
4)	Ki-tuš-ni dub-sar	the scribe Ki-tuš-ni
5)	*ù* Tir-[kù]	and Tir-kù (delivered?);
6)	12 ma-na [urudu]	12 minas [of copper],
7)	20 ma-na siki	20 minas of wool,
8)	Lugal-bur ⌜agrig⌝	Lugal-bur the agrig (delivered?);
9)	13 še gur	13 gur of barley,
10)	Ka-tar dub-sar	the scribe Ka-tar (delivered?);
11)	⌜*in*⌝-1-mu	in the first/current year.
12)	[x+]4 gín igi-4-gal [kù-babbar]	[x+]4 minas and ¼ shekel of silver,
r. 1)	23 2(b) 3(bàn) še gur	23½ gur of barley,
2)	Ki-tuš-ni dub-sar	the scribe Ki-tuš-ni
3)	*ù* Tir-kù	and Tir-kù (delivered?);
4)	*in* 2-mu	in the second year.
5)	[š]u-nígin 143 2(b) 3(bàn) še-gur *A-kà-dè*^{ki}	Total 143½ Akkad gur of barley;
6)	šu-nígin ⅓ ša lá igi-4-gal kù-babbar	Total 39¼ shekels of silver;

---

a summary of which is preserved in ITT I, p. 9, which records 210 guruš and 8 ugula, subordinates of Amar-su$_4$ and 8 ugula, subordinates of Šeš-da. It appears likely that 9 or 10 teams, each of between 15 and 20 persons headed by an ugula, made up the team of each nu-bànda, which must have numbered on average from 160 to 200 people. This means that approximately 4000/5000 workers could be recruited and provided rations by the é-gal and by affiliated institutions.

115. For the transliteration and a short commentary of this text, cf. B. R. Foster, "Selected Business Documents from Sargonic Mesopotamia," *JCS* 35 (1983): 106.

116. AOTb 198 is one of the unpublished documents of the Louvre of which J.-J. Glassner is preparing an edition. I thank J.-J. Glassner for having generously placed at my disposal his transliteration of the text. He also placed at my disposal all the references to scribes that occur in these texts, with their relevant context.

7)	šu-nígin 12 ma-na uru[du]	Total 12 minas of copper;
8)	šu-nígin 20 ma-na sík[i]	Total 20 minas of wool;
9)	x Ìr$^{?}$-e-za-am-^{d}[ ]	PN
10)	[La]gaš^{ki}-[ta$^{?}$]	from? Lagaš
11)	[*it*]-*ba-al*	carried away.
	(*1 or 2 lines destroyed*)	

This text, written in Akkadian, appears to be a two-year account (the current and the preceding years) of goods concerning various scribes.[117] In the extant portion, the text does not preserve the term that defines this relationship (presumably mu-túm or ì-na-sum). This was done by the official after the summaries and expressed by the term *it-ba-al*, indicating that the goods were brought from Lagaš.

L 5807 is a fragmentary text, a summary of which appears in ITT II "Liste de scribes pour un compte: Ur-^{d}Nin-dar; Lugal-a-ma-[ru]; Lugal-izi; Me-a-na-[ ]; Ur-ba-ba."[118]

AOTb 198

Obverse		Reverse	
1)	[x]	1)	[x]
2)	[dumu] Uš-di-nu	2)	[dumu] [x]
3)	GÌR	3)	[x].AN
4)	dumu Uru-nam-me	4)	dumu [x]
5)	Lú-šè-zi	5)	[x].AN.[x]-na
6)	dumu Ur-SI.A	6)	dumu [x]-x-[x]-x

117. Tir-kù is the only person mentioned concerning goods who is not accompanied by a title. This anthroponym is mentioned exclusively in L 4699, RTC 134, and CT 50, 172—all these references concern the visit of the royal family and their courtiers (cf. Foster, *JANES* 12 [1980]: 31–41). In L 3149 he is mentioned, with Šarru-ṭab, in connection to the delivery of livestock. The mention of these two officials could link L 3149 to the texts discussed in Foster, *JANES* 12 (1980). It would seem reasonable to suppose that the official mentioned in L 1095 (S6) and in the texts of Foster, *JANES* 12 (1980): 29–42 are the same person. Tir-kù, then, must have been a high-ranking official of the Crown, who was not necessarily resident in Girsu, but who could have come from Umma, where this anthroponym is frequently attested both in the Early and in the Classical Sargonic periods.

118. It is uncertain whether this document should be regarded as an administrative summary. It cannot be excluded, for reasons discussed below, that it is a school exercise.

7) Ur-giš
8) dumu Šu-da
9) Nam-maḫ-ni
10) dumu Da-<da>
11) Úr-ra-AN
12) dumu En-kù nagar
13) Ú-da
14) [dumu] [x].NE šitim
15) [Bar]-ra-AN
16) dumu Ur-ì-lí
17) Šeš-šeš
18) dumu Sipa-lú
19) Ur-[x]
20) dumu Ú-da
21) Ur-^{d}[ ]
22) [dumu] [ ]

7) Lugal-iti-da
8) dumu [x].x
9) [x]-x
10) [dumu] [x]
11) x-[x]
12) [dumu x]
13) [x]-da
14) dumu [x]
15) lú-[x]-da
16) lú-[x]-da
17) lú-[x]-ezen-[x]
18) KA.AN.[x]
19) dumu Lugal-ezen
20) A-tu dumu Ur-^{d}[ ]
21) x-x dumu [ ]
22) Lú-da-[x]
23) Ur-[ ]
24) [ ]
25) [ ]
26) [ ]

Left corner

šu-nígin 30 lá 1 dub-sar ugula Lú-^{d}Utu

These two texts and L 5807 indicate the importance and the role of scribes in the organizational system of the institution. If L 1095 and L 5807 demonstrate the activities of the scribes, AOTb 198, a unique text, reveals their organization into teams, headed by one or more ugula.[119] AOTb 198 lists 29 scribes, subordinates of Lú-^{d}Utu, a very high-ranking scribe, probably just below the dub-sar-maḫ. This document reveals the complexity and sophistication of the administration at Girsu. In fact, only administrations with such complexity, such as ED Šuruppak and Sargonic Girsu, need a hierarchical organizational system for scribes similar to that adopted for the guruš and the ugula.

119. The only exception is perhaps documented in the Fara texts, where an ugula dub-sar occurs. Texts have also been identified in which only a dub-sar occurs (EDATŠ 7; 8; 38–40).

Three officials, the énsi Lugal-ušum-gal and two dub-sar-lugal's, served a special function among the scribes mentioned in the Girsu documentation.

Lugal-ušum-gal, the énsi of Girsu to whom almost all the documentation under examination probably refer,[120] holds the titles dub-sar and énsi of Lagaš. He signs the copy of the List of Professions (ED Lu A), elegantly written on a six-sided clay prism,[121] ^{d}Nisaba Lugal-ušum-gal dub-sar éns[i] La[gaš^{ki}], "To the Goddess Nisaba Lugal-ušum-gal, the scribe, governor of Lagaš." In addition, he appears with this title in four clay bullae (RTC 165): ^{d}*Na-ra-am-*^{d}*Sin da-núm* DINGIR *A-kà-dè*^{ki} *šar ki-ib-ra-tim a*[*r*]*-ba-im* Lugal-ušum-gal dub-⌜sar⌝ énsi La[gaš^{ki}] "Narām-Sîn, the powerful one, God of Akkad, king of the four quarters, Lugal-ušum-gal the scribe, the énsi of Lagaš."[122] On the other hand, on RTC 162, an imprint of the seal of this governor during the reign of Šar-kali-šarrī makes no mention of the title of dub-sar, only that of énsi: *Šar-kà-lí-šar-rí da-núm šar A-kà-dè*^{ki} Lugal-ušum-gal énsi Lagaš^{ki} ìr-*sú*, "Šar-kali-šarrī, the powerful one, king of Akkad, Lugal-ušum-gal the énsi of Lagaš his servant."

The title dub-sar, which Lugal-ušum-gal uses, does not appear to be purely academic, as it seems to be in the case of some officials mentioned in the Ur III documentation.[123] If Lugal-ušum-gal is the author of the copy of ED Lu A, then we have here a scribe of the highest level with long experience in the art of writing. This means that Lugal-ušum-gal must have been one of the scribes of the é-gal before becoming énsi of Lagaš. It would not be surprising were he the dub-sar-maḫ or the nu-bànda of the é-gal in the administration of the preceding énsi. This, as well as the fact that the high-ranking

---

120. Lugal-ušum-gal is mentioned in about 50 texts in the archive; cf. Foster, *Inst. Land*, p. 18, n. 14.

121. Cf. W. Schileico, "Das sechsseitige Tonprisma Lugal-ušum-gal's aus der Sammlung Lichatschew," *ZA* 29 (1914): 78–84.

122. More recently RIM 2, p. 166; FAOS 7, pp. 42–43.

123. P. Michalowski, "Charisma and Control: Discontinuity and Change in Early Mesopotamian Bureaucratic Systems," in McGuire Gibson – R. Biggs, eds., *The Organization of Power*, SAOC 64 (Chicago, 1987), pp. 62ff.; see also W. W. Hallo, "The House of Ur-Meme," *JNES* 31 (1972): 87–95.

officials of the city administration, such as Lugal-giš and Lugal-èš governors of Adab, Me-ság administrator of a large estate, and Qinu-mupi énsi of Mugdan, and the great dignitaries of the empire, such as the šabra-é Šuaš-takal[124] and Iškun-Dagan[125] assume the title dub-sar, suggests that, at least in the Sargonic period, the governors of the Sumerian cities and the most important officials of the empire, for the most part, came from the category "scribe."[126]

Gal-zu-[ ] dub-sar-lugal occurs, in RTC 142 v II 4–5, as the person who, with the sa$_{12}$-du$_5$ Ur-^{d}Nin-gír-su, measured the lands.[127] There is no other reference to him.

Lugal-G[AR-x$^?$] dub-sar-l[ugal$^?$] is mentioned in L 1474 r. 1: "4 jars containing 10 sìla of oil, x jars containing 10 sìla of cow fat, 5 Akkad gur of cheese, Lugal-GAR.x$^?$, the royal? scribe brought to Akkad, (delivery from) Lugal-ušum-gal in (or énsi of) Lagaš."[128]

There is a group of scribes who, based upon title and context, was at the upper echelon of the category dub-sar.

The dub-sar-maḫ identified only by title is mentioned in texts of different typologies. He occurs in three documents concerning sheep:

---

124. Cf. Scheil, MDP 6, p. 6; RIM 2, pp. 164–65.

125. RIM 2, p. 198.

126. On this subject, cf. also Wu Yuhong, "High-Ranking 'Scribes' and Intellectual Governors during the Akkadian and Ur III Periods," *JAC* 10 (1995): 127–28. But this practice could have existed already in Pre-Sargonic times. At ED Girsu, Enentarzi, before his ascent to the throne, was sanga of Ningirsu. Besides, it is possible that Mes-e dub-sar-maḫ of Umma at the time of Lugalzagesi énsi, subsequently became the énsi.

127. A restoration gal-zu-[di-k]u$_5$ (suggestion by Glassner), an anthroponym known elsewhere, is possible.

128. [1+]3 dug 10 sìla ì-nun [ ] [d]ug 10 sìla ì-áb 5 ga-ḫar ⸢gur⸣ *A-kà-dè*^{ki} Lugal-G[ar-x] dub-sar-l[ugal$^?$] *A-kà-dè*^{ki}-šè ì-túm Lugal-ušum-gal Lagaš^{ki}.

In RTC 134 r. I 11', a document discussed in Foster, *JANES* 12 (1980), a certain Lugal-GAR is the recipient of a barley-fed kid. He also occurs with the title KA-gur$_7$ in CT 50, 187 o. 4–5, in which he received 60 gur of barley. It should be observed that this official immediately follows the šabra-é in the list of recipients. The latter official received 600 gur. The other recipients received much more modest amounts. Lugal-GAR also occurs in a texts from the Girsu region; cf. Foster, "Scattered Sargonic Texts," *VO* 6 (1986): no. 16, "record of the production of strands for basket making?"

L 1074 is a record of rams (that are to be) allocated to the sanga of ^{d}Nin-gír-su, ^{d}Nin-mar-ki, ^{d}Nin-dar-a, úru, É-bar$_6$-bar$_6$^{ki}, to the dub-sar-maḫ, and to the sa$_{12}$-du$_5$. The animals had not yet been handed over as can be seen from the clause following the summary: udu-ni[ga] [x] Lugal-KA nu-ta-è, "sheep fattened on barley which Lugal-KA has not yet out gone."[129]

L 3032 is an account of sheep, the contribution$^{?}$ (of/for) the dub-sar-maḫ, Lugal-bur, Da-ti, and Šu-na.

L 4375 is a record of an expenditure of sheep, a contribution for the goddess Baba, for the é-muḫaldim and Uruk, where the dub-sar-maḫ is the supervisor maškim of the transaction. He occurs, also, in a small document concerning cattle AOTb 306 f 3, 4 anše-libir-AL 3 anše-nita-AL dub-sar-maḫ mu-DU.DU (*blank*) [a]-rá–1-kam, "4 old donkeys, 3 male donkeys which the dub-sar-maḫ delivered, for the first time."

In L 5874; RTC 126 o. I 2'; AOTb 237 o. I 9'; 238 o. I 2' he is the recipient of bread and other goods[130]; in AOTb 247 o. I 2; r. I 6 of 2 he receives barley; in RTC 137 o. II 2 he receives a plot of land, perhaps to be cultivated for barley.[131]

He also occurs in L 1476, a record of 1,330 gur-sag-gál of barley and 55 shekels of silver (handed over? to the) dub-sar-maḫ, Lugal-bur and Šeš-šeš, probably two other scribes; in AOTb 249 o. I 2 he is in debt

---

129. The anthroponym Lugal-KA occurs frequently in the documentation as ga'eš, "trading river agent," in L 2952 o. II' 1'; L 4436; L 4512; 4461; RTC 78; 91; as má-laḫ$_4$, "sailor," in L 2917. Without any title, Lugal-KA occurs in L 1135 (S11); 1176 (S20); 1363; 3136; 3153; 4380; 5793; 5824; CT 50 98. In L 1176 (S20) r. 7 he seems to have at his disposal a large tract of agricultural land, aša$_5$-gu$_4$, which was distributed to other officials. Foster, *Inst. Land,* p. 43, proposes to identify this Lugal-KA with the namesake official mentioned in a letter with Ur-nu sanga (in L 1150 sanga ^{d}Nanše). It seems probable that he is a high-ranking official even if we cannot identify his profession. A namesake official is recorded in a text coming from Lagaš, perhaps a flour account (see R. Biggs, *Inscriptions from al-Hiba-Lagaš,* BiMes 3 (Malibu, 1976), n. 25: Lú-ba nu-bànda Lugal-KA u$_4$-zal-la-ke$_4$ *A-kà-dè*^{ki}-[šè?] ì-[DU], "goods in charge to Luba nu-bànda which Lugal-KA delivered to Akkad$^{?}$."

130. In RTC 126 I 2' he occurs at the head of a list of officials, among whom are several scribes.

131. Among the recipients in RTC 137 is the énsi-gal, the sukkal-maḫ, the sagi-maḫ.

regarding the administration of barley[132]; in L 5894 (S169) o. I' 2', a fragment of a list of silver paid as "court cost or bailiff's fees"[133]; in L 3152; 4447; 4701; 6750; 9442[134]; and in L 1405 o. 5, a list of witnesses.[135] From these references it is evident that all the administration's business had to pass through this official or his delegates, such as the énsi-gal and the ugula dub-sar.

In some cases, the dub-sar-maḫ is indicated not only by his title but also by name.

[x]-áš-ba-ak dub-sar-maḫ occurs in AOTb 184 o. I 6–7. This text is a fragmentary summary of dispersed or fugitive people (lú-zàḫ) under the responsibility of various officials, among whom is our dub-sar-maḫ, the dub-sar Lú-^{d}Utu, and another unnamed dub-sar. The people are of the category guruš, géme, dumu-nita, and géme-nam-ra-ak. The absence of any other reference, the etymology of his name, which unfortunately has been damaged, and the connection with the géme-nam-ra-ak, indicate he was not a dub-sar-maḫ from Girsu, but a foreign official present in Girsu for a special occasion.[136]

Lú-sa$_6$ dub-sar-maḫ is mentioned in CT 50, 123, 5. The text records (the enrolment of) "18 slaves belonging to En-ni, the sanga, to work (on behalf) of Lú-sa$_6$(g), the head of the scribes, (to) Lagaš, Warad-su-ni, the gala, brought."[137] In L 4590, a fragmentary text concern-

---

132. The text is a barley summary, probably to be paid by the holders of lands belonging to the administration for the current and for the preceding years, im-ma-kam, mu-a-kam. Deductions have been made as indicated by the clause after the summary: lá-NI-am$_6$ zi-zi-ga-bi íb-ta-zi.

133. For the bailiff's fee, nì-nam-maškim, and the other texts of this typology in the Girsu archive, cf. B. R. Foster, "Notes on Sargonic Legal and Juridical Procedures," *WO* 13 (1982): 21–24.

134. L 3152 is a school exercise transliterated and discussed in Foster, *ArOr* 50 (1982): 240. L 4477 is a fragmentary list of officials: dub-sar-maḫ, šu-i, gù-dè-a, Lú-ba, and Šeš-šeš. L 6750 records the allocation of ì-du$_{10}$-ga for the dub-sar-maḫ, the sa$_{12}$-du$_5$, and other officials. L 9442 records an expenditure of the dub-sar-maḫ in connection with a transaction concerning Ama-ar-gi$_4$-gar-ra.

135. Cf. Foster, *WO* 13 (1982): 15.

136. Names ending in -ba-ak occur elsewhere as officials of Elam or Susa.

137. 18 sag šu-ut en-ni sanga lú-sa$_6$ dub-sar-maḫ lagaš^{ki} á-ru warad-su-ni šu-gal$_5$-lá^{um}-e mu-túm. USP, p. 99 considers á-ru as the Akkadian verbal form *it-ru* from *waṭāru,*

ing personnel who were to live and reside with various officials,[138] he occurs only with the title dub-sar-maḫ. Also, the sequence in L 4590: Lú-sa$_6$ dub-sar-maḫ Šeš-šeš énsi-gal, compared with similar sequences in L 4701: dub-sar-maḫ, Šeš-šeš énsi-gal; L 4477: dub-sar-maḫ, šu-i, Gù-dé-a, Šeš-šeš énsi-gal; L 1476: dub-sar-maḫ, Lugal-bur, Šeš-šeš suggests that this unnamed leader of the scribes was Lú-sa$_6$. Quite possibly the dub-sar-maḫ who occurs without name in the majority of cases was Lú-sa$_6$.

Šeš-šeš dub-sar-ma[ḫ] is mentioned in RTC 142 II 1–2 as the recipient of several tracts of agricultural land. The recipients are described, after the mention of the third plot, as apin-lá-e íb-uru$_4$.[139] The text concludes with the notation: aša$_5$ ù dùg-ku$_4$ Ur-^{d}Nin-gír-su sa$_{12}$-du$_5$ gal-zu-[x$^?$] dub-sar-lugal-bi mu-gíd-éš. Our dub-sar-maḫ also occurs in the Post-Sargonic text, L 7333 (MVN 6, 319) r. I 3–4, a document like the preceding one, concerning plots of apin-lá íb-uru$_4$ land. In this text, Šeš-šeš dub-sar-maḫ is the official who, with Ur-sa$_6$ lú-éš-gíd-bi inim-bí-gar-éš, “released a declaration”$^?$[140]; the lands are described as aša$_5$ šuku-énsi.[141]

“to take away,” and translates the text “18 slaves belonging to Enni, the sanga, were taken to Lagaš by the dub-sar-maḫ, Waradsuni, the galla, delivered them (mu-túm).” En-ni without title occurs only in RTC 125 I 14, as the recipient of loaves of bread. Warassuni the galla does not occur elsewhere. The profession *šu-gal$_5$-lá-um* is discussed in USP, pp. 99; 112.

138. [ ] giš-a ib-ta-ti-e-éš Lú-sa$_6$ dub-sar-maḫ Šeš-šeš énsi-gal Ur-^{d}Nin-gubla$_x$ enku$_x$(zà) ab-tuš. Formulae similar to ib-ta-ti-e-éš occur in RTC 97: ì-da-ti; in L 1100 PN$_1$ PN$_2$ an-da-ti GN^{ki} ab-tuš. Cf. Foster, *Management*, p. 26. This subject will be discussed by G. R. Magid, “Micromanagement in the Queen’s Household: Notes on the Organization of the Labor at ED Lagash,” to appear in XLVe CRRAI (Harvard, 1998).

139. This clause is translated as “the lessee(s) cultivated (it)” in Foster, *Inst. Land*, p. 40. Foster includes the different interpretations of A. Deimel, G. Pettinato, and K. Maekawa.

140. For a discussion of this formula, cf. Foster, *Inst. Land*, p. 39.

141. RTC 181—a very fragmentary text from the time of the énsi Puzur$_4$-Ma-ma, recording the allocation of plots of land—contains similar subscriptions, gu$_4$-e íb-uru$_4$ and apin-lá íb-uru$_4$; cf. Foster, *Inst. Land*, p. 40.

This anthroponym occurs frequently and there are references to a namesake énsi-gal.[142] Šeš-šeš énsi-gal occurs in L 4701, a record of dead or fugitive slaves belonging to the dub-sar-maḫ's of two localities, to Šeš-šeš the énsi-gal, to the sa$_{12}$-du$_{5}$, and to Ur-nu sanga.[143] He also occurs in L 4590, a fragment concerning personnel allocated to Lú-sa$_{6}$(g) dub-sar-maḫ, Šeš-šeš énsi-gal, Ur-^{d}Nin-gubla$_{x}$ enku. Probably the untitled Šeš-šeš mentioned with a dub-sar-maḫ and Lugal-bur in L 1476, a barley and silver summary, is the namesake énsi-gal. In addition, our énsi-gal is mentioned in L 4489, a barley summary concerning various officials; in L 4514, a summary of cattle for high-ranking officials; and in a list of officials, L 6680.1, where Šeš-šeš énsi-gal occurs in the first position.[144]

Šeš-šeš without title occurs again with Lugal-bur in L 4421 (S118) o. 2, a record of two plots of land cultivated with sesame; and in L 4443, an account of sheep delivered by Ur-gi dam-gàr to Šeš-šeš, Lugal-bur, and Ur-sa$_{6}$.[145]

In L 3027, personnel belonging to Šeš-šeš and Ur-^{d}Ištaran are mentioned (lú Šeš-šeš lú Ur-^{d}Ištaran) concerning deliveries of sheep (L 2843 is a similar text). He is further mentioned in L 4401 (S116)

142. The earliest reference to this profession, whose meaning is uncertain, appears to be from ED II Ur (UET 2, 35 II 1). It is distinct from PA SI Urí^{ki}, which occurs in the same text. In the Fara texts, énsi-gal is an abbreviated form of énsi-gar-gal, the highest political authority in the city (cf. EDATŠ, pp. 17–19). It also occurs in ED IIIb Girsu texts in reference to a certain Amar-ezen (AO 4348 r. I 2–3, in NFT, p. 182) and in the Early Sargonic texts from Umma in reference to the scribe Ad-da, (cf. *supra*, p. 93). An unnamed énsi-gal occurs in the Sargonic documentation of Adab.

143. After the summary, these slaves are described as sag nu-mu-DU, "slaves who are not resident (gub)" or "who have not come (gín)"; cf. also ITT II, p. 39, "tous absents," nu-mu-gub. As similar clause appears also in L 1295, guruš nu-mu-DU. Because of its contents, L 4701 could be linked to three other worker lists: L 4616, CT 50, 107, and 108. Foster, USP, p. 65, translates nu-mu-DU, which occurs in L 3081—a similar lá-NI account of workers—as "not on duty/produced." One could compare nu-mu-DU to the opposite term in a list of guruš, L 1213, lú-gub-ba-me, and also in A 822 (OIP 14, 104) o. 2'–3', 34 an[še] [ ] gub-ba-[me].

144. Cf. L 4477 lists the dub-sar-maḫ, šu-i, Gú-dè-a, Šeš-šeš.

145. Ur-sa$_{6}$ probably is the namesake lú-éš-gíd mentioned in L 7333 (MVN 6, 319).

o. 2 as the official who makes a contribution in silver; in L 4667 (S143) o. I 7, a list of recipients of land plots[146]; in L 5676 (S152) o. 2, a very small tablet that records 350 sar of land for Šeš-šeš; and in CT 50, 100.1, in which he is recorded as having been in charge of guards (en-nu). In CT 50, 107 o. 5, Šeš-šeš ugula is charge of one guruš.

As Foster has observed,[147] L 7333 is similar to RTC 142. Because of the mention of a dub-sar-lugal in the latter, it should be dated in the Sargonic period, whereas L 7333 belongs to the Post-Sargonic period. Because of the contemporaneous mention of sa$_{12}$-du$_5$ Ur-^{d}Nin-gír-su in RTC 142 and RTC 181, these texts are very close chronologically. If we accept that the énsi-gal who frequently occurs after the dub-sar-maḫ or with officials who can be recognized as scribes must himself be a high-ranking scribe, possibly Šeš-šeš was the énsi-gal of the administration during the time Lugal-ušum-gal was énsi and at the end of the latter's reign or at the beginning of that of Puzur$_4$-Ma-ma, he became dub-sar-maḫ, probably in place of Lú-sa$_6$.

Lú-^{d}Utu ugula-dub-sar is certainly the highest-ranking scribe after the dub-sar-maḫ and perhaps the énsi-gal. He is mentioned with this title in AOTb 198, which lists 29 subordinate dub-sar's, identified by their patronymic. With only the title dub-sar, he occurs in L 3011, a receipt of fish. The tablet is signed by Lú-zàḫ kurušda and Lú-^{d}Utu dub-sar. They are the officials who supervise, probably on behalf of the é-gal, and compile the records of the receipt of goods. In CT 50, 158 r. 4–6 Lú-^{d}Utu is the official who, with Lú-zàḫ, gave sesame that had been received from Ur-pù and Lagaš.[148] In L 4673 (S144) Lú-^{d}Utu occurs twice; in r. 3 he is the recipient of a plot of aša$_5$-SUD land at 5 gur[149] and in r. 7 he is the official who, with Ur-^{d}Nin-gír-su sa$_{12}$-

146. Cf. Foster, *Inst. Land*, pp. 24–25.

147. Foster, *Inst. Land*, pp. 39–40.

148. The operation is indicated by the clause é-kišib-ba ùr-ra-ta PN$_1$ PN$_2$-bi ì-ne-sum. For this obscure clause, cf. *infra*, sub Lú-zàḫ.

149. For the meaning of the indications of barley that in some cases follow allocated land, and for the particular type of field to which texts of this type refer, cf. Foster, *Inst. Land*, pp. 23; 39–41.

du$_5$, measured the fields.[150] The lands are described as aša$_5$ šuku àga-uš, a notation similar to that of L 1135 (S11) and probably with the same meaning.[151] In RTC 134 r. II 9–10,[152] Lú-^{d}Utu is the official who delivered the gifts for the king and his entourage to Akkad, Lú-^{d}Utu dub-sar-e *A-kà-dè*^{ki}-šè mu-DU. Perhaps Lú-^{d}Utu was the official, whose anthroponym is partially lost, who delivers barley for Akkad in L 1076, [l]ú-[x] *A-kà-dè*^{ki}-[šè] mu-D[U] Lugal-ušum-gal Lagaš^{ki}. He is one of the witnesses in RTC 81 r. 2, a slave sale contract. Possibly he is the scribe mentioned in L 5893, whose name is partially lost, Lú-^{d}[x] dub-sar-me—this fragmentary text is written in Akkadian in an elegant chancery style.[153] Foster interprets it as an important land transaction[154]; the contracting parties are Šar-kali-šarrī (r. I' 5'–6') and a group of important officials from the Lagaš region, described as *be-lí pár-sà-ti* Lagaš^{ki}, "allotment holders from Lagaš(?)." Among them is a scribe, perhaps the sa$_{12}$-du$_5$ Ur-[^{d}Nin-gír-su?], and the sanga of Nanše, of Ninkimara, of the é-UD.UD, and perhaps the scribes Túl-ta and Lú-^{d}Utu (Túl$^{?}$-[ta] Lú-[^{d}Utu] dub-sar-me). These lands, purchased by the Crown, may have been granted in usufruct to royal officials. Because of its content, Foster has compared it to the inscription on the Maništusu obelisk. Lú-^{d}Utu occurs in AOTb 184 o. I 9 as the person in charge of the Lú-zàḫ personnel.

In many other documents Lú-^{d}Utu appears without title. But, on the basis of content, they all refer to our scribe.

Lú-^{d}Utu occurs as a bailiff (maškim) in L 4457 v. 2–3 in connection with a contribution of goods (perhaps barley) made by Me-ság,

---

150. This sa$_{12}$-du$_5$, in addition to L 4673, occurs in texts dated to Lugal-ušum-gal (L 4553 [S128]; 4695 [S149]; 6692; RTC 142) and one text from the period of Puzur$_4$-Ma-ma énsi (RTC 181).

151. The tablet contains many erasures and is crossed by two transverse lines. This could mean that it was a provisional record on which corrections were made and that probably had to be rewritten. Perhaps it was a school practice tablet (cf. Foster, *ArOr* 50 [1982]: 239).

152. Foster, *JANES* 12 (1980): 29–42.

153. Collated by Foster, *Inst. Land,* p. 31.

154. *Ibidem,* pp. 30–31.

the sagi-maḫ, which Ur-DU received on behalf of Akkad. In L 4548 (S127) 7' he is mentioned with Da-ti[155]; and in L 3050 with Me-ság in connection with the expenditure of urudu-kin. Lú-^{d}Utu is the official who incurred the expenditure in L 1113 and L 1357[156] and is the maškim in L 9281, an account of flour.

He also occurs in other types of texts: L 1283 (S40) r. 2 records wool belonging to Engar-zi, received by Lú-^{d}Utu; L 4562 (S129) r. 4 records bronze received by Lú-^{d}Utu and Lú-zàḫ[157]; in L 2856 and L 4375 Lú-^{d}Utu is mentioned with other officials concerning offerings of sheep; in L 1374 o. II 1 he is the recipient of a plot of 136 sar of land probably cultivated as a garden; probably the official, [Lú?]-^{d}Utu-ke$_4$, who delivered the brick molds for the account of the é-ki-gim in L 4679 (S146) r. 10' is our scribe; in L 1350, a list of guruš (^{d}En-líl-lá dumu Lú-^{d}Utu); in L 4551, a list of people (ìr, dumu-nita, dumu-mí, dumu-ga) in the charge of Ur-ba-gára, Ab-ba ì-du$_8$, and Lú-^{d}Utu; in RTC 139 o. 7, a record of work on canals. L 6753 is a letter from Ur-^{d}Nin-[ ] to Lú-^{d}Utu about a bailiff's fee.[158] The wife of Lú-^{d}Utu is mentioned in L 5817 v 11' as the recipient of golden objects.

Lú-^{d}Utu's high rank is clear from the activity witnessed in RTC 134 and L 4673. The fact that the texts in which he is mentioned are of quite varied typologies indicates that he has a direct supervisory function ranging across different sectors of the administration.

Lú-bàn-da dub-sar is mentioned with this title as a witness in two contracts, L 1040 o. 12–13 and RTC 81 o. 16. Both contracts record the purchase of a slave by the énsi, Lugal-ušum-gal, from two different vendors. Amar-kun sukkal and Bar-ra-AN dub-sar dumu Lú-šu-

---

155. L 4548 (S127) records two groups of allocations of lard; in the former, Lú-^{d}Utu is the maškim and in the latter Da-ti is the maškim— the recipients are of the highest rank, including Eṭib-Mer.

156. L 1113 (S12) records the receipt by Da-ba-ba muḫaldim of various spices and legumes, and written along its edge is: zi-ga Lú-^{d}Utu. L 1357 (S47) r. 2–3 concerns the allocation of ì-du$_{10}$-ga and ì-giš to three officials (Šeš$_4$-da-NI nu-bànda, the ugula of the šeš-gal, and Se$_{11}$-na) zi-ga Lú-^{d}Utu.

157. These two officials are also mentioned together in L 3011 and CT 50, 158.

158. See FAOS 19, pp. 109–10.

maḫ are also witnesses in both documents.[159] This official appears untitled in L 2917 o. 4–5 as the supervisor of the purchase of two slaves for which the bailiff's fee is paid.[160] In L 1368 (S49) r. 4–5 Lú-bàn-da dub-sar is the official who weighed the textiles and the wool delivered by the šabra Ur-mes. In L 1429 (S60) r. 7–8 in the é-gal he receives reed bundles and wooden objects (é-gal-la Lú-bàn-da dub-sar šu-ba-ti), a contribution from Ur-ba.[161] The first entry of L 1429 o. 1–2 (5 giš-ùr Ur-ki) is recorded also in L 4420 (5 giš-ùr Ur-ki mu-túm Lú-bàn-da dub-sar šu-ba-ti). He occurs in L 2915, described in ITT II. p. 6 summary as "listes de passagers? avec le nom du batelier: ni-na-e; Lú-bàn-da le scribe...ad-da etan le batelier." He occurs in AOTb 30 r. II 2, a personnel text where the scribe Lú-bàn-da seems to be in charge of a group of subordinates. AOTb 71 r. II 21–22 is a record of plots of agricultural land given in leasehold in which Lú-bàn-da is one of the lessees.[162] A household headed by Lú-bàn-da dub-sar is mentioned in RTC 92 o. II' 5' (and perhaps in the similar text, L 5885 o. I' 5'). This fragmentary text might be a record of the transfer of personnel (šul ugula Nina^{ki} bar é-Lú-bàn-da dub-sar ri-ri-ga-ka). But whatever the interpretation of the text is, the existence of such a household in the context of the palace administration indicates that Lú-bàn-da must have been a very high-ranking scribe, perhaps an ugula dub-sar like Lú-^{d}Utu.[163]

---

159. The last lines of the obverse and, with the exception of two lines, all those of the reverse of L 1040, where other witnesses were listed, are destroyed. Possibly many of them corresponded to those of RTC 81.

160. See Foster, *WO* 13 (1982): 21–22.

161. Ur-ba, who makes three different contributions, is an ugula; Ur-ki and En-uru-na are ugula or nu-bànda.

162. In this text, barley and sheep seem to be associated with each plot, perhaps as rent to the administration. Besides Lú-bàn-da, there is another scribe who is a lessee but whose name is lost. A third scribe is mentioned after the summary: [x] dub-sar [x] gíd-éš. It would not be surprising if this latter scribe were Lú-^{d}Utu. Possibly this text should be linked to RTC 142 and MVN 6, 319, discussed by Foster, *Inst. Land*, p. 39.

163. The ugula Lú-bàn-da is mentioned in L 1280; 2904; 2917; 5802; 9363: RTC 91; 93. The untitled official in L 5850 and CT 50, 95.7 may be the latter ugula.
A certain Lú-bàn-da ì-rá-rá in L 1330 o. 3 (S45) is the official with one subordinate (lú Lú-bàn-da ì-rá-rá), who contributes spices and herbs. He also occurs

Possibly this scribe is the namesake official without title who in L 2882 receives fish brought$^{?}$ from the boat of Šul-^{d}Ab-ba$_6$. If so, we have to add the references to this man in L 4446 r. 1 and L 5748, which deal with fish.

Túl-ta dub-sar is mentioned in L 3050 o. 2. In this document Túl-ta dub-sar and Lú-zàḫ ìr šu-i are mentioned in connection with wrought copper brought from Girsu by Šu-i-GA-[x]. Lú-^{d}Utu and Me-ság are the maškim's of the expenditure. He is also mentioned in CT 50, 98 r. I 6, which probably records a transfer or exchange of personnel.[164] In CT 50, 124 o. 2 Túl-ta dub-sar makes a delivery (mu-túm) of goods.[165] Túl-ta occurs in PUL 6 r. 2, a record of six measures of barley due as arrears (lá-NI) by six individuals that is about to be paid in Girsu (as can be seen from the subscription, še Gír-su^{ki}-a è-è-dam).[166] This document assures us that the scribe Túl-ta is one of the officials who has plots of agricultural land in usufruct from the administration. With the title of agrig, he is mentioned in RTC 96 r. III 4, a long text similar to CT 50, 98. He is mentioned in L 1114 o. 7' ([Túl]-ta dub[sar]), a tablet—damaged both in its

---

in L 5889, a summary of plots of land, some of which are burdened with a tax called máš-kù, "rent (of) silver" (cf. Foster, *Inst. Land*, p. 26); here, he is the recipient of a plot of land with rations of four gur of barley. The meaning of these indications of barley is still not clear in spite of considerable discussion, Foster, *Inst. Land*, p. 41, "I surmise, but cannot of course demonstrate, that some of these grain figures were schematized as a means of determining in advance rents or accountable yield and could thereby point to a 'future' or 'guaranteed income' on certain small, carefully accounted plots, accruing to the holder or the user."

164. CT 50, 98 r. I 6, is a damaged personnel list, identified by the sequence PN$_1$ dumu / ìr / šeš PN$_2$ ugula / ki PN$_3$ (PN$_1$ son or servant or brother of PN$_2$ in the place / from PN$_3$). The sequence in our case is Ur-^{d}Ištaran dumu Íl-me ki Túl-ta dub-sar.

165. The text is sealed on the reverse by En-ki-ág, an official who occurs without title in L 2954; 3030; 3095; 5832; 5839; 6681; RTC 125.

166. The term lá-NI is written only concerning the amount of barley owed by Lugal-gír-nun-né (2–3): lá-NI 30 lá 1 (b) še-gur. But it appears probable that the reason behind these amounts of barley owed (Gír-su^{ki}-a è-è-dam) by the same recipient is identical. For the term è-è-dam as "forthcoming," see USP, pp. 92–93.

upper and lower parts—listing a series of names, of which only 8 survive, not preceded by any numeral.[167]

Túl-ta occurs without title in L 1189 o. 3; 1201 o. 4; 1262 o. 4; 3008; 4406; and 5733 as recipient of sá-du$_{11}$. In L 1176 o. 3 (S20) he is the recipient of a plot of 1 bur of aša$_5$-gu$_4$; in L 4606 (S135) o. 3 the recipient of a tract of land with grain rations; in L 5824 (S163), 6 the recipient of 6 bur of aša$_5$ ki-duru$_5$; in CT 50, 182 o. 11 he is mentioned in connection with a plot of 2 iku of aša$_5$-g[u$_4^{?}$] on which arrears have to be paid which are still in the hands of the engar (lá-NI aša$_5$-g[u$_4^{?}$] *šu* engar-engar).[168] Túl-ta also occurs without title in oil and cattle texts: L 2912 (S77) r. 6'[169]; and in CT 50, 51 o. 8, a record of lard contained in 4 sìla jars, which are probably the contributions of the officials mentioned and are destined for the king.[170] He is mentioned in L 2869, a record of sheep; in RTC 136 o. II 8', a record of cattle probably belonging to Lugal-ušum-gal and managed by various officials; in CT 50, 167 r. 6 in connection with a number of unshorn sheep (udu nu-ur$_4$-ra-a). A certain Túl-ta dumu Igi-su$_4$ occurs as recipient in L 5848 o. I 4'–5', a record of the distribution of wool.[171] In L 2936 (S82) r. 4 he is the recipient of items, includ-

167. The list concludes perhaps with a professional name, [luga]l$^{?}$, with a summary and a clause that would indicate that this text was a summary of fattened sheep owed as arrears by di-ku$_5$ (PN?), followed by a unique year formula (cf. FAOS 7, p. 55): Ur-[x] Ur-^{d}En-líl Ur-^{d}En-ki Ur-èn Ur-gi-ni ta.še.mar$^{?}$ [Túl$^{?}$]-ta dub-sar Ur-^{d}N[in$^{?}$] [ ] [PN] [luga]l$^{?}$ udu-še di-ku$_5$-ka lá-NI-am$_6$ mu lugal Sar-kà-lí-šar-rí MUNUS?.TUKU? é-^{d}En-líl-ke$_4$ ì-DU. The peculiarities in the compilation of this text, the absence of numerical indicators, and other particulars suggest that this text was a school exercise.

168. Three of the engar's (Lugal-gír-nun-né, Íl, and Túl-ta) mentioned in PUL 4 occur in this text. Consequently, it appears that CT 50, 182 probably is a stage of the previous recording of PUL 4.

169. Probably a school text; cf. *infra*, p. 145.

170. In CT 50, 51, after the summary, the destination of the oil is indicated: ì-šaḫ Lugal-ra *a-na* ká-^{d}En-ki *in* mu ^{d}En-líl ^{d}*Šar-kà-lí-šar-rí* su x.ŠU$^{?}$.AB$^{?}$.x-su [ ], "lard for the king through the gateway of Enki in the year when to Enlil Šar-kali-šarrī his...." (cf. FAOS 7, p. 56).

171. On the edge of the tablet is recorded [ ] nu-⸢x⸣-[ ], perhaps to be restored: [udu] nu-⸢ur$_4$⸣-[ra]—the same clause as in CT 50, 167. Thus, this latter text should be regarded not as a record of sheep but as a wool distribution record.

ing silver,[172] bread, and ninda-sag; he is the recipient of various kinds of bread in L 5868. It seems probable that the untitled official who appears in these texts could, in some cases, be linked with the namesake scribe.[173] The wife of Túl-ta occurs in a juridical text, L 9313 o. 2.[174]

UŠ dub-sar and Lú-^{d}Utu are the two scribes most frequently mentioned. UŠ occurs in texts concerning such commodities as oil, cattle, barley, and copper. In L 1380 (S52) o. 3, he is involved with ì-giš and lard, which Bar-ra-AN had received from UŠ dub-sar. In L 2912 (S77) o. 7'; 10', perhaps a school document, in which UŠ is linked to a record of oil for the current and past years—but the recipient is missing.[175] L 4625 is a summary of oxen and asses in the charge of various officials and signed by UŠ dub-sar. In RTC 136 r. I 10' he is one of the officials in charge of one- and two-year-old cows. The text concludes with the mention of Lugal-ušum-gal énsi and with the date: mu KAS.ŠUDUN Unug^{ki}-a Nag-su^{ki}-a ba-gar-ra-a.[176] RTC 120 r. 6, is an account of barley (allocated) to persons perhaps connected with cult activities, which UŠ dub-sar received from the Lugal-un-ge$_{26}$ (perhaps the namesake dub-sar).[177] DCS 4, 36 o. 4, is

---

172. The text records clothes, barley, oil, silver, gur$_{11}$, de$_6$-de$_6$-ga, and other goods received by various officials (cf. STTI p. 3).

173. A certain Túl-ta also occurs with the title gala-maḫ in L 5901 (S170) r. I' 2 and with the title gudu$_4$ in CT 50, 108 o. 8. Finally, a certain Túl-ta occurs in RTC 96 r. II 7, a record of personnel similar to RTC 92.

174. See Foster, *WO* 13 (1982): 23.

175. Cf. *supra*, p. 144 no. 169.

176. This dating formula occurs also in L 1196; RTC 99; 176; and CT 50, 4, translated in FAOS 7, p. 57: "im Jahre, nach dem der kampf gegen Uruk in Nagsu ausgetragen wurde." It should be related to a similar year date of Šar-kali-šarrī: mu KAS.ŠUDUN Gu-ti-um ba-gar-ra-a, which occurs in L 1048; 1052; 1053; RTC 88; and *RA* 4 (1897): pl. V n.15 (cf. FAOS 7, p. 57).

177. Among the recipients are various persons from other places: Uruk, Adab, and Susa: 20 gur sá-d[u$_{11}$] dumu Lugal-šu-ma[ḫ], 10 Lugal-lú išib ^{d}Inanna, 10 gudu$_4$ é-^{d}Utu, 2 (gur) 2(bariga) šeg$_{12}$-kù nar, lú-Unug^{ki}-me, 10 ^{d}Nin-šubur, 5 išib ^{d}Nin-šubur, lú- Adab^{ki}-me, 15 Mùš-me Šušina^{ki}. The mention of the priest (gudu$_4$) of the temple of Utu, of the cantors from Uruk, and of the išib of Ninšubur coming from Adab suggests that these people were connected with cult activities and had come to Girsu for some particular event.

a record of barley that UŠ dub-sar delivered to the é-kéš.DU.[178] L 3129 (S106) o. 4 is a record of three large bronze objects for which UŠ dub-sar was responsible.[179] L 4417 r. 4 is an account of onions[180] extracted in one year from an allotment of 6 iku of the aša$_5$-kurušda delivered by UŠ dub-sar.[181] Along with other officials, he is the recipient in L 4584 of beer of the highest quality and dida-beverages. He occurs in L 9365 (S178) o. I 2', a fragment concerning plots of land for the sustenance of the staff of the énsi are listed. UŠ dub-sar is mentioned in CT 50, 100 o. 6, a list of guards in the charge of different officials[182] and in AOTb 258.

A namesake kurušda is mentioned in three cattle texts: L 1291, records that UŠ kurušda took into his charge a young heifer (belonging to) Lugal-ušum-gal[183]; L 4697 is a summary account of sheep (rams and kids) and cattle (oxen and heifers) for maš-da-ri-a, which

---

178. é-kéš.DU occurs only in L 5721: 4 kúš anše kúš é-kéš.DU-ta è-a-àm mu-túm, "four donkey hides, hides that have come from é-kéš.DU, delivered." It is difficult to establish whether é-kéš.DU is a place or a PN, but the former appears more likely.

179. Part (šà-bi-ta) can be found with a person whose name is lost and the rest with a certain KA-zi (ì-da-gál).

180. 30 gú sag-sum and 47 sum-uš. The term gú, in this case, may not mean "talent" but rather "recipient"; cf. OSP 2, p. 90. For the meaning of sag-sum and sum-ús, cf. H.Waetzoldt, "Knoblauch und Zwiebeln nach den Texten des 3 Jt," *BSA* 3 (1987): 29.

181. a-šà-bi 6 iku aša$_5$-kurušda sum ba-al-la mu-a UŠ dub-sar mu-túm. For the meanings of ba-al, "graben, ausgraben," cf. H. Waetzoldt, *BSA* 3 (1987): 23.

182. 24 Šeš-šeš 24 Lugal-bur 32 Ur-^{d}Nin-mar-ki 51 Amar-šùba 54 Šeš$_4$-da-ni 23 UŠ dub-sar šu-nígin 248 en-nu. Similar texts are L 1065; 4507; 5829; 5837; CT 50, 99 (cf. Foster, *Management*, p. 26). It should observed that at least four of the officials mentioned here occur elsewhere as scribes.

183. 1 amar-gir UŠ kurušda šu Lugal-ušum-gal énsi Lagaš^{ki} šu-du$_8$. Foster, *ZA* 72 (1982): 17, although translating "1 calf (to) PN$_1$ the fattener, (property) of PN$_2$ ensi of Lagaš, (a) pledge," does not exclude the possibility that the term šu-du$_8$ could stand for Akkadian *ilqa*. The term šu-du$_8$ occurs several times in the Sargonic texts in connection with cattle: MAD 1, 152; MAD 5, 25, 26; and F. Rashid, *The Ancient Inscriptions in Himrin Area*, Himrin 4 (Baghdad, 1981), A8 r. 16. For the meaning of šu-dù/du$_8$-a as "pledge" when referring to persons, as opposed to the meaning "to take possession" when referring to objects and animals, cf. TLAT, p. 108.

UŠ kurušda distributed (ì-da-gar); and L 5785 is a summary account of cattle and barley signed by UŠ kurušda. An unnamed kurušda, who probably is UŠ, occurs both in L 1104 r. 6; 10, a summary account of sheep brought by the kurušda and taken in charge by Ur-^{a}aza$_{x}^{za}$[184] when the énsi came from Akkad, and deducted from his summary account[185]; and in L 1425 o. 1, a list of tablet baskets (pisan-dub) probably connected with soldiers.[186]

UŠ kurušda occurs in L 1291, 4697, and 5785, which, on the basis of content, can be linked to RTC 136 and L 4625 in which the namesake dub-sar is mentioned. Moreover, the fact that both UŠ kurušda in L 1291 and UŠ dub-sar in L 9365 (S178) belong to the staff of the énsi, suggests that UŠ kurušda and UŠ dub-sar are the same person at different stages of his career.[187]

As a maškim supervisor, UŠ is mentioned in a transaction concerning highest quality beer (L 4452) and in the weighing/payment of goods in (L 5765 [S154]). He occurs in L 4690 r. I 8, a tablet basket concerning delivery of barley from UŠ. He is the recipient of bronze in L 3129 and of bread and beer in RTC 114 o. 5'.

Quite likely UŠ was in charge of the livestock of the énsi at one stage in his career and was promoted to another level within the palace administration, although he continued to deal with livestock.

The remaining scribes can be divided into three groups:[188]

---

184. For the reading ^{a}aza$_{x}^{za}$, see P. Steinkeller, *Sale Documents of the Ur-III-Period*, FAOS 17 (Franz Steiner Verlag: Stuttgart, 1989), p. 277.

185. udu kurušda mu-túm Ur-^{a}aza$_{x}^{za}$-ke$_4$ ì-dab$_4$ énsi *A-kà-dè*^{ki}-ta im-gín-na im kurušda-ta ib-[ta]-zi. The return of the énsi from a journey to Akkad ia also documented in L 4690 r. II 4': [1] pisan énsi *A-kà-d*[*è*]^{ki}-ta še ì-DU-a [u$_4$]-zal-la-ke$_4$-ne è-a, and in RTC 103 (cf. Foster, *ZA* 72 [1982]: 16). Ur-aga-za is the namesake sipa who is in charge of more than eight talents of wool received from the head of the weavers in L 4434.

186. Cf. Foster, *Management*, p. 27, no. 17.

187. Foster, *ZA* 72 (1982): 13 notes that "There is no way of determining whether or not these groups of references (between UŠ kurušda and UŠ dub-sar) refer to the same person."

188. This division, in itself a matter of opinion, is dictated by practical reasons of compilation and is not intended to divide scribes of different rank into three groups *a priori*. In fact, one cannot but notice that a scribe mentioned more than

(1) Scribes frequently mentioned with the title dub-sar

Bar-ra-AN dub-sar is mentioned with this title in three texts: RTC 81 r. 3, Bar-ra-AN dumu lú-šu-maḫ Ur-[d]Nin-gír-su dub-sar-me, as a witness in a sale transaction for a slave purchased by the énsi Lugal-ušum-gal[189]; RTC 99 o. 4', a summary account of urudu-kin zi-ra, "copper broken"[190]; and AOT 49 v. 3', as the recipient of bread and beer.[191]

Bar-ra-AN is mentioned without title in about 20 texts.[192] But it is possible to link this official to the namesake dub-sar only in a few cases: in L 3117, a contribution of silver and silver objects by five officials; in L 1380 o. 4, a record of ì-giš and lard in jars of 8 and 9 sìla, which UŠ dub-sar (gave) and Bar-ra-AN received; in L 1410, a summary account of sheep for slaughter taken in charge by different officials; in CT 50, 169 o. II 12, a summary account of sheep characterized by the terms ì-bí-za-kam; hé-dab$_5$-ba-kam; libir-àm, (Bar-ra-AN is mentioned in connection with 4 ì-bí-za-kam sheep)[193];

---

once is, in many cases, haphazard because the limits of the documentation, e.g., Da-ti and Ur-GAR, who are certainly scribes of the highest rank, although they are discussed in different sections.

189. In L 4588 o. 4 Bar-ra-[AN] is the buyer of one slave, 6 gín igi-2-[gál] nì-šám [I]Ur-èn bar-ra-[AN] dumu Lú-[d]Nin-[ ] ì-ši-lá.

190. This term probably occurs in L 4595. The destination of the goods is indicated by the final clause, urudu-kin šu-a-gi$_4$-a Bar-ra-AN dub-sar-kam Lú-zàḫ-e šu-ba-ti Gír-su[ki]-a é-gal-la ba-ku$_4$, "wrought copper which Bar-ra-AN the scribe restored/ brought back, Lú-zàḫ received in Girsu and brought into the é-gal." RTC 99 records the same date as L 1196; RTC 136; 176; and CT 50, 49.

191. In AOTb 198 r. 15–16, a certain Bar-ra-AN <dub-sar> dumu Ur-ì-lí occurs. He is a subordinate of Lú-[d]Utu, which seems to exclude the possibility that Bar-ra-AN dumu Lugal-šu-maḫ and Bar-ra-AN dumu Ur-ì-lí (who does not occur elsewhere) are the same person. A namesake šabra occurs in L 2924 (S80), but this latter text could be a school exercise (cf. STTI, p. 3). A certain Bar-ra-AN dumu É-da is a recipient of wool in L 5848 o. II 1–2.

192. Bar-ra-AN is mentioned as KU.KÙ.GI in RTC 127 r. I 11 and in CT 50, 75 r. 3 as a witness (*Na-bí-um* Bar-ra-AN Lugal-á-zi-da KU.KÙ.GI-me…lú-ki-inim-ma-bi-me); as nu-bànda in L 4507; as ugula in L 1352; CT 50, 90; and as šu-ku$_6$ in L 1465. In texts L 2915; 5873; RTC 90; 91, involving personnel, in which he appears without title, probably he is the namesake ugula as well as in the list of persons mentioned in L 3010 and 4558.

193. The terms ḫé-dab$_5$-ba-kam and libir-àm probably mean "sheep that have to be

in RTC 125 r. I 5', recipient of bread without title. L 5805 is a fragment recording the allocation of a land parcel of 6 bur to Bar-ra-AN. CT 50, 182 o. 6 records the arrears for a plot of land or gardens of 60 sar, still held by the engar's. Finally, the wife of Bar-ra-AN is recipient of a piece of gold jewelry (gú-za kù-sig_{17}).

Iliš-takal (Ì-lí-iš-tá-kál) dub-sar is mentioned in AOTb 206 o. I 4'–5' and 207 o. I 2'–3'. Both texts record a distribution of bread and beer for the people and of barley as fodder for the animals. In both texts, Iliš-takal is one of the recipients and occurs in the first position.

Iliš-takal occurs without title in L 4691, a text similar in content to AOTb 206 and 207; in L 1416 r. 4, Iliš-takal (receives?) a container of beer from(?) Ur-^{giš}gigir, and in L 9396, a similar beer summary account (ITT V, p. 37). Finally a namesake nu-bànda perhaps occurs in RTC 127 o. III 9' (Ì-lí-iš-tá-x$^{?}$ nu-bànda-bi) as the recipient of fish. The official mentioned in these three texts might well be our namesake dub-sar.[194]

Inim-ma-AN dub-sar is mentioned in RTC 127 r. III 11 as recipient of emmer and sliced/split fish[195]; and in RTC 98 r. 4, a tablet missing the upper part of the obverse, which lists 22 persons, of which only 16 names survive, including 4[+x] simug; 1 ašgab; 3 ì-du_8 [*A*]-*kà*-[*dè*$^{ki\ ?}$]; 1[+x] ì-rá-rá; 3 dub-sar; and 4 untitled officials. After the summary, the workers enlisted are described as "personnel employed in the work giš-kin-ti" (guruš giš-kin-ti-me).[196] A certain Inim-ma dub-sar,

---

taken in charge" and "sheep of the preceding account," whereas the term ì-bí-za-kam is perhaps a loan from Akkadian *ibissû*, "commercial loss" (see *CAD* I/J, p. 3), meaning perhaps "sheep that are strays?" (suggestion by B. R. Foster).

194. Because it cannot be excluded that Ì-lí-iš is an abbreviation of Ì-lí-iš-tá-kál, perhaps Iliš-Takal dub-sar is the scribe who compiled RTC 151 (cf. *infra*, p. 172).

195. A. Salonen, *Fischerei*, pp. 44, 267 "aufgespaltene Fische."

196. The giš-kin-ti workers were household personnel specialized in some professional activity (metal or leather working). The secondary meaning of giš-kin-ti is "workshop" (cf. USP, p. 11). Concerning this secondary meaning, it is possible that in this context guruš giš-kin-ti is an abbreviation of guruš é-giš-kin-ti. Established between the end of the reign of Narām-Sîn and the beginning of the reign of Šar-kali-šārrī, the é-giš-kin-ti seems to have been a permanent institution involved in the construction or reconstruction of temples in such cities as Adab, Zabalam, and Nippur (cf. OSP 2, pp. 26–29). If the 22 persons listed in RTC 98

probably an abbreviation for Inim-ma-AN, occurs in DCS 4, 44 r. 2, a document characterized by the clauses PN$_1$ PN$_2$, šu-du$_8$-a-ni ì-túm, "PN$_1$ PN$_2$ his guarantor, brought." The reason for the guarantee is unknown.[197]

Inim-ma-AN is mentioned without title in L 1278 as a recipient with an unnamed lú-Unug^{ki} of eight jars of beer.[198] In DCS 4, 31 o. 4 Inim-ma occurs as the official who returns textiles and wool weighed /paid for by Lugal-bur. In L 4412 r. 1, a record of fish, which Ur-sipa delivered and, on behalf of Inim-ma, brought into the é-GIŠ.NAG^{ki}.

Lú-zàḫ dub-sar is mentioned in L 4680 as the official who signs a summary account of 117 guards.[199] He also occurs in AOTb 248 o. I 11, concerning barley distribution. In this case, too, it is an issue of a frequently mentioned anthroponym.[200]

The references to Lú-zàḫ kurušda are of particular interest. With Lú-^{d}Utu dub-sar, this official occurs in L 3011, a summary account of different fish items. These officials without title occur together in two other texts; in L 4562 (S129) r. 3, a record of bronze

---

were enrolled for a such a project, the text does not indicate whether they were enrolled for a local construction project or to be sent to another city; but it should be observed that several of the anthroponyms mentioned in this text do not occur elsewhere. The contents of L 1066, a fragmentary list of 11 guruš giš-kin-ti, which contains the following clause after the summary: Dingir-a-zu šu-gal$_5$-la^{um} *A-kà-dè*^{ki}-šè mu-laḫ$_4$-ḫi-éš, "(11 guruš giš-kin-ti) sent by Dingir-azu, the constable, to Akkad," could suggest that the giš-kin-ti personnel were enlisted for work outside Girsu.

197. The three guarantors are two nu-bànda's (Lú-ba and Šeš-da) and a dub-sar. Probably our official was the superior of the person who needed the guarantee.

198. Inim-ma-AN is also mentioned in L 1365 o. 4; 1448 o. I 10, but the official mentioned in these texts should certainly be identified with an ugula who in L 1448 is a subordinate of the nu-bànda En-uru-na. An ugula Inim-ma is a subordinate of the same nu-bànda in L 1449 o. II 4. It is clear that it is the same official as in L 1448, whose anthroponym has simply been abbreviated to Inim-ma.

199. Cf. ITT II, p. 38. For a list of the en-nu texts, cf. Foster, *Management*, p. 26, n. 11.

200. A namesake nu-bànda-é-gal is mentioned in L 4497, a fragment that must be a record of one or more transactions involving this official (the maškim supervisor is Ur-^{giš}gigir sagi). With the title nu-bànda-gu$_4$ and probably to be identified with the previous one, he occurs in L 3079 (S94) o. 2, a small expenditure (ziga) record of urudu-kin.

that these two officials received on two occasions (Lú-zàḫ Lú-^{d}Utu-bi šu-ba-ti-éš)[201] and in CT 50, 158 r. 4–5, concerning two measures of sesame received by Ur-pù and Lagaš, which the two officials had been given by the ùr of the storehouse.[202] The comparison with L 3011 and the frequent mention of Lú-zàḫ with the scribe Lú-^{d}Utu suggests that the kurušda and the namesake dub-sar are the same individual. The circumstances are somewhat analogous to those of UŠ kurušda.

Lú-zàḫ kurušda also occurs in RTC 91 r. III 3', a personnel text.[203] It is likely that the official who occurs without title in L 2838, sheep deliveries by various officials, and in L 2955, a record of sheep in the charge of Amar-su$_4$ and Lú-zàḫ,[204] is this kurušda and probably, therefore, the namesake dub-sar. A namesake, but untitled official is mentioned in RTC 99, a text discussed concerning Bar-ra-AN dub-sar. On the basis of content, the text should be linked to L 4562 and consequently its Lú-zàḫ is the namesake dub-sar. Again, the circumstances are somewhat analogous to those of UŠ kurušda.

Finally, Lú-zàḫ untitled occurs in L 1212+4672 (S26) IV' 2 as the official, probably the dub-sar, who measured(?), [ì-g]íd, the listed gifts.[205]

---

201. A third recipient is also mentioned in the text, GIŠ-*ra-ra-bí*, who is not mentioned elsewhere (cf. STTI, p. 10).

202. é-kišib-ba ùr-ra-ta Lú-^{d}Utu Lú-zàḫ-bi ì-ne-sum. The meaning of ùr in this context is unclear. This term is discussed by P. J. LaPlaca – M. Powell, "The Agricultural Cycle and the Calendar at Pre-Sargonic Girsu," *BSA* 5 (1990): 79, concerning names of the month guru$_7$ kišib-ba (Nik I, 16) and gur$_7$ im-du$_8$-a (DP 114 and HSS I, 22) and to the clause that appears in the ED IIIb text RTC 55 r. III 2: zíz ùr é-ganba (KI.LAM)-ka-ka im-du$_8$-a. The authors suppose that the term ùr in RTC 55 "may not mean roof but merely some upper floor."

203. RTC 91 lists different groups of persons (each identified by the formula PN$_1$ (N. Prof$_1$) PN$_2$ (N. Prof$_2$), and the name of the ugula to whom each member of the group is subordinate.

204. Cf. ITT II, p. 9. L 2955 is dated to the reign of Lugal-ušum-gal and in the year of the construction$^?$ of the temple of Nanše: [mu]-x é-^{d}Nanše-ka [mu-dù$^?$]-a or in the following year.

205. Transcribed and discussed in Foster, *JANES* 12 (1980): 42.

Nam-maḫ/Nam-maḫ-ni dub-sar is mentioned in L 4676 (S145) o. 10, a record of arrears of goats, barley, and silver, probably due as taxes, which had still not been paid (lá-NI-àm ki-engar-e-ne-ta nu-mu-túm). Those in arrears, besides Nam-maḫ dub-sar, are Ur-šu (elsewhere dub-sar), Lú-ab-ba dub-sar, and Me-a engar.

Nam-maḫ should, in many cases, be considered an abbreviation of Nam-maḫ-ni.[206] Nam-maḫ dub-sar is mentioned in MLC 1224 o. 2[207] as the official who took fish from the storage facility of the place called Ambar^{ki}, and who made the deductions from the summary account.[208] The namesake dub-sar dumu DA, who occurs in AOTb 198 o. 9–10, a list of scribes subordinates to Lú-^{d}Utu, could be the namesake dumu Da-da nu-bànda who occurs in L 1105 o. 7, in connection with 15 anše libir and 2 anše kunga$_x$. A dub-sar with this name also occurs in MVN 6, 310 (ITT IV, 7321) r. II' 12', as the recipient of sheep, an expenditure of the é-gal. Since the text is dated in the year when Lú-Ba-ba$_6$ became énsi, we cannot be sure that he is the same scribe mentioned in the other texts.[209]

Nam-maḫ<-ni> as a *garde-peche* (ITT II, p. 13) appears in L 3065 and in L 1407; in L 4469 he occurs without title. All three texts concern summary accounts of fish. In particular, L 1407 and 4469 feature the same clause, "contribution by Nam-maḫ of fish that are in the boat" (Nam-maḫ má-a ì-gál mu-túm). A namesake má-laḫ$_4$ occurs in RTC 115 r. 1'–2' as the recipient of barley. Nam-maḫ occurs in connection with boats in L 3060, a summary account of 693 dug dida, "par la barque d'A-ni-ak Nam-maḫ apportés" (ITT II, p. 13). But all these texts should probably be linked to MLC 1224, where the namesake dub-sar is mentioned.

206. The ugula Nam-maḫ, subordinate to the nu-bànda Lú-ba, is mentioned in L 1448 o. II 11 and the ugula Nam-maḫ-ni in L 1449 r. I 7.

207. Unpublished, courtesy B. R. Foster.

208. [ ] ku$_6$-dar-ra Nam-maḫ-ni dub-sar-e ambar^{ki}-ta é-kišib-ba-ta ì-ku$_4$ zi-zi-ga-ta íb-ta-zi.

209. Nam-maḫ is one of the officials, such as Šeš-šeš, Ur-ba-gára, and Ur-^{d}Nin-gír-su, who seem to occur both in Sargonic texts and in those of the following period. This and other examples confirm that many of the texts in the Girsu archive should be dated to the final years of the reign of Šar-kali-šarrī.

Nam-maḫ occurs without title in L 2841 as a recipient, Nam-maḫ and Nina[ki] receiving an amount of emmer; in L 4370 (S 111) o. 2, a contribution of [giš]ḫašḫur received by Nam-maḫ and [ ]-gu$_4$; in L 9441 (S182) r. I 5' as the recipient of a parcel of 12 iku of agricultural land for šuku (perhaps to be connected with L 4676). He also occurs in L 1410 as the official who takes charge of a sheep destined for slaughter; in L 1467 r. 1, a list of three 3 ìr-lugal whom Nam-maḫ took into his charge and whom Beli-ṭab énsi captured in KA.DIM[ki] [210]; in L 4514, a summary account of cattle put into the charge[?] of Nam-maḫ and various other officials. He also occurs in L 1303 r. 4, a summary account of bread and dabin with the clause "the seal of the énsi has been impressed,"[211] an expenditure by Nam-maḫ. A contribution of dabin belonging to Lugal-ušum-gal, which Šu-ilisu received from Nam-maḫ, is recorded in RTC 117.4.[212] Finally Nam-maḫ appears in L 6753, a letter previously discussed. However, it is quite possible that there were several scribes with this name during the same general period, for Nam-maḫ is one of the more common anthroponyms both in the Girsu documentation and in that of the whole of Mesopotamia in the third millennium.

Si-da dub-sar is perhaps mentioned in RTC 126 r. I 5 as the recipient of bread[213] and in RTC 127 r. IV 4 involving the allocation of 1 sìla of lard and 2 GÁxGI$_4$ containers of fish to I-sar-sar-rí. It is not indicated whether Si-da is the maškim of the transaction or the recipient

---

210. ìr-Lugal-me Nam-maḫ-e ì-dab$_5$ Be-lí-ṭab énsi-ke$_4$ ba-da-kar KA.DIM[ki]-ka. For the infix -da- as an alternative to the infix -ta- with the verb kar, cf. M. L. Thomsen, *The Sumerian Language,* Mesopotamia 10 (Copenhagen, 1984), pp. 226–27.

211. kišib-énsi-ka íb-ra. For the meaning of the clause kišib-PN íb-ra, "the seal of PN was rolled," cf. P. Steinkeller, *Sale Documents of the Ur-III-Period,* FAOS 17 (Franz Steiner Verlag: Stuttgart, 1989), p. 113.

212. 1 dabin gur šu Lugal-ušum-gal Lagaš[ki] Nam-maḫ mu-tú[m] ŠI.[ ] *Šu-ì-lí-su imḫur.* Nam-maḫ gal$_5$-lá-gal occurs in L 1228; 4404.3; 4604. There is also a namesake nu-bànda in L 4495. In L 1105 Nam-maḫ-ni dumu Da-da nu-bànda occurs. He appears in personnel lists, L 4558; 5813; 5834. Personnel in the charge of Nam-maḫ-<ni> appear in L 3073 and 5858. It is possible, from a comparison with L 4404, to identify this latter Nam-maḫ-ni with the namesake gal$_5$-lá-gal. Finally Nam-maḫ occurs in L 4414 and CT 50, 169 as the recipient of sheep.

213. 12 Si-da [d]ub-[sa]r[?] (but a reading Si-da um-me is possible).

with I-sar-sar-rí.[214] Possibly Si-da is a hypocoristic form of Si-da-ba-ri/ḫu (suggestion by Foster), who occurs in CT 50, 104 o. 4 as the official (ugula) in charge of employed (lú-gub-ba) guruš; in L 4640 (S142) o. 4 as the recipient of garments; and in L 3123 o. 5, a record of canal(?) measurements.

Ur-^{d}En-ki dub-sar in L 1183 r. 2–3 is the official who brought doors, wooden beams, and ladders[215]; in L 2911 (S76) r. 1–3, a record of contributions of sheepskins, which [Ur]-^{d}En-ki dub-sar has with him[216]; in CT 50 168 r. 6, a summary account of sheep allocated to various officials, among whom is our dub-sar.[217]

Probably the namesake official mentioned without title in the following texts is our dub-sar. In L 1114 o. 3, a summary of sheep (already discussed); in L 4423, a text with lacunae, which must have recorded the delivery of one sheep to Ur-^{d}En-ki and of 6 mina of šim-mun to another official by an unknown dam-gàr (ITT II, p.23); in L 5848 (S164) r. II 5', a summary account of the distribution of wool in which [Ur]-^{d}En-ki is probably the official who distributed the wool. On the basis of the attestations presented, L 2911, CT 50, 168, and perhaps L 1114, L 4423, and L 5848, Ur-^{d}En-ki may have been involved in the management of livestock and its by-products. A certain Ur-^{d}En-ki is the recipient of a land parcel of 5 bur in PUL 23 o. 4. He occurs also in L 9270 r. 5'.

Ur-GAR dub-sar is mentioned in RTC 127 r. I 14–15 as the maškim supervisor of an allocation of fish[218] and in PUL 23 o. 11, a text concerning land allocations in which the only recipient with a title is Ur-GAR.[219] After the summary, the recipients are described as lú-a-šà

---

214. Both texts belong to the group of documents listed by Foster, *JANES* 12 (1980): 29–42. A certain Si-da nin occurs in an anomalous list of witnesses, L 1405 o. 5 (cf. Foster, *WO* 13 [1982]: 15).

215. 27 ig 42 giš-ùr 3 ^{giš}kun$_{5}$ níg-gál-la sìla-du$_{10}$-kam Ur-^{d}En-ki dub-sar-e ba-túm iti mu-šu-du$_{8}$ 2 u$_{4}$ mu-gál.

216. 20 kúš [udu] 63 kúš gukkal 19 kúš máš 81 kúš máš-ga 60 kúš ^{mí}áš-gàr mu-túm.

217. The text must have concluded with the clause [udu zi-ga]-àm.

218. Cf. Foster, *JANES* 12 (1980): 26. It should be noted that the maškim of the transactions recorded in this text are ugula, nu-bànda, and dub-sar elsewhere.

219. The text is discussed by Foster, *Inst. Land*, p. 46.

DU-mu.[220] Ur-GAR appears in a seal imprint in L 5907: Ur-GAR dub-sar dumu Da-ti. The existence of a seal with the name of this scribe indicates that he was a very high-ranking official. The Da-ti of whom Ur-GAR is the son or subordinate may be the namesake scribe.[221]

This anthroponym with or without title is rather common.[222] A namesake sagi and sukkal are mentioned.[223] In L 1316 (S48) o. 3, where Ur-GAR holds a parcel of 15 bur of the aša$_5$ da-sal$_4$ for the current year, he is probably a high-ranking official who could be either the dub-sar or the namesake sukkal. In the case of L 4382 r. 4 and 4480 r. 3, two texts about the same transaction of barley, malt, emmer, flour, *sà-tum,* and dida-beverages brought by Ur-su and received by Ur-GAR, he could be the dub-sar or the namesake sagi.[224] The fragment L 4638, a summary account of ninda, ninda-

---

220. The term DU, mentioned also in MVN 3, 34, as compared to dab$_5$ (the term more commonly used to describe landholders), is discussed by Foster, *Inst. Land,* p. 51: "DU was used when land was actually worked by someone and the term dab$_5$ was used when land was not necessarily cultivated by the person holding." Foster adds on p. 52, "Were the lands in PUL 23 domain lands they produced labor for (DU) in return for lands they held elsewhere?" Even if the arguments adopted by Foster, *Inst. Land,* were convincing, it is difficult to imagine that an institutional scribe, like Ur-GAR, whose education was long and costly, could then spend his time cultivating the land parcel allocated to him as holder.

221. Cf. *infra*, p. 171. Another seal impression has the inscription Ur-^{d}Lamma dub-sar dumu Ur-GAR. If in this case dumu means "son," these inscriptions could indicate the existence of a family where the grandfather, Da-ti, his son, Ur-GAR, and his grandson, Ur-^{d}Lamma, were all scribes.

222. At least three namesake ugula's, each a subordinate to a different nu-bànda: (1) a subordinate of Amar-su$_4$ mentioned in L 1448 o. I 2 and L 1449 o. I 3; (2) a subordinate of En-uru-na in L 1448 o. I 10 and L 1449 o. II 5; (3) a subordinate of Da-da in L 1210 [S25] r. 3; a nu-bànda (mentioned in L 1448 r. I 11; 2863; 2907; 3079; 4433; 4557; 5781; RTC 80 r. 15; CT 50, 89 o. 4; 103 r. 4), a má-gín (L 1451 o. 3; 4703 [S151] o. II' 6').

223. Ur-GAR sagi is mentioned in L 4514 r. 7'; 5699; RTC 81 v 7; Ur-GAR sukkal in L 2954 (S86) r. II 13; 4516. Both the sukkal and the dub-sar occur as maškim's (the former in L 4516 and the latter in RTC 127). Thus, it is difficult to identify the namesake official when he occurs without title.

224. L 4382 records the receipt of goods, ki-Ur-su-ta Ur-GAR-e šu-ba-ti; L 4480 records that the goods received from Ur-GAR were in his possession$^{?}$: ([x]...ì-gál) di [x$^{?}$]-ba-da-ak [dum]u$^{?}$ Ur-GAR and were received at the beginning of the month of

gu, and sag-ninda for the énsi, Ur-GAR, and other officials, may be linked to RTC 103 o. 7. This document lists officials including Lugal-iti-da, Šu-na, and Ur-GAR, who are recipients of wool and contains the final clause "gone out from the household of the sagi-(maḫ?) on the occasion of the journey of the énsi to Akkad."[225] Perhaps L 4638 and RTC 103 indicate that Ur-GAR was part of the staff that accompanied the énsi to Akkad. We cannot identify the Ur-GAR mentioned in L 3144 (S108) o. 4', a summary of land.

Ur-ki dub-sar occurs in RTC 126 r. I 7 as a recipient of bread. He also occurs in AOTb 238 r. I 7', a short document that records the expenditure of a goat for Ur-ki dub-sar, one sheep for the god Giš-bar-è, and one lamb for the god Ningirsu, and in AOTb 295 o. 2–3.[226]

---

the feast of Baba: [ki-Ur]-su-ta [Ur-GAR šu-b]a-ti [x] [x?]-ba-da-ak [dum]u? Ur-GAR ì-gál sag iti ezen-dBa-ba$_6$-ka-ka šu-ba-ti. While in L 4382 o. 1, 5 gur-maḫ of barley brought by Ur-su are recorded, in L 4480 o. 1 only 3 gur-maḫ-sag-gál (the gur-maḫ-sag-gál [of which the gur-maḫ in L 4382 is certainly an abbreviation] must have been a gur of 240 sìla) are so recorded. But since the amounts of all the other goods listed coincide in both texts, the discrepancy apparently results from an error in the ITT copy or because the numbers in the tablet were erased.

225. é-sagi-ta è-a énsi *A-kà-de*[ki]-[šè?].

226. A namesake gudu$_4$ occurs in CT 50, 108 o. 9, a census of dead slaves; àga-uš in L 4432, concerning his contribution of fish; and ugula in L 1448 o. II 16 and L 4579. He occurs without title in L 1086 o. 4, a record of a contribution of fish and salt for Akkad from Ur-ki; L 1429 (S60) o. 2 and L 4420 o. 2 (the only item of this latter text that corresponds to the first item of L 1429), a record of a contribution of giš-ùr, "wooden beams" from Ur-ki, received by Lú-banda dub-sar; L 2855, a summary account of sheep, beer, and gú for/from various officials; L 4622, a summary account of livestock for/from three officials. This text is signed by Nam-tar-ré šabra, an official not mentioned elsewhere. (Perhaps this official is the namesake scribe and administrator of the god Enki, ìr Lugal-giš, in a seal from Adab, or the namesake scribe who occurs in the "Onion Archive" of Nippur.) A certain Ur-ki, as maškim supervisor, occurs in L 4486 (S148) o. III' 7' (cf. Foster, *JANES* 12 [1980]: 31). Ur-ki is the recipient in L 2907 (S74) o. 6 of a parcel of šub-šub-ba land and a parcel of SU$_7$ land (for aša$_5$ šub-šub-ba as "fallow" and SU$_7$ as "wasteland," cf. Foster, *Inst. Land*, pp. 22; 34). Finally, he appears in L 3009 and L 5882. A certain Ur-ki-gu-la occurs in an account of oxen and cows (see F. Thureau-Dangin, *RA* 3 [1892]: 127, 17–19).

The references to this anthroponym without title could refer to all three namesake officials, the gudu$_4$, the dub-sar, and the àga-uš.

Ur-^{d}Nin-dar dub-sar is mentioned in L 4437, a record of goods that Ur-^{d}Nin-dar(a) dub-sar brought; in L 4586, a summary account of sheep and goats involving various officials; in L 4679 (S146), a record of the distribution of brick molds to different officials[227]; and in L 5807, a list of scribes.

In addition, this anthroponym occurs without title in other texts. In the already cited summary account of oil, L 2912 (S77) r. 4'; in L 2876 as one of the recipients of jars of beer; in L 4443, a text recording officials who received sheep brought by Ur-gi dam-gàr; in RTC 126 r. II 3 as the recipient of bread and sag-ninda.[228] A namesake official is the recipient of a plot of land of 27 iku in L 3144 (S108) r. 4. But it is difficult to identify the official mentioned in these texts with the namesake dub-sar.

Ur-^{d}Nin-gír-su dub-sar is mentioned in RTC 81 r. 5–7 as a witness to a contract in which the énsi Lugal-ušum-gal is the purchaser and in RTC 127 o. VI 10–11 and r. I 22–23, as the maškim supervisor of two allocations of fish. Since RTC 81 is dated to the énsi-ship of Lugal-ušum-gal and RTC 127 (because of the mention of Eṭīb-Mer in o. I 3' in the first position)[229] can be dated to Šar-kali-šarrī, we can establish the approximate period during which the scribe served.

Ur-^{d}Nin-gír-su is one of the most common names in Girsu documents in all periods.[230]

---

227. In the text, two persons are mentioned who share the anthroponym with our scribe: (1) in o. 2', this anthroponym is listed with other officials mentioned elsewhere as ugula (Lugal-e; En-ni-lu; Lú-^{d}Nanše); he should be identified with the namesake ugula who occurs in L 1280; 1353; 2929; 3155; 4572; 5802; 5823; 9363; RTC 93; and probably in CT 50, 101; and (2) in o. 9' he is listed as Ur-^{d}Nin-dar dumu dub-sar-ra$^{?}$-ke$_4$ (Foster, STTI, p. 9, interprets dub-sar-ra as a personal name). Possibly the Ur-^{d}Nin-dar mentioned here is the son of or the subordinate to the dub-sar<-maḫ> and would therefore be the namesake dub-sar.

228. In L 4443, the officials Lugal-bur and Šeš-šeš are among recipients elsewhere noted as scribes, while in RTC 126 two scribes and the dub-sar-maḫ occur among the recipients, as well as an àga-uš and a šabra.

229. A little more than ten lines are missing from the first column of the text. From a comparison with CT 50, 172, the gifts for the king, queen, and perhaps the šabra-é may have been recorded there.

230. A sanga with the same name as in our text occurs in L 1403, a document concerning a contribution of fish signed by this official. The official without title in

An official who might be our scribe is the namesake sa$_{12}$-du$_5$, who occurs in the Late Sargonic and immediately following documents. In L 4673 (S144) r. 8; L 4695 (S149) r. I 1–2; RTC 142 r. II 2–3; perhaps L 4569 (S130) r. 2; and L 6692 o. 4', this official measures land.[231] In L 4673, this operation is performed with Lú-^{d}Utu dub-sar and in RTC 142 with Gal-zu-[x] dub-sar-lugal. In addition, he occurs in L 4553 (S128) o. 3 as the recipient of an ass and cattle hides. This official occurs with the same title in RTC 181 r. I' 1'–2', a document dating to the time of Puzur$_4$-Ma-ma énsi. Probably the Ur-[ ] sa$_{12}$-⸢du$_5$⸣ who occurs in L 5893 o. II 4'–5' is Ur-^{d}Nin-gír-su. A namesake official without title occurs in L 1196 o. 2, a fragment dating to Šar-kali-šarrī,[232] and in L 4690 r. I 7: "1 basket of barley records, barley which Nimgir-èš and Ur-^{d}Nin-gír-su transferred to."[233] Possibly the scribe of RTC 81 and the sa$_{12}$-du$_5$ who seems to have worked for a long time within the administration of Girsu are the same person. In this case, Ur-^{d}Nin-gír-su must be considered as an official of the same rank as Lú-^{d}Utu, Lú-bàn-da, Šeš-šeš, Túl-ta, and UŠ.

(2) Scribes mentioned once only

Ab-ba dub-sar is mentioned in DCS 4, 45 r. 3, which records goods in connection with various officials. But, in fact, a series of elements, such as words beginning with nin (nin-maš-e; nin-lú; nin-zi) and groups of signs repeated in two consecutive lines in different order (ma-àm-ma and àm-ma-ma) indicate that this is probably a school exercise tablet. Thus, the dub-sar Ab-ba mentioned there could be a

---

L 5722 r. 3–5, a text which concerns his arrears of fish that were not recorded in the general account summary and that were added: lá-NI Ur-^{d}Nin-gír-su im-dagal-a nu-sar daḫ-ḫe-dam, is, perhaps, to be identified with the individual in our text. There is also a nu-bànda in L 2968 (recipient of a sheep) and in L 4486 (S123) o. 1' (recipient of wool). An ugula with this name occurs in L 1193 (S23) o. 2 as the recipient of a parcel of land.

231. Foster, *Inst. Land*, p. 27.

232. Cf. FAOS 7, p. 57, sub D-43.

233. 1 pisan še nimgir-èš Ur-^{d}Nin-gír-su mu-bal-éš-a. The anthroponym Nimgir-éš occurs several times: (1) without title in L 1058; 2867; 3051; 4365; 4422; 4519; 469; (2) as gudu$_4$ in L 4703; CT 50, 107; (3) as šabra in CT 50, 107; and (4) as dub-sar-DI on CT 50, 172.

mere invention of the apprentice scribe who compiled the tablet. But the signature Ab-ba or zi-ga Ab-ba in some texts, all of the same typology, suggests that Ab-ba was in reality an official working within the administration. These texts are L 2823, an account of flour signed by Ab-ba; L 2979, a summary account of barley, emmer, gú, sag-ninda, KAL, and ZI.GAZ signed by Ab-ba; L 3094, a summary account of ba-ba flour, gú, and *sà-tum*, disbursed by Ab-ba; L 5738 and CT 50, 143 r. 4, a summary account of various types of flour, disbursed by Ab-ba.[234] In L 2906 and L 2944, a certain Ab-ba é-ḪAR occurs. But it is not clear whether é-ḪAR is a part of the PN or indicates the characteristic element of Ab-ba. In this case, however, it is most probable that Ab-ba worked for the administration of the mills. Because L 2944 is a list of personal names, the former hypothesis appears more likely. Ab-ba could perhaps be a shortened form of Ab-ba-é-ḪAR. L 2906 records a transaction of barley given to Ab-ba é-ḪAR.

Amar-su$_4$ dub-sar is mentioned in L 5847, a summary account of 150 rams and 150 ewes that Amar-su$_4$ dub-sar took into his charge. A namesake nu-bànda occurs in some records that refer to guard duty (L 1065, 4507, CT 50, 99) and in personnel lists.[235]

Amar-su$_4$ occurs without title in L 2955, a summary account of various types of shorn sheep belonging to the é-énsi involving Amar-su$_4$ and Lú-zàḫ. Based on the contents, this official may be our scribe. In that case, Amar-su$_4$ would have been a scribe belonging to the administration that managed sheep.

Amar-šùba dub-sar occurs in AOTb 259 o. II 2, a summary account of grain and flour.[236]

234. A namesake šabra occurs in L 3130, 9 as the recipient of sheep.

235. L 1149; 1162; 1448; 1449; 2859; 4448; 4458; 4502; 4670; 5796; CT 50, 103; BIN 8, 225. Amar-su$_4$ nu-bànda occurs also in ration texts (L 1237) and in texts concerning equids (L 1430; 1431; 4441). Note that anthroponyms that occur in some texts as nu-bànda (e.g., Amar-su$_4$; Amar-šùba, Bar-ra-AN; Lú-zàḫ; Lugal-iti-da, Nígin; Ur-GAR; Ur-^{d}Nin-gír-su) occur in others as dub-sar. In some of these instances the dub-sar is responsible for en-nu, "guards," (e.g., UŠ in CT 50, 100).

236. The text concludes with the clause: [ ] še-bi íb-zi. AOTb 258 and 259 are similar summary accounts; but AOTb 258 has a different final clause, ki-UŠ dub-sar-ta.

Amar-šùba occurs without title in L 3113 (S100) v. 1, a summary account of hay and reeds, as the father or superior of LUL-g[u-ak]; and in CT 50, 100 o. 4 as the official in charge of 51 guards (en-nu). It is likely that this official is the namesake nu-bànda.[237]

Beli-rabi (Be-lí-ra-bí) dub-sar occurs in L 3072 as the recipient of a sheep. His occurrence among the recipients of Ur-mes di-ku_5, who also is in L 4699 o. I ii 7,[238] and the method of recording the single allocations by the formula PN_1 Prof PN_1 PN_2 maškim that is adopted in RTC 127, suggest that this text is linked to the texts of Foster, *JANES* 12. Beli-rabi, in this case, would have been a royal official not in the employ of the administration of Girsu.

Du-du dub-sar URUxGÁNA*tenû*^{ki} is mentioned in L 1176 (S20) r. 6', a record of two groups of land parcels.[239] One section lists eight parcels of $aša_5$-še for eight officials, with a summary; the name of the holder of the parcels ($aša_5$-še PN-kam) is in the lacuna. The other section lists [x]+3 parcels of $aša_5$-gu_4 belonging to Lugal-ka. After these lists the text contains the clause Du-du dub-sar URUxGÁNA*tenû*^{ki} mu-DU, "Dudu, the scribe of U., produced/did labor."[240] This anthroponym occurs frequently in the Girsu documentation, but the title dub-sar URUxGÁNA*tenû*^{ki} precludes identification with others having the same name.[241]

Eden-bi-šè dub-sar is a witness in RTC 80 r. 5, a family group sale contract, in which Lugal-ušum-gal, the énsi, is the buyer and Šu-ilišu,

---

237. Amar-šùba nu-bànda occurs in L 1206 as the official who makes a contribution of two asses, of which Ur-nìgin takes charge: 2 anše-nita kùnga Amar-šùba nu-bànda mu-D[U] Ur-nìgin ì-dab_5. This nu-bànda is the untitled namesake who occurs in L 4503, a text which records a contribution of sheep by Amar-šùba.

238. Foster, *JANES* 12 (1980): 40.

239. For the reading of the toponym URUxŠÈ*tenû* (URUxGÁNA*tenû*)^{ki} as uru_x^{ki}(b) = *Uruba^{ki}, see K. Volk, "Lesung von URUxŠÈ*tenû*," *NABU* (1997): 60.

240. Cf. Foster, *Inst. Land*, pp. 51–52.

241. Du-du occurs as ašgab in L 1463; gala in L 4550; kurušda in L 4699; maškim in RTC 124; nu-bànda in L 3132 and 5690$^?$; sipa in RTC 96; šabra$^?$ in L 2924; šu-gal_5-lá in L 5709; 9353; CT 50, 154; ugula in L 1448; 1449; mí-us-sa Lugal-ušum-gal in L 1071; without title in L 1241; 1372; 2891; 3030; 3148; 4580$^?$; 5788; RTC 95; 96; CT 50, 98. In RTC 80 he is the father of $Puzur_4$-^{d}Iškur and brother of Šu-ilisu di-ku_5.

the judge, is the seller.[242] A namesake official without title occurs as the maškim supervisor in RTC 127 o. IV 16'–17'. A certain Eden-bi occurs in L 4488, a list of people.

En-an-na-túm dub-sar is mentioned in L 4405 o. 4, a record of his payment of onions and grasses.

This official is mentioned without title in L 4550 r. 5–6; RTC 115 r. 5; and CT 50, 159 r. 4. L 4550 r. 5–6, an account of seed barley for two land parcels located in the fields aša$_5$-maḫ and aša$_5$-tur[243] undersigned by En-an-na-túm. According to RTC 115 En-an-na-túm received 237 gur-sag-gál and 3 bariga of barley from Ur-^{giš}gigir for four allocations to four sailors, probably as rations for the personnel serving on the boats. In CT 50, 159 he receives four measures of emmer from Ur-^{d}Sàman.

GÌR-dalla dub-sar is mentioned in L 1190 as the official receiving barley, perfume, malt and flour. Probably GÌR <dub-sar> dumu Uru-nam-ma listed in AOTb 198 o. 3–4 is the same official. A certain GÌR also occurs in L 2891 as the recipient of barley.

Íl-ga dub-sar is mentioned in RTC 143 o. 2, as the recipient of a land parcel in the field aša$_5$ du$_6$-sír-[ra].[244] Perhaps in some instances this anthroponym has been abbreviated to Íl.[245]

Ki-tuš-ni dub-sar is mentioned in L 1095 (S6) o. 3'; r. 2'. He occurs untitled in L 5889 (S168) o. II' 4, as the father or the superior of a recipient of a land parcel: Uru-[ki] dumu Ki-túš-[ni]. Uru-ki probably is the namesake scribe.

---

242. Cf. SRJ, pp. 94–96, no. 46.

243. According to this interesting text, for 24 iku about 4 gur-sá-du$_{11}$ of seed barley was necessary. Assuming that the gur-sá-du$_{11}$ was equal to 240 sìla (cf. PPAC, pp. 65–66), 40 sìla of barley was needed for every iku of land; this must also have included barley fodder for draft animals and barley for workers' rations. A similar result can be found by comparing barley expenses for seed, animal fodder, and rations in BIN 8, 122; 123; 131 (cf. Foster, *Agriculture*, pp. 120–23).

244. In RTC 143, the recipients are Íl-ga, a šitim-lugal, the énsi of Elam^{ki} and Šušin^{ki}, a lú-eme, engar's; a sa$_{12}$-du$_5$ whose anthroponym is lost, and others without title (cf. Foster, *Inst. Land*, p. 19).

245. Cf. CT 50, 51 o. 4; 98 r. I 5; 182 o. 8.

Lú-^{d}Ab-ba$_{6}$ dub-sar is mentioned in L 4976 (S145) o. 4, a record of barley and silver arrears. A namesake official without title occurs in L 4641, a record of livestock (rams, ewes, goats, and asses) contributed by the sa$_{12}$-du$_{5}$, Lú-^{d}Ab-ba$_{6}$, Lugal-sa$_{6}$, and Maš-dà; in RTC 102 r. II 3, an account of various goods, including clothes, silver, flour, oil, and sheep, which covers one or more years in connection with various officials[246]; and in RTC 138 r. 1–2, a contribution by Lú-^{d}Ab-ba$_{6}$ on the occasion of the festival of the god URUxGÁNA*tenû*^{ki} or of the forthress of URUxGÁNA*tenû*^{ki} (ezem/bàd URUxGÁNA*tenû*^{ki}).

Lugal-an-na-túm dub-sar is mentioned in AOTb 41 o. 6–7 as the recipient of bread and beer. A namesake official without title is mentioned in L 4539, a list of persons, and in CT 50, 126 o. 2 as an official who delivers sheep.[247]

Lugal-bur agrig is mentioned in L 1095 (S6) o. 7'. This anthroponym without title occurs frequently in the texts. He is mentioned in several documents with other dub-sar's: L 1476, a record of barley and silver concerning the dub-sar-maḫ, Lugal-bur and Šeš-šeš; L 3032, deliveries of sheep for the dub-sar-maḫ, Lugal-bur, Da-ti, and Šu-na; L 4443, deliveries of sheep by Ur-gi dam-gàr for Šeš-šeš, Lugal-bur, and Ur-^{d}Nin-dar; L 4421 (S118).4, a record of two land parcels cultivated with sesame allocated to Šeš-šeš and Lugal-bur; and CT 50, 100.2, a list of guards in the charge of different officials. In addition, Lugal-bur occurs in L 1125 (S7) r. 8, a summary account of metal objects and military equipment, including helmets and spears for the sanga NIM, Ur-nu, and the sanga of ^{d}Nin-dar, contributed by Lugal-bur; in L 3098 (S98) o. 3, a record of a large number of rolls of gu-sa fibers (bundles of string), brought by Lugal-bur; in L 3139 (S107) r. 4', amounts of gold, silver, and bronze brought by Lugal-bur, part of which [ ]-ta è-a, "gone out from...."; in L 4462 (S121) o. 3'–4', a fragmentary summary account of copper and wool[248] brought by Lugal-bur. Finally, he is the recipient of a land parcel for sustenance in L 9441 (S182) r. II 7'. If the official

246. This text may be related to those of Foster, *JANES* 12 (1980).

247. A namesake ugula occurs in L 1350.8, and a šitá in RTC 96 r. II 9.

248. Cf. ITT II, p. 26.

listed above is our namesake scribe, then Lugal-bur was involved in the management and distribution of metals.

Lugal-ḫi-li dub-sar is one of the officials enrolled for the giš-kin-ti in RTC 98 r. V 5–6.

Lugal-iti-da <dub-sar> dumu [x] occurs in AOTb 198 r. 7–8. With different titles or without any title at all, this anthroponym occurs frequently in the documentation.[249]

The official who may be the scribe of AOTb 198 is the Lugal-iti-da who in L 1158 (S16) makes an expenditure in the é-gal of wool for the past and present years. Probably the official who occurs in L 1364 o. 3 in connection with arrears of wool that is in his possession is the same person as in L 1158[250] and in L 9317 o. 4, an account of wool that Lugal-iti-da paid/weighed out to the énsi. He also occurs in L 5848 (S164) o. II 4, concerning an allocation of wool received from Šeš-ša[g$_5$] dumu Lugal-iti-da and in RTC 103 o. 5 concerning second class wool characterized by the formula é-sagi-ta è-a énsi A-kà-dè^{ki}-[šè]. Possibly the namesake túg-du$_8$-gal who occurs in L 4616, a list of slaves, is our dub-sar.

Lugal-izi dub-sar is mentioned in L 5807, a scribal list already discussed. Note that there is a Lugal-izi$^?$ on a seal imprint on RTC 177, but there is no compelling reason for identifying him with our scribe.

Lugal-un-ge$_{26}$ dub-sar is mentioned in L 5893 r. II 5',[251] in which, with Si-DU and Ur-^{giš}gigir, he is one of the witnesses. The three scribes are subordinates of Da-ti: Lugal-un-ge$_{26}$ Si-DU Ur-^{giš}gigir dub-sar-me *šu* Da-ti.

---

249. A namesake nu-bànda occurs in DCS 4, 34 o. 2; šabra in L 2925; má-laḫ$_4$ in L 1436 o. 4. Lugal-iti-da occurs without title in L 1182 o. 5; 1245 (S31) o. I 5'; 1256 o. 6; 1364 o. 3; 1365 o. 5; 2889 (S72) o. 4'; 2969$^?$; 3058; 3117 r. 6; 4455; 5729; 5780; 5801 (S160) r. 2; 5854; 5862; 5873; 5882; 6680; 9270; 9303 o. 2; 9421 (S180) o. II' 5'; RTC 139 r. I 8; 142 o. II 7; CT 50, 51 o. 7; 75 r. 7; 76 r. 1–2; 85 r. I 9; 106 o. II 3'; 163 o. 2; 182 o. 4; 184 r. 7'; MVN 3, 34 o. 5.

250. Cf. USP, p. 94.

251. Cf. Foster, *Inst. Land*, pp. 29–31.

In RTC 120 r. 6 Lugal-un-ge$_{26}$ receives barley from the scribe UŠ, for the payment of officials who seem to have been connected with the cult and to have come from Uruk, Zabalam, and Adab.

Me-ság-zu dub-sar is mentioned in RTC 98 r. 3, a record of the recruitment of giš-kin-ti personnel.[252] In the documents—usually written Me-ság—both a namesake sagi[253] and a namesake kurušda[254] occur, but neither of these officials, on the basis of available data, can be identified with the namesake dub-sar. On the other hand, it is perhaps possible that the maškim official mentioned in L 3015, a transaction concerning Lugal-kù dam-gàr, and in L 3050 r. 4, a record of urudu-kin concerning Túl-ta dub-sar and Lú-zàḫ that Šu-i-x brought from Girsu, where he was a supervisor with Lú-^{d}Utu, should be connected with our scribe.[255]

Mes-zi dub-sar occurs in L 3145, a barley record from MI.RA-núm šabra and from the é-duru$_5$ of the énsi and received by Sipa-si-in-TAB.BA and Mes-zi dub-sar.[256] The text also records a payment made by the nagar to MI.RA-núm šabra. The document dates from the reign of the énsi Lugal-ušum-gal. Mes-zi, the šabra MI.RA-núm, and the two recipients of the barley in the text do not occur elsewhere.

Nabium (Na-bí-um) dub-sar is mentioned in L 1077 o. 6–v. 1, a summary account of the withdrawal of sheep offered to Šul énsi, Dada šabra, Nabium dub-sar, and to the gods Ningirsu and Utu-Kisurra. A namesake šagina occurs L 1472 o. II 2' and CT 50, 172 o.

---

252. Cf. *supra, sub* Inim-ma dub-sar.

253. Me-ság/Me-ság-zu sagi occurs in L 1454 o. 2–3 (a summary account of fish) and as sagi-gal in L 4457 o. 2 (in which he is taking goods to Akkad). Probably the namesake official mentioned in L 1360; L 1561; and CT 50, 165 o. 3 in connection with fish, and in L 4464 and 4561 in connection with uz-tur, is this latter sagi. We have identified a certain Me-ság sagi who occurs in the Adab texts with the namesake scribe who occurs in the same documents (cf. *infra*, p. 185). There is the possibility that this official was not in the employ of the administration of Girsu.

254. Me-ság lú kurušda lugal occurs in RTC 112 o. 6–7.

255. For the seal of this scribe, see D. O. Edzard, "Die Inschriften der Altakkadischen Rollsiegel," *AfO* 22 (1968/9): 14, lines 13 and 17.

256. Unpublished transliteration courtesy of B. R. Foster.

II 8' as the recipient of eggs and fish, respectively. A namesake KU.KÙ.GI with Bar-ra-AN and Lugal-Á-zi-da appears as lú-ki-inim in CT 50, 75 r. 2.[257]

He occurs without title in L 5861, a fragmentary summary account of barley and in L 9441 (S182) o. I' 2', an account of large plots of land. The reference in L 1077 makes it probable that Nabium dub-sar and the namesake šagina are the same person, a direct subordinate of the ruler and not of the énsi of Girsu.

NÌGIN dub-sar[258] is mentioned in L 2914, a record of cattle, as the maškim supervisor. This anthroponym occurs elsewhere as ugula or nu-bànda,[259] officials who should probably be distinguished from the namesake dub-sar. He occurs without title in different flour and grain texts: in L 2874 he receives barley and fine flour with Ur-šu and Lugal-id-NE; in L 5703 and 5720 and probably in L 5698 he receives the same goods with Ur-mes[260]; in L 5712 o. 3; r. 3 he receives flour from Šeš-kur-ra, goods for which Šeš-kur-ra compiled the summary account but which had not yet reached NÌGIN[261]; in L 2980, a record of the allocation of 30 sìla of fine flour as the sá-du$_{11}$ to Ì-sa$_6$-sa$_6$, disbursed by NÌGIN; and in CT 50, 144 r. 4, an allocation of fine flour and ninda ḫar-ra, disbursed by NÌGIN. He is also mentioned in L 4682, a record of goat hairs from the house of the énsi. These goat were the arrears which had not yet been deduced or withdrawn from the previous and current years. As the recipient of beer and dida, he occurs in L 4584 with Lugal-ig-gal and UŠ dub-sar. Finally, the wife of NÌGIN receives five containers of beer in RTC 114 o. 2. If the official in L 2874; 2980; 5698; 5703; 5712; 5720 and

---

257. Some KU.KÙ.GI may also be scribes. It may be another “overlap” similar to that previous discussed (suggestion by Foster).

258. The alternate name forms Ur-NÌGIN and Ur-NÌGIN.GAR (CT 50, 144) suggest the readings nigar$_x$ for NÌGIN and nigar$_x^{gar}$ for NÌGIN.GAR (courtesy of J. Bauer).

for nigar$_x$ M. Krebernik ZA 1986 199

259. NÌGIN ugula occurs in L 1448 r. I 13; the namesake nu-bànda occurs in L 3006; 4448; 4579; BIN 8, 225.

260. Perhaps Ur-mes is the namesake šabra who occurs in L 1172 (S18) r. 10'; 1368 (S49) r. 2; 1399 (S56) 3. This anthroponym occurs without title in about 20 texts.

261. Literally “the goods are outside NÌGIN,” ki-Šeš-kur-ra-ta NÌGIN šu-ba-ti Šeš-kur-ra níg-kas$_7$-bi ba-da-ak bar NÌGIN-ka ì-gál.

CT 50, 144 was our scribe, he would probably be one of the officials in charge of cereals and their derivatives imported and exported by the palace of the énsi.

Nimgir-èš dub-sar is mentioned as the recipient of fish in CT 50, 172 r. I 19.[262] He is mentioned without title in L 2867, a text concerning the receipt of bread, munu$_4$, and beer bread; in L 3051, a summary account of flour concerning various officials; in L 4422 where deliveries of sheep, ì-nun, ga-ḫar and fish to the wife of Nimgir-èš are recorded; in L 4519, a contribution of sheep by various officials, including Nimgir-èš; and in L 4690 r. I 7, in connection with Ur-^{d}Nin-gír-su. With the exception perhaps of L 4422, it is impossible to recognize our dub-sar in any of the officials listed without title.

Puzur$_4$-šùba dub-sar occurs in L 4548 (S127) r. 3–4. The text is a short record of allocations of lard and oil for anointing ^{d}Nisaba-an-dùl,[263] Sipa-da-ri, Gabium, Eṭib-Mer, and Puzur$_4$-šùba dub-sar. Lú-^{d}Utu is the maškim supervisor of the first three and Da-ti of the last two. L 4548 could be linked to those in Foster, *JANES* 12. Possibly the namesake official who is the recipient of bread and other goods in CT 50, 147 o. 7' and of flour in L 9271 o. 6 is our scribe.

Rīm-Ḫaniš (Ri!(ḪU)-im-ḫa-ni-iš) dub-sar is mentioned in RTC 122 o. 6–7 as a recipient of barley. The recipients mentioned in the texts are probably foreigners or, at least, not residents of Girsu: Da-kum-[x] lú-ka[s$_4$]; Ì-lí-iš-m[a-ni$^?$] énsi Šušin^{ki}; AN-zu-zu; and Zu-zu lú-Šušin^{ki}. These men may have constituted a foreign delegation present in Girsu. The Rīm-Ḫaniš who occurs in L 1371,[264] an expenditure of bread, beer, and flour, is likely the scribe in RTC 122.

---

262. Foster, *JANES* (1980): 31. Nimgir-èš is mentioned with the title šabra in CT 50, 107 r. 4, a list of dead slaves who must be replaced: sag ba-daḫ Ambar^{ki}, "slaves he added in Ambar" (CT 50, 108 is a similar list but refers to the city Nina). A namesake gudu$_4$ is mentioned in the same text (v. 3); he also occurs in L 4703 (S151) r. IV' 3' as the recipient of ì-nun and lard.

263. ^{d}Nisaba-an-dùl should be identified with the namesake official, perhaps a šagina of the king, mentioned in L 2903 (S73), a letter in Sumerian concerning the movement of troops (see FAOS 19, pp. 78–79).

264. ITT I, p. 23.

Si-DU dub-sar occurs in L 5893 r. II 6' as a witness.[265]

Šu-ili (Šu-ì-lí) dub-sar is mentioned in L 1317, a small fragment. Although its contents cannot be determined, Šu-ì-lí dub-sar is legible. This anthroponym occurs in L 2899 and L 5895. In L 2899, he is the recipient of beer.[266] In L 5895, he is the official in charge of a group of persons listed according to the name of their place of residence.[267]

Ú-da dub-sar is mentioned in L 2906[268] as the maškim supervisor in a transaction concerning barley given to$^{?}$ Ab-ba é-ḪAR.[269] He also occurs in AOTb 198 o. 13–14, a list of scribes subordinate to Lú-^{d}Utu.[270]

---

265. Cf. *supra, sub* Lugal-un-ge$_{23}$. Si-DU sag-apin-na occurs in L 2920, a summary account of cattle delivered by various officials to Da-da (perhaps the namesake šabra and šabra-é). Si-dù ugula occurs in L 1448; 4677; 4683. In L 4652 he is an ugula šu-ku$_{6}$ ("si-DU chez le pècheur," see ITT II, p. 36). A namesake šíta occurs in RTC 96 and L 5853; a namesake igi-nu-du$_{8}$ occurs in L 4630.

266. Of the recipients mentioned in L 2899, only Sarru-bani occurs elsewhere in the documents (RTC 127 r. III 21). The anthroponym of another of the recipients, Ì-lí-iš-me-ni may be linked to the name of the énsi of Susa Ì-lí-iš-ma-[NI] mentioned in RTC 122 r. 1–3.

267. Possibly Šu-[ ] dub-sar mentioned in L 1469 (S63) r. 1' (a fragment that seems to record copper used for a trip to Elam, as well as for something in Guabba [STTI p. 3]) could be Šu-[ì-lí]. But other restorations are also possible.

268. Unpublished transliteration, courtesy B. R. Foster.

269. In L 2906, according to the summary in ITT II, p. 5, another scribe, A-da-mu, occurs. This anthroponym is not mentioned elsewhere.

270. This anthroponym occurs without title in L 5874, a fragmentary record of bread for the dub-sar-maḫ, Ur-šu, and Ú-da; in L 1059.9, a summary account of cattle with this clause after the final summary: áb Lugal-u na-gada áb Lugal-kam Ú-da ù Ú-a Unug^{ki}-šè ì-laḫ$_{4}$, "cattle that Lugal-u, the cowherd of the king, with Ú-da and Ú-a, took to Uruk." L 1047 is a similar transaction concerning sheep that have the same destination.

The sag-apin-na mentioned in MVN 3, 87 o. 3–4, which concerns four oxen and a plow, should be distinguished from the namesake dub-sar of L 2906, but should be connected to Ú-da mentioned in L 3070 (S93) o. 2 and RTC 140 o. 2; 5. L 2906 and L 3070 are two records of days of work in an onion field (cf. Foster, *Inst. Land*, p. 27).

Ur-nu dub-sar occurs in RTC 82 o. 4; 9, a difficult juridical document, which records a statement concerning two oxen and seven asses that were taken into charge on a ship. Ur-nu is one of the contracting parties.[271]

He occurs without title as the maškim supervisor in L 3000 and 4348 o. 3 in connection with the allocation of a kid goat to the énsi of Umma[272] and in CT 50, 152 in connection with sheep offerings to gods. With the exception of the above references, Ur-nu occurs several times as sanga. The sanga Ur-nu is the recipient of metal objects and arms in L 1125 (S7) r. 4; of "ducks" in L 1157; and of sheep and other goods in RTC 114 r. 3. He is also mentioned in L 5892, a summary account of barley payments by the sa_{12}-du_{5}, Ur-nu sanga, and others; and in L 1150, a small tablet that has a seal imprint on one side and the legend Ur-nu sanga ^{d}Nanše on the other. He also occurs in L 1135 (S11) o. 2, a letter concerning a plot of 5 bur of land in the field DU_{6}-pù-ra that Ur-nu had inspected[273]; in several personnel texts: L 1253 and CT 50, 91 o. 2, two parallel texts concerning a textile worker; CT 50, 88 o. 4 in connection with a guruš, a subordinate of Ur-nu, and a géme from Lagaš[274]; and in CT 50, 108 o. 3, a census of dead slaves.

Ur-šu dub-[sar] is mentioned in L 4703 (S151) r. III' 1, a long record of allocations of oil and fats. A namesake šabra occurs in L 4684, a lú-mar-sà list.

He occurs without title in L 1416, perhaps as the recipient of beer (a contribution by Gala) with Puzurum and Iliš-takal. In RTC 101 o. 9 and L 4626 (S138) o. 10 a certain Lú-ba dumu Ur-šu occurs.

Ur-TAR dub-sar occurs in L 3152, a school exercise tablet.[275] As in the case of Ab-ba, it is possible that the name of the dub-sar in this text is the invention of a young scribe. One could perhaps identify this

---

271. Cf. SRJ, p. 143, no. 87.

272. L 4348 should collect the two items of L 3000.

273. Cf. LEM, p. 25 and FAOS 19, p. 23.

274. 1 guruš Ur-^{d}Šer$_{7}$-da nu-bànda Lú-ba lú Ur-nu sanga 1 géme Lagaš^{ki} daḫ-ḫe-dam (probably concerning dead people who have to be added).

275. Discussed by Foster, *ArOr* 50 (1982): 240.

scribe with the maškim supervisor who occurs with Lú-^{d}Utu in the same role in L 9271 o. 7 and L 9181 r. 3, summary accounts of flour. Ur-TAR also occurs in L 2834 and 3051 o. 2, summary accounts of the receipt of flour and its derivatives. In L 4690 r. II 5', a dub-pisan text discussed by Foster,[276] Ur-TAR is mentioned concerning a basket of tablets. A namesake official occurs in texts concerning sheep and wool: L 1229 (S28) r. 1; 4519; CT 50, 166 o. 3; 169 r. I 10.

Zu-zu dub-sar lu[gal$^{?}$] is mentioned in RTC 127 r. IV 10–11 as the recipient of various goods. This anthroponym occurs also in L 4482; 5838; CT 50, 85, but the type of references preclude his being the scribe mentioned in RTC 127, who must be regarded as a high-ranking royal official.[277]

For references to scribes for whom we cannot identify a role in the administration (A-da-mu, En-šeš, Ka-tar, Lú-^{d}Igi-ama-šè,[278] Lú-šè-zi, Lugal-a-ma-[ru], Lugal-dub-sag-ki,[279] Lugal-su$_4$, Me-a-na, Ur-ba-ba,[280] Ur-giš, Úr-ra-AN,[281] Za-ni-ni[282]), see TABLE 13.[283]

---

276. Foster, *ZA* 72 (1982): 15–19.

277. Perhaps this is the same scribe who is frequently mentioned at Gasur (suggestion by B. R. Foster).

278. He occurs in AOTb 143 (private communication from J.-J. Glassner).

279. Lugal-dub-sag-ki is mentioned in L 4544, ITT II, p. 30: "2 chevraux Lugal-dub-sag-ki le scribe, chevaux pour défricher 18 gan de terrain?, *ṭa-bi* le dub-sag et ^{d}Nin-sar-al-mu le dub-sag." The first part of the text is unclear; perhaps it concerns the allocation to an official of two equids to work one bur of agricultural land. However, if so, the subsequent mention of two dub-sag's is incomprehensible to us. Adding to our difficulty in understanding this passage is the strange repetition of the element dub-sag, both in the name of the scribe and in the professional names. We are unaware of any other occurrence of these three anthroponyms in the Girsu archive. Perhaps L 4544 is a school exercise.

280. Lugal-a-ma-[ru], Me-a-na, and Ur-ba-ba are three of the five scribes who occur in L 5807. But while the other two anthroponyms (Ur-^{d}Nin-dar and Lugal-NE/IZI) have been previously discussed, the other three are not mentioned elsewhere in the texts. Unfortunately, it is not possible to establish the nature of this document, since only a very brief summary appears in ITT V. The well-founded suspicion that this document could be a school exercise takes nothing away from its value.

281. Úr-ra-AN <dub-sar> dumu En-kù nagar occurs in AOTb 198 r. 11–12. A namesake simug occurs in RTC 98 o. 5 as a guruš giš-kin-ti. This simug may be the

(3) Scribes mentioned in the seals

There are eleven scribes mentioned in seal impressions. Some of these impressions contain the name Narām-Sîn, during whose reign they apparently were active. It is understandable in the light of our above analysis that there are no other attestations of these scribes. Other imprints have the name Šar-kali-šarrī and thus it is possible that traces of them remain in the documentation. The scribes of these seal impressions must have been very high-ranking officials. Only in a few cases are we fairly secure in identifying these scribes with officials mentioned in texts.

Abi-išar (*A-bí-i-šar*) dub-sar and *I-sí-núm* dub-sar are two scribes of Bin-kali-šarrī, son of Narām-Sîn. The former occurs in RTC 169, ^{d}*Na-ra-*

---

namesake official who occurs without title in several texts relating to metals: L 2878 (S61) o. 3; RTC 101 o. 3; L 4634 (S140) o. 2 (these three texts seem to be related); and L 5763. Úr-ra-AN is the maškim supervisor in all four texts and occurs in another text of the same typology (L 1388 [S54] r. 1). A namesake sag-apin, a subordinate of Ur-NÌGIN, occurs in L 4618. He also occurs without title in a group of texts concerning products derived from grain (L 1311; 2971; 3019; 3022; 4374; 5685). He is mentioned as the recipient of barley in CT 50, 187 r. 4, and of monthly distributions in L 5800. He also occurs in L 2971, a text of sá-du$_{11}$.

282. Za-ni-ni dub-sar occurs in AOTb 134 r. I 5'–6'. This text is a small fragment of a text that originally had 2x2 columns recording "liste di personnel dont plusieurs noms cassés qui sont dub-sar, comme, ailleurs, igi-nu-du$_8$" (private communication from J.-J. Glassner).

283. It is surprising that about 20% of the scribes mentioned occur once only in documentation the size of that of Sargonic Girsu. In fact, four of them could only have been born of the imagination of a beginner scribe. Seven others (Beli-rabi; Rim-Ḫaniš; Šar-ḫili; Nabium, Puzur$_4$-šùba, Šu-ili, and Zu-zu) seem to have been foreign scribes or at least not connected with the administration of the é-gal. The remaining scribes could have been officials working in the Girsu region but outside the é-gal, or scribes mentioned in texts that were not contemporaneous with the majority of the documentation that has reached us. The vast majority of documents of the archive we have analyzed in this section belong to the Late Šar-kali-šarrī period, although older documents from the Narām-Sîn period and later ones from the period of the énsi Puzur$_4$-Ma-ma, who succeeded Lugal-ušum-gal, are present as well as. Thus, the real limit is our present inability to establish the internal chronology of the archive. This inability has led us to treat the documents of the archive as if they were contemporary, with all the methodological limits that implies.

am-^{d}*Sîn* ^{d}*A-kà-dè*^{ki} *Bi-in-ga-lí-sar-rí* dumu-*sú* *A-bí-i-sa*[*r*] dub-sar ìr-*sú*. The latter occurs in a seal which must have been at the Metropolitan Museum of New York at one time, but whose present location is unknown: *Bi-in-ga-lí-sar-rí* dumu-lugal *I-sí-núm* dub-sar ìr-*sú*.[284]

Ad-da dub-sar appears in RTC 164,[285] *Ša*[*r-kà*]-⸢*lí*⸣-*šar-rí* lugal [*A-k*]*à-dè*^{ki} ⸢Ad-da⸣ dub-sar ⸢*ìr-sú*⸣.[286] None of the namesake officials who occur in the documentation, the má-laḫ$_4$ (L 2915); the nagar (L 4399); the sukkal (L 4353); without title (L 4512; 4703; RTC 116), can be connected to the scribe in RTC 164.

Beliti (*Be-lí-ti*) dub-sar occurs in RTC 175, on which the seal of the scribe had been rolled twice. There is no mention of the name of the king or énsi. A namesake official without title occurs in RTC 127 r. IV 21[287] and in RTC 131 o. 2 in connection with sheep. The officials mentioned in the text besides Beliti are: *Sar-ru-ì-lí*, x-ša$_6$, Úr-KU.KU and Si-DU.[288] Possibly the Beliti who occurs in RTC 127 and 131 is the same as in RTC 175. In this case, he is certainly an official who does not belong to the administration of Girsu.

Da-ba-ba dub-sar occurs in CT 50, 84, a bulla with the cartouche of the scribe, Da-ba-ba dub-sar dumu [PN], inside the representation. Outside there is the inscription GÁxGI$_4$ šim-gam-ma. This must mean that the bulla was probably used with perfume containers.

Da-ti dub-sar is mentioned in RTC 176, a tablet with the sealing of the scribe in the center and a partially abraded inscription in the upper

---

284. The inscriptions are discussed in RIM 2, pp. 178–79 (nn. 2022–23); and FAOS 7, p. 40, with other inscriptions by Bin-kali-šarrī.

285. Cf. RIM 2, p. 203, n. 2008.

286. The reading of this anthroponym is uncertain. The reading Ab-ba, a scribe who occurs in the texts, cannot be excluded.

287. Foster, *JANES* (1980): 27.

288. Of these officials, Sarru-ili occurs in RTC 121, a summary account of two amounts of barley received by Ilum-dan, Sarru-ili, and by an official of Lugal-ušum-gal, *iš-dè* é-úr *ši* Lugal-ušum-gal. A subordinate of Sarru-ili (lú *Sar-ru-ì-lí*) occurs in two anše texts, L 1106 and 2853; Si-dù in L 1434 (s62) o. 4 records a shipment of logs shipped by canal; Ur-KU.KU does not occur elsewhere in the documentation.

part. It records a transaction that apparently involved the king and the énsi. It concludes with expenditures, and in the lower part there is the date formula: (mu [KAS].ŠUDUN [Unug^{ki}-a] ⸢nag-su-a⸣^{ki} [ba-gar-ra-a]). In L 5907, an identical inscription in three bullae is also mentioned: Ur-GAR dub-sar dumu Da-ti. The dating of these latter bullae is uncertain; it is possible that they belong to the Post-Sargonic period. Our dub-sar may be the untitled namesake official who occurs in L 5893, as the superior of three scribes who were witnesses to a transaction. Similarly, the official who in L 1207 (S24) r. 4 surveys the lands listed in the text could be none other than the namesake dub-sar. Also, the Da-ti who occurs in L 3032 (a record of sheep for the dub-sar-maḫ, Lugal-bur, Da-ti, and Šu-na) and in RTC 137 o. I 4' (a record of the allocation of land, whose recipients include Da-ti, the dub-sar-maḫ, the énsi-gal, the sukkal-gal, the sagi-maḫ) may be our scribe. Perhaps our official is the person who occurs in CT 50, 180 r. 8. The text lists 12 plots of land, summarized as approximately 40 bur, a large area, with the name Da-ti, the official who is the holder of the listed lands.[289] In CT 50, 179 r. 3, Da-ti is the official who signs the summary account of goods.[290]

Iliš (*Ì-lí-iš*) dub-sar is probably the scribe who drew a map of a plot of land in RTC 151.[291] It is possible that the *Ì-lí-i*[*š*] who receives gifts in CT 50, 172 II 2' is the same Iliš as in RTC 151.

Lú-mar$^?$ dub-sar occurs in L 5905, a bulla containing the inscription: en-^{d}Nanna *ba-ni* Lú-mar$^?$-bi dub-sar dumu-nita-bi (ITT II, p. 53). This anthroponym does not occur elsewhere in the documentation. The seal probably belongs to the Post-Sargonic period.

Sarriš-ṭakal (*Sar-rí-iš-ṭá-kál*) dub-sar occurs in RTC 170, ^{d}*Na-ra-am-*^{d}*Sin* ^{d}*A-kà-dè*^{ki} *Sar-rí-iš-ṭá-kál* dub-sar ìr-*sú*.

---

289. Cf. Foster, *Inst. Land*, p. 47.

290. Da-ti occurs in other texts of the Girsu archive (L 1075; 2952; 2954; 3005; 4533; 4597; 5799; CT 50, 92; 97; 106), but the contents of these documents does not enable us to establish the identity of the official.

291. This parcel of land is part of the field aša$_5$ ad-da-[ ] gal-UN and is bounded by three canals of a river. A tract of 40 sar of very poor quality (murgu) lay between a river (ìd ì-lí-tab-ba) and a canal (e-sù aša$_5$), probably for irrigation.

Ur-da dub-sar occurs in RTC 173, a seal from the period of Narām-Sîn.[292]

Ur-^{d}Lamma dub-sar occurs in the bulla L 10040,[293] Ur-^{d}Lamma dub-sar dumu Ur-GAR, and probably belongs to the Post-Sargonic period.

The period of activity of two scribes, Ur-ba-gára dub-sar and [Uru]-ki dub-sar, is very controversial.[294] The two scribes are mentioned respectively, probably as recipients, in AOTb 321 o. III 13'–14' and o. II 11'.[295]

Ur-ba-gára, who occurs without title in almost 40 texts, is described in RTC 221 as nu-bànda é-gal. Uru-ki occurs without title in about 15 texts. In addition to AOTb 321, Ur-ba-gára and Uru-ki occur together in 11 other texts, nine of which have the same context,[296] summary accounts of flour and bread for which Ur-ba-gára is responsible and beer and beverages for which Uru-ki is responsible, probably regular allocations. In some texts of this typology (L 1332; 1455; 4384) Ur-^{giš}gigir is mentioned with Ur-ba-gára instead of Uru-ki.[297] In L 3057 both Uru-ki and Ur-^{giš}gigir occur with Ur-ba-gára. Ur-ba-gára and Uru-ki probably occur together in L 1062, which concerns slaves and cattle belonging to Lugal-ušum-gal and in L 1129, which concerns wrought copper received in$^{?}$ Girsu.[298] Ur-ba-

---

292. Cf. FAOS 7, p. 43.

293. See ITT V, p. 67.

294. It is the period of the compilation of RTC 221–23, (cf. *supra*, p. 128, n. 112).

295. AOTb 321 was "Grand texte de 2x6 colonnes, 3 cassè; compte d'une matière dont le nom est perdu, mesurée en sicles et en minas; parmi les gens cités: šu-ku$_6$-me et mušen-dù-me, sipa-anše-me, gala-maḫ, nu-bànda-gu$_4$" (private communication by J.-J. Glassner).

296. L 2824; 3057; 4431; 5732; 5886; CT 50, 146; 147; 157; MVN 3, 47.

297. Ur-^{giš}gigir should probably is the namesake sagi who occurs in L 4497. Ur-^{giš}gigir occurs about 20 times, more frequently without title (L 1416; 2833; 2981; 4354; 4406; 4427; 4539; 4545; 4670; 4689; 5824; 5892; 9441; RTC 115; CT 50, 129; 186) or with the title ugula (L 1305; 1448). The maškim supervisor who occurs in RTC 127 o. I 4' is this latter official. A namesake má-laḫ$_4$ occurs in L 1436.

298. Both in L 1062 and in L 1129, the name Ur-ba-gára has been restored (L 1062 2 Ur-[ba-gá]ra; L 1129 o. 4 Ur-ba-[gára]). This restoration has been suggested by the contemporary presence of Uru-ki in L 1062 o. 4 and in L 1129 (S9) o. 5. In Foster, *JANES* (1980): 36 a mention of Ur-ba-gára is indicated in L 3124, but the summary of ITT II, p. 16, does not list this official.

gára occurs in L 4539 with Ab-ba ì-du$_8$ and Lú-^{d}Utu (perhaps the namesake scribe) in connection with dumu-nita, dumu-mí, and dumu-ga for whom the three are probably responsibility. Our official may be the Ur-ba-[x] in RTC 124 r. II 4', a summary account of enormous quantities of barley, dated to the reign of Šar-kali-šarrī. Uru-ki also occurs in RTC 91 r. II' 2'–3' and RTC 125 r. II 4' as the recipient of bread; and in L 4360 as the maškim supervisor of a consignment of sheep to Ur-sa.[299] Uru-ki also occurs in L 6682 o. 4, a letter written by [Sin-ru]puš to Lugal-ušum-gal,[300] and in DCS 4, 32, a summary account of garments in the possession of Uru-ki (Uru-ki-da ì-da-gál).

Ur-ba-gára was probably the person in charge of the flour needed to make bread and of the bread itself that was regularly allocated to the highest-ranking officials by the administration.[301] Ur-ba-gára may later have been the nu-bànda é-gal in RTC 221. Uru-ki was in charge of beverages.

A certain Ur-ba-gára was the official who incurred expenditures in a group of documents, the greater part of which are certainly Post-Sargonic: DCS 4, 30; MVN 6, 12; 22; 86; 250. In MVN 6, 29 he is the recipient of ì-du$_{10}$-ga and in MVN 6, 77 the maškim supervisor.[302]

The wealth and size of the Sargonic archive of Girsu enables us to establish a hierarchy among the scribes mentioned in the administrative documents:

---

299. In L 4360 another maškim, Ur-èn, is mentioned. This official also occurs with Uru-ki in RTC 91 and perhaps in L 6682. In L 4360, the nu-bànda é-gal is also mentioned as a recipient. It is likely that this nu-bànda is Lú-zàḫ, who occurs with this title in L 4497, where the sagi Ur-^{giš}gigir occurs as the maškim supervisor rather than Ur-ba-gára.

300. Kienast and Volk, FAOS 19, p. 66, regard Uru-ki as an indication of place (uru^{ki}). The official's anthroponym [x]-li, which occurs in line 6, could perhaps be integrated as [Ur]-èn (cf. previous note).

301. Cf. for example, RTC 124–27.

302. A more detailed analysis of the Ur-ba-gára archive and of the career of this official will be the subject of further study by the writer.

(1) at the head of the institution were the dub-sar-maḫ Lú-sa₆(g), his ugula Lú-ᵈUtu, and the énsi-gal Šeš-šeš.

(2) the second tier consisted of the scribes Da-ti, Lugal-bur, Lú-bàn-da, and perhaps Ur-ᵈNin-gír-su (if the identification with the namesake sa₁₂-du₅ can be established). While Da-ti and Lugal-bur were linked to the administration of various goods, Lú-bàn-da was apparently involved in the administration in charge of fish.

[margin note: England JAOS 122 500 doub? This 4-t? system]

(3) the third tier is comprised of the scribes Túl-ta, Ur-ᵈNin-dar-a, UŠ, and Lú-zàḫ—all four involved in the management of cattle.

All the officials in these three groups were holders of large parcels of agricultural lands.

(4) There may have been a fourth tier of scribes, who appear to have been specialized in particular sectors of administration and production, but who do not seem to be as important as those in Group (3). For example, Ur-GAR and Nam-maḫ(-ni) were involved in the administration of fishing and means of navigation; Amar-su₆, Lú-Ab-ba₆, Ur-ᵈEn-ki, Ur-nu, and perhaps Ur-ki were involved in the administration of sheep and goats and their by-products; and Ab-ba, En-an-na-túm, and NÌGIN were involved in the distribution of flour and grain. Ur-ba-gára seems to have had a role in this latter activity but at a different level. Uru-ki may have been connected to the household of the sagi-maḫ and to the administration of beverages.

Several scribes occur elsewhere as šabra's (Ab-ba, Du-du, Nimgir-èš, Ur-šu), gudu₄'s (Nimgir-èš, Ur-ki), and sanga's (Ur-ᵈNin-gír-su, Ur-nu). It is often difficult to identify these officials with the namesake dub-sar, but in some cases it appears likely that they are scribes of temple households linked to the é-gal.

In addition to these four groups, it is possible to identify eleven scribes (Beli-rabi, Rim-Ḫaniš, Íl-ga, Ka-tar, Ki-tuš-ni, Lugal-gar, Lugal-NE/IZI, Nabium, Puzur₄-šùba, Šu-ili, Zu-zu) who were certainly not part of the staff of the é-gal. Most may have been scribes from other cities, such as the scribe Zu-zu from Gasur, or scribes in the entourage of the king or of royal dignitaries. But in some cases it is possible that they were officials operating in the Girsu region outside the administration of the é-gal; albeit, at times, employed by that institution.

3. The Scribes of Adab

The Sargonic archive of Adab contains about 900 tablets and fragments. Three hundred form part of the collections housed in the Oriental Institute of the University of Chicago; the remaining 600 tablets are housed in the Istanbul Museum. Most of the Sargonic documents in the Oriental Institute were published in the 1930s by D. Luckenbill.[303] Subsequently, Yang Zhi published the remaining texts as well as newly collated texts that had appeared in OIP 14.[304] Zhi, in PPAC 1, analyzes text typologies and proposes a reconstruction of what must have been the main administrative structures of Adab during the Sargonic period.[305]

The 600 tablets of the Istanbul Museum remain unpublished, although a brief description of their contents has been given by F. R. Kraus.[306] In addition, several seal inscriptions were found, a copy and transcription of which were originally published by R. M. Boehmer[307] and republished in RIM, 2.[308]

According to the excavation records of E. J. Banks,[309] who excavated the site between 1904 and 1905, the majority of the tablets from the

---

303. D.D. Luckenbill, *Inscriptions from Adab*, OIP 14 (Chicago, 1930), nos. 78–198. Subsequently, Yang Zhi, *Sargonic Inscriptions from Adab*, PPAC 1 (Changchun, 1989).

304. Yang Zhi, *op. cit.*; collated PPAC 1, pp. 285–389.

305. Using the sigla in PPAC 1, the texts of the Chicago Oriental Institute collections are designated with a number preceded by the letter A and those of the Istanbul Museum by a number preceded by Ad.

306. F. R. Kraus, "Istanbuler Tontafelsammlung," *JCS* 1 (1947): 100–1.

307. R. M. Boehmer, *Die Entwicklung der Glyptik während der Akkad Zeit* (Berlin, 1965).

308. In 1998 several hundred tablets, both Sargonic and Pre-Sargonic—surely from Adab, coming from illicit digs by local Arabs, appeared on the market. I could see about 30 Fara-type tablets coming from Adab, on sale in the United States in 1998. M. Molina informed me that he had bought about 300 Sargonic tablets, probably from Adab, in London some months ago.

309. E. J. Banks, *Bismya or the Lost City of Adab* (New York, 1912). A reworking on the

Sargonic period came from two findspots. The largest lot of tablets was found on the floor of a room in a building located in Mound IV, which is situated in the central part of the site.[310] This fact, coupled with internal evidence, indicates that here was a single archive, probably that of the Sargonic administration of the city, which must have had its center in Mound IV. The building where the tablets were found, therefore, may have been that of the énsi.[311] Banks found a smaller lot of tablets in different rooms in Mound III, which is situated at the edge of the excavation, to the northwest. This lot is comprised of several small tablet collections that could have come from several archives and may not, therefore, be directly connected with the administration of the city.[312]

The vast majority of the tablets date to the reign of Šar-kali-šarrī; only a few to the reign of Narām-Sîn.[313]

The Sargonic archive of Adab in the Oriental Institute is constituted primarily of administrative records, legal documents, letters, memoranda, and labels.[314] The administrative archive contains records of land, grain and grain products, beer, animals (e.g., sheep, cattle, pigs), metals, textiles, oil, and fats.[315]

Nineteen dub-sar's and one dub-sar-maḫ are mentioned in this documentation. The anthroponyms of two other dub-sar's are not preserved. A dub-sar Nibru^{ki}, whose name has been lost, is mentioned once. Possibly at least two other dub-sar's, never mentioned with this title, occur in the documentation. The documents in which these scribes are mentioned all come from the site of Mound IV, headquarters of the administration of Adab.

---

basis of the excavation records made by Banks with a more accurate reconstruction of what the site must have been like has recently been published by Yang Zhi, "The Excavation of Adab," *JAC* 3 (1988): 1–21.

310. For a map of the excavation, see Yang Zhi, *op cit.*, p. 6.

311. Cf. PPAC 1, pp. 29, 270.

312. Cf. PPAC 1, pp. 29, 270.

313. Cf. PPAC 1, pp. 29–34.

314. PPAC 1, pp. 115ff.

315. For the full details of the typologies of texts, see PPAC 1, pp. 139–223.

Six other scribes whose seal imprints or whose seals have survived should be added to the scribes mentioned in the administrative documentation. These seals come from Mounds III and IV.

In addition to the dub-sar-maḫ, who is always unnamed, three scribes (Enlil, Inim-ma, and UN-íl), who are mentioned numerous times in the documentation, seem to have played a special role in the Sargonic administration of Adab when Lugal-giš was énsi.

En-líl dub-sar is mentioned in many texts of varied contents. He occurs in one group of homogeneous texts: A 646 o. I 7'–8'; 683+869 r. 16'–17'; 707 r. 8; 944 r. 3–4; 965 r. 3–4.

A 707, 944, and 965 record the receipt of the monthly sá-du$_{11}$, "regular offerings," of barley and emmer or only emmer; they conclude with the clause "the regular offerings for the gods, En-líl, the scribe, received."

A 683 is a *Sammeltafel* that collects all the sá-du$_{11}$ offerings for nine months, from the first month, that of the Akiti festival, to the ninth month, when the barley was cut.[316] The text ends with the clause kú-a En-líl. The En-líl of this clause, keeping in mind similar clauses in A 707, 944, 965, assuredly is the namesake scribe.[317] Possibly the term kú-a does not refer to En-líl, as Zhi suggests,[318] but to sá-du$_{11}$-dingir-e-ne.[319] In this case, the entire clause could be translated "the regular offerings to the gods consumed, En-líl (the scribe received/had in charge)."[320]

316. sá-du$_{11}$-dingir-e-ne 9 iti iti á-ki-ti-ta iti še-kin-ku$_{5}$-šè. For the Sargonic calendar of Adab, see PPAC 1, pp. 53–57.

317. Cf. PPAC 1, p. 243, no. 26. En-líl does not seem to refer to the namesake god or to the city of Nippur, since, if the god, the divine determinative is missing, and if the city, the place determinative is missing.

318. PPAC 1, p. 243.

319. Cf. the similar clause in A 730 r. II 9.

320. A similar formula is recorded in A 998 r. 5 (OIP 14, 89). This text lists two items: the first concerns sá-du$_{11}$ offerings of beer for the seventh day, the second of bread and perhaps beer specified by the clause é-maḫ kú-a ^{d}En-líl iti á-ki-ti. This clause, by analogy with A 683, may mean: "For the food of the é-maḫ, Enlil (the scribe received) in the month of Akiti."

A 646 contains two sections that record grain and silver, presumably due as taxes.[321] The first section collects entries of grain and silver, probably field taxes,[322] and the second section contains only one item, a record of barley concerning the sá-du$_{11}$ offerings to the gods. The scribe En-líl deposited the barley recorded in the first section in the storage facility of the new palace.[323] The name of the scribe who deposited the barley recorded in the second section (I 9), relative to the sá-du$_{11}$, and the third item (I 13) is lost in the lacunae.

En-líl dub-sar occurs in A 674 r. 6–7 in which he receives from several engar's threshed barley probably due the recording institution. In A 637 o. II 2'–3' En-líl is the maškim supervisor who collects the rents for institutional lands. Since En-líl maškim performed the same function (receiving and maintaining the accounts for the payment of revenues to the institution) as the dub-sar's UN-íl and En-líl (A 1121 and A 646),[324] it seems probable that En-líl maškim and En-líl dub-sar are the same individual.[325] Furthermore, in A 637 barley is collected by the scribe UN-íl. In A 981 Lú-^{d}En-líl ("subordinate of En-líl," probably the namesake scribe) and lú Ilsu-dan ("subordinate of Ilsu-dan," who, in turn, was a subordinate of the dub-sar-maḫ) are recipients of beer.[326] In A 923 o. 4 En-líl dub-sar delivers onions for Akkad. The fragmentary tablet A 1012, 2' contains "from the enigga En-líl (the scribe) has received in the month when the barley is harvested."[327]

---

321. Cf. PPAC 1, pp. 231–32.

322. The tax maš-ašag$_x$ is discussed in PPAC 1, pp. 226–27; 232–35. The maš-da tax in PPAC 1, p. 230.

323. [x]+34 lá 1 še gur [é]-kišib-ba é-gibil-ka [an]-si ^{d}[E]n-líl-lá dub-sar. For an-si, "it is filled," cf. PPAC 1, p. 232. The same term occurs in the similar text, A 1121. The recording scribe in this case is UN-íl.

324. Cf. PPAC 1, pp. 231–32.

325. Another dub-sar, Inim-ma, occurs as bailiff in A 684 o. I' 6.

326. Zhi, PPAC 1, p. 261 regards Lú-^{d}En-líl as an anthroponym. While this cannot be excluded, the contemporary mention of a subordinate of the dub-sar-maḫ, Ilsu-dan, and the fact that this anthroponym is mentioned only in A 650 o. 1, [L]ú-^{d}E[n-líl$^{?}$], makes it more probable that the lú is not part of the anthroponym and means "a subordinate of" En-líl.

327. é-níg-gur$_{11}$-t[a] En-líl šu-ba-ti iti še-kin-ku$_{5}$.

Inim-ma dub-sar is regarded by Zhi to be the scribe in charge of cult expenditures.[328] In fact, Inim-ma is often mentioned in the body of texts concluding with the clause zi-ga Inim-ma dub-sar. The texts characterized by this clause are: A 865 r. 5, a text recording amounts of barley flour and emmer (zì-ZÍZ.AN) for the nì-^{giš}kiri$_6$ festival and bread and flour distributed by Igi-zi (ne-ne-gar Igi-zi); A 1002 o. 3 – v. 1 and X 1, which record, respectively, zì-gu and emmer for the god Iškur[329]; A 1021, which records beer breads sent to Ur-Èr-ra for the perfume-maker[330]; A 1026, which records zì-gu for ^{d}EN.ZU-lugal-ni, the nu-èš; and A 1113, which records lentils (gú-gú-gal-gal) for Lugal-ezen.[331]

Inim-ma is also mentioned in A 707, a text recording various deliveries of grain[332]; in A 745, which records amounts of harvested grain which Lugal-igi-tab and Lugal-giš, cultivators from the fortress of Ur-èš, delivered to Inim-ma and which were deposited in the house of the armed forces for the second time[333]; in A 816 o. 6, which records "x donkeys belonging to Lugal-á$^{?}$-da-DU the nisku, which have been brought by UN-íl dub-sar, Inim-ma dub-sar have taken in charge for plow from the palace"[334]; in A 624 o. 10, summary

---

328. PPAC 1, pp. 264–66.

329. M. A. Powell, "Sumerian Cereal Crops," *BSA* 1 (1984): 54ff., translates zì-gu as "a finest quality-*ḫišiltu* flour." Zhi, PPAC 1, p. 177 considers zì-gu a special type of food for feasts allocated to high-ranking officials, e.g., the énsi, the nu-èš.

330. In A 1019, the same person receives kaš-GIN delivered by the é-lùmgi for the same purpose.

331. It is also possible that A 1082, a text recording allocations of flour and lentils to UN-íl, was issued by Inim-ma. Unfortunately the name of the official to whom it was disbursed has been lost.

332. In A 707, a first group of five surviving entries recording barley and emmer from the field of the goddess Šeraḫ, ends with a total (šu-nígin) and with the clause Inim-ma dub-sar. A second group, consisting of only one delivery from the same field, after a blank line, ends with the clause sá-du$_{11}$-dingir-e-[ne] En-líl dub-s[ar].

333. [še-gi]š-ra-a engar-e-n[e] bàd-Ur-èš^{ki}-ta Inim-ma dub-sar-e mu-túm é-á-^{me}mè-ka an-si a-rá 2-kam.

334. [x] $^{\text{[an]še}}$dusu-giš [Lu]gal-á!-da-DU *ni-is-ku* UN-íl dub-sar mu-túm Inim-ma dub-sa[r] $^{\text{[giš]}}$apin é-gal-ta ì-dab$_5$. For a discussion of the term *nisku*, see B. R. Foster, "ni-is-ku," *RA* 75 (1981): 190 and USP, p. 85.

accounts of barley, emmer, and lentils for the past and current years, which Sipa-an-né, the muḫaldim, received for the kitchens of the énsi. Portions of the grain were supplied by Inim-ma, UN-íl, and an unnamed group of scribes (še dub-sar-ne-kam); in A 684 o. I 6 Inim-ma is the maškim supervisor of one of the transactions—the text concerns copper, sheep, and large quantities of barley, all due for the maš-ašag$_x$ tax; in A 690+876 r. 10 Inim-ma is in charge of, or more probably the one who pays perhaps En-líl nu-èš a fee for, the transport of barley along the i$_7$-^{d}Nin-mu-DU canal[335]; in X 3 (PPAC 1, p. 388) Inim-ma received barley that Lugal-[ ] returned (šu-a gi$_4$-a).

UN-íl dub-sar is regarded by Zhi as "the scribe in charge of grain and flour supplies for travellers,"[336] based on the his mention in A 919 and 1014, which concern travellers and contain the phrase "disbursement of UN-íl." A 919[337] records allocations of flour for the Gutian,

---

335. A group of texts involving fees for the transport of barley on the i$_7$-^{d}Nin-mu-DU canal is discussed in PPAC 1, pp. 232–37. Each item of these texts has three numbers (x, y, and z) in the following sequence: x še gur y; z addir$_x$ má-laḫ$_4$ PN. The number y is not specified, but the second z is specified as addir$_x$ má-laḫ$_4$. The following relationship exists: x=40 y and y=3 z and so x= 30 (y+z). In the summary, the numbers y and z are added separately and received by the nu-èš ^{d}En-líl-lá. The number x indicates the quantity of barley transported, the number y a fee or tax paid to the temple or to the administration, and the number z the fee paid to the transporter. Zhi, PPAC 1, p. 238, n. 18, suggests that y and z might only be the cost of the transport of the goods and not proper fees or taxes, y the hire of the boat, and z the hire of the boatman—but this would raise the problem as to who was the owner of the boats and who was the boatman's superior. There are no similar texts in the Pre-Sargonic and Sargonic documents, but contracts for the hiring of boats for transport of goods have been found in the Ur III period.

Another text connected with transport ships in which Inim-ma is mentioned is A 726. In this text two large amounts of barley (240 gur each) are mentioned in connection with má En-an-né and má Inim-ma. This probably concerns barley loaded onto the ships of En-an-né and Inim-ma—barley given by a certain Da-da-izkim and[?] by a dub-sar from Nippur whose name is lost in the lacuna, and the dub-sar Lú-làl, who drew up the balanced account but did not debit Da-da-izkim: ki Da-da-i[zkim-x] [ ] dub-sar Nibru^{ki} [ ] an-na-s[um] Lú-làl dub-sar nì-kas$_7$ ba-na-ak Da-da-izkim-ra nu-na-zi.

336. PPAC 1 p. 267.

337. Discussed by P. Steinkeller, "The Old Akkadian Term for 'Easterner'," *RA* 74 (1980): 7–8.

(and) foreigners travellers/transporters from the east, issued by UN-íl."[338] A 1014 concerns flour allocations[339] to the travellers/transporters of MAŠKIM-*ì-lí*.[340] UN-íl is mentioned in other barley texts: A 624 o. 11 records a barley delivery by UN-íl the scribe for the kitchens of the énsi; A 773 o. 5 and A 862 o. 3, two similar texts in which an unnamed dumu Be-lí-gú in Adab receives barley in A 773 and silver and barley in A 862. The officials who delivered the goods apparently were UN-íl, Šul-gi, and Ur-é in A 773; UN-íl and Ur-é in A 862. In A 968 r. 1 he is mentioned in connection with amounts of barley perhaps for baking bread.[341] He is mentioned in A 1121 o. II 4, in which UN-íl deposits barley in the palace storehouse—probably from the engar's as a kind of tax; A 805 r. 2, an account of sheep delivered by people described as uru^{ki}-ke$_4$-ne, "citizens," in which UN-íl is entrusted by Lugal-e with the task; A 816.4, which concerns ^{anše}dusu that UN-íl dub-sar brought; A 1045 r. 1–2, a record of the delivery of a sheep to Pà-da disbursed by UN-íl.

In A 897+908 o. 4, a very fragmentary text, é-UN-íl occurs, an office or household headed by UN-íl.[342] The text records the receipt$^?$ of minas of silver and containers of ì-dug contributed$^?$ by Inim-ma.

---

338. gu-ti-um-me gìr-gin-na *sa*$_{12}$*-ti-um* zi-ga UN-íl. For *sa*$_{12}$*-ti-um*, see P.Steinkeller, *RA* 74 (1980): 1–9.

339. zi-ga UN-íl [g]ìr-gin-na [MAŠ]KIM-*ì-lí*. The allocated flour is described by the term da-bulug^{ninda}, which also occurs in A 750 o. 3 and 1007 o. 4; v 1, but not preceded by dabin. Without the determinative ninda, but preceded by the term banšur, it also occurs in A 809 o. 5 in connection with pigs and pig skins. Zhi, PPAC 1, p. 180, supposes from the context of A 750; 1007; and 1014, that da-bulug^{ninda} is a particular type of bread. The hypothesis proposed by P. Steinkeller, *RA* 74 (1980): 6, n. 7, appears more convincing; he regards da-bulug^{ninda} as "a type of receptacle in which breads and arrows could be stored." This seems to be confirmed by the occurrence of da-bulug^{ninda} in texts from Girsu (L 2880) and Susa (MDP 14, 7; 22) and by da-bulug concerning arrows in MDP 14, 86.

340. MAŠKIM-*ì-lí* is considered by Zhi, PPAC 1, p. 180, to be a personal name. But perhaps it indicates the bailiff of the (temple of the) god.

341. Cf. PPAC 1, p. 267.

342. Here, perhaps, it is an anthroponym. It is possible also that UN-íl is a professional name and therefore é-UN-íl designates a guild of porters.

dub-sar-maḫ is head of the scribes and is always mentioned in texts without name. Zhi identifies the dub-sar-maḫ of Adab as Ilsu-dan,[343] an official who occurs in a small text, A 1010 r. 4–5, concerning non-identifiable goods: [ ] lú Umma^{ki} 1 Lugal-šutur (TÚG.NÁM) lú Nibru^{ki} Ur-^{d}Inanna an-na-sum 1 Ìl-su-dan dub-sar-maḫ [an-na]-sum. But this identification is to be rejected. As a matter of fact, the recipients of the goods are the people signed by the ciphers, [PN] lú-Umma^{ki}, Lugal-šutur lú-Nibru^{ki}, and Ilsu-dan, while Ur-^{d}Inanna and the unnamed dub-sar-maḫ not signed by cipher and following the names of the recipients are the officials who delivered the goods. Then, we can translate the text "1 (to) PN, the man of Umma; 1 (to) Lugal-šutur, the man of Nippur; (from) Ur-^{d}Inanna were given. 1 (to) Ilsu-dan (from) the dub-sar-maḫ was given."[344] This unnamed dub-sar-maḫ is mentioned again in A 784 o. 1 as recipient of a parcel of 10 bur of irrigated land (aša$_5$ ki-duru$_5$)[345]; in A 839 o. 1 he, and his subordinate Ur-^{d}Ištar, lú-u$_5$, an unnamed lú-éš-gíd, and others whose names are lost in lacuna, supervise work on the i$_7$-^{d}eš$_5$-peš-ša$_4$ canal; and in A 969 r. 2, which mentions containers being stored with him (ki dub-sar-maḫ-ka al-gál).

Other scribes mentioned in the documentation are:

Lú-làl dub-sar occurs in A 726 r. 51 as the official who compiled the balanced account of barley loaded onto the ships of En-an-ni and Inim-ma.

A namesake official without title occurs in A 1209 o. II.6 in charge of arrears incurred for the boatmen for the sustenance of the énsi and of the priestess of ^{d}Nin-šubur. The mention of Lú-làl and boatmen in the same text in both A 726 and A 1209 suggests

343. PPAC 1, p. 435.

344. Ilsu-dan also occurs without title in A 981 o. 3, a text we have already discussed concerning the scribe En-líl, as the official whose subordinate is a recipient of beer (lú Ìl-su-dan). Noting lú Umma^{ki} and a lú Nibru^{ki} in A 1010, possibly Ilsu-dan was not originally from Adab.

345. The text does not say whether this parcel was allocated for sustenance or was rented from the institution. It should be noted that the recipients of parcels of land are all high-ranking officials (énsi-gal; sagi-gal, etc.; cf. PPAC 1, p. 152).

that the official mentioned in A 1209 is the namesake scribe and that he belongs to the boatmen's office.

Lugal-é dub-sar is mentioned in A 842 o. 7, which contains nine entries concerning barley to individuals[346] and in A 991 o. 3 (OIP 14, 120) which records a delivery by Lugal-é dub-sar of two goats and their young, managed by Ur-ur sipa.

The reference to Lugal-é dub-sar in A 991 enables us to identify him with the namesake official who occurs untitled only in goat texts: A 805 r. 7 records the receipt by Lugal-é of seven goats from various officials (sagi, sipa, sipa-anše, šitim); A 922 r. 1 records ten sheep given to Ur-^{d}Dumu-zi sipa-udu by Lugal-é; A 844.7 records the delivery of lambskins and goatskins by Amar-kù and Lugal-é; A 1022 r. 1 records the delivery of 225 sickles of wool that Lugal-é received and stored in the palace[347]; A 1086 r. 2–3 (OIP 14, 99) is a record of the contribution by Ur-ur of one goat as a maš-da-ri-a, which Lugal-é took into his charge. All these records indicate that the scribe Lugal-é was the receiver in the é-gal of goats and their by-products from the husbandry stations.

---

346. The lines following the summary are lost; they probably contained the clauses regarding the destination or the provenance of the barley.

Of the nine officials mentioned in A 842, three are identified only by title (gala-gal; lú-éš-gíd; lú-še-bala-[ ]), three by their anthroponym and the characterizing element expressed by a professional name (dub-sar; lú-ganun), or by blood relationship (ama En-an-na-túm). The remaining individuals are identified only by anthroponym. Some of the amounts of barley recorded in the text are signed in the box under the name, in smaller characters, using the term zi-ga; others use the term PAP, and one uses the term a-tag. Only one other text, A 916, has signatures for single items in the same box, but in this case the term used is diri, "in excess." Zhi, PPAC 1, p. 37 observes: "both of these texts are only partially preserved, making it impossible to ascertain the exact meaning of these remarks by working through the equation of the amounts. In general PAP, a-tag, and zi-ga in A 842 seem to be different categories of debit from the storehouse's account." Other texts contain analogous signatures (A 652; 674; 683; 699; 850), but in these cases the remarks are made up of numbers expressed in thinner cuneiform signs when compared with the rounded ones in the upper part of the box. These thin cuneiform signs probably indicate the arrears, or that part of the total indicated in the entry is an arrears.

347. Cf. PPAC 1, p. 195.

Lugal-iti-da dub-sar is the recipient of gú-gú-gal in A 972 o. 5–r. 1.[348] A namesake sukkal is mentioned in A 712 o. 3 and 795 o. 2.[349] Lugal-iti-da in A 772 o. 2 is recipient of 2 iku of arable land.[350]

Lugal-NI n[u-èš$^{?}$] dub-sar occurs in A 790 o. 5 (OIP 14, 114), which records maš-bi and udu-bi taxes due from the recipients of a parcel of land from the field called x.ŠIR.BUR^{mušen}.

Me-ság/^{sá}sag$_7$ dub-sar is mentioned in A 940 o. – r. 15, one of the twelve documents discussed in Foster, *JANES* 12, as recipient of fish delivered by Ur-[ ] šu-ku$_6$ in the [é$^{?}$]-mar-ma-ta.

In A 937 o. 2 and 978 o. 5 a namesake sagi is mentioned. Me-ság without title occurs in several texts.[351] On the basis of typology and content, Me-ság in these documents is the namesake sagi. Me-ság sagi appears in A 978 o. 5 (OIP 14, 93) in charge of the é-bappir of the énsi and in transactions concerning beer of differing qualities.[352] Me-ság without title signs A 925 r. 2 (OIP 14, 92) and A 970 r.

---

348. Besides Lugal-iti-da there are other recipients: Ur-^{d}Ištaran lú-u$_5$, who is a subordinate of the dub-sar-maḫ (cf. A 839 o. 1); Lugal-maḫ, an official never mentioned elsewhere; and Ur-NÌGIN, perhaps the namesake dub-sar mentioned in A 936 o. 2. For the meaning of gú-gú-gal and gú-gú-tur as "chick peas and lentils" cf. M. A. Powell, "Sumerian Cereal Crops," *BSA* 1 (1984): 61. For a different interpretation of gú-gú-gal as "broad beans," cf. M. Stol, "Beans, Peas, Lentils and Vetches in Akkadian Texts," *BSA* 2 (1985): 128–29.

349. Lugal-iti-da, who occurs without title in A 677 o. 5—a text exactly like A 712 and 821 (cf. PPAC 1, p. 259)—should be the namesake sukkal. He also occurs without title in A 725 o. 5, a text recording the delivery of še eštub and še-kur to Badtibira by engar's, among whom was Lugal-iti-da; the goods were received by Belam-nupiq (še giš-ra engar-[e-ne] *in* Pa$_5$-ti-bí-ra[^{ki}] *Be-lam-nu-pi-i*[*q*] *im*-[*ḫur*]). A namesake muḫaldim occurs also in A 690 o. 3.

350. It is surprising that the existence of two namesake officials, one a dub-sar and one a sukkal, did not lead the scribe who compiled A 677, 725, and 772 to specify to which of the two officials he was referring. This leaves open the possibility that they were the same person.

351. The name of the official is sometimes written Me-ság(PA.GAN), but more frequently Me-^{sá}sag$_7$(GAN). But without doubt it is always the same anthroponym.

352. muš-túm é-bappir énsi-ka me-^{sá}sag$_7$ sagi. The term muš-túm, which is characteristic of the beer texts, is discussed in PPAC 1, pp. 187–88, where it is rendered: "fully fermented beer." (For muš-túm=*naparkû*, see *CAD* N, p. 279; for different orthographies for this term, see A. Falkenstein, AnOr 28 (1978), pp. 28–29.)

4 (OIP 14, 101), texts concerning beer, with the clauses: è Me-ság; zi-ga Me-^{sá}sag$_7$ "out-going/expense by Me-ság." In A 937 o. 2 (OIP 14, 100) Me-ság sagi receives bronze objects, while Me-ság without title in A 777 r. 5 (OIP 14, 103) distributes bronze objects. The Me-ság mentioned in A 669 o. 5, a text concerning barley for the é-muḫaldim and the é-bappir of the énsi, and in A 938, in which he receives barley from the storehouse to make ninda-ḫar-ra, an expenditure of Enanatum should be identified with the namesake sagi. Thus, the Me-ság mentioned in the documents, except for A 940, is a sagi. Probably, then, the scribe Me-ság and the namesake sagi were the same individual. Of course, it is possible that our scribe was from another town.

Ur-é-maḫ dub-sar is mentioned only in two texts: A 721 r. 4–5 records his receipt of various kinds of bread and beer delivered to the palace for the festivals of bára-^{d}En-líl and ^{d}Dumu-zi; A 1008 o. 4–r. 1 is a record of 60 sìla of barley, perhaps intended as fodder for draft$^{?}$ donkeys (še-anše-giš) received by Ur-é-maḫ the scribe in the é-gu$_4$.

Ur-é-maḫ occurs without title in four texts. In A 986 r. 1–2, he receives three sìla and one sìla of ì-giš from Puzur$_4$-Ma-ma and Nin-sa$_6$[353]; in A 984 Ur-é-maḫ is the recipient of two parcels of land[354]; in A 933 r. 2–3 Ur-é-maḫ is the official who disbursed sesame and zì-níg-nag$_x$ (KUM/GAZ)-gá[355]; in A 963 o. 3 Ur-é-maḫ is the addressee of a letter sent by En-abzu, probably his subordinate.[356]

This group of texts is characterized by the term muš-túm and never contains the clause è or zi-ga and therefore are not distribution texts (PPAC 1, p. 187).

353. Puzur$_4$-Ma-ma is mentioned as the šeš *i-ma-ru-um* in a text (A 944 o. 4) concerning emmer delivered as offerings for the gods to En-líl dub-sar. Nin-sa$_6$ is not mentioned elsewhere.

354. In the same text Igi-bar is mentioned as one of the recipients of a parcel of land of 4 iku ašag$_x$. This official sent a letter to Šar-kali-šarrī (A 874 o. 1), complaining that he had not received a ki-duru$_5$ parcel of land and begging the king's intervention so that he would receive it (cf. FAOS 19, pp. 58–60; LEM, p. 32).

355. Perhaps a by-product of the sesame plant; cf. PPAC 1, p. 183.

356. For the transliteration and translation of this letter, cf. LEM, p. 33; FAOS 19, pp. 52–53. En-abzu is mentioned in A 684, 2 with the scribe Inim-ma as the maškim in charge of a delivery of barley due as tax.

Ur-NÌGIN dub-sar is mentioned in A 936 o. 2 as the recipient of beer delivered by the é-sukkal-gi-<si>.[357]

In A 972 r. 2 Ur-NÌGIN without title and the scribe Lugal-iti-da are the recipients of 20 sìla of gú-gú-gal legumes (... Lugal-iti-da dub-sar ù Ur-NÌGIN). As discussed above, recipients of this type of goods are generally high-ranking officials; thus it is probable that the title dub-sar applies to our official as well as to Lugal-iti-da. Ur-NÌGIN is mentioned in A 756 o. 4 as the official who delivered two minas of bronze to the sagi Me-ság and in A 707 o. 6—a record of sá-du$_{11}$-dingir-e-ne signed by the scribes Inim-ma and En-líl—in connection with barley and še-muš.

Ur-zikum-ma dub-sar is mentioned in A 846 o. 7. He and Lugal-má-gur$_8$-e receive 95 sìla of barley, (feed?) for ducks, an expenditure by En-an-na-túm.

This anthroponym is mentioned in A 699 o. 9 in connection with 3 gur and 2 bariga of barley, probably due as an obligation (ašag$_x$ maš-da ì-[kas$_7^?$]).

Last, an unnamed énsi-gal is the recipient of two containers for dates in A 714 o. 6[358] and of a plot of land measuring 10 bur in A 784 o. 3. In A 784, the recipients are ordered: dub-sar-maḫ, énsi-gal, sagi-maḫ, Ur-mes dam-gàr and an unnamed lú-éš-gíd. This order is similar to that in some references to Šeš-šeš énsi-gal in the Girsu texts.[359] An unnamed énsi-gal occurs in A 826 o. 1, which concerns unspecified goods.

Three scribes occur only once in the texts from Adab:

I-ku-bu-sa! dub-sar is mentioned in A 662 r. 3, a record of the delivery of sheep to the king, the queen, the šabra-é, and the šabra giš-kin-ti, probably for the king's journey to Sumer.

Si-dù dub-sar is mentioned in A 672 o. 3. Each entry in the text contains the quantity of goods, in some cases the purpose of the

357. Zhi, PPAC 1, pp. 261–62, considers é-sukkal-gi-si's department as a separate brewery from that of the énsi.

358. In the same text, listed among the recipients are the sanga of Iškur, the sagi-maḫ, and UN-íl nu-èš.

359. Cf. *supra*, sub Šeš-šeš dub-sar-maḫ.

allocation[360] and, with but one exception, the name of the official in charge of the transaction. From context, Si-dù was in charge of the delivery of three jars of lard for the šabra's journey, perhaps a military expedition to Elam (suggestion by B. R. Foster).

Šu-ni-DINGIR dub-sar is mentioned in A 661 o. 6, a damaged letter from Nam-tar-ré, in which an ass belonging to the UN-gal was taken by Šu-ni-DINGIR dub-sar and brought by Ì-sa$_6$-sa$_6$ to the estate of Ur-^{giš}gigir, son of Lugal-KA, for (work on) a field of 18 iku cultivated for sesame, which the šabra-é had given him.[361]

The absence of other references to these anthroponyms and the particular content of these texts suggest that these officials did not work for the énsi of Adab, but rather depended either directly on the king, on the šabra-é, or perhaps even on the administration of another city.

In addition to those mentioned in the administrative texts, there are scribes known only from their seal impressions:

[A]-ba-an-da-sá dub-sar is mentioned on a stone seal kept at Istanbul, Ad 771, in connection with an énsi whose name is only partly preserved.[362] He is not mentioned elsewhere.

Amar-šùba dub-sar is mentioned in Ad 769, a bulla kept at Istanbul dating from the Late Sargonic period: Du-du *da-núm šàr A-kà-dè*^{ki} Amar-šùba dub-sar [i]r$_{11}$-*sú*.[363]

Du-du dub-sar is mentioned in A 530, a seal imprint found in Mound III.[364] The seal of a namesake official, described as UN-gal in A 529, was found at the same site. Thus, they may be the same individual.

---

360. šabra-<é$^{?}$> kaskal-me Si-dù dub-sar, "it is (the lard as provision for the) journey of the šabra-é (to Elam?), in the charge of Si-dù, the scribe"; nam-ra-ak Elam-ke$_4$ ib-še šabra-é maškim, "used for anointing the prisoners from Elam, the šabra-é is the maškim supervisor"; lú-uru maškim <ib?>-še, "used to anoint? LU-uru is the maškim supervisor"; Ur-^{d}En-lí-lá ì-⌈rá$^{?}$-rá⌉, "to Ur-Enlil the perfume-maker."

361. Cf. FAOS 19, pp. 55–57; LEM, pp. 30–31.

362. The passage in question is: [ ].AB énsi adab^{ki} [a]-ba-an-da-sá dub-sar ir$_{11}$-su. The discovery of some yet unpublished sealings enables us to restore the name of the énsi as Lugal-èš (cf. p. 189, sub Lugal-èš).

363. Cf. Frayne, RIM 2, p. 212.

364. Cf. Yang Zhi, "The Excavation of Adab," *JAC* 3 (1988): 11.

Iškun-^{d}Dagan dub-sar is mentioned in the seal impression, NBC 4142: ^{d}*Šar-kà-lí-šar-rí šar bù-u-la-ti* ^{d}En-líl *Tu-tá-šar-li-bí-íš* nin *Iš-ku-un-*^{d}*Dagan* dub-sar šabra [é]-ti-[sá] ìr-[*sú*] "Šar-kali-šarrī, king of the subjects of the god Enlil. Tuta-šar-libbiš, the queen. Iškun-Dagan, scribe and her majordomo, (is) her servant."[365]

A namesake official is mentioned in AO 4419, a letter sent by Iškun-^{d}Dagan to Puzur$_{4}$-aš-tár. Since it is likely that the recipient of this letter is the official who signed some of the tablets found in Mound III (A 709; 975), it is also probable that Iškun-Dagan is the namesake dub-sar šabra-é of NBC 4142.[367] Iškun-^{d}Dagan appears also in PUL 21 r. 8'.

Kirbanum dub-sar is mentioned in A 917: *Šar-kà-lí-šar-rí šar A-kà-dè*^{ki} *Kir-ba-núm* dub-sar ir$_{11}$-*sú*.[366]

Lugal-èš dub-sar was énsi of Adab during the reign of Šar-kali-šarrī. He occurs in three unpublished seals (recently appearing on the market), which span the career of this scribe. In the first of these seals he is indicated as a dub-sar, a subordinate of Šar-kali-šarrī (as crown prince) during the reign of Narām-Sîn. In the second he was a dub-sar when Šar-kali-šarrī became king. In the third he was titled dub-sar and énsi of Adab. Surely he is the énsi who occurs in Ad 771. It is likely he succeeded Lugal-giš as governor of Adab late in the reign of Šar-kali-šarrī. He does not occur elsewhere in the archive.[368]

Lugal-giš dub-sar was the énsi of Adab during the early reign of Šar-kali-šarrī.[369] His seal impressions, housed in Istanbul, Ad 767, 768, have the inscription [*Š*]*ar-kà-lí-šar-rí* dingir ur-sag *A-kà-dè*^{ki} Lugal-giš dub-sar é[nsi] Ad[ab^{ki}] ìr-*sú*, "Šar-kali-šarrī the god, the hero of Akkad/the divine hero of Akkad, Lugal-giš scribe and governor of

365. Cf. RIM 2, p. 198.

366. *Ibidem*, p. 204.

367. *Ibidem*, p. 184 ii; see previously G. Biga, *RSO* 53 (1975): 204; Foster, *JNES* 37 (1978): 275.

368. Private communication of Foster, who could read the sealings in question and the bulla of Ur-èš dub-sar (see below, p. 190).

369. Cf. PPAC 1, p. 30.

Akkad, is his servant." This inscription should be compared with those of Lugal-ušum-gal énsi of Lagaš, discussed above.

Nam-tar-ré appears in a seal imprint:[370] Lugal-giš énsi Adab^{ki} Nam-tar-ré dub-sar sanga ^{d}En-ki ir$_{11}$-da-ni, "Lugal-giš énsi of Adab, Nam-tar-ré the scribe, sanga of Enki (is) his servant." As in the case of Iškun-^{d}Dagan, the official is identified by his double title as both the scribe and the administrator of the god Enki.[371]

A namesake official who could be identified with our scribe was the sender of the letter A 661.[372] This anthroponym is not mentioned elsewhere in documents from Adab, while he occurs frequently in the texts from Nippur, in particular, a namesake dub-sar is mentioned in OSP 2, 133 r. 10, a text from the "onion" archive.

Ur-èš dub-sar appears in an unpublished bulla dedicated to Narām-Sîn dingir A-kà-dè^{ki} (courtesy of Foster). He does not occur elsewhere, but the mention of bàd Ur-èš, "the fortress of Ur-èš," in A 745 could refer to this official.

Ur-mes is mentioned in the stone seal A 889, found in Mound III, [PN *šàr ki-ib-ra-tim*] *ar-ba-im* Ur-mes dub-sar ir$_{11}$-*sú*. D. Frayne[373] restores the name of the king as Narām-Sîn, because of the formula *šàr ki-ib-ra-tim ar-ba-im* and because of its provenance, Mound III. Nonetheless, there is the possibility that the royal name was Šar-kali-šarrī.[374]

---

370. Cf. Y. Kuga, "An Inscribed Sargonic Cylinder Seal in the Atarashi Collection," *ASJ* 14 (1992): 103–23.

371. It is not clear whether ^{d}En-ki is an abbreviation for é-^{d}En-ki, which, in this case, would refer to the temple of the god Enki where Nam-tar-ré was sanga. There is only one reference to ^{d}En-ki in A 680 (OIP 14, 142), a text concerning sheep allocated to the é-maḫ, the temple of bára-^{d}En-líl, and to other divinities, among whom is Enki, and to other persons. It is signed with the clause, en-né íl-la, "raised for ancestors" (PPAC 1, p. 194; Y. Kuga, *ASJ* 14 [1992]: 110).

372. Cf. *supra*, sub Šu-ni-DINGIR dub-sar. Y. Kuga, *ASJ* 14 (1992): 120, n. 17 is of a different opinion.

373. RIM 2, p. 171.

374. Ur-mes dam-gàr is mentioned in A 784 5 as recipient of 6 bur of ki-duru$_5$ land. A namesake official without title is the recipient of 1 iku of garden in the du$_6$ ^{dgiš}Bíl-ga-mes^{ki} in A 693 o. 5' and of 120 sìla of barley in A 893 o. 3'.

As noted above, the documentation places particular emphasis on the activity of the scribes En-líl, Inim-ma, and UN-íl. Zhi regards the scribe En-líl as the scribe in charge of the distribution of the sá-du$_{11}$ for the gods; Inim-ma as the scribe in charge of cultic deliveries; and UN-íl as the scribe in charge of the allocations of barley and flour for journeys.[375] The roles Zhi assigns to these three scribes are too restricted. These scribes seem to have had more important roles. In fact, they appear to have been the managers over a wide range of commodities, not just barley, grain and it by-products, and onions, but also of silver and cattle. They pay out or receive goods on behalf of the city administration or perhaps in the wider sphere of inter-city commerce. The officials En-líl and UN-íl occur in the documentation with the title nu-èš,[376] a high-ranking temple official linked to the énsi's administration. Another nu-èš, Lugal-NI, is mentioned in A 947.7. In addition, a namesake official with the title x-[ ] dub-sar occurs in A 790.5 (OIP 14, 144). The sign Luckenbill reads as "x" from his copy seems part of the sign nu. A comparison with A 947 suggests restoring the title Lugal-NI in A 790.5 with n[u-èš] dub-sar, thus identifying the dub-sar with the namesake nu-èš. Similarly, we could identify the dub-sar's En-líl and UN-íl with the namesake nu-èš. On the basis of this reconstruction, they would therefore be the scribes in charge of the administration of the temple households connected with the administration of the é-gal. In that function, they record the income and expenditure of these households and were probably, as well, responsible for the management of the institutional lands that were either granted or leased. The particular role these two scribes performed within the administration of Adab also is indicated by their being mentioned separately, compared to other dub-sar's who in A 624 record the expenses for the kitchens of the énsi.

It is possible to identify the activities of two other dub-sar's. Lugal-é was the scribe in charge of sheep breeding. Me-ság dub-sar and sagi were in charge of the allocation of beverages to the officials of the institution and of the purchase of these goods for the é-gal. Ur-é-maḫ seems to have been in charge of the allocation of bread and beer on festive

375. PPAC 1, pp. 248, 267.

376. With the title nu-èš, Enlil occurs in A 658 r. 14; 751 r. 4; 793 o. 6; 825 r. 3; 828 9; UN-íl in A 714 r. 4–5.

occasions and also connected with agricultural activities. Lú-làl was the scribe in charge of the management of boatmen on whose behalf he received from and delivered goods to the administration.

Two other officials, Lugal-šutur and En-an-na-túm, who always occur without title, were probably scribes.[377] The Lugal-šutur appears to have been responsible for the é-bappir, a center of the é-sukkal-gi-si, while En-an-na-túm was in charge of the storehouse of the é-gal.[378]

4. The Scribes of Nippur

The site of Nippur was excavated at the end of the last century by the Babylonian Expedition of the University of Pennsylvania. The most important excavations were carried out in the region of the Ekur. Unfortunately, the Sargonic settlements in the region of Ekur were almost completely destroyed due to the reconstruction of the Ekur during the reign of Ur-Nammu. From the Sargonic period private houses were found in an adjacent site, the so-called scribal quarters.

Most of the documentation from the Classical Sargonic period of Nippur were published by A. Westenholz, mainly in OSP 2. In addition, there are 30 texts, published in ECTJ and in OSP 1, that date to the reign of Narām-Sîn.[379] Of these 30 documents, 11 are ration lists of

377. Lugal-šutur is an anthroponym mentioned in texts concerning beer. In A 1033; 1037; 1078 he is the official who disburses the beer; in A 1096 he is the official who delivers kaš-sig$_5$ from the brewery of the énsi; and in A 982 o. 2, in which 80 gur of barley is delivered to Úr-ra-ni the sukkal. According to Zhi, PPAC 1, pp. 186–87; 256, Lugal-šutur was one of the officials appointed by the énsi to oversee the beer business.

En-an-na-túm, probably in charge of the é-kišib, signs A 938. This official occurs in A 748 r. 1–2; 846 r. 1–2; 938 r. 2–3; 973 r. 2–3; 994 o. 2–3; 1015 r. 1–2; 1100 4 with the same function. He also occurs in A 646 o. I 3; 652 r. 6; 692 r. 3; 802 o. 4.

378. Cf. PPAC 1, pp. 256–58; 261–64.

379. The OSP 1 documents are, with some rare exceptions, from the Late ED and Early Sargonic periods. OSP 1, 47 is one of these exceptions. The text, which records a list of 60 persons (dumu-dumu-UŠ) organized into three teams of 20 supervised by an ugula, can be dated to the reign of Narām-Sîn (cf. OSP 1, p. 9 nn. 20; 36).

barley,[380] which probably should be connected to a "large ration list from Ekur" from the period of Narām-Sîn that will appear in OSP 3.[381]

The 181 texts published in OSP 2, the 30 in ECTJ and OSP 1, and the roughly 400 texts that will be published in OSP 3 seem to belong to four distinct archives, each with quite distinct paleography, prosopography, and content: (1) the Akkadian archive; (2) the En-líl-e-ma-ba archive and family archives; (3) the "onion" archive; and (4) the Narām-Sîn ration lists.[382]

In all, 23 scribes are mentioned. In some texts the anthroponym is not preserved and an unnamed dub-sar-maḫ occurs (see TABLE 15).

4.1 *The Akkadian Archive*

The majority of tablets from the Akkadian archive (OSP 2, 1–35) were found in the "courtyard of the Ekur" in Mound III during the excavations of the Second and Third Expeditions. The remaining tablets, among which are six seal imprints, must have come from the same area or from neighboring areas.[383] The contents of the texts leave no doubt that most of them belong to the archive of an Akkadian institution involved with the Ekur, probably in connection with reconstruction work at the Ekur begun during the reign of Narām-Sîn and concluded during that of Šar-kali-šarrī.[384] All the texts have the characteristic Akkadian *ductus* and many are written in Akkadian. Those with a preserved date are dated by the Akkadian calendar rather than by the local one. Three scribes are mentioned in these documents by their seal impressions.

---

380. Cf. ECTJ, pp. 10–12.

381. Cf. OSP 2, p. 7. From Nippur we have not only the texts mentioned above, but also some 300 in Istanbul, as well as a number from more recent excavations (private communication by A. Westenholz).

382. The Akkadian archive (AA) consists of OSP 2, 1–43; ECTJ 13; 51; 126; 205. The ^{d}En-líl-e-ma-ba archive and family archives (EA) consist of OSP 2, 44–65; 66–78; The "onion" archive (OA) consists of OSP 2, 79–181. The Narām-Sîn ration lists (NRL) consist of ECTJ 29; 34; 37; 39; 44; 148; 185; 186; 189; 191; 196 and about 400 documents to appear in OSP 3.

383. Cf. OSP 2, pp. 22–23.

384. Cf. OSP 2, p. 24.

Ṭappu-alim (Du$_{10}$-pù-URU.KI^{im}) dub-sar[385] occurs in a seal imprint. D. Frayne identifies the "fill of an Old Babylonian drain in WA near the southeast corner of Mound I" as the findspot.[386] The inscription states: *Šar-kà-lí-šar-rí* dumu-lugal *Du*$_{10}$*-pù-*URU.KI^{im} dub-sar ir$_{11}$-*sú*, "Šar-kali-šarrī son of the king, Ṭappu-alim the scribe (is) his servant."[387] There are no other references to the scribe Ṭappu-alim in the documentation.

Udatum (Ú-da-tum) dub-sar is mentioned in OSP 2, 36, which groups together identical seal impressions from the fragments of four jars: Ú-da-tum dub-sar Puzur$_4$-aš-tár dumu-*sú*!. Between the names of Udatum and Puzur$_4$-aš-tár is the figure of a lion, a figure which identified the seal of the scribe Udatum. This seal was probably inherited by his son Puzur$_4$-aš-tár,[388] probably also a scribe.

Ur-^{d}EN.ZU dub-sar is mentioned in OSP 2, 3, a seal impression placed on the tablet envelope recording the receipt by Šu-Ma-ma of 222 Akkadian gur of barley for the sanga (of the Ekur), brought by Maš.[389]

4.2 *The Enlile-maba Archive*

There is no information from the excavation documents that would enable us to identify the findspot of the texts comprising the ^{d}En-líl-e-ma-ba archive (OSP 2, 44–65). Some elements, however, seem to indicate that they were found by the Fourth Expedition and that they came

385. For a different reading and for the possible Hurrian derivation of this anthroponym, cf. OSP 2, p. 24, n. 18.

386. RIM 2, p. 178 (n. 2021).

387. From this inscription it would seem that Šar-kali-šarrī was governor of Nippur before he ascended to the throne (cf. RIM 2, p. 178), but, more likely, his presence in Nippur is linked to the reconstruction of the Ekur.

388. Cf. OSP 2, p. 53.

389. The barley was stored in containers measured in gur-sag-gál of Marad. For this interpretation, see OSP 2, p. 32. A certain Šu-Ma-ma is mentioned in OSP 2, 13 r. I 1, a text that lists workers under the supervision of an ugula and nu-bànda. But he does not appear to be identifiable with the namesake official in OSP 2, 3. Maš is not mentioned elsewhere.

from sites other than the courtyard of the Ekur.[390] The archive concerns a group of private money lenders and real estate owners who rarely did business with public institutions. Regularly mentioned are the dam-gàr's ^{d}En-líl-e-ma-ba, É-lú, Amar-ezinu, various artisans, and others. Of particular interest is the position of Šeš-ku-li nu-bànda kù-dím, who, presumably, was the head of the city's silversmiths' guild. All these people appear to have a connection with the é-ad-da (literally, "father's house"); this was perhaps a family type institution with a common fund, the dusu é-ad-da, "the family basket." Individual members of the family could borrow from this fund, and were obliged to repay with interest in annual installments over a certain period of time; it is impossible to determine the interest rates. Family members succeeded each other as head of the household: Lugal-inim-giš-tuku, Ur-^{d}Nammu, É-lú, and finally ^{d}En-líl-e-ma-ba. The archive dates to the reign of Narām-Sîn and perhaps some texts to the end of the reign of Maništusu.[391] Archives similar to that of ^{d}En-líl-e-ma-ba must have existed, but have not survived. Pieces of such archives could be OSP 2, 66 and 67, two texts concerning a certain Lugal-inim-gi-na and OSP 2, 68–71, four texts that record a series of speculative commercial ventures concerning the dam-gàr Lugal-iti-da. In the ^{d}En-líl-e-ma-ba archive two scribes are mentioned.

En-eden-né dub-sar is mentioned in several texts of the ^{d}En-líl-e-ma-ba archive. OSP 2, 46 o. 5 is a document recording "the statement of Ur-Nammu's account with the 'family basket' and its transfer to Elu."[392] In this document En-eden-né received ½ mina of silver from the family fund (^{giš}dusu) from Ur-^{d}Nammu. OSP 2, 47 o. 5 is a similar document recording "the statement of É-lú with the dusu" where En-eden-né received from É-lú silver from the family fund, ^{giš}dusu. OSP 2, 50 r. I 3 is a document recording the sale of two slaves, property of a single seller, to separate purchasers. En-eden-né was one of the witnesses of the transaction and likely the scribe who wrote the document.

390. Cf. OSP 2, p. 59.

391. For more details on the characteristics of this archive and its socio-political implications, cf. OSP 2, pp. 59–61.

392. Cf. OSP 2, p. 63.

En-eden-né is mentioned without title in OSP 2, 54 r. 6, a document concerning the ownership of a 9 iku parcel of land and two houses, as well as a loan for 21 years guaranteed by En-eden-né.[393] He occurs in OSP 2, 62 o. I 12, which summarizes a series of transactions between É-lú and ^{d}En-líl-e-ma-ba—some of the entries of OSP 2, 62 are recorded in other texts[394] and En-eden-né was the supervisor of one or two of these transactions.[395] OSP 2, 63 o. I 3; r. I 2, is similar to OSP 2, 62, which summarizes a series of payment records into the "family fund." So too in this case some of the entries corresponding to entries recorded in OSP 2, 63 have been identified.[396] In OSP 2, 63 En-eden-né makes two payments of silver into the ^{giš}dusu.

The En-eden-né in all five of these OSP texts is the same dub-sar, and his texts are part of this family archive. In this archive, he occurs both as the recipient of silver goods paid out by the family fund, probably a six-year loan, received by Ur-^{d}Nammu and confirmed by É-lú,[397] and as one of the persons who deposited silver into the family fund, probably as a loan repayment or as the annual loan instalment. We do not know whether he was also in the employ of the civil administration, but most certainly he is the first scribe whose activity outside of public institutions can be documented.

Lugal-bára dub-sar is mentioned in OSP 2, 44 o. II 4 as a witness to the transfer of objects belonging to Lugal-inim-e, head of the "family," to AN-lú, perhaps through Úr-<ra>-ni, his representative. The reason for the transaction is not given.[398]

4.3 *The Onion Archive*

The exact findspot of the "onion" archive cannot be established. But as in the case of the texts from the ^{d}En-líl-e-ma-ba archive, indirect

393. For ab-gi-né "guarantees," cf. OSP 2, p. 70, differently SRJ, p. 123.

394. These are OSP 2, 46; 47; 48; 52; 54; 55; 59; 60; 61; 63.

395. Ur-^{d}Nammu BE-dè in-tag$_4$ é-lú in-lá u$_4$-ba En-eden-né ugula-ni.

396. OSP 2, 47; 51– 55; 58–62.

397. Cf. OSP 2, 47 o. 3' mu-6-šè.

398. AN-lú (probably an abbreviation of the anthroponym AN-lú-maḫ, father? of Lugal-en-nu) occurs only in OSP 2, 51 r. 1; 52 r. 13; 63 r. I 13; 64 o. 5.

evidence indicates that the lot of tablets came from an area "in the broad and deep trench carried into the South-East side of Mound I along the side as far as the corner between Mound I and Mound IV" near the area where the great temple WA was excavated.[399]

Many of the tablets contain dates from the beginning of Šar-kali-šarrī's reign, and so it is probable that the entire archive is from this period. However, it is possible that some texts date from the end of the reign of Narām-Sîn.[400]

The Onion archive consists of documents about the cultivation, harvesting, and distribution of different types of onions (sum-sikil, sum-gaz, sum-TU.LÚ, sum-GAM.GAM), turnips (lu-sar), and coriander (še-lú). The same individuals, many referred to as lú-sar-ra, occur throughout these documents dealing with cultivation and harvesting (OSP 2, 80–112).[401] Lugal-nì-BE-du$_{10}$ gal-kiri$_6$ receives the produce harvested by the lú-sar-ra; is in charge of the payment of taxes[402] due on the produce[403]; and is in charge of allocating the produce (OSP 2, 114–81).[404] The recipients, all of high rank, receive either regular monthly allocations (sá-du$_{11}$) or occasional ones, for which the reason is often stated.

The officials who supervise or receive the delivery of the goods on behalf of the administration often are titled maškim, more rarely dub-sar.[405] The regular allocations are for Ninurta and the tables of the énsi and the king.[406] The occasional contributions, which are the more frequent, are for officials and members of the institution, among whom are many scribes and sagi's. Many of the sagi allocations are in connec-

---

399. OSP 2, pp. 87–88; see OSP 2, p. 88, fig. 2.

400. OSP 2, p. 89.

401. OSP 2, p. 90.

402. Cf. OSP 2, pp. 91–93. For the close relationship between the "onion" archive, belonging to the énsi, and the temple of Ninurta, see OSP 2, pp. 97ff.

403. íl-taxes in OSP 2, 113 10.

404. All of these texts have the following subscriptions: ki-gal-kiri$_6$-ta al-zi/ ki-Lugal-nì-BE-du$_{10}$-ta al-zi/ ki-Lugal-nì-BE-du$_{10}$ gal-kiri$_6$-ta al-zi.

405. It is unclear whether in this latter case the meaning is PN dub-sar <maškim> or PN recorded the onion delivery.

406. banšur énsi; banšur lugal, OSP 2, pp. 96–97.

tion with persons who are about to make or have just made a journey (kaskal-šè)—the destination is not always mentioned. Other occasions for allocations were religious festivals or important events in the life of the city, such as a visit by the royal family and their entourage or the coronation of the en. The identity of the officials who were the recipients shows that the office of the gal-kiri$_6$[407] was part of a larger bureaucratic organization of the royal administration of the region of Nippur.

Eleven scribes and one dub-sar-maḫ are mentioned in these texts:

[Du]-du dub-sar is the recipient of an allocation of sum-gaz in OSP 2, 141 o. 6. A nu-bànda and a namesake sagi occur in the documentation. The nu-bànda was the recipient of onions in OSP 2, 122 o. 6 and the sagi received 2 gú of onions in OSP 2, 147 o. 5.

The mention of three high-ranking officials with the same name does not enable us to identify the namesake official who occurs without title in the documentation.[408]

Du$_{11}$-ga-ni dub-sar in OSP 2, 134 r. 2; 142 o. 6; and 149 o. 9 is the supervisor for a contribution of onions (Du$_{11}$-ga-ni dub-sar <maškim-bi>). In OSP 2, 164 he is the recipient of a monthly allocation of onions in the e-eren-na[409] beginning in the first month, disbursed by Lugal-nì-BE-du$_{10}$; the reason for this allocation is not stated—perhaps as supervisor for the maintenance of the e-eren-na canal.

He occurs without title in OSP 2, 122 o. 5 and in records concerning harvesting various fields belonging to the administration.[410] Possibly this latter untitled official is our scribe.

Inim-kù dub-sar is the maškim supervisor of two allocations in OSP 2, 128 r. I 5; 10 and of one allocation in OSP 2, 130 o. I 12. He is a recipient of onions in OSP 2, 126 o. II 1[411] and OSP 2, 152 o. 3. In OSP 2,

407. Onion Office, OSP 2, pp. 93–97.

408. Du-du occurs without title in OSP 2, 84 v I 3; 93 r. II 3; 96–97 r. I 9; 160 o. 4; and 178 r. 3.

409. x sum líd-ga e-eren-na-a du$_{11}$-ga-ni dub-sar-ra an-na-ág iti-da 2(b) 3 (bàn)-ta [iti bára-z]à-gar-ta. E-eren-na is, in all likelihood, the name of a canal (cf. OSP 2, p. 171: "perhaps the canal's name is i$_7$-e-eren-na.") The meaning of the small wedge that follows this term escapes us.

410. OSP 2, 95 o. III 4; 96–97 r. II 7; III 5; 98 o. II 8; 100 r. I 12.

411. The recipients include the scribe Inim-kù, the énsi, the sa$_{12}$-du$_5$ Nam-tar-ré,

140, with the title of ša$_{13}$-dub-<ba>, "archivist," he is the recipient of káb-ku$_{5}$ containers of onions.

Probably the namesake official mentioned without title in several harvest records is our scribe/archivist.[412] A namesake dumu Ù-mu-ni-ni is mentioned as a recipient in OSP 2, 123 o. 5 and 155–56 r. 3'.[413]

Lugal-sa$_{6}$ dub-sar is mentioned in OSP 2, 179 o. 4, which has three entries, each concerning three varieties of onions: sum-sikil, sum TU.LÚ, and sum-gaz. The text ends with the name of the scribe, Lugal-sa$_{6}$. It is not clear whether he should be regarded as a recipient of the onions listed in the three entries, as the official who supervised the transaction, or the scribe who compiled the tablet. It is highly likely that [ ]-sa$_{6}$ dub-sar who occurs as a recipient in OSP 2, 126 o. I 11 is our scribe.[414]

Nam-tar-ré dub-sar in OSP 2, 133 occurs in o. 12 as the maškim supervisor of an allocation of onions and in r. 10 as the recipient of sum-gaz and sum-sikil.

A namesake sa$_{12}$-du$_{5}$ is the recipient of four káb-ku$_{5}$ of onions in OSP 2, 126 o. II.7.

Without a title, he is the recipient in OSP 2, 129 r. II.5 (in this text perhaps the professional name is lost in the *lacuna*) and in 154.11.[415] He is also mentioned in several harvest records.[416] In OSP 2, 80 II.12 he receives onion seed (numun-sum).[417]

---

another scribe, perhaps Lugal-sa$_{6}$, a sagi, the dumu-en, and the šeš of the sagi-gal.

412. OSP 2, 80 o. I 9; 84 o. I 10 = 96–97 o. IV 5; 93 o. I 8.

413. For the reading Ù-mu-ni-ni, cf. P. Steinkeller, "Observations on the Sumerian Personal Names in Ibla Sources and on the Onomasticon of Mari and Kish," *Studies Hallo*, p. 238.

Possibly the Ù-mu-ni-ni in OSP 2, 123 and 155–56 is linked to a scribe mentioned in an unpublished text from the NRL archive, where only a part of the anthroponym is preserved (cf. *infra*, p. 203).

414. Cf. OSP 2, p. 137.

415. In this latter text he is the recipient of 1 bariga of sum-gaz equal to that received by the namesake dub-sar in OSP 2, 133 (in this latter text, however, he also received 2 bariga of sum-sikil).

416. OSP 2, 80, 84 r. I 11; 94 r. I 6; 96–97 r. I 9; II.6.

417. It is possible to link our scribe with the namesake dub-sar mentioned in the

Nita dub-sar is mentioned in OSP 2, 147 o. 9 as the recipient of two bariga of onions. Nita is probably an abbreviation for Nita-zi—two officials named Nita and Nita-zi occur in this archive with the same title.[418] Since only scribes and a few high-ranking officials, such as the šabra, had their own seals, it is likely that Nita-<zi> dub-sar and the namesake ugula-é are the same person. Nita and Nita-zi without title occur in harvest records (OSP 2, 84 o. II.8; 86 o. I.6; 96–97 o. IV 15; 105 o. I.5) and in allocation texts (OSP 2, 124 o. II.7; 182 r. 7). But an identification of these officials with the namesake dub-sar cannot be made with any certainty.[419]

Šu-ilisu (Šu-ì-<lí>-su) dub-sar giš-kin-ti occurs in OSP 2, 133 o. 5; 8; 140 r. 5–6 as the recipient of onions. Without a title he occurs in OSP 2, 141 o. 8 and perhaps in 168 r. II 3 as the recipient of onions.

This scribe may be the official to whom workers were allocated in a text from Girsu, RTC 91 o. II 14; III 6; r. III 14.[420] The description of this official as "the scribe of the workshop" occurs only in these texts. Another official connected with this office is the šabra-<é>-giš-kin-ti, who seems to have been one of the highest-ranking dignitaries in the kingdom, subordinate only to the king, queen, and the šabra-é.[421] The é-giš-kin-ti at Nippur seems to have been totally involved in the reconstruction of the Ekur. This could have

---

Adab archive (cf. *supra,* p. 190) and the namesake šabra who occurs in a seal from the Girsu archive, L 4622.

Given the mention of Nam-tar-ré in both the Adab and Nippur archives, we cannot exclude an identification with this unnamed dub-sar-maḫ who occurs only in OSP 2, 136 o. 2.

418. Nita ugula-é is mentioned in OSP 2, 134 r. 10 and is the recipient of bunches of sum-sikil and sum-gaz as provisions for a journey to Akkad: Nita ugula-é *A-kà-d*[*e*^{ki}] du-ni šu-ba-ti; Nita-zi ugula-é occurs in a seal imprint, OSP 2, 187, as the father/superior of a certain UN-íl: Nam-maḫ-abzu énsi Nibru^{ki} UN-íl dumu Nita-zi ugula-é, and probably in OSP 2, 168 v II 7' ([Nita$^{?}$]-zi ugula-é), as the official who signs the tablet (cf. OSP 2, p. 173).

419. A certain Nita dumu Mes-é occurs in several texts (OSP 2, 124 r. I.3; 126 r. I.14; 134 o. 10; 174 7), but we are unable to distinguish between this official and the namesake dub-sar.

420. Cf. OSP 2, p. 95.

421. For this official in the texts of Adab and Girsu, cf. Foster, *JANES* (1980): 29ff.

been a unit set up by Narām-Sîn for managing the reconstruction of principal temples in cities, such as Adab, Zabalam, and Nippur. This official, in the direct employ of the Crown, must have been responsible for the management of goods and personnel for that organization.

Ur-^{d}Da-mu dub-sar in OSP 2, 139 o. 2 received 2 bariga of onions on the occasion of the énsi's journey to Akkad.[422] Possibly Ur-^{d}Da-mu received the onions on behalf of the énsi. In OSP 2, 154.2 he delivers one bariga of sum-sikil and one of sum-gaz for the wedding of the king's son, probably in connection with a journey to Marḫaši.[423] Ur-^{d}Da-mu may have been the official whose anthroponym is partially lost in OSP 2, 115.1, 2 (bàn) Ur-$^{⌜d⌝}$[ ] *A-kà-dè*$^{[ki]}$ du-ni šu-ba-ti.[424]

Ur-^{d}Da-mu may have been responsible for providing high-ranking officials with provisions for their journeys. Possibly he is the namesake sagi[425] who in OSP 2, 128 o. II 14; 131 r. I 6' e 132 r. II 3 delivered onions to Puzur$_{4}$-Sîn, a high-ranking Akkadian official.[426]

Ur-^{d}En-ki dub-sar is mentioned in OSP 2, 145 o. 3 as the official who delivered$^{?}$ sum-sikil and sum-gaz for one of the énsi's journeys.[427] His role appears similar to that of Ur-^{d}Da-mu.

A certain Du-du dumu Ur-^{d}En-ki is mentioned as a recipient in OSP 2, 129 o. I 15; 134 r. 6–7 and 135 r. 3'. If this Du-du is the dub-

---

422. Ur-^{d}Da-mu dub-sar-e énsi *A-kà-dè*^{ki} du-ni šu-ba-ti; cf. OSP 2, p. 154.

423. dumu lugal dam-[tuku] ba-túm-ma-a Ur-^{d}Da-mu dub-[sar] ba-túm. Cf. OSP 2, pp. 97; 165.
Another allocation of onions in connection with a journey to Marḫaši made by the lugal's son is recorded in OSP 2, 133.13: 1 (bariga) sum-sikil 1 (bàn) sum-gaz dumu-lugal Mar-ḫa-ši ì-gín-na-a Šeš$^{?}$-ne šu-ba-ti.

424. For the reading du-ni, which also occurs in OSP 2, 129 III 3 and 134.23, instead of gín-né, cf. OSP 2, p. 130 and also USP, p. 20. For the *marû*-form, cf. also M. L. Thomsen, *The Sumerian Language* (Copenhagen, 1984), p. 131.

425. Ur-^{d}Da-mu sagi also occurs in OSP 2, 115 r. 2; 123 r. 4; 126 o. I 13 as the recipient of onions. A namesake untitled official is also mentioned in harvest summary accounts (OSP 2, 80 o. I 11; 98 o. I 8; 107 r. 4).

426. Cf. OSP 2, p. 94, Table of Akkadian Officials.

427. [Ur-^{d}E]n-ki-ka dub-sar [x-k]am-šè énsi kaskal-šè [x-gá]-gá-a-a.

sar previously discussed, it is probable that Ur-^{d}En-ki is the namesake dub-sar.

4.4 *The Narām-Sîn Ration Lists*

The ration tablets from the Narām-Sîn period were probably excavated by the Third and Fourth Babylonian Expeditions. The majority of these tablets must have come from the area of the Ekur[428]—but there is no evidence in the excavation reports that can confirm this.

In the 11 documents published in ECTJ, two scribes are mentioned:

Gissu(GIŠ.MI) dub-sar is mentioned in ECTJ 34 r. III 12, a record of barley rations for the um-ma, dumu-nu-síki, and géme-šáḫ personnel. Our scribe is mentioned at the end of the list of géme-šáḫ personnel. He is separated from the list by a space and thus seems to have been in charge of these categories of people. After the summary, this clause occurs: še-bi 15.3 NI-ga lú-ganun ugula-bi. This lú-ganun official was probably in charge of the barley rations.

Zà-mu dub-sar is mentioned in ECTJ 185 r. III 5–6. This text, like the previous one ECTJ 34, lists the rations to um-ma and géme-šáḫ personnel. The clause that concludes the text, še-bi Zà-mu dub-sar ugula-bi, when compared with that in ECTJ 34, suggests that the scribe Zà-mu is the lú-ganun in the latter document.

In about 200 ration lists from the Ekur, to be published in OSP 3, three scribes occur.[429]

Lugal-iti-da dub-sar is mentioned in a fragmentary ration text, CBS 7952 r. II' 6'–7', as the recipient of one bariga, probably of barley.[430]

[Ù-mu$^{?}$]-ni-ni dub-sar is mentioned in CBS 8272 I' 3', a small text of unclear typology (perhaps concerning goats). This restoration is

428. OSP 1, p. 3.

429. A. Westenholz kindly placed at my disposal the copies of some unpublished tablets of Nippur that mention scribes.

430. Officials with this rather widespread anthroponym, without a characterizing element or with a different characterizing element, are mentioned in the ^{d}En-líl-e-ma-ba archive (cf. OSP 2, p. 197, *sub voce*). This archive is near in time to the archive in question, but we cannot establish any connection.

proposed because of his possible connection with Inim-kù dub-sar.[431]

[ ] dub-sar is mentioned in another ration text CBS 353+ III' 2' similar to the previous one, CBS 442+.

Finally, two unnamed dub-sar's, who receive rations of 2 bariga each from Ur-nin nu-bànda, occur in CBS 182* o. III' 3'. This text is similar to ECTJ 34 and 185. The personnel listed are essentially: um-ma, géme, and dumu-nu-síki.

5. The Scribes of Isin and Tell al-Wilaya

5.1 *The Isin Archive*

A group of about 50 texts, scattered throughout museums and collections, seems, on the basis of prosopography, topography, and content, to have come from the same site. F. J Stephens, E. Sollberger, and others have surmised that this group of texts comes from Nippur.[432] However I. J. Gelb expressed his doubts.[433] A more recent analysis by J. N. Postgate shows that they came from Isin.[434] This provenance seems to be confirmed, at least for several of the documents, by the mention of high-ranking officials from Isin (e.g., Gissu sanga; Nam-maḫ énsi). Although the provenance of some records has been settled, Foster addresses the possibility that "Isin-type" tablets may actually come from Nippur.[435] This group of tablets, which includes legal and commercial documents, is the remains of several family archives, identified and listed by Foster, who dates the whole group to the period of Šar-kali-šarrī.[436] Four other

431. Cf. *supra*, sub Inim-kù. A restoration [Mu]-ni-ni, an anthroponym that occurs in OSP 1, 29 II 5, [Šu-mu]-ì-lí or [Ù]-ì-lí cannot be excluded. For a personal name Ne-ne in the Mari sources, cf. P. Steinkeller, *Studies Hallo*, p. 238.

432. F. J Stephens, BIN 8, p. 7; E. Sollberger, *BiOr* 16 (1959): 115ff.

433. I. J. Gelb, MAD 4, p. XVII.

434. J. N. Postgate, *Sumer* 30 (1974): 209.

435. Foster, *BiOr* 46 (1984): 361.

436. Foster, *ZA* 72 (1982): 6–7. These are: BIN 8, 34–40; 43; 44; 66; 80; 154; 159; 166–

texts have been published as TLAT nos. 4–6; 46. Steinkeller and Postgate see two distinct groups in this lot of tablets.[437] The first group, consisting of 34 tablets,[438] dates to the Classical Sargonic period (Narām-Sîn to Šar-kali-šarrī), the second group, of 16, dates to the Early Sargonic period.[439]

Two scribes are mentioned in the first group of texts.

Lugal-šùd dub-sar is mentioned in MAD 4, 150 r. 5, a contract for the sale of an individual,[440] in which our scribe was one of the witnesses to the transaction.

Me-šeš-šeš dub-sar is mentioned in MAD 4, 15,[441] a contract for the sale of 10 gur of dates. The name of the scribe is written on the left edge of the tablet, Me-šeš-šeš dub-sar-bi, and probably indicates that he wrote the tablet.[442]

A namesake official without title is mentioned in MVN 3, 1 o. II 6; III 5, annual summary accounts of silver. This text is included in the list in Foster, *ZA* 72 (1982), but not in TLAT.

In BIN 8, 163 r. 4 [x-š]eš-šeš delivered dates from the é-^{giš}gigir/túl$^{?}$. This text does not appear in either of the two lists.

68; 170–76; 177'; 213; 241; MAD 4, 14–16; 36; 37; 64; 69–71; 77; 78; 80; 81; 150–53; 155; 158; 169; 170; MVN 3, 1; 52; 57; 63.

437. TLAT, pp. 7–8.

438. BIN 8, 66; 158; 162; 164; 167–68; 171–72; 174–75; 178–80; MAD 4, 14–15; 37; 77; 78; 80–81; 150–51; 155; 158; 169–70; MVN 3, 25; *JCS* 20 (1966): 126; NBC 10197 (unp.); NBC 10198 (ELTS n. 168); NBC 10202 (unp.); NBC 10204 (unp.); YBC 8463 (unp.) and TLAT 46

439. BIN 8, 34; 37; 39; 80; MAD 4, 152–53; MVN 3, 13; 36; 53; 67; Lambert Tablet; Böhl Coll. 929; NBC 6844 (ELTS n. 194); TLAT nos. 4–6.

Not all the texts mentioned by Foster, *ZA* 72 (1982), can be found in Steinkeller's list (BIN 8, 35; 36; 38; 40; 43; 44; 154; 159; 166; 173; 176; MAD 4, 16; 36; 37; 64; 69; 70; MVN 3; 1; 52, 57; 63). On the other hand, Steinkeller includes some texts not mentioned by Foster (BIN 8, 158; 162; 164; 178–80; MVN 3, 13, 25; 36; 53; 67).

440. Cf. NSRJ p. 233, no. 14; ELTS no. 187.

441. Cf. NSRJ p. 247, no. 21; ELTS no. 224.

442. Mention of the scribe who compiled the contract is quite rare in the documentation. In these cases, he often received a gift (cf. ELTS 7.11.3, p. 238).

Two scribes are mentioned in the second group. An unnamed dub-sar occurs in BIN 8, 35 o. 7, which records silver in connection with or to officials indicated by name or profession (saḫar-kam, dub-sar) or according to destination (*A-kà-dè*^{ki}-<šè?>).

Šà-ga-ni dub-sar is mentioned as a lú-ki-inim in MAD 4, 36 r. 7, and is included only in Foster, *ZA* 72 (1982). J. Krecher considered this to be a record of sale of an individual,[443] whereas Gelb thought it was a witnessed loan of silver.[444] The provenance of this document is very uncertain; on the basis of prosopography, it may even be part of the Umma B archive.

5.2 *The Tell al-Wilayah Tablets*

Scribes are mentioned in the documentation discovered at Tell al-Wilayah, a site excavated in 1958 by the Iraqi Directorate-General of Antiquity. The excavation brought to light a brick-built palace situated in the southwest of the site and dated by T. A. W. Madhloom to the Sargonic period,[445] and by J. Margheron as Pre-Sargonic.[446] In all, there were 22 tablets and fragments, seals and seal imprints dating from the Sargonic and Ur III periods. Postgate published copies of the documents and, on the basis of the archaeological and epigraphical evidence, proposed that the site be identified with the ancient city of Kesh.[447] Of the 22 tablets and seals with inscriptions only eight are from

---

443. NSRJ p. 252, no. 23.

444. Cf. MAD 4, p. 26.

445. T. A. W. Madhloom, "Les Fouilles de Tell Wilayah dans le district de Kuta," *Sumer* 16 (1960): 67–68.

446. J. Margueron, *Recherches*, pp. 145ff.

447. J. N. Postgate, "The Inscriptions from tell al-Wilayah," *Sumer* 32 (1976): 77–100. The combination of the dates in question seems to indicate, in Postgate's opinion, that, in the ED period, Keš and Adab had control of the main waterways connecting the Sumerian cities with the northeast, Elam, and the high plateau of modern Iran. This seems to agree with the importance these cities had in the Pre-Sargonic period and their gradual decline in subsequent periods. This decline can be attributed to a change in one of the main waterways, which must have hindered the Nash-river from being a communications channel. The identification with Larak, proposed by some scholars, seems, however, improbable

the Sargonic period, the others from Ur III. From the paleography and from the form of the signs ŠU.NÍGIN, the Sargonic texts date to the Classical Sargonic period. They include records of barley deliveries, barley and silver for various purposes,[448] goats and wool, and seal imprints and seals containing the names of three scribes:

Šu-da-ti dub-sar appears on a cylindrical seal (*Sumer* 32 [1976]: 88, n. 19).

Šu-Ma-ma dub-sar appears on a seal imprint on a jar (*Sumer* 32 [1976]:87, n. 17).

Šu-Eš$_4$-tár um-mi-a appears in the same imprint as the father of Šu-Ma-ma.

The administrative context in which these scribes worked cannot be discerned. But a comparison with texts from neighboring sites, such as Adab and Girsu, shows that they were high-ranking officials, since each possessed a seal.

6. The Scribes of Central Mesopotamia

6.1 *The Kiš Archive*

The Sargonic archive of Kiš, published by Gelb,[449] consists of 68 documents now housed in the Ashmolean Museum. The tablets were found by the Field Museum - Oxford University Joint Expedition to Kiš in the C trenches at Ingharra—an area that must have been the seat of government in the Sargonic period, an area much smaller than during the ED period.[450]

---

because Larak must have been totally abandoned during the ED period and was resettled only in the first millennium.

448. *a-na* šám šaḫ, "to buy fats"; *a-na* še-numun, "(to buy?) seed barley"; *a-na* šám ì, "to buy oil"; *a-na* má, "to (pay price? for) ship."

449. MAD 5, 1–66; 114–16. To these add some Sargonic tablets from Kiš published recently by J.-J. Grégoire in AAICAB I 1: Ash. 1928, 439; 440; 1930, 173; 1931, 1446; Ash. 1932, 1126a and 1126b will be published in AAICAB I 2.
Gelb had included IM 23302; 23304–5 (MAD 5, 102–4) among the texts from Kiš, but did not include Foster, *ZA* 72 (1982): 7.

450. For greater detail, cf. Mcguire Gibson, *The City and Area of Kish* (Miami, 1972), pp. 90; 109 n. 207.

The archive contains four letters, one incantation, one school text, and four loan or sale contracts,[451] and 58 administrative texts. Of these latter texts, 27 concern personnel,[452] ten the allocation and purchase of barley,[453] seven involve goats and other animals,[454] four deal with flour and/or other goods,[455] and one deals with silver.[456] Two are field texts. The first field text, MAD 5, 12, concerns the location of ten large parcels of land, totalling 3,132 iku. The second (MAD 5, 40) is a fragment concerning a parcel of land measuring about 60 iku. Given the fragmentary nature of at least seven of the texts preserved, their contents cannot be accurately described.[457]

Given that the preponderance of texts concern personnel and barley, it is probable that the majority of the documentation consisted of summary accounts of one or more institutional households. Among the high-ranking officials an unnamed énsi is mentioned,[458] I-mi-DINGIR šabra-é (MAD 5, 56 o. III 13–v. I 1), and a šabra-é whose anthroponym is lost (MAD 5, 58.5). A certain Sar-a-ti-gu-bi-si-in is mentioned in MAD 5, 2, a long and unusual sequence concerning an order to return a slave: "Adi-lum (who is) with Ilum-danu, (dependent) of Šu-ilišu, the head of the cadastre in the service of Ilum-bani the merchant maidservant in the service of Saratigubisin, must be taken away."[459] This sequence

---

451. Letters: MAD 5, 1, 2, 20; 54; incantation text: MAD 5, 8; school text: MAD 5, 37; contracts: MAD 5, 21, 30, 40, 65.

452. MAD 5, 4; 5; 7; 11; 13–16; 18; 19; 22; 28; 29; 33; 34; 36; 45; 46; 49; 50; 53; 56–58; 60; 62; 116.

453. MAD 5, 3; 6; 9; 24; 31; 44; 52; 59; 64; 115.

454. MAD 5, 25; 26; 41; 42; 55; 63. MAD 5, 114 concerns cattle.

455. MAD 5, 10; 23; 43; 61.

456. MAD 5, 17. This text concerns barley; MAD 5, p. 20 "Receipt of barley (instead of silver) by nine *bêlu*" (šu-nígin 1⅓ ša ma-na 4 gín 1 ma-na-tur 7½ še [*be*]-*lu* še *i-ma-ḫa-ru*).

457. MAD 5, 27; 32; 35; 38; 39; 47; 51.

458. Cf. MAD 5, 42 r. 1, a small account of goats received by the sagi of the dam-gàr of the énsi and by other officials ([PN] sa[gi] dam-gàr énsi *im-ḫur*).

459. ^{I}*A-ti-ilum iš-dè* ^{I}*Ilum-dan ši Šu-ì-lí-su* sa$_{12}$-du$_{5}$ ir$_{11}$ *Ilum-ba-ni* dam-gàr ir$_{11}$ *Sar-a-ti-gu-bi-si-in u-ša-ab li-ru-nim.* For other precative forms of *warawum/tarawum* in Sargonic texts, cf., MAD 3, p. 59.

indicates a hierarchical chain in which the last-mentioned official is the head. A namesake official is mentioned in a Sumerian votive inscription: nam-ti Sar-a-ti-gu-bi-si-in Lugal-la-na-šè, and in a seal: Sar-a-ti-gu-bi-si-in dumu-lugal.[460] Gelb identifies the person mentioned in the votive inscription and in the seal as the official at the head of the sequence in MAD 5, 22.[461] If we accept his identification, the unnamed énsi might be Saratigubisin, the unnamed official mentioned in the sequence in MAD 5, 42, [PN] sagi dam-gàr énsi, and the official whose name is lost could have been the sagi of the business agent of the énsi.[462] The organization of power at Kiš may have been similar to and perhaps connected with that of Mugdan, a large estate under the direct control of the royal family and officials of the highest rank (šabra-é). If so, perhaps MAD 5, 12 is a list of the landed property administered by this household.

Only three scribes are mentioned in the Sargonic documentation of Kiš.

A-mur-DINGIR dub-sar is mentioned in MAD 5, 9 r. II 14, which records the allocation of barley rations totalling 40 sìla (with the exception of one person who received 80 sìla in r. I 22) among four groups of guruš (identified by their patronymic, PN_1 dumu PN_2), each under the supervision of an ugula. One group consists of šitim, one group of persons described as *za-gi-ru* (a profession which remains obscure), and four other persons identified by their patronymic or professional name, like the scribe in question, who received 40, 80, and 30 sìla. The summary records the number of guruš (38) listed in the text,[463] and the barley and silver allocated.[464] After the summary the text apparently contained an indication of the date, which has not been completely preserved.[465]

---

460. Cf. RIM 2, pp. 250–51.

461. MAD 5, pp. XVII–XVIII.

462. MAD 5, p. 105, by describing *Sar-a-ti-gu-bi-si-in* as a"ruler," implicitly makes this hypothesis.

463. There are, in fact, 45 persons listed in the text; cf. MAD 5, p. 12.

464. The silver is not mentioned in the allocations recorded in the text. Possibly some people were paid with the silver mentioned in the summary and equivalent barley was recorded in the various entries.

465. Cf. MAD 5, p. 18.

A namesake official, without title, receives 67 Akkadian gur of barley in MAD 5, 3 o. 5. The text records four large quantities of barley: the first concerns the payment of the price *iškinū* to the owners of the field[466]; the second is given to our scribe, for a journey to an unspecified destination; the third concerns the purchase of 450 shekels of silver[467]; and the fourth indicates barley present but not yet spent. The summary contains the clause DINDIR-GÚ *a-na* LUGAL-É *u-sa-lim*, "DINDIR.GÚ for Lugal-é/the house of the king made good."[468] In MAD 5, 10 r. 5 A-mur-DINGIR is the official who has taken (*it-ba-al*) different kinds of goods (barley, goats, salt) and one or two slaves in three different places (Uru-sag-rig$_7^{ki}$, Dur(BÀD)-^{d}EN.ZU^{ki}, Kiš^{ki}). Finally, MAD 5, 61 is a record of fish involving A-mur-DINGIR. The A-mur-DINGIR mentioned in the last three texts certainly is the namesake dub-sar.

Dingir-a-zu dub-sar is mentioned in MAD 5, 45 r. II 13. The text is a list of guruš úš and ḪAL (dead or fled/dispersed) during the year in a place called Šitu-niše. Dingir-a-zu dub-sar is the šeš of Watrum. This anthroponym is mentioned elsewhere, but there are no elements for identification with the namesake scribe.

Lugal-iti-da dub-sar is mentioned in MAD 5, 31 o. 2' as the recipient of barley. A namesake scribe is mentioned in a text, of unknown provenance, in the Ashmolean Museum, MAD 5, 108 o. 6, in which he is the recipient of barley and silver.

6.2 *The Mugdan Archive*

Ancient Mugdan, modern Umm el Jir, is a small site near Kiš from which a lot of 45 or 46 tablets were found.[469] The identification of Umm

466. For the additional price of a field or house (*iškinū*) and specific reference to this text, cf. ELTS p. 220.

467. Cf. MAD 3, p. 198.

468. MAD 3, p. 272. Lugal-é is a personal name that occurs in many Sargonic Sumerian archives. However, in this context, it is unlikely that it designates a personal name.

469. Thirty-six of these are kept in the Ashmolean Museum and were published by Gelb in MAD 5, 66–101. In addition, Gelb recognized that BIN 8, 144, was

el Jir with ancient Mugdan was first suggested by Gelb on the basis of the frequent references to this city in the texts.[470] This identification was confirmed by archaeological in the excavation reports of McGuire Gibson.[471]

The Mugdan archive, with the exception of the texts published in TLAT, has been analyzed by Foster.[472] In essence, it contains records, all written in Akkadian, of land, barley and other grains, various goods, and letters and school texts.[473] From a prosopographic analysis, the archive appears to be homogeneous, the remains of the official and private documents of a large household or of an estate controlled by members of the royal family or directly by the king during the Narām-Sîn period.[474]

Three or perhaps four scribes are mentioned in the Mugdan documentation.

Aḫi-ṭab (*A-ḫi-ṭá-áb*) dub-sar is mentioned in MAD 5, 80 o. 2, which records four measures of barley that four officials received. Of the four anthroponyms mentioned only one, Pù-pù, is mentioned elsewhere in the documentation.

Belili (*Be-lí-lí*) agrig is mentioned in MAD 5, 88 o. 2, "16½ shekels of silver Belili, the controller of the tablets, has received (payment equivalent to/on account of ?) 230 Akkadian gur of barley, out-go, 'old' barley in arrears."[475]

---

certainly another of the documents from this archive, on the basis of numerous parallels (MAD 5, p. 14). To these tablets should be added eight other tablets, five from the Australian Institute of Archeology in Melbourne published by B. R. Foster, "An Agricultural Archive from Sargonic Akkad," *ASJ* 4 (1982): 41–46 and three from the Iraq Museum published in TLAT 47–49. Probably TLAT 73 comes from Mugdan (cf. TLAT, p. 79).

470. MAD 5, p. XIV.

471. McGuire Gibson, "Umm el Jir, a Town in Akkad," *JNES* 31 (1972): 237–94.

472. Foster, *ASJ* 4 (1982): 7–51.

473. *Ibidem*, p. 7.

474. *Ibidem*, p. 36.

475. *Ibidem*, p. 33,16½ gín kù-babbar *Be-lí-li* agrig *im-ḫur* 240 lá 10 še gur *A-kà-dè*^{ki} è-a še libir.

Belili, without title, occurs in MAD 5, 70 r. 7, as the official who, with Išma-Aštar, gave barley to four people.[476] MAD 4, 86 o. 3, is a note concerning silver that Belili has (is with Belili): "15⅓ shekels of silver in the possession of Belili."[477] Since there are no other persons with this anthroponym in the archive, most likely the Belili in question is the agrig of MAD 5, 88.

Qí-nu-mu-pí dub-sar is mentioned in MAD 5, 69 o. II 7', a damaged tablet concerning agricultural lands and other goods. Qí-nu-mu-pí is involved in a transaction concerning various kinds of goods: asses, sheep? and barley, (in) *Bil*$_x$*-lum*-TUR^{ki}, a place whose name follows that of the scribe.[478] The reason for this transaction, which must have been in the initial part of column iii obverse, which is damaged, may have concerned the purchase of rights to fields of the royal household.[479]

A namesake énsi is mentioned in BIN 8, 144 r. II 11–15 (šu-nígin 585 aša$_5$-sig$_5$ *iš-tum Qí-nu-mu-pí* énsi Lu-lu *ú-šé-ṣí*) and in AIA 8 r. II 7–10 (še-giš-ra-a *šu* 3-mu *ù-ì-lí na-ba-al-kà-at* dub *Qí-nu-mu-pí* énsi). Gelb proposed that Qí-nu-mu-pí énsi and the namesake dub-sar were the same person.[480] In effect, his being mentioned in MAD 5, 69 suggests that Qí-nu-mu-pí was a high-ranking scribe, perhaps on the same level as the énsi Qīšum mentioned in the same text in I 5'.

[x-s]ag dub-sar is mentioned in TLAT 73.11 as the witness to a controversial transaction. Steinkeller and Postgate suggest that this text comes from Mugdan.[481] In fact, a certain Qīšum, the judge in the controversy, is mentioned in the text; he must be the namesake énsi of MAD 5, 69, because of the mention of Qīšum énsi di-ku$_5$ in BIN 8,

476. x (gur) sag-gál PN$_{1-4}$ *im-ḫur* šu-nígin še x sag-gál *Iš-má-aš-tár Be-lí-li i-ti-na.*

477. 15 gín 1 ma-na-tur kù-babbar *iš-dè Be-lí-li i-*[*b*] *a-šè.* MAD 5, p. 75 "Memo concerning a large amount of silver borrowed by one person."

478. D. R. Frayne, *The Early Dynastic List of Geographical Names,* AOS 74 (New Haven 1992), pp. 19–20, considers the possibility that *Bil*$_x$*-lum* is an early writing of the city of Babylon.

479. Cf. Foster, *ASJ* 4 (1982): 21.

480. MAD 5, p. 14.

481. TLAT, p. 109.

121 o. I 12–14, *et passim.*[482] Moreover, other officials in this text who serve as witnesses occur elsewhere in the Mugdan texts.

It is difficult to establish precisely the role and the capacity of the scribes who occur in the documentation of the households of Kiš and Mugdan. But their being mentioned along with the highest-ranking dignitaries of the realm suggests that they were involved at a very high level in the management of their respective institutions.

7. The Scribes of the Diyala Region and Gasur

In the Diyala region many inhabited sites have been found, both large and small, that show signs of settlement from very ancient times. In particular, from the ED period there are four such sites, which, thanks to their particular position along the route linking Babylonia with the north of Mesopotamia, the region of Susa and the upper Tigris region, reached the dimensions and characteristics of large urban structures: Akšak (Tell ʿUmair), Sippar (Habu-Habba), Tutub (Khafaja), and Ešnunna (Tell Asmar). The site of Tell Ağrab should be added to these settlements, although its ancient name is unknown, and those in the Himrin region, among which is Tell el-Suleimah, discovered during the Himrin Salvage Project. It is uncertain whether Tell el-Suleimah should be identified with ancient Awal or Batiri. Of these sites, only Tell Asmar, Tell Ağrab, Khafaja, and Tell el-Suleimah have yielded tablet archives from the Sargonic period.

Tell Asmar, Tell Ağrab, and Khafaja were extensively excavated by the Oriental Institute of University of Chicago Expedition from 1930 to 1938. The sites in the Himrin region were excavated by joint international expeditions during the 1970s. Uch Tepe was excavated by the Chicago-Copenhagen Expedition to the Hamrin, and Tell el-Suleimah and sites nearby by the Iraqi Expedition to the Hamrin.

The site of Yorghan Tepe, the Sargonic city of Gasur, is situated in the northeast of Mesopotamia, near the Lower Zab river. The site was excavated by the Harvard-Baghdad School Expedition at Nuzi from 1928 to 1931. All the Sargonic tablets, with the exception of nos. 224–27, were discovered during the season 1930–31.

482. Cf. D. O. Edzard, "Qišum énsi von Kazallu," in G. Van Driel – Th. J. H. Krispijn – M. Stol – K. R. Veenhof, eds., *Zikir šumim*, Fs. F. R. Kraus (Leiden, 1982), pp. 26–33.

Scribes occur only in the texts from Tell Asmar, Tell el-Suleimah, and Yorghan Tepe.[483]

7.1 *The Ešnunna Archive*

Part of the Tell Asmar excavation report was published by P. Delougaz and S. Lloyd.[484] In OIP 88, particular attention was devoted to the area of the Northern Building, situated in the northern part of the site (OIP 88, fig. 36), and to the nearby so-called "private houses." Almost all the tablets published in MAD 1, 1–195 come from these two sites.[485] The largest lot of Sargonic tablets from Ešnunna comes from the area of the Northern Building.[486] This building shows a series of reconstructions from the ED to Isin-Larsa periods.[487] This series of reconstructions

483. The Tutub tablets, with those from Ešnunna and Tell Ağrab, were published in MAD 1, nos. 196–266 and should be dated, at least the most important lot, to Narām-Sîn's reign, as can be seen from the date formula on some of the tablets (cf. MAD 1, pp. XVIIIff.). At least three of these documents seem to be of particular importance: MAD 1, 217 and 220, which contain the date formula: in 1 mu ^{d}*Na-ra-am-*[^{d}*Sin*] x* *Si-m*[*u*]*-ur*$_4$ [*in*] KI.RA.[È.N]I.PI [*iš*$_x$*-a*]*-ru ù* Ba-ba [é]nsi *si-mu-u*$_4$ [Dub$^{?}$]-ul$^{?}$ énsi *A-ra-*[*ma*^{ki}] *ik-mi-ù*, "In the year that Narām-Sîn battled Simurrum in...and captured Baba the énsi of Simurrum (and) Dubul$^{?}$, the énsi of Arame" (see M. E. Cohen, "A New Narām-Sîn Date Formula," *JCS* 28 [1976]: 227). Also MAD 1, 220 mentions an inspection made by Nabu-Ulmaš, son of Narām-Sîn, *Na-bí-ùl-maš in Tu-tu*^{ki} *ib-rí* (Foster, *Archives*, p. 50). In addition, MAD 1, 235, a sheep text with the mention of a certain Rigmum, (x máš *šu-ut Sá-lim-a-ḫu ši Iš-nun*^{ki}*-im Rí-ig-mu-um ik-su-am*, "kids belonging to Salim-aḫu, a men of Ešnunna, which Rigmum has fattened"), seems to correlate with two texts from Ešnunna, MAD 1, 317 and 324, which record, respectively, sheep and wool and in which a namesake official occurs. The only three tablets from Tutub, MAD 1, 267–69, date to the reign of Šar-kali-šarrī. W. Sommerfeld, *Die Texte der Akkade-Zeit 1. Das Dijala-Gebiet: Tutub* (Munster, 1999) has recently republished all the Tutub tablets.

484. P. Delougaz, *et al.*, *Pre-Sargonid Temples in the Diyala Region*, OIP 58 (Chicago, 1942) in which the structure and area of the Abu-temple in Tell Asmar (see OIP 58, pp. 156–217) are described; and P. Delougaz, *et al.*, *Houses and Graves in the Diyala Region*, OIP 88 (Chicago, 1967). The preliminary report was published by H. Frankfort, *Third Preliminary Report of the Iraq Expedition*, OIC 17 (Chicago, 1934), pp. 23–39.

485. Foster, *ZA* 72 (1982): 7, suggests that the only texts clearly coming from Ešnunna are: 1–163.

486. The findspots of the tablets are within areas E15–16, F17, and D16.

487. A dating to the Classical Sargonic period of the main level of the Northern

shows that for a period of several centuries the area was an important center of the city even though the building does not seem to have been the headquarters of the palace administration.[488] The specific function of the "northern building" is unclear from archaeological evidence.[489]

The second lot of tablets was found in the area of the "private houses," a series of small rooms and buildings near the Northern Building (area G-K 18–21). One part of this lot was found in stratum IVb and another part in the stratum immediately following, stratum IVa. The tablets of stratum IVa can be dated to the Late Sargonic period because of the presence of two bullae with the seal of Šudurul.[490] Other tablets were found in other areas of the site.[491]

MAD 1, 1–165; 173; 182 belong to the first lot and MAD 1, 166–172; 174–181; 183–190; 192; 194 to the second. Although the first lot contains some contracts and the second lot includes some school tablets, they share many of the same anthroponyms. It appears, therefore, likely that the documents of the second lot, at least those of stratum IVb, were a product of the administration that compiled the first lot.

A second collection of tablets from clandestine excavations, MAD 1, 270–336, was purchased from the inhabitants of the area by the Chicago

---

Building has been proposed by McGuire Gibson, "A Re-evaluation of the Akkad Period in the Diyala Region on the Basis of Recent Excavations at Nippur and in the Hamrin," *AJA* 86 (1982): 533–35. In addition, he also establishes that this level was contemporaneous with stratum II of the temple of Abu and with stratum IVb of the "houses" (*ibidem*, p. 537).

488. The excavators suggest that the palace, both in the Sargonic period and in subsequent periods, should be identified with a building situated in the central part of the site, OIP 88, fig. 36, area K-Q 26–32.

489. H. Frankfort, OIC 17, p. 23, regards the building of the most recent period as the private residence of a rich and powerful man. Lloyd, OIP 88, p. 181, thinks it was a residential center linked to the palace administration and had a military garrison. Delougaz, OIP 88, p. 198, on the other hand, considers it a "manufacturing establishment" probably connected with weaving and jewelry. And finally, J. Margueron, in his *Recherches sur les Palais mésopotamiens de l'Age du bronze* (Paris, 1982), pp. 122–44, connects the activity of this center to that of the nearby temple areas (J. Margueron, *op. cit.*, fig. 85 Temple d'Abu, area D–E 17) and considers the two buildings to be one architectural and organizational complex.

490. Cf. MAD 1, p. XV. The seal was most recently published in RIM 2, p. 213.

491. Unfinished Building K-L 26–27 (MAD 1, 191–94); Town Wall K-L 13–14 (MAD 1, 195).

Oriental Institute in 1930. On the basis of internal evidence, this collection is related to the first lot of texts.[492] Most assuredly, then, the tablets purchased by the Chicago Oriental Institute come from the area of the Northern Building and are part of the same text archive as the first lot.[493]

Besides the texts in MAD 1, other tablets, purchased on the clandestine market, come from Ešnunna. Some of these texts, housed in museums and private collections, were published prior to the appearance of MAD 1,[494] while others were published later.[495] But Ešnunna as the

492. On one hand, in the texts in this collection and in those of the first lot the same anthroponyms occur; on the other, close parallels can be seen in some cases that would connect the texts of the first lot with the documents of the collection in question. For example, MAD 1, 23; 102; 117+133, which belongs to the first lot, and MAD 1, 273; 284; 293; 295; 330, which are part of the tablets excavated clandestinely, constitute a homogeneous group of še-gu_4 texts.

493. MAD 1, p. 16 dates 336 (a sale contract for a parcel of 15 iku of land) probably to the ED period, but the anthroponyms mentioned in that contract, Ilum-dan, Ili-aḫi, and UD-kum are also frequently mentioned in the remaining documents. This suggests the same date for this text as for the other texts in the collection (cf. ELTS, p. 191).

494. These are UCP 9/2, 76; 83; 89, which come from the Lowie Museum of Anthropology of the University of California at Berkeley and are part of a small group of tablets, the remainder of which are still unpublished and *An.Or* 7, 732 (MM 497) from the Museum of the Monastery of Montserrat in Barcelona.

495. The five texts from the Museum of Montserrat have been published: one (MM 401) by P. Steinkeller, "Two Sargonic Sale Documents Concerning Women," *Or*NS 51 (1982): 362–64; and four (MM 526; 560; 697 and 987) by M. M. Molina, "Tablillas Sargónicas de Museo de Montserrat, Barcelona," Fs. M. Civil, *AuOr* 9 (1991): 141–47. The four tablets from the Kelsey Museum of Ancient and Medieval Archaeology of the University of Michigan were published in MVN 9, 192; 193; 194 and by Steinkeller, *Or*NS 51 (1982): 355–62. The three tablets from the National Museum of Copenhagen were published by A. Westenholz, "Old Sumerian and Old Akkadian Texts in the National Museum of Copenhagen," *JCS* 26 (1974): 74–76. One text from the Nies Babylonian Collection (NBC 10920) was published by M. E. Cohen, "A New Naram-Sîn Date Formula," *JCS* 28 (1976): 229–31. And finally, three or perhaps four texts probably from Ešnunna belonging to the John Frederick Lewis Collection were published in MVN 3, 60; 79; 102[?]; 111. Two texts from the Iraq Museum of Baghdad are in TLAT, 51; 52. Possibly other texts published in MVN 3 may come from Ešnunna. Steinkeller, *Or*NS 51 (1982): 366 has indicated, in the case of MVN 3, 27; 57; 65; 78; 80; 83; 101; and 104, a provenance from the Diyala region based upon prosopography and language.

provenance for the 53 texts of Chicago's Field Museum of Natural History and of the eight texts of the Louvre Museum published by Gelb in OAIC and MAD 4, 2–9 is uncertain, although there is no doubt that their provenance, in general, is the Diyala region.[496]

The Sargonic texts from Ešnunna, which have never been analyzed in detail, contain about 90 barley texts: 30 texts concerning livestock, wool, and skins; 15 ì-nun texts; 15 texts concerning various other goods; ten texts concerning personnel; less than ten land texts; and six silver texts. The content and typology of about ten texts cannot be determined because of their fragmentary state. The remaining texts are contracts, other legal texts, letters, and school exercises.

From a preliminary analysis of the barley documents at least four groups of homogeneous texts are recognizable by the people involved and the destination of goods.[497]

The first group of barley texts contains about 20 ration lists. In one of these, MAD 1.163, which appears to be the *Sammeltafel* of the other texts of the group, the final clause after the summary indicates that the document is a monthly record of barley rations allocated to low- and mid-ranking personnel (105 guruš and 585 géme listed with their professional names) belonging to an institution indicated simply by the term é. The personnel given rations by this institution are employed in weaving (géme-uš-bar, TÚG.NI, azlag$_4$), husbandry (ša udu-UŠ; sipa šáḫ; ša anše), craft work and in industry (DUB.NAGAR; lùmgi), and probably also in agriculture (sa$_7$-a).

The second group of barley texts is comprised of ten documents concerning transactions of large quantities of barley. Almost all these tablets are fragmentary, but fortunately some of the texts in this group, MAD 1, 2 and 86, have preserved clauses that enable us to establish the nature of these texts. They are probably records of barley due the administration, which compiled the tablets concerning those who had

---

496. It is very probable that these texts come from Ešnunna, but the fact that no scribes are mentioned in these documents has precluded their analysis in this study.

497. For a more detailed analysis of the barley texts and of the correlated documentation of Sargonic Ešnunna, cf. G.Visicato, "A Temple Institution in the Barley Records from Sargonic Ešnunna," *ASJ* 19 (1997): 235–59.

agricultural lands belonging to it leased or in usufruct.[498] From the amount of barley due (about 2,500 gur in MAD 1, 86 and more than 3,000 gur in the surviving items of MAD 1, 2) it seems clear that they were large tracts of land.

On the basis of prosopography, three lot of texts constitute the second group: three seed barley texts; three texts about asses and oxen delivered for agricultural work, and three texts of barley delivered, perhaps, for rations to personnel involved with cattle.[499]

The third group of eight texts concerns the monthly allocation of barley as fodder for oxen (še-gu$_4$ še 1 iti) and for asses (še-ba anše).

The fourth group concerns the delivery of barley to persons and as food for goats.

Textual data and archaeological evidence indicate that the same institution drew up the tablets of the Northern Building and those of the so-called "private houses." This institution provided rations for at least 700 persons working in various activities. This institution, in addition, owned large tracts of arable land, which it gave in usufruct in exchange for part of the yield. The seed barley and fodder for the draft animals was supplied by the institution.[500] This institution may be the é-DINGIR[501] in whose service was the gal-sukkal Uṣium, mentioned in NBC 10920 o. I 1–2 and MM 497 o. III 3–4, those whose sealings have been

---

498. This conclusion is based upon the clause recorded in MAD 1, 86: lá-NI engar-engar, "arrears of the farmers" and from the mention in two other texts of this group (MAD 1, 2; and 35) of clauses concerning the payment of taxes by these engar's to the administration and by the fact that this group of texts is like Group C.2b from Umma, analyzed in USP, pp. 91–93.

499. The seed barley texts are: MAD 1, 289; 297; 329; the texts of asses and oxen are: MAD 1, 47; 136; 138; the barley texts are: MAD 1, 16; 20; 57.

500. It is different in other Sargonic archives. The barley for seed and fodder was advanced by the holders and deducted as expenses from the part of the yield due to the institution (cf. USP, p. 95; Foster, *People,* pp. 93–94).

501. Gelb, "The Arua Institution," *RA* 66 (1972): 4, identifies this institution with the é-géme, an administrative center mentioned in a letter (MAD 1, 290 o. 8). In charge of the é-géme was the official é-GI$_4$.A, a professional name that occurs also in the Old Babylonian period in two letters from Ešnunna. It was considered "a kind of cloister" similar to an Old Babylonian institution in Sippar. It is more likely that this institution was more extensive in scope, while the é-géme was only one of the structures, like the é-^{munus}tigi$_x$-di.

found,[502] and the dub-sar Šurus-kin mentioned in NBC 10920 o. I 3–4. In the term é-DINGIR, the DINGIR sign is an abbreviated form of ^{d}Tišpak, the tutelary divinity of Ešnunna, as we can see from a seal imprint containing the legend, *U-ṣi-um* gal-sukkal-^{d}Tispak.[503]

This administrative structure must have operated at various levels within the ever-changing political circumstances from the ED to the of Isin-Larsa period.[504] It is not possible to establish what relationship this administrative structure had with the énsi Engik-Ḫaniš mentioned in UCP 83 III 11–13, whose residence was situated in the central area of the site. Possibly this administrative structure was controlled directly by the Crown. In these documents, just 12 scribes are mentioned.

Beli (*Be-lí*) dub-sar is mentioned as dumu Ši-a-za in UCP 9/2, 89 o. 6, of which only 15 lines on the obverse are preserved. This text contains a list, of which only eight names have survived, in the format: PN_1 dumu PN_2 or as PN_1 Prof. name or PN_1 Prof. name dumu PN_2. Beli without title, which is normal for the majority of the people mentioned in the Sargonic texts from Ešnunna, occurs in MAD 1, 80 o. 1' as one of the people who has received (PN *im-ḫu-ru*) goods not clearly specified and in MAD 1, 86 r. II 2 as one of the holders who owes the administration 60 gur in arrears.[505]

Da-ti dub-sar is mentioned in MAD 1, 319 r. 8 as the father of or the official to whom A-ḫu-DINGIR is a subordinate and probably the recipient of barley. The text concludes with the clause *šu Zi-lu-lum,*

---

502. H. J. Frankfort, *Stratified Cylinder Seals from the Diyala Region,* OIP 72 (Chicago, 1955), n. 593.

503. Cf., M. M. Molina, "Tablillas Sargónicas de Museo de Montserrat, Barcelona," Fs. M. Civil, *AuOr* 9 (1991): 144. A similar type of abbreviation, AN for ^{d}Sùd, had already been widely used in the Fara texts (cf. EDATŠ, p. 211).

504. Large temple institutions are documented in the Old Babylonian period in the Diyala region: the temple institution of the god Sin at Tutub (cf. R. Harris, "The Archive of the Sin Temple in Khafajah," *JCS* 9 [1955]: 31–120) and of the goddess Ištar-Kiti at Ishchali (cf. M. deJong Ellis, "The Archive of the Old Babylonian Kitittum Temple and Other Texts from Ishchali," *JAOS* 104 [1986]: 757–86).

505. In the texts of Group C.2b from Umma, among the engar's who are in debt to the administration are officials such as the dub-sar-maḫ, sukkal, and gala (cf. USP, p. 91).

which could indicate that these persons were subordinates of Zilulum or that the barley paid out belonged to Zilulum.[506]

A namesake šagina is mentioned in MAD 1, 150 o. 2, concerning the receipt of 30 gur of barley: 30 še gur *Da-ti* šagina dumu-a *En-na-núm im-ḫur.*

In addition, this anthroponym occurs in MAD 1, 23 o. 2' as one of the engar's who was in debt. He is also mentioned in MAD 1, 102 o. 4; 273.3; 284 o. 4 and 293 o. 4, all recording deliveries of barley for oxen. Perhaps this official should be identified with our dub-sar. In fact, among the people who receive še-gu$_4$, high-ranking officials like the AB×ÁŠ, the "elder," occur.

Dab$_4$-si-ga dub-sar is the scribe who compiled ([*š*] *a-ṭi-ir*) the contract UCP 9/2 83 r. II 2–4.[507] The text is dated to the time when Um-mi-mi was munus-sagi and Enpik-Ḫaniš was énsi of Ešnunna.[508] Dab$_4$-si-ga appears to be mentioned in MAD 1, 321 o. 9–10 in connection with 5 gur of barley that Dab$_4$-si-ga probably received as a payment on a previous loan.[509]

⸢I⸣-[da]-pi$_5$-ì-li um-mi-a occurs in MAD 1, 336 r. 8 as one of the witnesses to the measurement of chairs of a house-lot (é-^{giš}GU.ZA), perhaps a preliminary procedure for evaluating property whose ownership is to be transferred. In all probability, the text belongs to a group of related documents, all perhaps from Ešnunna. They have in common both the identity of the seller, a certain Dabalum/Dabilum, and the structure of contracts characterized by the use of the verb *šadādum*, "to measure."[510]

---

506. A certain [Zi$^?$]-lu-lum is mentioned in MAD 1, 97 o. 2' as one of the engar's in debt to the administration.

507. For other scribes who wrote private contracts and the fees they received, cf. ELTS, p. 238.

508. For this date formula, cf. ELTS, p. 249.

509. The text, of which only one fragment has survived, lists two entries: 5 še gur Dab$_4$-si-ga dub-sar *ḫu-bu-lu*[*m*] 62 še gur *Na-bí-um* dam-gàr *im-*[*ḫur*] *a-na ša-bu-u*[*l-ti*], "5 gur of barley Dab$_4$-si-ga the scribe (for the) debt; 62 gur of barley Nabium, the trading agent, has received for exchange" (for the rendering as "exchange," cf. CAD Š III, p. 320, sub *šupêltu, šapûltu*).

510. They are a group of five texts collected in ELTS, p. 209, nos. 242–46. See also TLAT, p. 89.

A namesake official is mentioned in a list of persons, MAD 1, 72 o. 2, among whom are persons mentioned in the second group of barley texts.[511]

Isarum (*I-sa-ru-um*) dub-sar is mentioned in MAD 1, 322, a summary of the receipt/delivery of barley by various officials, among whom is *I-da*-DINGIR šabra-é and *Pù-su*-GI dub-sar. The dub-sar Isarum is mentioned in two entries in the text, in o. 4–6, without title where he receives$^?$ 120 gur of barley: *a-na* še-ba é, literally "for rations (for the personnel) of the household" and in r. 4, with his title where he receives$^?$ another 120 gur of barley. There does not seem to be any doubt that we are dealing with the same person.[512] This document should be linked to MAD 1, 334, a barley text with the same structure (*a-na* še-ba ir$_{11}$) and in which both Isarum and Pusu-kin occur.[513]

A namesake official is mentioned in the barley texts of the second group as one of the engar's who are in debt to the administration. A namesake occurs in MAD 1, 126 o. 4', a fragmentary document about fields, and in MAD 1, 332 o. 4 as the recipient of a land parcel measuring 2 bur. In TLAT 51, o. I 7', a tablet of which only the central part has survived, Isarum is the recipient of goods not clearly described, perhaps clothes. Some of the recipients in TLAT 51 also occur in MAD 1, 138, a text concerning barley for oxen.

Pusu-kin (*Pù-su*-GI) dub-sar is mentioned with Isarum in MAD 1, 322 and, like the latter, received 120 gur. Although the destination is not specified, the barley must have been for še-ba ir$_{11}$. This official, in

---

511. A namesake ugula occurs in OAIC 12 r. 7, where, before witnesses, he makes a declaration about something he said to Ginunu, probably the merchant of the namesake archive (cf. B. R. Foster, "Commercial Activity in Sargonic Mesopotamia," *Iraq* 39 [1977], p. 32).

512. We cannot determine unequivocally whether this text concerns the receipt or delivery of barley. But the fact that three of the entries refer to rations (še-ba é; še-ba ba-ba; [še-ba$^?$] arád) and rations to the šabra-é suggest that this is a receipt of barley by officials. It should be taken into account that the last entry records 10 gur of barley to Na-ni, which is indicated as a receipt$^?$ for debt payment (*ḫubullum*).

513. MAD 1, 322; 334 with MAD 1, 299; 321; 326 seem to constitute a single group of texts concerning še-ba ir$_{11}$.

fact, occurs without title in MAD 1, 334 o. 3, a document similar to MAD 1, 322,[514] as the recipient of barley with the same destination. He is the namesake official who receives 2 gur in MAD 1, 326 r. II 2, "barley of Ilulu," an official who also occurs in MAD 1, 334.

Šu-ili (*Šu-ì-lí*) dub-sar is mentioned in a contract in which he receives as a gift 1 BA.AN (container) perhaps of oil and clothes ŠAG$_4$.GA.DÙ,[515] probably because he compiled the contract. This anthroponym is not mentioned elsewhere. It is possible that this document came from Ešnunna, but its provenance from the Diyala is certain.

Šu-Ma-ma dub-sar tigi$_x$-di is mentioned in NBC 10920 o. I 13–14 as a witness.[516] Women described by the professional designation munus-tigi$_x$-di[517] frequently occur in contracts or legal texts from Ešnunna,[518] both as witnesses and as persons directly involved in sale contracts of barley and fields. An administrative structure or a household, é-munus-tigi$_x$-di, occurs in MM 497 II 3'. Probably the é-munus-tigi$_x$-di was connected to or was part of the é-géme. In fact, a certain Šu-Ma-ma wrote two letters (MAD 1, 282, 290) to the é-GI$_4$.A, the official whose relationship with the é-géme has been discussed previously. Probably the same Šu-Ma-ma received a letter from Uṣium (MAD 1, 298 o. 3). This anthroponym occurs frequently in the Sargonic documentation of Ešnunna, particularly with regard to cattle (MAD 1, 112; 285, 2; 301, 2; 311, 2). But we are unable to establish a connection between this official and the namesake dub-sar.

Šurus-kin (*Su-ru-*[*ús*]-GI) dub-sar é-DINGIR is mentioned in NBC 10920 o. I 2–3 as witness to a declaration made by A-ḫa-ti-ku-ku ABxÁŠ uru^{ki}. A namesake official without title is mentioned in MAD 1, 149.2, which concerns 12 *su-ba-rí-ù* belonging to Šurus-kin, who are recipients of oil.

514. Cf. *supra, sub* Isarum dub-sar.

515. For the meaning of this term, cf. P. Steinkeller, *Or*NS 51 (1982): 362.

516. Cf. M. E. Cohen, *JCS* 28 (1976): 229.

517. Akkadian **šāriḫtum, širḫu*, "wailing women" (cf. P. Steinkeller *Or*NS 51 [1982]: 365).

518. Cf. Molina, *AuOr* (1991), p. 143, *sub* II 2'–3'.

In addition to the scribes mentioned, three other scribes occur in NBC 10920[519]: [ ]-ì-šum and Lú-sa_6 dub-sar-me mentioned in o. I 7–9 and Ìl-sù-GAR dub-sar in II 8. None of these anthroponyms is mentioned elsewhere in the archive.

7.2 *The Tell el-Suleimah Texts*

Tell el-Suleimah was excavated by an Iraqi expedition from 1977 to 1984 in the context of a project for safeguarding the Hamrin basin. This basin, which covers an area 40 km long and 15 km wide is situated between Jebel Hamrin and Jebel Jubbah in the center eastern part of Iraq. The site is near the Diyala and about 50 km northeast of Ešnunna, in the direction of the Zagros mountains. Forty-seven Sargonic tablets were found in 1980 in one of the rooms of a structure situated in the southern part of the site, probably used as an administrative office.[520] All 47 Sargonic tablets were published by F. Rashid, who identified the Tell el-Suleimah site as ancient Awal, a city mentioned in Sargonic texts and those of the Ur III and Old Babylonian periods.[521]

The shape of the tablets and their paleography seem to indicate a date between the Umma A and Umma B archives.[522] Probably the Tell el-Suleimah archive dates to the beginning of the reign of Narām-Sîn, in any case, prior to his administrative reform.

---

519. M. E. Cohen, *JCS* 28 (1976): 237.

520. Cf. S. S. Rmaidh, "The Tell Sleima Excavations (Second Season)," *Sumer* 40 (1981): 57–58.

521. F. Rashid, *The Ancient Inscriptions in Himrin Area*, Himrin 4 (Baghdad, 1981).
D. R. Frayne, *The Early Dynastic List of Geographical Names*, AOS 74 (New Haven, 1992), pp. 56ff.; 67ff., suggests that the evidence indicates that Tell el-Suleimah is ancient Batiri, a town that occurs twice in the Tell el-Suleimah archive (A29 and A42).
Cf. *Rép. géogr* 1, pp. 20–21, and P. Steinkeller, "Early History of Hamrin Basin in the Light of Textual Evidence," Appendix I in McGuire Gibson, ed., *Uch Tepe* I (Chicago and Copenhagen, 1981), pp. 164–66.

522. For the dating of these archives, cf. USP, pp. 2–7. A much more important date indicator is the form of the signs ŠU.NÍGIN. In some texts from Tell el-Suleimah the two signs are separated, in others joined, and in two texts both forms occur. For the shape of ŠU.NÍGIN in the Sargonic period, cf. A. Alberti, "šu-nígin: Ein neuer Anhaltspunkt zur Datierung der Texte der Akkade-Zeit," *WO* 18 (1987): 22–25.

Several categories of texts have been identified in the documents of Tell el-Suleimah. However, the great majority of texts can be grouped into two categories: (1) loans of barley at interest to animal breeders of the region, which comprise 50% of the texts; (2) the second, texts recording distribution of barley rations to workers and perhaps soldiers, which comprise 20% of the documentation.[523]

Proposographic analysis suggests that the entire documentation was compiled by a single household.[524] In such a household, as A1 and A7 document,[525] about 80 workers receive rations. Furthermore, there are at least ten officials called *bēlū*-BAR.E, among whom are some dub-sar's. These officials were probably the controllers and administrators of the household. This household, according to A1, owned many draft oxen and asses. The people mentioned in A3,[526] a personnel text, should belong to this same household.

The Hamrin region lies outside the rainfall agriculture area. Because of low rainfall and the torrid summer climate, it is incapable of support-

---

523. On the basis of content and the purpose for recording and distributing goods, there are eight categories of texts: (1) eight texts concerning personnel (lists of workers: A1, A7; list of individuals: A40; records of deliveries of grain and rations to personnel [A25, A41, A45–46]; one record concerning assignment of personnel [A3]); (2) 24 texts concerning barley loans (A2, A4, A6, A10, A11, A13–14, A16–24, A26–28, A30–31, A33, A37, A39); (3) six texts concerning sheep (three receipts of sheep for barley loans [A9, A32, A35]; three transactions concerning sheep and other goods for the purchase of barley [A5, A12, A34]); (4) two transactions of goods to purchase or to hold land (A42, A44); (5) two allocations of plots of land (A36, A47); (6) two records of livestock (A8, A29); (7) one record of chairs (A43); (8) two records of various goods (A15, A38).

524. P. Steinkeller, "Early Political Development in Mesopotamia and the Origins of the Sargonic Empire," in *Akkad* (1993): 122, n. 41, discusses these texts. For an in-depth analysis of the Sargonic texts of Tell el-Suleimah, see R. Dsharakian, "Altakkadische Wirtschaftstexte aus Archiven von Awal und Gasur," *ZA* 84 (1994): 1–10 and G. Visicato, "The Sargonic Archive of Tell el-Suleimah," *JCS* 51 (1999).

525. A7, which lists 33 people, corresponds, in parts, to A1 VI 8–VII 17.

526. A3 lists three groups of subordinates in three different places—a total of 30 people—with partial summaries for each group. In the first group, which records in the summary 23 guruš, four are subordinates of the nu-gal (certainly a syllabic writing for lugal), one of the nin of the god Enlil, two of the šabra-é, two of the énsi of *Ša-bu-e*^{ki}, and one of the énsi of *Ib-ra-at*^{ki}.

ing significant irrigation agriculture, despite the immediate proximity to the Diyala. Thus the only activity possible is animal husbandry, which the people of the region practice today.[527] The geo-climatic condition of the region could not have been very different in the Sargonic period. The fact that only two texts in the Himrin documentation, A36 and A47, deal with agricultural land and that the recipients in A36 are the énsi, a scribe, and a third probably high-ranking official, seems to confirm that the area was essentially used for sheep breeding and the small amount of arable land was utilized only by the highest authorities.

The main activity of the local institution seems to have been providing barley at interest to sheep breeders. Our household must have been identified with this institution, whose subordinates received barley in A42 v.11–12 (še ìr-é *im-ḫu-ru* è-a) and monthly rations in A41 r. 11–12 (še-ba…guruš *šu* 1 iti). Thus the household to which the documentation refers is an organization of an institutional kind. As can be deduced from the references to subordinates of the lugal, the nin of Enlil, the šabra-é, various local énsi's in A3, and the strategic importance of the region, it is probable that this household was directly controlled by the Crown.

Five scribes are mentioned in the texts, three of them in A1, the most frequently mentioned personnel text. One is mentioned in a barley text and the last in a text concerning fields.

Pù-pù dub-sar is mentioned in A33 o. 2 in relation to barley in A-ba-bi^{ki}. The document lists four people. Our scribe and the dam-gàr Damiq-ilum are involved with 60 and 130 gur respectively, while the other two, 1 and 2 gur each. The reason for the record is not specified. A namesake official without title is mentioned in A35 r. II 11, which records sheep delivered for a loan at interest. He is also mentioned in A9 r. 10 concerning the receipt of 8 ud_5 in Purkulum; they were counted in Durūm and received by a certain Zu-zu.

En-na-núm dub-sar is mentioned in A1 o. I 12–13, as being in charge of guruš. A namesake official in A6 o. II 10 received, *a-na* ur_5-kam, 120 sìla of barley with Da-rí-ša dam I-bí-al-sú.

Šunium (*Šu-ni-um*) dub-sar is mentioned in A1 r. III 16–17 and A7 r. I 13–14, probably as being in charge of the guruš and géme.

---

527. Cf. Mcguire Gibson, *Uch Tepe* I (Chicago and Copenhagen, 1981), pp. 13–15.

Imtalik (*Im*$_4$*-ta-lik*) is mentioned with Šunium dub-sar in A1 and A7. He occurs without title in A8 r. 2, which concerns cattle and in A35 r. II 6 in the section where Pù-pù is mentioned.

⌜x⌝-SAG/KA$^{?}$-a-ni dub-sar is mentioned in A36 o. 7–10 as the recipient of a parcel of 7 iku of arable land. Among the recipients mentioned are the énsi Be-lí-lí and a certain I-bí-^{d}A-bí, who is not mentioned elsewhere.

7.3 *The Gasur Archive*

The site of Yorghan Tepe in the northeast of Mesopotamia, is the ancient Hurrian city of Nuzi, whose name in the Sargonic period was Gasur. The first Sargonic tablets were found during the season 1928–29 by the Harvard-Baghdad School Expedition at Nuzi, beneath the area of the Hurrian palace in a shaft excavated in room L 4. During the season 1930–31 the shaft was excavated until virgin soil was reached; the majority of the remaining tablets of the Sargonic period were discovered in subsequent strata. It was almost immediately apparent that, since the 224 tablets from this period constituted a homogeneous archive, they must have come from a single stratum that was disturbed by later builders. The texts were published a few years after their discovery by Th. J. Meek,[528] who dated the archive to the Early Sargonic period. Because of the appearance and paleography of the tablets and the systematic use of the Akkadian gur as the unit of measurement for seed barley, Foster has suggested a date in the Classical Sargonic period, more precisely, between the end of the reign of Narām-Sîn and the beginning of that of Šar-kali-šarrī.[529]

The 224 Sargonic documents that consitute this archive are, with the exclusion of twelve letters and nine school texts, mainly records connected with agricultural activity, that is, with the allocation of land parcels, seed, and barley fodder; and of carts for use in agriculture—there are also transactions of barley, emmer, and other harvested grains.

528. Th. J. Meek, *Old Akkadian, Sumerian and Cappadocian Texts from Nuzi,* HSS 10 (Cambridge, 1935).

529. B. R. Foster, "Administration of State Land at Sargonic Gasur," *OrAn* 21 (1981): 39.

In addition, there are barley and emmer ration texts and nì-ḫar-ra and MUN.ŠÀ allocation texts.[530] The documents regarding cattle and personnel are fairly representative; only a few texts deal with silver, beer, and other goods. Prosopography and content indicate that the surviving documentation is all that remains of the archive of an institutional household over a short time span. Foster concluded "that the records belonged to a domain administered by a certain Zuzu, a cadaster official, who served, indirectly at least, the interest of royal accountability."[531] Foster identified two series of barley texts and outlined the relationships among the persons mentioned in these groups of texts. These persons can be divided into four principal groups:

(1) personnel connected with the land and its exploitation. This consists of those who received land grants, seed barley, or threshed barley.

(2) personnel connected with produce who do not occur in the first group. This consists of those who received nì-ḫar-ra and goods for sustenance, and barley and emmer rations.

(3) personnel connected with the harvest. This consists of those who received barley šu-peš$_5$-ri-a "coming from the division of the harvest." These people occur both in Groups (1) and (2) and are the linked between the two groups.

(4) personnel connected with éš-gar, "allocated work," which Foster regards as that part of the production and resources of the estate that were due the Crown. The persons who occur in this group occur in at least one of Groups (1), (2), and (3).

From an economic point of view, these people can be divided into three large classes: (a) producers, holders of large tracts of land; (b) administrators, managers of large amounts of barley; (c) wage earners, those who had no access to the land or its products but were rationed by the

530. Foster; *People,* p. 101 regards MUN.ŠÀ as "presumably a local term for sustenance."

531. Foster, "People, Land and Produce at Sargonic Gasur," in D. I. Owen – M. A. Morrison, eds., SCCNH 2 (Winona Lake, 1987), p. 90.

The term "accountability" is used here in the sense of "obligation to keep records for property that is not one's own. So far as I can see, accountability exists in the third-millennium archives only in institutional contexts" (Foster, *OrAn* 21 [1981]: 47, n. 16).

household for their work. In the Sargonic documentation from Gasur five scribes are men-tioned.

[D]a-ti [dub]-sar is mentioned with professional name only once, in HSS 10, 160 o. I 12 in connection with allocations of barley, flour, and dida received in Assur. Among other things, the text records an allocation of dida for Ur-^{d}Gibil$_6$ to taste (*a-na la-tá-ki-im*). This note and the mention of Zu-zu sa$_{12}$-du$_5$ and of other scribes among the recipients suggests that the persons listed in the text were part of a delegation of officials who had gone to Assur, perhaps in connection with the visit of an important person, either the king or the šabra-é.[532]

A namesake official without title occurs in HSS 10, 55 r. 2 and 108 r. 8. HSS 10, 55 lists amounts of barley in connection with various people, described as še-libir, "barley (of the) old (harvest? or account)"; after the summary, the clause *si-tum*, "expenses" is recorded. HSS 10, 108 is a text regarded by Foster as dealing with "raw rations,"[533] in which amounts of barley are listed for various people. After the summary, a clause is recorded: *a-na Ga-sur*^{ki} ⸢*x*⸣ KU.UR-ma *ù Da-ti ìr-da-a*, tentatively translated "(barley) to Gasur KU.UR-ma[534] and Da-ti brought/accompanied it."[535] In HSS 10, 65 r. 4 the latter is the recipient of 10 gur of še-è barley. In HSS 10, 155 r. I 12 he is the recipient of 3 bariga of MUN.ŠÀ. Finally, he occurs again in HSS 10, 175 III 11 concerning one ass's hide. The text is signed by Zu-zu sa$_{12}$-du$_5$.[536] The fact that this name is common makes it difficult to establish whether Da-ti without title is the namesake scribe.

532. See below, p. 229, n. 541.

533. Foster, *People*, p. 102.

534. KU.UR-ma is an official who also occurs in HSS 10, 62, which concerns barley, emmer, and malt belonging to him: *šu* KU.UR-ma *in Ga-sur*^{ki}.

535. A similar formula is recorded in HSS 10, 65 o. 5–10. For the meaning "bring / accompany," cf. *AHw* p. 965 sub *redû*.

536. A certain Da-ti also occurs in HSS 10, 107 o. 6, as the person receiving a loan with interest from Zu-zu (cf. Foster, "Selected Business Documents from Sargonic Mesopotamia," *JCS* 35 [1983]: 164-65).

Ili (Ì-lí) dub-sar is mentioned in three texts. In HSS 10, 45 r. 1–2 and 47 o. 4-v. 1 he receives barley from the harvest (še šu-peš$_6$-ri-a) in Maš-gán^{ki}; in HSS 10, 142 o. 2 he is the recipient of 2 bariga of unspecified goods, perhaps nì-ḫar-ra.

This anthroponym occurs frequently without title in the documents of Gasur. In particular, a certain Ili is the recipient of several letters sent by Da-da, probably the namesake šabra-é (HSS 10, 5–7) and by Ur-sa$_6$ (HSS 10, 8, 10). These letters deal with the management of goods and personnel. In HSS 10, 92 r. 2 he is the official who delivers barley and other goods to a certain Ba-zi for the city of Ḫubni.[537] HSS 10, 93 is a summary account from the office of Ili of threshed barley and grain for the current year, (še gig giš-ra-a é *ì-l*[*í*] [*š*]*u* mu-a-kam). In HSS 10, 120 r. 1 he receives barley and malt from Ba-a-ti and Ma-ma-ḫu. In HSS 10, 144 there is an expenditure in nì-ḫar-ra by Ili, the recipient of which is Ire-Šamaš; Ili occurs also as a recipient of barley, emmer, and other grain; in HSS 10, 153 o. III 2, a summary record of šu-peš$_6$-ri-a, he receives barley and MUN.ŠÀ; in HSS 10, 154 r. I 13, he is mentioned in a long allocation text of threshed barley; and in HSS 10, 155 r. III 2, as the recipient of dabin and MUN.ŠÀ. He perhaps occurs with Ili-mešum and Pù-zu-zu as the recipient of 10½ iku in HSS 10, 15 o. 3.[538] If the Ili of this text is the namesake scribe, it would be one of the few cases where an administrator also occurs as a holder of agricultural lands.

Ilsu-dan (Ìl-su-dan) dub-sar šabra-é is mentioned in HSS 10, 205, 17–18. The text probably records the transfer or the recruitment of eight servants, seven as subordinates of Zu-zu, the sa$_{12}$-du$_5$, and one as a subordinate of Ikunum, an official mentioned in HSS 10, 72 o. II 11–13 with the title of šabra dumu énsi. The text is concluded by the clause "in Dur-šargal Aḫarši and Ilsu-dan, the scribe of the šabra-

537. For this toponym, cf. *Rép. géogr.* 2, p. 76; *Rép. géogr.* 3, p. 99.

538. Foster, *People*, p. 91, considers the sign *ù* that precedes *ì-lí* to be part of the name and reads this anthroponym as U'ili. But the repetition of the conjunction *ù* before Pù-zu-zu, the anthroponym that follows *ì-lí*, suggests that the first *ù* has the same meaning.

é, marked (the servants) (in) the ship of Dakum...."[539] A certain Il-dan, probably an abbreviated form of *Ìl-su-dan,* is mentioned in HSS 10, 71 o. 2 as the official who took 10 gur of barley on behalf of the šabra to provide rations for 30 ass drivers at 25 sìla a day.[540] To clarify the role of Ilsu-dan we note that HSS 10, 56 records disbursements of barley and grain delivered to various officials. Among them are *I-ku*$_x$*-num* dam-gàr (elsewhere šabra dumu énsi: HSS 72 o. II 1), Zu-zu sa$_{12}$-du$_5$, and an unnamed šabra-é. A quantity of barley is delivered as še-ba ir$_{11}$-lugal, "rations for the king's servants." There is a similar clause in HSS 10, 134: *Ga-sur*$^{\langle ki\rangle}$ lugal libir-ù še-ba *šu-ut Da-da,* "(from) Gasur to the king (delivery of) the 'old' barley and (barley) for rations to the (personnel) belonging to Da-da." This Da-da is the namesake šabra-é mentioned in HSS 10, 220 r. 1–2 and dumu dumu-mí lugal in HSS 10, 109 r. 1–2. Consequently Ilsu-dan, scribe of the šabra-é Da-da, did not belong to the household to which the surviving documentation belonged, but instead came to Gasur as part of the entourage of Da-da for an inspection or with the visit of the king.[541]

Šu-ilisu (Šu-ì-lí-su) dub-sar is mentioned in HSS 10, 160 o. II 11 (a text discussed under Da-ti dub-sar). This anthroponym, often without title, occurs frequently in the Gasur documentation. But although there is abundant evidence that within the administration of Gasur several namesake officials worked, it is probable that the Šu-ilisu

---

539. *in* BÀD.LUGAL^{ki}-gal *A-ḫa-ar-ši ù Ìl-su-dan* dub-sar-šabra-é zag šuš má *da-kum* NE.U. The meaning of the term NE.U escapes us. A similar clause occurs in HSS 10, 206, 5–6: 1 ir$_{11}$-lugal sag-šuš MÁ *da-kum en-a-ru,* (tentatively translated in MAD 3, p. 191, *sub na'arum,* as "to mark in the form of branding? [piercing])" and in HSS 10, 197 o. 5. For the meaning of the term zag-šuš, and occurrences in other Sargonic sources, cf. ELTS, p. 243 and A. Foxvog, "Sumerian Brand and Branding Irons," *ZA* 85 (1995): 1–7.

540. 10 še gur *Ìl-dan a-na Su*$_4$*-a-a* šabra *u-ba-al* 30 guruš *kà-sa-ru.* For *kassāru,* "walker, bleacher," cf. MAD 3, p. 154.

541. HSS 10, 6 is a letter in which Da-da asks Suma-il to carefully check the flour in his possession because the king is about to arrive: [e]n-*ma Da-da* [*a-n*]*a Su*$_4$*-ma-ìl* dabin *šu iš-té-šu li-su-ur šarrum*^{um} *è-la-kam* (cf. FAOS 19, pp. 180–81; LEM 35, p. 35). Documents such as HSS 10, 66; 109; 110; 134; 205; 206; and 208 may be related to this visit. For more details, cf. G. Visicato, "A Journey of a Sargonic King to Assur and Gasur," XLVe CRRAI, Harvard, 1998 (forthcoming).

who occurs without title should be identified with the namesake scribe.[542] This is probably true of the Šu-ilisu mentioned in HSS 10, 169 r. 2, who received 1 sìla of lard in Assur. In addition, Šu-ilisu, without title, occurs as the holder of lands in HSS 10, 31 r. 1. He is the recipient of barley in HSS 10, 35 o. 6 and 68 o. 2 and of nì-ḫar-ra in HSS 10, 154 r. I 20 and 155 o. I 4. In HSS 10, 104 o. 4 and 203 o. 7 he receives a cart; in HSS 10, 173 o. 2 he is mentioned concerning a pig; in 179 o. 3 he is mentioned concerning ten sheep. He is mentioned in HSS 10, 193 o. 8 concerning his receipt of guruš and géme workers. In HSS 203 o. 2, he receives workers and a cart for transport.

Ur-zu dub-sar is mentioned in HSS 10, 109.12. The text is a record of fattened oxen, lard, and barley owed to high-ranking officials, among whom were the énsi of Gasur and Da-da—nephew of the king (probably Šar-kali-šarrī). These allocations were debited to Zu-zu sa$_{12}$-du$_5$. The general summary of these goods is also recorded but without the names of the recipients in HSS 10, 110, *ḫu-bu-lum šu-al Zu-zu* sa$_{12}$-du$_5$ *i-ba-še-ù*. HSS 10, 110 perhaps collects other texts besides HSS 10, 109. Probably HSS 10, 109 and 110 were related to

542. The namesake officials are: Šu-ilisu ABxÁŠ Uru^{ki} (HSS 10, 49 o. 2; 139 r. I 9; 142r. 3; 153 o. V 20; 154 o. I 2; 161 o. 10; 162 o. 3; 167 o. 3); Šu-ilisu simug (HSS 10, 158 r. I 6); Šu-ilisu *šu* Mumu (HSS 153 r. I 13; 158 o. III 16; 161 o. 9; 164 o. 4); Šu-ilisu *šu* Zu-zu (HSS 10, 153 r. II 17); Šu-ilisu *šu* Abua (HSS 10, 153 o. IV 13). Šu-ilisu often occurs without title. In particular, Šu-ilisu (without title) and Šu-ilisu ABxÁŠ Uru^{ki} occur in the same text (HSS 10, 154 o. III 20 and I 2); Šu-ilisu and Šu-ilisu simug in HSS 10, 158 o. II 11 and r. I 6; Šu-ilisu and Šu-ilisu *šu* Mumu in HSS 10, 158 o. II 11 and r. I 16. This would preclude Šu-ilisu without title being identified as the namesake ABxÁŠ, simug, and *šu* Mumu. The mention of Šu-ilisu ABxÁŠ; Šu-ilisu *šu* Abua; Šu-ilisu *šu* Mumu and Šu-ilisu *šu* Zu-zu in the same text, HSS 10, 153 o. V 30; IV 13; r. I 13; II 17, and Šu-ilisu simug and Šu-ilisu *šu* Mumu in HSS 10, 158 r. I 6 and o. III 16, suggests that they are different officials. By exclusion, the Šu-ilisu who occurs without title might be identified only with the namesake dub-sar or the namesake *šu* Zu-zu or *šu* Abua. The identification with Šu-ilisu *šu* Abua appears improbable. In fact, this latter official, like Abua, his boss, occurs only once. If Zu-zu, the boss or father of Šu-ilisu, is the namesake sa$_{12}$-du$_5$, it is likely that Šu-ilisu dub-sar and Šu-ilisu *šu* Zu-zu are the same person. In conclusion, this would mean that the Šu-ilisu who occurs without title should, in most cases, be identified with the namesake scribe who belongs to the household managed by the cadastre Zu-zu.

the king's visit to Gasur. Thus, the scribe Ur-zu could have been a member of the entourage of the king or of the šabra-é, and may not have been a member of the household.

This anthroponym occurs only one other time in a personnel text, HSS 10, 158 r. I 10.

In summary, Ili and Šu-ilisu belonged to the household managed by the sa_{12}-du_{5} Zu-zu. They must have been officials ranking just below Zu-zu, especially if Ili was really the recipient of the letters from the šabra-é Da-da. It is quite possible that the other scribes did not belong to this household. Some are high-ranking royal officials like Ilsu-dan, and perhaps Da-ti and Ur-zu.

CONCLUSIONS

Continuity and Change in the Role of the Early Mesopotamian Scribes

From earliest recorded times, the scribes headed the institutional organizations of power. This prosopographic study supports the contention of other scholars[1] that the first scribes of the Mesopotamian institutional administrations were the sanga. At first, they did not bear the title dub-sar, "scribe," which would eventually be applied to scribes throughout the remainder of the third millennium. The sanga officials fulfilled two roles simultaneously, that of administrators and compilers of administrative documents and that of teachers in the scribal schools. The tablets from Fara demonstrate this dual responsibility, many scribes (dub-sar) who are attested to in administrative texts and sale contracts are also mentioned in the lexical texts. A similar situation appears to have occurred at Abū Ṣalābīkh and, perhaps, at Archaic Ur.

Although scribes would remain a pillar of institutional organization—even during the subsequent Ur III period—functional and hierarchical change, in concomitance with the transformations and crises in the society in which they worked, can be detected in the documentation.

The first of these changes is the emergence of the dub-sar. The sanga had been the official who compiled the documents during the Uruk III and Jemdet Nasr periods, but it was the dub-sar who performed this function from the Archaic Ur period onwards. The documentation does not enable us to pinpoint the social or historical events that led to the emergence of the dub-sar, side by side with the sanga. We do know, however, that the sanga official continued to occupy a primary role, as discerned from the position of the sanga-GAR just below that of the énsi-

1. Cf. *supra*, pp. 2–3.

GAR-gal at Fara, and from the various sanga's of the temple institutions in the ED IIIb and Sargonic archives.

In the course of the centuries the dub-sar gradually gained control of all productive and administrative sectors. They were in charge of the harvesting and distribution of grain and grain products, cattle breeding, the wool industry, textiles, metal, fishing, aromatics, and all the services connected with the transport of goods and people. Ultimately, they became responsible for all the people serving in these sectors.

Although we cannot know the definite causes for the evolution of the dub-sar's position and functions, there are at least two important factors in this period that should be considered. First is the sudden growth in the number and size of written documents from Early ED Ur to ED IIIa Fara. Of the 335 tablets and fragments from Early ED Ur, there are approximately 290 administrative documents. With the exception of about 15 texts, they are small records, some containing only one or two entries. These documents span a brief period, perhaps no more than a few years. On the other hand, the roughly 500 administrative documents from Fara, most of which cover only one year, are of quite different dimension. In general, 20% of the texts record between 25 and 50 entries, 45% record between 10 and 25 entries, and only 25% record less than 10 entries. At least 10% of the documents have more than 50 entries and some of them, like the general summary documents, contain over 100 entries. Documents recording just one or two entries are rare. To these documents, the first homogeneous group of sale contracts should be added.[2] The relationship among the primary documents, the partial summary documents, and general summary documents[3] enables us to conclude that the surviving documentation is only a fraction of that which was compiled in the course of an administrative year at Fara, perhaps no more than 20% to 25% of the total. Thus, at a minimum, the combined annual production of primary and summary documents for the administration of ED III Fara must have been more than 2000 documents.[4] The demand for scribes had clearly become enormous.

---

2. Some contracts belonging to a previous period have been found, but these are isolated cases outside the main context.

3. Cf. EDATŠ, pp. 21–24, 32.

4. The reason for differences between the texts from ED II Ur and those from ED

A second consideration is the diminished supply of river water, particularly from the Euphrates, which began in the Late Uruk period.[5] Beginning during the Jemdet Nasr period in Babylonia, this event caused dislocation and a profound change in the structure of settlements. Most dramatic was the period between ED I and II, when, in southern Babylonia, almost all the settlements now distant from a source of water disappeared, causing a remarkable growth in settlements along the remaining channels. In fact, the settlement of Uruk reached its maximum size in this period.[6] In central and northern Babylonia, sites that had been founded in the Jemdet Nasr period, such as Kiš and Šuruppak, were transformed from simple villages to large urban settlements.[7] At the same time, in the Diyala region, sites previously abandoned in the Archaic and Late Uruk periods, were resettled, giving rise to significant urban development.[8] This new distribution of settlements set in motion great social and economic transformations. The populations from the abandoned sites flooded into new sites, which rapidly expanded and caused a remarkable increase in population and organizational and social problems deriving from a more and more marked social stratification and from continuing differences in the distribution of wealth. Institutional response to this challenge was the greater centralization of power, leading to the extraordinary growth of administrative bureaucracy. The appearance of a new figure, the dub-sar, an official flanking the sanga, should be dated to this period. The need for increased institutional management of goods, arable land, and a non-specialized work force, resulted in an ever-increasing need for written documents.[9]

III Šuruppak may be other than the mere growth and refinement of bureaucracy. The tablets from Ur were found as ancient rubbish, while those from Šuruppak were found *in situ* among the ruins of a burned-down city. These circumstances favored the preservation of large tablets from Šuruppak, while the Ur tablets would have become scattered bits (suggestion by A. Westenholz).

5. See Nissen, *Protostoria,* pp. 141ff.

6. *Ibidem,* 77.

7. *Ibidem,* pp. 81–84; figs. 20–21.

8. *Ibidem,* pp. 141–49.

9. *Ibidem,* pp. 103–6.

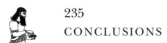

Unfortunately, the data that has survived from Šuruppak and Ur are uneven samplings. The available texts date, almost exclusively, to either the initial stages of this process—from Ur, which at that time was probably a peripheral site—or from a period in which the process was practically complete—from Šuruppak (Fara), a city violently destroyed. At the beginning of this phenomenon, at Early ED Ur, only two dub-sar's occur. At the end, in Šuruppak, the category of scribes was so deeply rooted in institutions, it had developed its own hierarchy: dub-sar-maḫ, ugula dub-sar, dub-sar sanga-GAR, dub-sar-sa$_{12}$-du$_5$, etc. These officials were certainly those who benefited most from the resources of society. In fact, they received allocations of goods considerably greater than did others, being given plots of arable land together with laborers and the necessary equipment.

At Šuruppak the highest-ranking scribes in the administration initialed the lexical texts and taught at the schools and, conversely, schoolmasters (um-mi-a) served as dub-sar-aša$_5$ and lú-é-éš-gar, those who measured land and houses in sale contracts. Perhaps as early as this period, but definitely during the Sargonic and Ur III periods, the majority of governors and kings arose from the category of the scribes. There are some indications that Kiš was one of the centers where this great scribal tradition had originated.[10]

Between ED II and ED III, the Euphrates once more changed course.[11] The channel that flowed from Nippur to Uruk, passing near Šuruppak, began to reduce the volume of its flow and became a secondary waterway. The principal channel now passed by Adab, Umma, and

10. We know little about Kiš except for some votive inscriptions of its kings and the mention of Mesalim in the cones of Entemena. The archaeological evidence indicates that during ED II and III Kiš reached its greatest development and became the largest settlement in Mesopotamia (cf. MacGuire Gibson, *Kiš*, pp. 48, 58 and 268, fig. 27A). This city exercised a leadership role over Babylonia during this period and had developed a political and organizational system similar to that of Šuruppak—possibly the system then current at Šuruppak was derived from Kiš. About 80 tablets from the ED period were found in Kiš. For a brief description of them, see I. J. Gelb, "Ebla and the Kišh Civilization," in L. Cagni, ed., *La Lingua di Ebla* (Naples, 1981), p. 55. Twenty-four of these tablets are published in AAICAB I, 1: Ashm. 1924: 462–69; 1928: 16; 427–38; 441; 442; 1930: 339a; 1931: 146; 147. The remaining tablets will be published in AAICAB I, 2.

11. Cf. R. Adams, *Heartland of Cities* (Chicago, 1981), figs. 29–31.

Lagaš, enabling the development of these sites to the detriment of those along the old channel, which had become secondary.[12] It is not coincidence that the first significant archives come from Girsu and Umma, about 150 years after the fall of Šuruppak.[13]

The about 1,600 tablets from ED IIIb Girsu are all that remains of the archive of the é-mí, probably one of the most important administrative structures that governed the state of Lagaš. This archive spans about 25 years, between the reigns of Enentarzi and Urukagina. Using the same model that was applied to Fara, we can establish that the annual production of tablets by the é-mí could not have exceeded 400 documents.[14] Despite allowances for a wide margin of error, it is clear that this number is far below that of Fara.[15] Based upon a comparison of barley rations, we suggest that the scribe in ED IIIb Girsu occupied a lower position than had the scribe at Fara. Nonetheless, as at Fara, they received plots of land and other goods. So too, all the important heads of the administration seem to have risen from the category of the

---

12. Cf. *Bureau,* pp. 144–47.

13. The only exception is the lexical archive of Abū Ṣalābīkh, which is later than that of Fara. The excavations also revealed a group of administrative texts. Their small number, however, does not permit an analysis of the historical processes now under examination.

14. This approximation is based on the assumption that we have only 20%–25% of the tablets and that the production in the various years was uniform. In fact, this latter assumption cannot always be verified. The documentation from L1 and L6 is certainly greater than that from L4 and L5. Production from Ue, U1, and U2 is greater than that from U5 and U7. But despite these differences, the application of statistics to a period of about twenty years, with all its limitations, should be fairly accurate.

15. The é-mí was not the only administrative structure in ED IIIb Girsu. The mention of different dub-sar-maḫ's who worked contemporaneously (cf. *supra,* pp. 74–75) indicates that, besides the é-mí, the é-gal had its own administrative structure and staff of scribes (cf. Westenholz, *Circulation,* p. 18, n. 1), and that other temple and non-temple centers existed—but no documentation from these centers has, as yet, been found. It is probable that most of the archives of the ED énsi's (and perhaps a Sargonic archive) still lie buried under the Ur III building in the Tell du Tablettes. Therefore, it is unlikely that the original number of tablets produced by the administration of Girsu would have been far less than that of Šuruppak. Perhaps, then, the above analysis is inadequate after all. Rather, this is only a working model of the possible evolution of Mesopotamian society, rather than a point of view.

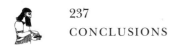

scribes. Enentarzi was the sanga of the temple of Ningirsu before becoming énsi. The scribe A-ba-DI seems to have been the son of Šubur, the nu-bànda é-gal, who was probably a scribe himself. The nu-bànda é-mí, En-ig-gal, was the official who compiled the tablets with the kurušda En-kù. The official who initialled the tablets, when En-ig-gal no longer occurs in the documentation, was the agrig En-šu-gi$_4$-gi$_4$.

The number of tablets produced by the administrations in the Early Sargonic period seems to have remained at the same level as in the previous ED IIIb period. However, during the Classical Sargonic period significant changes occurred. As before, the new dimensions of the empire and the need to manage it presented new challenges to which the institution once again responded by centralizing the organizational system of its administration. But, in contrast to earlier historical periods, the thrust of Narām-Sîn's response was at the regional and local levels. This led to the creation of administrative structures, such as the šabra-é, that overlapped existing ones and the presence of Sargonic institutions within local administrations. It is, therefore, understandable, as can be seen in the Girsu archive, that from the end of the reign of Narām-Sîn to the beginning of Šar-kali-šarrī's rule, there was a sharp increase in both documentation and the number of scribes. On the basis of interconnections among texts, we suggest that the vast majority of the approximately 2,000 documents that have reached us were almost certainly compiled in a rather brief period of time, perhaps in less than ten years during the reign of Šar-kali-šarrī.[16]

The role of the scribes in this period differed considerably from the past. The royal scribe (dub-sar-lugal) appears for the first time.[17] He is the official who, during tours of inspection, controlled and ratified transactions of various types executed by local administrations on behalf of the king. It is probable that other officials without that title had anal-

16. The findspot of the tablets—construction fill used in the subsequent period—and analysis of the archive itself suggest that the 2,000 Sargonic tablets are only a fraction of the original quantity. If the majority of the tablets cover a period of ten years, the annual production of written documents during the Sargonic period at Girsu would be comparable to that of the ED period at Šuruppak. It is probable that this calculation is also applicable to the archives of Umma and Adab.

17. Officials with the title maškim-lugal or kurušda-lugal are attested, for the first time, in texts at Umma and Girsu.

ogous functions in cities such as Girsu, Nippur, Adab, and Gasur. In the large households owned by the local énsi, the scribe may have continued his traditional role. But, as seen in the private archives and in the archives of estates granted by the king, such as that of Me-ság, the scribe may well have functioned in a new and different capacity.

As before, local governors and high-ranking royal officials, such as the šabra-é and šagina, came from the category of the scribes. But now it assumed far greater proportions and was much more visible—a policy that would continue into the Ur III period.[18]

Many scribes had a military role in the Sargonic period. At least six scribes (out of 16) are nu-bànda's in the early Sargonic archive of Umma,[19] and others in the Sargonic archive of Girsu.[20] In some instances, scribes were in charge of guard duty.[21] Scribes with military authority over guruš seem to be attested already in the Fara documents.[22]

THE SCRIBES AND THE ORGANIZATION OF MESOPOTAMIAN SOCIETY

Various developmental models of Mesopotamian society and of its administrative organization have been proposed during the last fifty years.[23] A. Deimel developed a temple-state hypothesis—later modified by A. Falkenstein—that assumed that cultivated land was owned by the temple institutions, thereby giving them control of the entire economy of southern Mesopotamia. The Soviet model proposed that land, at least originally, belonged to the collective and that the temple institutions possessed only a fraction of the land. I. J. Gelb posited a significant presence of private property, even from earliest times.[24]

---

18. Cf. Yuhong Wu, "High-Ranking 'Scribes' and Intellectual Governors during the Akkadian and Ur III Periods," *JAC* 10 (1995): 129ff.

19. Cf. *supra*, p. 95, n. 306.

20. Cf. *supra*, p. 159, n. 235.

21. Cf. Foster, *Management*, pp. 26–27.

22. Cf. *Bureau*, pp. 51; 85ff.

23. For analysis of these models, see B. R. Foster, "A New Look at the Sumerian Temple State," *JESHO* 24 (1985): 225–41.

24. Cf. Foster, *JESHO* 24 (1985): 228–29. For the bibliography relative to these models, cf. Foster, *id.*, nn. 2–4, 9–11. For a more recent discussion of these models, cf. G. Pettinato, *I Sumeri*, pp. 238–46; 251–56.

Our analysis of the archives permits the following observations:

(a) The Early ED archive of Ur shows the existence of temple organizations that owned or managed arable land. The occurrence in these texts of a governmental figure, the PA.SI Urí^{ki}, raises the possibility that temple structures depended on institutional power.

(b) The archives of ED IIIa Šuruppak (including the unpublished archives of the University Museum) provide evidence of an organizational system of the local affairs that appears as a capillary network of family and professional households that were working on behalf of or inside the temple households, which, in turn, were supervised by the énsi through the é-géme. The foreign affairs were managed directly by the é-gal, which, in contrast to the local cooperative system, appears to be a centralized organization with Šuruppak the center of the Hexapolis league (cf. EDATŠ, pp. 10–17, and texts 1–13).

(c) The archive of ED IIIb Girsu documents the existence of several administrative centers. Some institutional centers, such as the é-gal, the é-mí, and the é-nam-dumu, were controlled by members of the royal family. The temple institutions operated with officials called sanga or dub-sar-maḫ. But the fact that the é-Ningirsu and é-Baba seem to be synonyms for the é-gal and the é-mí and that the sanga of the é-Ningirsu, Enentarzi, became the énsi, the political head of the city, suggests that, in reality, all these administrative centers operated under a single political and economic center.

(d) The archives of Late ED and Early Sargonic Umma and Ur indicate that the administration of the énsi was the economic and political control center of the city. The only exception is seen in the archive of Nippur, according to which the economic power may have been wielded by the sanga of Enlil— a result, perhaps, of the special status of this "holy city" of Sumer.

(e) The archives of the Classical Sargonic period indicate that in the south, in Girsu, Umma, and Adab, economic power was wielded by the administrations of the local énsi's[25] under the control and supervision of the Sargonic king. In Nippur, however, the function of the énsi was carried out by the sanga of Enlil. In central Mesopotamia, in Kiš and Mugdan, this power was vested

25. At Adab it is possible that temple institutions were present and functioned within the administration of the énsi; cf. *supra*, p. 191.

> in the estates that were controlled by the royal family. In the Diyala (Ešnunna), Himrin (Awal or Batiri), Tutub, and the north (Gasur), economic power seems to belong to institutions connected to the Crown.

No one model hitherto proposed provides a coherent interpretation of the data from all these archives. Only a model that, at a minimum, integrates aspects of each model and takes into account both the centrality of the political institutions and local differences could, perhaps, bring together into a coherent picture data from the archives of the various centers.[26]

---

26. P. Steinkeller, "Land-Tenure Conditions in Third Millennium Babylonia: The Problem of Regional Variation," in *Urbanization and Land Ownership in the Ancient Near East*, p. 290, working on the basis of the early studies of A. Deimel, AnOr 2 (1931) and A. Falkenstein, "La Cité-Temple Sumérienne," in *Cahiers de l'Histoire Mondiale*, 1 (1954): 784–814, outlines a "working model" of the socio-economic organization of the Sumerian city-state as "a pyramid of temple based communities, each community being administratively and economically tied to a different temple estate or temple household." In this drawing "temple community was organized hierarchically" but "it was not a hierarchy of individuals, but of nuclear or small extended families. In other words the temple community formed a pyramid of individual families or households" (*idem*, p. 294). All temple communities were linked together to form one super-community headed, on behalf of the city god, by the énsi and his family. G. R. Magid, "Micromanagement in the Queen's Household: Notes on the Organization of the Labor at ED Lagash," to appear in XLVe RAI (Harvard, 1998), in his study of ED IIIb Girsu documents, stressed that the family households are presumed to differ in scale, rather than model, from the main temple household. Magid suggests they maintained subordinate workers in their separate residential households. The high-ranking members of the community who seem to have had persona/family households, received šuku lands and in the period of their obligation (ranging from four to six months), they were given food and clothing allotments. Once free of obligation to the estate, these households operated for their own benefit. The existence of households managed by scribes is not surprising. Actually, such households are attested in all the documents we have considered in this study. In ED IIIb Girsu: é-Îl dub-sar-maḫ (see, p. 74); in ED IIIb Umma: é-Giš-šà sanga (see p. 91); in Sargonic Girsu: é-Lú-bànda dub-sar (p. 141); Adab: é-UN-íl dub-sar (p. 181); Gasur: é-Ì-lí dub-sar (p. 228). Some households in ED IIIa Šuruppak, like é-Al-la and é-Úr-NI, may have been similar to them. Also many scribes were sellers or buyers in sale contracts and in private transactions. Certainly, as we have observed elsewhere (G. Visicato – A. Westenholz, "Some Unpublished Sale-Contracts from Fara," *Memorial Cagni* [forthcoming]), the Fara documents indicate that the scribes belonged to an "elite" that managed institutional power, estates, and properties.

Since writing had become absolutely essential for the management of power, scribal bureaucracy had a vital role in Mesopotamian society. This role became more marked in the ED I period with the almost total disappearance of minor centers and the tremendous growth of large urban centers. The scribal bureaucracy, now fully ensconced into all facets of activity throughout the country, was part of the system of power and control, which had become centralized and autocratic.[27] Although this autocratic and bureaucratic system was necessary to coordinate and

27. M. T. Larsen, "The Role of Writing and Literacy in the Development of Social and Political Power. Literacy and Social Complexity," in B. B. Gledhill – M. T. Larsen, eds., *State and Society. The Emergence and Development of Social Hierarchy and Political Centralization* (London, 1988), pp. 173–91, outlines some of the principal models that analyze the relationship between the development of the state and the birth of writing in the ancient Near East, in particular, the models proposed by C. Levi-Strauss, *Tristes Tropiques* (Paris, 1925), pp. 265–66, "the claim is that writing appears to be necessary for a centralized state to reproduce itself" and by S. Goody, *The Logic of Writing and the Organization of Society* (Cambridge, 1986), p. 92, "writing was not essential to the development of the state, but a certain type of state, the bureaucratic one." Larsen, *op. cit.*, pp. 177ff. compares these models of relationships with models of other areas and other periods. Dealing with the development of the state in China, P. Wheatley, *The Pivot of the Four Quarters. A Preliminary Enquiry into the Origins and Character of the Ancient Chinese City* (Edinburgh, 1971), p. 377, states that "the claim that writing was a prime mover in the development of complex societies or a bureaucratic state appears to spring from a conviction that it was of fundamental importance for the promotion of the homogeneity of the ruling classes, as the prime instrument in the consolidation of their power and as the principal disseminator of their value systems." E. L. Eisenstein, *The Printing Revolution in Early Modern Europe* (Cambridge, 1983), p. 273, suggests that the invention of printing should not be regarded as the agent but as only one of the agents that brought about the change and development of the modern European state. In his conclusions, M. T. Larsen, *op. cit.*, p. 187, states that "the emergence of writing does not create or cause social complexity, the rise of the state, urbanism, slavery or freedom. It is, on the other hand, an enabling factor." His conclusion does not agree very well with that of M. W. Green, "The Construction and Implementation of the Cuneiform Writing System," *Visible Language* 15 (1981): 387, who regards writing as the fundamental technology for the creation of the bureaucratic state that emerges in Mesopotamia in the third millennium B.C.E., "The emergence of a large-scale, centralized, bureaucratic institution, however, might itself have been a consequence of the creation of the tools which empowered its functioning. Certainly, writing enabled the administration to grow and, through written liability, to maintain direct authority over even the lowest levels of personnel and clientele."

perform a whole series of collective activities, it may have been the Achilles' heel of Mesopotamian society. The maintenance of such a large and expanding bureaucracy may have become, at particular moments in history, an intolerable burden. We can, in fact, observe that the major collapses of Mesopotamian society of the third millennium, in the ED IIIa, Sargonic, Ur III, and perhaps in the Late Uruk periods, all coincide with the maximum production of tablets and the highest number of scribes.

In this work we have not discussed the impact of the scribe throughout all facets of Mesopotamian society. We have limited our study to the scribe's role in the institutional and bureaucratic systems, in part, because almost all the documentation that has reached us derives from institutional structures, such as the é-gal or temple households—especially in the ED period.

Nevertheless, scribal ties to private households, some perhaps belonging to scribes (é-PN dub-sar), are mentioned in documents from ED IIIa Šuruppak and ED IIIb Girsu. In the Sargonic period more households managed by scribes appear. Many scribes were involved in sale contracts as sellers or buyers, or in other commercial activities.

Scribal family relationships are attested (PN_1 dub-sar dumu PN_2 dub-sar dumu PN_3 dub-sar) and family relationships (PN_1 dub-sar dumu PN_2 dub-sar) link some scribes to both the Šuruppak and Girsu archives. Only a few families had the resources, both money and time, to provide a scribal education. Quite likely the earliest scribal educations were provided within the family unit itself. Thus the earliest scribes belonged to the families of the elite, having wealth and wielding power within Mesopotamian society. Scribes could rise to the highest political positions, as governors and rulers, in both the ED and Sargonic periods.

Our subject merits further in-depth study. We hope this book will be a solid resource for other scholars in their quest for more information about those who held the power and the writing in early Mesopotamia.

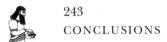

Tables of the Scribes

TABLES 1 & 2

TABLE 1

Scribes of Early ED Ur

NAME	TEXTS
Ma-za <-LA>	dub-sar: UET 2, 297 ————: UET 2, 70; 109; 212; 226; 252; 353
Ma-zi	dub-zu: zu.SAR: UET 2, 93 ————: UET 2, 87; 226

TABLE 2

Scribes of ED Šuruppak

NAME	ADMINISTRATIVE TEXTS	SALE CONTRACTS	LEXICAL TEXTS
A-du$_6$	dub-sar: EDATŠ 121; 127; 128; 134		
A-na-da-ak		agrig: Ung. 4	
A-geštin	dub-sar na-gada ^{d}Sùd: EDATŠ 37 dub-sar: EDATŠ 134; 135; 146	———: WF 30	NTSŠ 229$^{?}$ (a-dam-geštin)
A-ḫar-ši		dub-sar: WF 32; MVN10, 84; BAOM 5 dub-sar-aša$_5$: Ung. 1	
A-ḪU/RI-ti	dub-sar: EDATŠ 68; 69; 121; 132; 183; 195; TSŠ 936; WF 121	dub-sar: Ung. 2; WF 30; 37	
A-me-te		dub-sar. *ArOr* 39, p. 15	
⌜A$^{?}$⌝-NI	dub-sar: EDATŠ 26		
A-pa-è	dub-sar: WF 138		

TABLE 2 

Abzu-ki-<dúr>-du$_{10}$	dub-sar: EDATŠ 14; 68; 71; 74; 121; 135; ———: EDATŠ 173; 174	dub-sar: WF 42(1)	
Ad-da-da	dub-sar: TSŠ 90. ———: EDATŠ 8; [74]		SF 16; 20; 77; NTSŠ 229
AK-girin$_x$ or Girin$_x$-AK	———: EDATŠ 19; 20	dub-sar: WF 33; 36	
Amar-é-^{d}Gibil$_6$	dub-sar: EDATŠ 116; 139		
Amar-^{d}Gú-lá		dub-sar: WF 33; 37	
Amar-ḪA.A		um-mi-a: MVN 10, 82; 83; PBS 9, 3 ———: A 33676	
Amar-kù	dub-sar sanga-GAR: EDATŠ 10 ———: EDATŠ 7; 8		
Amar-NÁM	———: EDATŠ 7		SF p. 6*, 1; TSŠ 46R; 80; 124
<Amar>-sag-TAR	dub-sar: EDATŠ 115; 121; 122	(dub.sar:) A 33676	
Amar-šùba	dub-sar: EDATŠ 12; 115; WF 138 gal-unken: EDATŠ 7; 35; 116 ugula é-géme: EDATŠ 46	dub-sar: TLAT 1	SF37
Amar-[ ]	dub-sar: WF 138		
AN.DA-zu$_5$		dub-sar: WF 35	
AN.DU$_6$.GU.NA		dub-sar: RTC 13	
AN-nu-me	———: EDATŠ 7		SF 13; 16; 39; 44
AN-sag-tuku/ sag-dingir-tuku	dub-sar: EDATŠ 20; 27; 121; 122; 138		SF 13; 18; 29; 33; 36; 42; 55; 58; 63; 64; 69; TSŠ 124

TABLE 2

AN-úr-šè	dub-sar: EDATŠ 37; 68; 72; 73; 115; 122; 123		SF 59; 64
Bil$_x$-<á>-nu-kús	dub-sar: EDATŠ 68; 72; 74; 76; 82; 121; 123; 134; 135; 140	dub-sar: *WO* 8, 180	TSŠ 46R
Bil$_x$-anzu	dub-sar: EDATŠ 12; 141		
Da-du-lul	dub-sar: EDATŠ 19 ——: WF 149		
Du-du	maškim dub-sar-maḫ: TSŠ 627	dub-sar-aša$_5$: YBC 12305	
Dub-ḫul-tar	dub-sar: EDATŠ 14; 15 <ugula>-agrig: EDATŠ 3; 68; 73; 134; 181 ——: EDATŠ 38; 39; 40		NTSŠ 229
Dumu-nun-šita	dub-sar: WF 135; TSŠ 649		
E-ta-e$_{11}$		dub-sar-aša$_5$: CBS 8830 ——: A 33676	
É-du$_6$	dub-sar tigi$_x$-di: EDATŠ 10		
É-gù-nun	EDATŠ 38–40 dam-kas$_4$: TSŠ 964$^?$		
É-ḫur-sag	dub-sar: 116; 121; 122; 123		
É-na-lu-lu	dub-sar: EDATŠ 115; 144		
É-^{d}Nanna	dub-sar: EDATŠ 132; 136 ——: EDATŠ 8	dub-sar-aša$_5$: NBC 6842	
É-pa-è (cf. É-zi-pa-è)		dub-sar: TSŠ X; Ung. 2	
É-saḫar-ra\ta-è	dub-sar: EDATŠ 14; 15		
É-šùd-du$_{10}$	dub-sar: EDATŠ 132; TSŠ 423 dilmun-gal: WF 136 ——: EDATŠ 187; TSŠ 775; 928		SF 39: é-[ ]-du$_{10}^?$

TABLE 2

É-zi-<pa-è>	dub-sar: EDATŠ 68; 70; 136; 172; 212 ———: EDATŠ 82; 96	um-mi-a: TMH 5, 71	
Eden-si	dub-sar: EDATŠ 127; 128.		
En-nagar-šà	dub-sar: EDATŠ 7 ———: EDATŠ 116; 121		
EN.PI		dub-sar-aša$_5$: RTC 14	
GAR-du-la	dub-sar: EDATŠ 29; 116 ———: WF 151		
Gissu-šè		dub-sar: MVN 10, 83	SF 36; 69
Gú-ni-mu-MUŠENxBURU$_5$		dub-sar: Or 44, 436	
Ḫar-tu-^{d}Sùd	dub-sar: EDATŠ 11 ———: EDATŠ 8	sa$_{12}$-du$_5$: A 33676	SF 1
Ig-ge-nu-gi$_4$		dub-sar-aša$_5$: Ar Or 39, 14; Ung. 2; 3	
Íl		dub-sar: TMH 5, 75 ———: WF 33	
KA-lugal-da-zi		———: WF 34	TSŠ 46R; 80; NTSŠ 294
KA-ni-zi	dub-sar sa$_{12}$-du$_5$: EDATŠ 10 dub-sar: EDATŠ 19 nì-si$_4$: EDATŠ 7; 8 ———: EDATŠ 38; 39		cf. KA-zi SF 37; TSŠ 80
KA-^{d}Sùd-da-zi		dub-sar-aša$_5$: WF 34 dub-sar: A 33676	
Ka-tar-ni-ga		dub-sar: WF 30 dumu UR.UR: *WO* 8, 18	

Lu-lu	dub-sar: CT 50, 20 agrig: EDATŠ 10 nimgir-abzu: EDATŠ 7		
Lú-na-nam		dub-sar: TLAT 1 ———: WF 37; 38	
Lugal-á-maḫ	dub-sar: EDATŠ 212 ———: EDATŠ 38; 39		
Lugal-é-si		dub-sar-aša$_5$: WF 33. dub-sar maškim: TSŠ X	
Lugal-ezen		dub-sar: TMH 5, 71	
Lugal-ir-nun		dub-sar. Ung. 1	
Lugal-ki-dúr-du$_{10}$	dub-sar: EDATŠ 121; 123; 141; NTSŠ 258 ———: EDATŠ 38; 39; 40	dub-sar: WF 42	NTSŠ 294; SF 62
Lugal-u$_4$-su$_{13}$-šè		dub-sar: RTC 14	
Lugal-UŠ.ŠIM		dub-sar-aša$_5$: A 33676 ———: WF 40; *SEL* 3, p. 11	
Lum-ma	dub-sar-anše sa$_{12}$-du$_5$: EDATŠ 7 dub-sar-<é>-géme: EDATŠ 121; 122 dub-sar: EDATŠ 116; 117; 128; 164 ———: EDATŠ 78; 79; WF 120	———: WF 37	SF 16; 27; NTSŠ 294
Mes-nu-šè	dub-sar: EDATŠ 14; 15		
Mu-ni-da	dub-sar: EDATŠ 115		
Mu-ni-ùri		dub-sar: MVN 10, 82	
Munus-ki-nu-zu	———: WF 151	dub-sar: WF 42	

Nam-maḫ	dub-sar: TSŠ 881 ——: EDATŠ 38; 39	um-mi-a lú-é-éš-gar: RTC 13; TLAT 1 dub-sar: MVN 10, 85; ——: A 33676	
Nam-maḫ-^{d}Sùd-da		um-mi-a lú-é-és-gar: de Marcellis tablet	SF 39; NTSŠ 294
Nin-ig-gal		dub-sar: SRJ p. 31, no. 6	
^{d}Nin-unug-^{d}anzu		dub-sar: de Marcellis tablet	
<Pa$_4$-á>-nu-kúš	dub-sar-udu: EDATŠ 47; WF 121 dub-sar: EDATŠ 19; 115; 121; 122; 123; 132; 146; CT 50, 17; 25 ——: 38; 39	dub-sar: *WO* 8, 180 ——: BAOM 5, 28	
<Pa$_4$>-é-kur-pa-è	dub-sar: EDATŠ 127; 143, TSŠ 936		
Sag-a-DU-ba-sum	.	dub-sar: A 33676	
Si-dù	agrig: EDATŠ 152 dumu abzu-ki-du$_{10}$ dub-sar: EDATŠ 14 ——: EDATŠ 38; 39; 40		
^{d}Sùd-anzu	(a) dub-sar sanga-GAR: EDATŠ 10 dub-sar: WF 138 en-nagar-šà dub-sar: EDATŠ 7 en-nagar-šà: EDATŠ 116; 121 (b) Ur-dumu-zi dub-sar: 14; 35 dumu ^{d}En-líl-pà: 120 dub-sar: 15	dub-sar: TSŠ X; DeMarcellis ——: WF 30; 37	SF 39
^{d}Sùd-šer$_7$-zi	dub-sar: EDATŠ 127; 128		
Šà-ge-TAR	dub-sar: EDATŠ 23; 24; 25		
Šeš-ama-na	dub-sar: TSŠ 627 ——: EDATŠ 38; 39		

TABLE 2

Šeš-ki-na	dub-sar: WF 149		
Šeš-kur-ra		dub-sar-aša$_5$: RTC 15	
Šeš-tur	dub-sar: EDATŠ 121; 123; 128; 129	dub-sar-aša$_5$: RTC 15	TSŠ 973
Šita	dub-sar: EDATŠ 116; 117; 124; 138; 154; WF 149 ———: EDATŠ 35; 216; WF 151		
Šita-AK		———: A 33676	
Šubur	dub-sar sanga-GAR: TSŠ 430 ugula-dub-sar: EDATŠ 116; (WF 147) *bur-su-ma:* EDATŠ 195; (41) dub-sar: EDATŠ 19; TSŠ 897; WF 153	dub-sar: WF 36 ———: WF 30	SF 33; 39
Ul$_4$-la	dub-sar: WF 138		
Ur-abzu\abzu$_x$	———: EDATŠ 37$^?$; TSŠ 775; WF 116	dub-sar: Ung. 2; 3	
Ur-$^{\langle d\rangle}$Dumu-zi	dub-sar: EDATŠ 14; 15; 19; 35; 68; 71; 73; 93; 124; 140; 143; 173; 174		
Ur-^{d}En-ki		dub-sar: PBS 9, 3. ———: MVN 10, 83	
Ur-^{d}Gú-lá		dub-sar: Ung. 3; MVN 10, 86 ———: Or 44, 436	
Ur-kin-nir	———: EDATŠ 212	dub-sar-aša$_5$: SRJ p. 31, no. 6	
Ur-Nin-unug		dub-sar-aša$_5$: WF 32	
Ur-^{d}Nusku		dub-sar: *SEL* 3, p. 4	

Ur-^{d}Sùd		um-mi-a: MVN 10, 85; 86; Ung. 2	TSŠ 4 6R
Ur-^{d}Šer$_7$-da	dub-sar: EDATŠ 68; 72; 74; 75; 77; 79; 115; 147		
Ur-túl-sag	dub-sar-<é->géme: EDATŠ 7	——: WF 35; 39	TSŠ 46R
UR.UR	dub-sar: EDATŠ 116; WF 108	dub-sar-aša$_5$: WF 37 dub-sar: WF 33	SF 39; TSŠ 46R
Utu-á-maḫ	dub-sar-maḫ: CT 50, 19 ——: EDATŠ 68; 70; 74; 124		
Utu-šita	dub-sar: EDATŠ 116; 117; 146; 157; TSŠ 70 Pa$_4$-^{d}anzu: EDATŠ 7; 8$^?$; 37		SF 77
Zà-ta	dub-sar sanga-GAR: EDATŠ 10 ——: EDATŠ 7		SF 77 Zà-ta-ḫar-tu: SF 33
[ ]	dub-sar-šùš: EDATŠ 10		
unnamed	dub-sar-maḫ: EDATŠ 23; 27; 94; TSŠ 420; 679		

TABLE 2a

Lexical Texts with Names of Scribes of the Fara Administration

NAME	GROUP A	GROUP B	OTHER TEXTS
A-geštin			NTSŠ 229
Ad-da-da	a1: a2: SF 77 a3:	SF 16	SF 20; NTSŠ 229
Amar-NÁM	a1: a2: a3: TSŠ 124	TSŠ 46; 80	
Amar-šùba		SF37	
AN-sag-tuku	a1: a2: SF 36; 69 a3: SF 18; 29; 33; 42; 55; 63; 64; TSŠ 124	SF13	SF58
AN-nu-me	a1: a2: a3: SF 13; 16; 39		SF 44
AN-úr-šè	a1: a2: a3: SF 59; 64		
Bil$_x$-á-nu-kúš	.	TSŠ 46R	
Dub-ḫul-tar			NTSŠ 229
É-šùd-du$_{10}$		SF 39: É-[ ]-du$_{10}$	
Gissu-šè	a1: a2: SF 36; 69 a3:		
Ḫar-tu-^{d}Sùd			SF1

TABLE 2a

KA-lugal-da-zi		TSŠ 46R; 80; NTSŠ 294	
KA-ni-zi		cf. KA-zi: SF 37; TSŠ 80	
Lugal-ki-dúr-du$_{10}$		SF 62; NTSŠ 294	
Lum-ma		SF 16; NTSŠ 294	
Nam-maḫ-^{d}Sùd-da		SF 39	
^{d}Sùd-anzu		SF 39	
Šeš-tur			TSŠ 973
Šubur	a1: a2: a3: SF 33	SF 39	
Ur-^{d}Sùd		TSŠ 46R	
Ur-túl-sag		TSŠ 46R	
UR.UR		SF 39; TSŠ 46R	
Utu-šita	a1: a2: SF 77 a3:		
Zà-ta	a1: a2: SF 77 a3: Zà-ta-ḫar-tu: SF 33		

TABLE 3

Scribes of Abū Ṣalābīkh

Name	Administrative Texts	Lexical or Literary Texts
A-DU	dub-sar: IAS 494	
A-geštin-abzu	cf. A-geštin-⌜x⌝: IAS 516	IAS 34; 39; 46; 91; 117; 131;142; 268; 476; 480
A-UZU-gal	IAS 495	cf. A-ul$_4$-gal: IAS 298
Bí-bí-um/Bí-bí-ù/ I-bí-um	IAS 531	IAS 116; 254; 480
Gu-NI-sum	IAS 498	IAS 126
I-gi/gi$_4$-ì-lum	IAS 503	IAS 18; 20; 59; 124; 126; 163
I-ku-<gu>-il	IAS 503	IAS 61; 113; 268; 479; 481
Il-LAK 647	IAS 515	IAS 116; 283
Im-ri-i-rúm	IAS 518	cf. [ ]-i-rúm: IAS 141
Puzur$_4$-il	IAS 503	IAS 13; 142; 268

TABLE 4

Scribes of ED IIIb Girsu

NAME TITLE	ENENTARZI TEXTS	LUGALANDA TEXTS	URUKAGINA TEXTS	UNDATED TEXTS
A-ba-DI<ì-e/bé> dub-sar	DP 195; AWAS 75(2)	RTC 75(1); DCS 8(1); DP 542(1); 231(2$^{?}$); 622(2); 641(2); 623(3); Nik 79(3); AVG I, 40(3); DP 645(3); AWL 68(4); 130(4); DP 657(4); AVG I, 101(5); DP 132(5); 192(5$^{?}$)AVG I, 41(6); DP 193(6); AVG I, 39(7); DP 584(6); RTC 54(6); DP 192(4/5); AVG I, 103; AVG II, 25(6$^{?}$)	DP 194(e); AWAS 5(e); 37(e); 19(e); 30(e); DP 637(e$^{?}$); AWAS 74(1); 39(1); TSA 23(1); DP 133(1); TSA 5(2); AVG I, 79(2); 95(2); AVG II, 6(2); AWL 19(2$^{?}$); AWAS 6(2); TSA 20(2); AWAS 68(3); 10(3); 7(3); 8(3); 9(3); DP 130(3); 603; 545 (4); TSA 7(4$^{?}$); DP 257(4$^{?}$); 567(4$^{?}$); TSA 8(4$^{?}$); DP 121(6); AWAS 81(6); 12(6); 11(6$^{?}$); DCS 7(?); DP 137(?)	AVG II, 4; 71; Nik I, 30(1$^{?}$)
A-ba-mu-na-DU dub-sar				DP 31 (Entemena)
A-li-ì-ba dub-sar		Nik 213(6)		
Amar-Gírid^{ki} dub-sar		DP 657(1); 622(2); 641(2); 623(3); 624(3); 179(4); AVG I, 101(5); 39(6); RTC 54 (6); AVG I, 39(7)	AWAS 5(e); DP6 37(e$^{?}$); AVG I, 70(1); 79(2); 93(2$^{?}$); AWAS 6(2); TSA 20(2); AVG II, 6(2); AWAS 68(3); 7(3); 10(3); 9(3); DP 130(3); 603(4); 647(4$^{?}$); 121(6); AWAS 81(6); 12(6); 11(6)	AVG II, 96(2)

TABLE 4

Aš$_{10}$-né dub-sar	AWAS 75(2); DP 617	DCS 8(1); DP 657(1$^?$); Nik 125(2); DP 622(2); 641(2); DP 231(2$^?$); Nik 79(3); DP 623(3); AWL 68(4); 130(4); AVG I, 101(5); DP 132(5); 192(5$^?$) AVG I, 41(6); DP 193(6); RTC 54(6); DP 192(5$^?$); AVG I, 39(7)	DP 194(e); DP 567(4); Nik 20(5)	AO 4348
Bára-zi-<šà-gal> agrig			AWAS 6(2); Nik 13(2); AVG II, 6(2); 13(2); DP 130((3); AWAS 7(3); 10(3); 118(3); 8(3); 9(3); 7(4); Nik 52(4); DP 647(4$^?$)	
Du-du dub-sar		RTC 44(6$^?$)	AWAS 39(1)	CIRPL 62: 8
E-ge-<a-na-ak> dub-sar			TSA 7(4$^?$); TSA 8(?)	
E-ta dub-sar	DP 617			AO 4348
É-an-né-mud dub-sar				NIK 102; AWL 169(3)
É-gu$_4$-gim-saḫar-ra dub-sar	RTC 17			
É-li-li dumu Ki-ti dub-sar	RTC 17			
É-me dub-sar		Nik 44(-)		Nik 44
En-an-na-túm-sipa-zi agrig	CIRPL, EN 12;			AO 4156 (Ent. 19)

En-bi-<sà-ga> dub-sar		RTC 54(6); AVG I, 39(6); AVG II, 7(6)	AWAS 5(e); 37(e); DP 637(e); AVG I, 70(1); 74(1); 79(2); 87(2); 93(2); AVG II, 6(2); 13(2); 96(2); AWAS 6(2); TSA 20(2); AWAS 68(3); 7(3); 10(3); 8(3); 9 (3); DP 130(3); 603(4); 647($4^{?}$); 121(6); AWAS 81(6); 12(6); 11($6^{?}$)	
En-da-<mu>-gal-di dub-sar		DP 132(5)	Nik 9(e); AWAS 52(e); 119(e); DP 113(2); AWAS 121(3); 6(3); 12(4); TSA 14(4); Nik 2(4); TSA 15(4); DP 114(5); DCS 1(6); AWAS 121(6); TSA 16(6); AWAS 23(6); 17(6)	
En-DU dub-sar			DP 258(e)	
En-ig-gal dub-sar	AWL 138(4)	Nik 324($6^{?}$)	Nik 325($1^{?}$)	DP 137
En-ki-šár-ra dub-sar	AWL 32(2)			
En-kù dub-sar	RTC 17	AVG I, 40(3)		

TABLE 4

En-kù <dub-sar> kurušda		DP 81(1); AVG I, 48(2); AWL 160(2); DP 61(2); 64(2); 90(2); Nik 167(2); 168(2); 172(2); 173(2); RTC 42(2); 46(2); AWL 175(3); DP 104(3); 246(3); RTC 47(3); DP 199(4); 200(4); 205(4); 208-210(4); 212(4) 218(4); 219(4); Nik 157(4); AVG I, 30(5); 64(5); AVG II, 41(5); DP 85(5); 201(5); 202(5); 206(5); 207(5); 211(5); 217(5); 246(5); 247(5); 248(5); Nik 148(5); 149(5); 153(5); 197(5); 312(5); DP 193(6)	AWAS 37(e$^?$); DP 194(e); 637(e); AVG I, 70(1); AWAS 53(1); TSA 23(1); AWAS 6(2); AVG II, 6(2); 96(2); TSA 20(2); DP171(2); 638(2$^?$); 639(2$^?$); Nik 13(2); DP 130(3)	
En-kù um-mi-a			DP 158(2); Nik 60(2); 64(2); TSA 34(3); Nik 63(3); TSA 36(3); AWAS 52(4)	
En-lú-[ ] dub-sar				*RA* 74 (1980): 45
En-šu-gi$_4$-gi$_4$ agrig			DP 416(1); TSA 3(2); AVG II, 40(5); Nik 57(6); DP 114(6); 149(6); AVG II, 1(6); AWAS 53(6); 7(6); DP 121(6); 150(6); TSA 16(6); AWAS 6(6); 81(6); 12(6); 69(6); 11(6); 23(6); 7(6); 22(6); TSA 13(6); 17(6); AWAS 13(6)	

TABLE 4

Gìri-né-ba-tuš dub-sar	ITT V, 9242(2)			
Gú-bé dub-sar	RTC 17 (untitled)	Nik 33(4$^{?}$)		Nik 177(4); Nik 118
Gú-bé sanga	AWAS 79(2)	Nik 125(2); AWL 175(3)		AWL 182 (EN/L$^{?}$)
Gú-ú dub-sar		CT 50, 29; 30		
Ìd-lú-sikil dub-sar				A 3604 (Enanatum)
IGI$^{?}$.ḪUŠ$^{?}$ dub-sar		DP 179(4)		
Igi-mu-<an-šè-gál> dub-sar		RTC 75(1); DP 577(2$^{?}$); Nik 157(4)	TSA 2(1)	
Ki-ti-<la-né/na> dub-sar	RTC 17; DP 39(4$^{?}$)	Nik 158(1); DP 352(3$^{?}$); 354(3$^{?}$)		RTC 16 (Ent. 19); DP 31
Ki-tuš-lú dub-sar		CT50, 28; 32		
Lugal-a dub-sar		Nik 44(?)		
Lugal-èš-du$_{10}$-ga dub-sar			AWAS 42(3)	
Lugal-Kèš^{ki} dub-sar			Nik 90(3); AWL 77(3$^{?}$); AWAS 124(3): 26(3); 6 8(3); Nik 16(4); DP 116(4); 117(4); CT 50, 35(4); Nik 20(5); DP 118; AVG II, 77(-)	
Lugal-mu <dub-sar>		Nik 44(1)		Nik 177(4)$^{?}$
Lugal-nam-gú-sù dub-sar	L 9249 (2)	DP 59 (3)		

Lugal-pa-è dub-sar		DP 645(3$^?$); AVG I, 101(5)		
Lugal-šà-lá-tuku dub-sar			CT 50, 36(3); AWAS 121(3); 16(3); 120(4); TSA 14(4); Nik 2(4); TSA 15(4); DP114(5); 115(6); TSA 16(6); AWAS 17(6)	
Lugal-šà-lá-tuku lú-é-éš-gíd ^{d}Nin-gír-su		DP 59(3)		
Lum-ma-mes-ni dub-sar				CIRPL, An 2
Lum-ma-šà-tam dub-sar		Nik 44(1); RTC 75(1)		
Maš-dà dub-sar	DP 617	DCS 8(1); DP 145(1); Nik 44(1); AVG I, 8(1); DP 622(2); 641(2); 645(2); AVG I, 32(2); DP 231(2); Nik 125(3); 79(3) DCS 6(3); AWL 42(2); DP 623(3); RTC 52(3); Nik 97(3$^?$); AWAS 77(3$^?$); AWL 130(4); AVG I, 101(5); RTC5 1(5); Nik 83(5$^?$); DP 192(5$^?$); 193(6); AVG II, 7(6); AWAS 45(6); RTC 54(6); TSA 10(6); AVG I, 41(6); 43(6); RTC 55(7); AWAS 29(7); AVG I, 39(7)	AWL 43(e); DP 152(e); CT 50, 33(e); DP 155(e); DP 156(e); AWAS 19(e); 30(e); DP 194(e); 163(e); AWAS 37($^?$1); DP 637(1$^?$); AVG I, 66(1); AWAS 31(1); AVG I, 70(1); AVG II, 71(2)	Nik 30(1); DP 488(2); AO 4197(2); AVG II, 4(-)

TABLE 4

Maš-dà agrig			AWAS 4(e); (e); 3 9(1); AVG I, 74(1); TSA 23(1); AWAS 6(2); AVG II, 11(2); TSA 20(2); DP 158(2); Nik 60(2); 13(2); AVG I, 79(2); DP 630(2); 130(3)	
Nam-maḫ dub-sar		AWL 6(1+x); Nik 48(6)		
Nì-lú-nu-DU dub-sar				Nik 30; SRJ p. 66, no. 30
NÌGIN-mud dumu Na-na dub-sar	RTC 17			
NÌGIN-mud dumu Gú-bé dub-sar	RTC 17			
Puzur$_4$-Ma-ma agrig			AWL 156(2+x)	
Šeš-lú-du$_{10}$ dub-sar		DP 226(4)	AWAS 52(e); 119(e); 14(e); 15(e); Nik 9(e); 123(e); DP 113(2); CT 50, 36(3); AWAS 121(3); 1 6(3); TSA15(4)	
Šeš-tur dub-sar		AVG I, 41(6)		DP 32 (Entemena)
Šubur-<tur> dub-sar	DP 93(5): Schileiko, 4(6)			DP 576
Šul-ig-gal dub-sar			DP 591 (5)	
Šul-me-<šár-ra-DU> agrig	DP 42(3)	DP 516(1); AWL 177(2); [176(2)]; Nik 182(3); DP 512(4); AWL 5(4)		

TABLE 4

^{d}Šul-utul$_{x}$-men agrig			DP 167 (2)	
Ur-igi-gál dub-sar			AWAS 52(1); DP 130(3)	
Úr-mud agrig			DP 630(2); 488(2); Nik 127(2); 13(2); AVG II, 6(2); AWAS 20(2); 6(2); 4(2); DP 112(2); Nik 64(2); 1(2); DP 548(3); 644(3); AWAS 7(3); 8(3); TSA 18(3); 34(3); AWAS 9(3); 25(3); Nik 59(3); 63(3); DP 130(3); AWAS 26(3); 32(4); CT 50, 34(4); DP 116(4); AWAS 33(4); DP118(4);Nik6 (4); DP 117(4); AWAS 57(4); Nik 15(4); DP 647(4); CTNMC 3(5); TSA 12(5); AWAS 21(5); 34(5); 3 5(5); TSA 35(5); DP 149(6); 121(6); AWAS 81(6); AVG I, 69(6); AWAS 12(6); 11(6$^{?}$); 23(6); 22(6); TSA 13(6); DP 500(?); 550(?); AVG II, 1(6)	
Ur-^{d}Nin-gír-su dub-sar	DP 617	DP 226(4)		
Ur-sag agrig		AWL 122(3); H.G.12(-)		
Ur-su dub-sar	RTC 17			
Ur-túl dub-sar		DP 657(1$^{?}$)		

Ur-túl-sag agrig			TSA 23(1); AVG I, 70(1); 74(1); 79(1); AVG II, 13(2)	
Ur-^{d}[ ] dub-sar				*RA* 74 (1980): 45
Ú.Ú agrig		AWL 108(2); DP 338(2); 218(4); Nik 280(4); DP 430(5); RTC 51(5); 67(6); AVG I, 71(6); 11(6); DP 425(7); AWAS 29(7)	DP 155(e); AWAS 30(e); 119(e); 15(e); Nik 9(2); DP 152(e); AWL 43(e); 14(e); AWAS 52(1); AVG I, 66(1); AWAS 31(1); DP 158(2); Nik 60(2)	
Ú.Ú (agrig)-kurusda			AVG II, 85(3); CT 50, 36(3); AWAS 16(3); 120(3); 121(3); TSA 34(3); Nik 59(3); TSA 36(3); Nik 63(3); 2(4); CT 50, 37(4); AWAS 32(4); 33(4); 36(4); 65(4); TSA 14(4); 15(4); AWAS 34(5); 35(5); CTNMC 3(5); DP 114(5); TSA 35(5); Nik 57(6); AWAS 17(6); 23(6); 36(6); DP 115(6); TSA 13(6); 17(6$^{?}$)	

TABLE 4

Ú.Ú dub-sar		RTC 54(6); AWL 6(1+x)	DP 637(e); AWAS 5(e); TSA 23(1); DP 133(1); TSA 5(2); DP 113(2); CT 50, 36(3); AWAS 121(3); 16(3); DP 130(3); AWAS 120(4); TSA 14(4); AWAS 64(4); TSA 15(4); Nik 2(5); DP 114(5); 115(6); AWAS 122(6); 23(6); 17(6); DP 137(?)	
[x].A.NI-du$_{10}$ dub-sar		AWL 175(3)		
x.x$^{?}$ -[s]ikil$^{?}$			DP 82 (1)	
unnamed dub-sar				Nik 177(4)

TABLE 5

dub-sar-maḫ of Girsu ED IIIb

NAME	ENEN-TARZI	LUGALANDA	URUKAGINA	UNDATED OR PREVIOUS
Amar–šùba	DP 42(3)	DP86(2?); AWL 177(2); 175(3); DP59(3); Geneva1(3); 3(4); RTC 39(5); DP131(6); H.P.12(-)		
Íl		AVG I, 5(1?)	AWAS 39(1); AVG I, 70(1); 93(2?); DP592 (4?) (only dub-sar)	DP 32 (Entemena) (only dub-sar)
Lugal-ḫé-gál-sù dub-sar-maḫ				Bi Mes 3, 10 (Enanatum) (Enanatum)
Lugal-šùd-dè	DP 42(3)	DP 578(1?); 59(3)	DP 133(1); 591(5)	CT 50, 44
Nigìn-mud	RTC 17 (only dub-sar)		TSA 2(1)	VAT 4845

TABLE 5a p.76

sanga-GAR and sanga-é-gal in ED IIIb Girsu

NAMES	ENENTARZI	LUGALANDA	URUKAGINA	UNDATED
Úr-mud sanga-GAR	DP 42 (3)	DP 59 (3); DP 399 (4); AWAS 50 (5)		AWL 124
unnamed sanga-GAR		AWL 182 (1); 176 (2); H.P. 12(-)	Nik I (2); TSA 4(2)	Nik I, 30
Šà-TAR sanga-é-gal	DP 42 (3)	DP 134 (1); Nik I, 53(1); RTC 61(1); DP 578(-); AWL 175(3)	AVG II, 72 (2)	
Ur-é-zi-da sanga-é-gal		Nik I, 125(2); DP 218 (4); H.P.12(-)		
Ú.Ú sanga-é-gal			AWAS 7(3); 8(3); 9(3); 10(3); 16(3); 33(4); 34(5); TSA 35 (5); TSA 7(4); 28(3?); AWL 76(4)	

TABLE 6

Scribes of Late ED and Early Sargonic Nippur

NAME	TEXTS	PERIOD
AN-šeš-mu	dub-sar: OSP1, 101	Late ED (Enšakušana)
^{d}Inanna-ur-sag	dub-sar: OSP1, 122 ——: OSP1, 121	Late ED (Enšakušana)
Lugal-al-sa$_{6}$	dub-sar-maḫ: ECTJ1, 66	Late ED (Lugalzagesi)
ḪA.N[I]	dub-sar: ECTJ 1, 53	Early Sargonic$^{?}$
Lugal-ùri	dub-sar: OSP1, p. 92 ——: OSP1, 38, 56; 85	Early Sargonic$^{?}$
Ur-tur	dub-sar: OSP1, 12	

TABLE 7

Scribes of ED IIIb Umma

NAME	TEXT AND DATE	PROFESSIONAL NAME
Lugal-an-né	*HUCA* 49, 2 (L)	dub-sar
Lugal-gu_4	BIN 8, 26 (L)	dub-sar
Lugal-ki	BIN 8, 104 (l)	dub-sar
Lugal-mas-sú	BIN 8, 102 (l)	dub-sar
Má-gur_8	BIN 8, 51(l); 52(l); 116(l 7)	dub-sar
Mes-é	BIN 8, 47(l); 61(l 7); 86(L7); Bryn Mawr 6(L7)	dub-sar dub-sar-maḫ
Ne-sag	AOAT 25 (L7)	dub-sar
Tir-kù	BIN 8, 51(l); 62(l ?); 82(L?); 109(l); 111(l); Bryn Mawr 7(L7); BIN 8 120[L]	dub-sar um-mi-a
Ur-é-zi-da	*HUCA* 49, 3(L); BMC 7(L7); BIN 8, 52 (l)	dub-sar
[ ]	BIN 8, 76(l); *HUCA* 49, 3(L); 7(l)	dub-sar

Note: We have followed the notation used in *HUCA* 49 (1978): 30. The symbol "L" indicates that the name of Lugalzagesi énsi appears on the tablet; the symbol "l" indicates that the attribution to Lugalzagesi is virtually certain, even if the name of the énsi does not appear.

TABLE 8

Scribes of Early Sargonic Umma

NAME	TEXTS AND YEARS
Á-kal-lé	um-mi-a: Nik II, 14 (?)
Ad-da	dub-sar: CHÉU 53 (5); CST 11 (5) énsi-gal: Nik II, 56 (2); 59 (4); 61 (4); 60*(4); 62*(?); 63*(5); BIN 8, 309 (5)
Bára-ga-ni	dub-sar: Nik II, 51 (1) PA.É: Nik II, 22; 55
En-ki-ág	dub-sar: CST 8 (4); BIN 8, 332 (4)
Giš-šà	dub-sar: USP 15 (?)
Lú-giš	dub-sar: Nik II, 35 (5)
Lugal-gaba	dub-sar: Nik II, 46 (5) maškim: CHÉU 53 (5)
Má-gur$_8$	dub-sar: Nik II, 56 (2); 59 (4); 61 (4); BIN 8, 332 (4); CST 8 (4); AO 5657 (4); Nik II, 47 (5)
NIM	dub-sar: Nik II, 61 (4)
Tir-kù	dub-sar-maḫ: Nik II, 14 (?) dub-sar: Nik II, 51 (1); USP 2 (1)
Ur-^{d}Al-la	dub-sar-dingir-ra: Nik II, 55 (4–6)
Ur-bi	dub-sar: Nik II, 54 (-)
Ur-é-maḫ	dub-sar: Nik II, 19 (-); ugula <dub-sar>: CHÉU 54 (5)
Ur-^{gis}gigir	dub-sar: Nik II, 40 (3)
Ur-lú	dub-sar: Nik II, 42 (3)
Ú-URUxA	dub-sar: Nik II, 14 (?)

TABLE 9

Scribes of Late ED and Early Sargonic Ur

NAME	TEXTS	PERIOD
Amar-[sa]nga$^{?}$	dub-sar: UET 2, Suppl., 2	Fara
Lugal-KA-sì-ga	dub-sar: UET 2, Suppl., 16	ED IIIb to Early Sargonic
Lugal-šùd-dé	dub-sar: UET 2, Suppl., 43; U 4382; 4393 ———: UET 2, Suppl., 36 (written Lú-šùd-dé)	ED IIIb (Šubur archive)
Lugal-šu-luḫ-kú-an-ne	dub-sar: UET 2, Suppl., 44; U 4388	ED IIIb (Šubur archive)
Ù-x	dub-sar: UET 2, Suppl., 2	Fara

TABLE 10

Scribes of Ur-^{d}Šára Archive of Umma

NAME	TEXTS
Gala	dub-sar: BIN 8, 287; USP 24; MAD 4, 104 ———: MAD 4, 72; 167
Me-zu	dub-sar: MAD 4, 21
Šà-da	dub-sar: MAD 4, 41
Ur-gidri	dub-sar: MAD 4, 74 ———: MAD 4, 167
Ur-^{d}Šára	dub-sar: MAD 4, 24; 61

TABLE 11

Scribes of Me-ság Archive

NAME	TEXTS
Ama-bára	dub-sar-maḫ: BIN 8, 123; 254; TLAT 42 dub-sar: BIN 8, 265 ———: BIN 8, 123; 182; 184; 192; 195; 200; NBC 5920
Da-da	dub-sar: BIN 8, 268; YBC 12139 ———: BIN 8, 136; 143; 148; 152; 183; 184; 193; 194; 196; 199; 204; 233; 236; 243; 266; 269; 276; 343
Dur$_8$-mu-pi$_5$	dub-sar: BIN 8, 274; 283; 284; 285 (sealings) ———: BIN 8, 118; 273; NBC 6947
Gala	dub-sar: BIN 8, 152 ———: BIN 8, 148; 182; 183; 194; 199; 243; 269; 276
Ìl-mu-da	dub-sar-maḫ: BIN 8, 195; 196; TLAT 33 ———: BIN 8, 203
Me-ság	dub-sar sa$_{12}$-du$_5$: YBC 12139
Ur-^{d}Al-la	dub-sar: BIN 8, 152 ———: BIN 8, 251
Ur-me-ga	dub-sar: BIN 8, 152; YBC 12139 ———: BIN 8, 165; 194
Ur-ù	dub-sar: BIN 8, 203

TABLE 12

Scribes of Classical Sargonic Umma

NAME	TEXTS
É$^{?}$-abzu	dub-sar: BIN 8, 303 ——: Nik II, 70; USP 46
En-ùri	dub-sar: MCS 9, 251 ——: CT 50, 188
Gu-gu-uz	dub-sar-lugal: USP 18
IŠ	dub-sar-sagi: CT 50, 58
Kar-dù	dub-sar: BIN 8, 306
Lugal-^{giš}gigir	dub-sar: BIN 8, 335; 340 ——: CT 50, 23; TLAT 28; USP 73
LUL-gu-ak	dub-sar: BIN 8, 190 ——: CT 50, 53; MCS 9, 236; 237; Nik II, 76; USP 22
Me-ság	dub-sar: USP 23
Na-id-maḫ-ra-áš/ Na-id-maḫ-ar-šum	dub-sar: MCS 9, 240 ——: MCS 9, 241; Serota 20; 25
Nam-zi	dub-sar: USP 53 ——: USP 47; 55
Pu-ḫa-lum	dub-sar: BIN 8, 190
Sipa-sa$_6$-ga	dub-sar: Serota 2
Šeš-šeš	dub-sar: USP 54 árad dub-sar-maḫ: TLAT 30 ——: MVN 3, 110; S. 378
Ur-gidri	dub-sar-maḫ: CT 50, 52; BIN 8, 335 dub-sar: BIN 8, 312 ——: CT 50, 188

Ur-giš	dub-sar: BIN 8, 307; 312 ——: BIN 8, 320; 338
Ur-^{d}Lamma	dub-sar: MCS 9, 266 ——: AAS 1; CST 10; 21
Ur-me-ga	dub-sar: BIN 8, 190; MCS 9, 266 maškim: USP 17; Ur-um-me-ga maškim: Nik II, 78; USP 27
[ ]	[dub]-sar: MM 021
unnamed	dub-sar-maḫ: MCS 9, 236; 238; Nik II, 76; TLAT 30; USP 22; 57
unnamed	dub-sar-maḫ-šabra-<é>: Serota 18
unnamed	dub-sar-gal: Serota 35
unnamed	dub-sar a-šà-gu$_4^?$: TLAT 33

TABLE 13

Scribes of Sargonic Girsu

NAME	TEXTS
A-bí-i-sar & I-sí-núm	dub-sar: RTC 169
A.DA.MU	dub-sar: L 2906
A-tu	dumu Ur-^{d}[x]: AOTb 198
Ab-ba	dub-sar: DCS 4, 45 ———: L 2979; 2823; 3094; 5738; CT 50, 143
Ad-⸢da⸣	dub-sar: RTC 164 (sealing)
Amar-su$_4$	dub-sar: L 5847 ———: L 2955
Amar-šùba	dub-sar: AOTb 258 ———: L 3113; 4503; CT 50, 110
Bar-ra-AN	dub-sar: RTC 81; AOTb 49 dub-sar dumu Lú-šu-maḫ: RTC 99 <dub-sar> dumu Ur-ì-lí AOTb 198 ———: L 1380; 1410; 3117; 5805; RTC 125; CT 50, 169; 182
Be-lí-ra-bí	dub-sar: L 3072
Be-lí-ti	dub-sar: RTC 175 (sealing) ———: RTC 127, 131
Da-ba-ba	dub-sar: CT 50, 84 (bulla)
Da-ti	dub-sar: RTC 176 (sealing) Ur-GAR dub-sar dumu Da-ti: L 5907 ———: L 1207; 3032; 5893; RTC 137; CT 50, 179; 180
Du-du	dub-sar URUxGÁNA*tenu*^{ki}: STTI 20 V 6'
Eden-bi-šè	dub-sar: RTC 80 V 5 ———: RTC 127

En-an-na-túm	dub-sar: L 4405 ——: L 4550; RTC 115; CT 50, 149
En-šeš	dub-sar: AOTb 199
Gal-zu-[ ]	dub-sar-lugal: RTC 142
GÌR	dumu Uru-nam-ma: AOTb 198 ——: L 2891
GÌR-dalla	dub-sar: L 1190
Ì-lí-iš	dub-sar: RTC 151
Ì-lí-iš-tá-kál	dub-sar: AOTb 206; 207 ——: L 1416; 4691; 9396
Íl-ga	dub-sar: RTC 143
Inim-ma-AN	dub-sar: RTC 98, 127; DCS 4, 44 (written Inim-ma) ——: L 1278; 4412; DCS 4, 31
KA.AN.[ ]	dumu Lugal-ezen: AOTb 198
Ka-tar	dub-sar: L 1095
Ki-tuš-ni	dub-sar: L 1095; 1380 v 1-2
LU-[x-x]	dub-sar: L 1094
Lú-^{d}Ab-ba$_{6}$	dub-sar: L 4976 ——: L 4641; RTC 102; 138
Lú-bàn-da	dub-sar: L 1040.11; 1368; 1429; 2915; 4420; 5885; RTC 81; 92; AOTb 30; 71 ——: L 2882; 2917; 4446; 574 8
Lú-da	[dumu X]: AOTb 198
Lú-^{d}Igi-ama-[šè]	[du]b-sar: AOTb 143 (perhaps Late or Post-Sargonic)
Lú-mar$^{?}$	dub-sar: L 5905 (bulla)
Lú-sa$_{6}$	dub-sar-maḫ: L 4590; dub-sar-maḫ Lagas^{ki}: CT 50, 123

TABLE 13

Lú-šè-zi	dumu Ur-SI.A: AOTb 198
Lú-^{d}Utu	dub-sar: L 1076$^{?}$; 1368; 3011; 4673; 5893$^{?}$; RTC 81; 134; AOTb 184 ugula <dub-sar>: AOTb 198 maškim: L 3050; 4457; 4548; 9281 ———: L 1113; 1283; 1357; 1374; 2856; 4375; 4562; 5817; CT 50, 158
Lú-zàḫ	dub-sar: L 4680; AOTb 248 dub-sar-maškim: L 9457 kurušda: L 3011; RTC 91 ———: L 1212; 2838; 2955; 4562; RTC 99; CT 50, 158
Lú-[x]	dub-sar: AOTb 249
Lú-[x]-da	dumu Lugal-ezen: AOTb 198
Lú-[x]-ezen-x	dumu Lugal-ezen: AOTb 198
Lugal-a-ma-ru	dub-sar: L 5807
Lugal-an-na-túm	dub-sar: AOTb 41 ———: L 4539; CT 50, 126
Lugal-bur	agrig: L 1095 ———: L 1125; 1476; 3032; 3098; 3139; 4421; 4443; 4462; 9441; CT 50, 100
Lugal-dub-sag-ki	dub-sar: L 4544
Lugal-GA[R-x$^{?}$]	dub-sar-lu[gal$^{?}$]: L 1474 ka-gur$_7$: CT 50, 187 ———: RTC 134; Foster, *VO* 6, 16
Lugal-ḫi-li	dub-sar: RTC 98
Lugal-iti-da	<dub-sar> dumu [x]: AOTb 198 ———: L 1158; 1364; 5848; 9317; RTC 103
Lugal-izi	dub-sar: L 5807; RTC 177$^{?}$
Lugal-lam	dub-sar: *AfO* 22, p. 14, 13.14
Lugal-su$_4$	dub-sar: AOTb 30

Lugal-un-ge$_{26}$	dub-sar: L 5893 ———: RTC 120
Lugal-UŠ$^?$	dub-sar: RTC 177
Lugal-ušum-gal	dub-sar éns[i] La[gaš^{ki}]: RTC 165; G. Shileico, *ZA* 29 (1914): 79
Me-a-na	dub-sar: L 5807
Me-ság-zu	dub-sar: RTC 98 maškim: L 3015
Mes-zi	dub-sar: L 3145
Na-bi-um	dub-sar: L 1077 šagina: L 1472; CT 50, 172 ———: L 5861; 9441
Nam-maḫ-<ni>	dub-sar: L 4676; L 7321; MCL 1224 dumu DA: AOTb 198 dumu Da-da <nu-bànda> L 1105; 1467 ———: L 1303; 1407; 3060; 3065; 4469; RTC 117
NÌGIN	dub-sar: L 2914 ———: L 2874; 2980; 4584; 4682; 5698; 5703; 5712; 5720; CT 50, 144; RTC 114
Nimgir-èš	dub-sar DI: CT 50, 172 ———: L 2867; 3051; 4422; 4519; 4690
Puzur$_4$-šuba	dub-sar: L 4548 ———: L 9271; CT 50, 147
Ri-im-Ḫa-ni-iš	dub-sar: RTC 122.6–7 ———: L 1371
Sar-ḫi-li	dub-sar: RTC 98
Sar-rí-iš-tá-kál	dub-sar: RTC 170 (sealing)
Si-da	dub-sar: RTC 126; 127
Si-DU	dub-sar: L 5893

TABLE 13

Šeš-šeš	dub-sar-maḫ: RTC 142; L 7333 <dub-sar> dumu sipa-lú: AOTb 198 énsi-gal: L 4489; 4514; 4590; 4701; 6680 ——: L 1476; 3027; 4401; 4420; 4423; 4467; 5676; CT 50, 100
Šu-ì-lí	dub-sar: L 1317 ——: L 2899; 5895
Šu-[ ]	dub-sar: L 1469
Túl-ta	dub-sar: L 1114; 3050; CT 50, 98; 124; PUL 6 agrig: RTC 96
Ú-da	dub-sar-maškim: L 2906 <dub-sar> dumu [x].NE šitim: AOTb 198 ——: L 1059; 5874
Ur-ba-ba	dub-sar: L 5807
Ur-ba-gára	dub-sar: AOTb 321 nu-bànda-é-gal: RTC 221-223 ——: L 1062; 1129; 1332; 1455; 2824; 3057; 4384; 4431; 4539; 5732; 5886; CT 50, 146; 147; 157; MVN 3, 47
Ur-da	dub-sar: RTC 173 (sealing)
Ur-^{d}En-ki	dub-sar: L 1183; 2911; CT 50, 168 ——: L 1114; 4423; 5848; PUL 23
Ur-GAR	dub-sar: PUL 23; RTC 127 Ur-GAR dub-sar dumu Da-ti: L 5907 (sealing) Ur-^{d}Lama dub-sar dumu Ur-GAR: L 10040 (sealing)
Ur-giš	<dub-sar> dumu Su-da: AOTb 198
Ur-ki	dub-sar: RTC 126; AOTb 238; 295
Ur-^{d}Lamma	Ur-^{d}Lama dub-sar dumu Ur-GAR: L 10040 (bulla)
Ur-^{d}Nin-dar	dub-sar: L 4437; 4586; 4679: (dumu dub-sar-ra-ke$_{4}$) ——: L 2876; 2912; 3144; 4443; RTC 126; CT 50, 101

Ur-^{d}Nin-gír-su	dub-sar: RTC 81 (dub-sar dumu Lugal-mu-n[ir$^{?}$]): RTC 127 sa$_{12}$-du$_{5}$: L 4553; 4673; 4695; 5893$^{?}$; 6692; RTC 142; 181 ——: L 1196; 4690
Ur-^{d}Nin-[ ]	dub-s[ar] L 1063
Ur-nu	dub-sar: RTC 82 maškim: L 3000; 4348; CT 50, 152 sanga: L 1125; 1135; 1150; 1157; 1253; 5892; RTC 114; CT 50, 88; 91; 108
Ur-šu	dub-[sar]: L 4703 šabra: L 4684 ——: L 1416; 4696; RTC 101
Ur-TAR	dub-sar-maḫ: L 3152 (lexical text) maškim: L 9181; 9271 ——: L 1229; 2834; 3051; 4519; 4690; CT 50, 166; 169
Ur-^{d}[x]	dub-sar: AOTb 198
Ur-[x]	<dub-sar> dumu Ú-da: AOTb 198
Úr-ra-AN	<dub-sar> dumu En-kù nagar: AOTb 198
[Uru]-ki	dub-sar: AOTb 321 ——: L 4360; 6682; RTC 91; 125; DCS 4, 32
UŠ	dub-sar: L 1380; 2912; 3129; 4417; 4584; 4625; 9365; RTC 120; 136; CT 50, 100; MCL 1136; DCS 4, 36; AOTb 258 maškim: L 4452; 5765 kurušda: L 1291; 4697; 5785 ——: L 1104; 1425; 3129; 4690; RTC 114
Za-ni-ni	dub-sar: AOTb 134
Zu-zu	dub-sar lu[gal$^{?}$]: RTC 127 v. IV 10–11
[x].AN	<dub-sar> dumu [X]: AOTb 198
[x].AN.[x]-na	<dub-sar> dumu [X]: AOTb 198
[x.x]-áš-ba-ak	dub-sar-maḫ: AOTb 184

[x]-da	<dub-sar> dumu [X]: AOTb 198
[ ]-^{giš}gigir	dub-sar: L 5893 IV 4'
[ ]-gu$_4$	dub-sar: STTI 182 II 5
[-^{d}]Nisaba	dub-sar: L 5893 IV 3'
[x]-zu	[dub]-sar: AOTb 321
[ ]	dub-sar: L. 2890; L 9457 (courtesy of Foster); AOTb 71; 75; 104; 184; 198; SRJ 30
unnamed	dub-sar-maḫ: L 1074; 1405; 1476; 3152; 3032; 4477; 4499; 4701; 5874; 5894; 6750; 9442; RTC 126; RTC 137 r. II 2; AOTb 230; 237; 238; 247; 249; 306 dub-sar: AOTb 91

TABLE 14

Scribes of Sargonic Adab

NAME	TEXTS
[A]-ba-an-da-sá	dub-sar: Ad 771 (sealing)
Amar-šùba	dub-sar: Ad 769 (bulla)
Du-du	dub-sar: A 530(sealing) unken-gal: A 529(sealing)
En-an-na-túm	———: A 646; 652; 692; 748; 802; 846; 938; 973; 994; 1015; 1100
En-líl	dub-sar: A 646; 674; 683; 707; 923; 944; 965; 1016 nu-èš: A 658; 751; 793; 825; 828 maškim: A 637 ———: A 640; 883; 981; 998; 1012
I-ku-bu-sa	dub-sar: A 662

Kir-ba-núm	dub-sar: A 917 (sealing)
Inim-ma	dub-sar: A 624; 707; 745; 816 nu-èš: A 714 maškim: A 684 ——: A 646; 690; 726; 865; 1002; 1021; 1026; 1113; X3
Iš-ku-un-^{d}Da-gan	dub-sar šabra-é: NBC 4142 (sealing) ——: AO 4419 (letter)
Lú-làl	dub-sar: A 726 ——: A 1209
Lugal-é	dub-sar: A 842; 991 ——: A 805; 844; 922; 1022; 1086
Lugal-èš	dub-sar énsi Adab^{ki}: (unpublished seals)
Lugal-giš	dub-sar énsi Adab^{ki}: Ad 767; 768 (sealings)
Lugal-iti-da	dub-sar: A 972 sukkal: A 712; 795 ——: A 677; 725; 772
Lugal-NI	n[u-èš] dub-sar: A 970 nu-èš: A 947
Lugal-šutur	——: A 982; 1033; 1037; 1078; 1896
Me-^{sá}sag$_{7}$ / ság	dub-sar: A 940 sagi: A 937; 978 ——: A 669; 777; 925; 938; 970
Nam-tar-ré	dub-sar sanga ^{d}En-ki: *ASJ* 14 pp. 103–23 (sealing) ——: A 661
Si-dù	dub-sar: A 672
Su-ni-DINGIR	dub-sar: A 661
UN-íl	dub-sar: A 624; 816; 1121; Ad 401 nu-èš: A 714 ——: A 637; 773; 802; 805; 862; 864; 919; 957; 968; 1014; 1045; 1082 é-UN-íl: A 897

TABLE 14

Ur-é-maḫ	dub-sar: A 721; 1008 ———: A 903; 933; 963; 984; 986
Ur-èš	dub-sar: (unpublished bulla)
Ur-mes	dub-sar: A 889 (sealing) ———: A 693; 893
Ur-NÌGIN	dub-sar: A 936 ———: A 707; 756; 972
Ur-zikum-ma	dub-sar: A 846 ———: A 699; 975
[ ]	dub-sar: A 813 (sealing); 1209 dub-sar Nibru^{ki}: A 726
unnamed	dub-sar-maḫ: A 784; 839; 969; 1010

TABLE 15*

Scribes of Sargonic Nippur

NAME	TEXTS	ARCHIVE DATE
Du$_{10}$-pù-URU.KI (Ṭap-pù-alim)	dub-sar: RIM 2, p. 178, n. 2021 (sealing)	AA$^{?}$ (Narām-Sîn)
Du$_{11}$-ga-ni	dub-sar: OSP 2, 134; 142; 149; 164 ———: OSP 2, 95-98; 100; 122	OA (Šar-kali-šarrī)
Du-du	dub-sar: OSP 2, 141 ———: OSP 84; 93, 96-97	OA (Šar-kali-šarrī)
En-eden-né	dub-sar: OSP 2, 46; 47; 50 ———: OSP 2, 54; 62; 63	EA (Narām-Sîn to Šar-kali-šarrī)
Gissu	dub-sar: ECTJ 34 cf. OSP 2, 69; 70	NRL (Narām-Sîn)
Inim-kù	dub-sar: OSP 2, 126; 128; 130; 152; 157; 167 dumu Ù-mu-ni-ni: OSP 2, 123; 155-156 ———: OSP 2, 80: 84; 93; 96-97; 140	OA (Šar-kali-šarrī)
Lugal-bàra	dub-sar: OSP 2, 44	EA$^{?}$ (Narām-Sîn to Šar-kali-šarrī)
Lugal-iti-da	dub-sar: CBS 7952	NRL (Narām-Sîn)
Lugal-sa$_{6}$	dub-sar: OSP 2, 126; 129; 179	OA (Šar-kali-šarrī)
Lugal-⌜x⌝	dub-sar: OSP 2, 182	OA (Šar-kali-šarrī)
Nam-tar-ré	dub-sar: OSP 2, 133 maškim: OSP 2, 132 sa$_{12}$-du$_{5}$: OSP 2, 126 ———: OSP 2, 80; 84; 94; 96–97; 129; 154	OA (Šar-kali-šarrī)

TABLE 15

Nita-<zi>	dub-sar: OSP 2, 147 ugula-é: OSP 2, 134; 138; 187 (seal)	OA (Šar-kali-šarrī)
Šu-<ì>-lí-su	dub-sar giš-kin-ti: OSP 2, 133; 140 ——: OSP 2, 141; 168	OA (Šar-kali-šarrī)
Ú-da-tum	dub-sar: OSP 2, 36 (sealing)	AA (Narām-Sîn)
[Ù-mu]-ni-ni	dub-sar: CBS 8272	NRL (Narām-Sîn)
Ur-^{d}Da-mu	dub-sar: OSP 2, 139; 154 sagi: OSP 2, 115; 123; 126	OA (Šar-kali-šarrī)
Ur-^{d}En-ki	dub-sar: OSP 2, 145 ——: OSP 2, 129; 134; 135$^{?}$	OA (Šar-kali-šarrī)
Ur-^{d}EN.ZU	dub-sar: OSP 2, 3 (sealing)	AA (Narām-Sîn)
Zà-mu	dub-sar: ECTJ 185	NRL (Narām-Sîn)
unnamed	dub-sar-maḫ: OSP 2, 136	OA (Šar-kali-šarrī)
[ ]	dub-sar: OSP 2, 152	OA (Šar-kali-šarrī)
[ ]	dub-sar: CBS 182+	NRL (Narām-Sîn)
[ ]	dub-sar: CBS 353+	NRL (Narām-Sîn)

* *AA=Akkadian Archive; EA=Enlilemaba Archive; NRL=Narām-Sîn Ration Lists; OA=Onion Archive*

TABLE 16

Scribes of Isin and Tell al-Wilaya

NAME	TEXTS	PROVENIENCE
Lugal-šùd	dub-sar: MAD 4, 150	Isin, Classical Sargonic
Me-šeš-šeš	dub-sar: MAD 4, 15	Isin, Classical Sargonic
Šà-ga-ni	dub-sar: MAD 4, 36	Isin, Early Sargonic
unnamed	dub-sar: BIN 8, 35	Isin, Early Sargonic
Šu-da-ti	dub-sar: *Sumer* 8, p. 87, n. 19	Tell Al Wilaya
Šu-eš$_4$-tár	um-mi-a: *Sumer* 8, p. 87, n. 17	Tell Al Wilaya
Šu-Ma-ma	dub-sar: *Sumer* 8, p. 87, n. 17	Tell Al Wilaya

TABLE 17

Scribes of Sargonic Kiš and Mugdan

NAME	TEXTS	PROVENIENCE
A-mur-DINGIR	dub-sar: MAD 5, 9 ——: MAD 5, 3; 10; 61	Kiš
DINGIR-a-mu	dub-sar: MAD 5, 45	Kiš
Lugal-iti-da	dub-sar: MAD 5, 31 ——: MAD 5, 108$^{?}$	Kiš
A-ḫi-ṭa-áb	dub-sar: MAD 5, 80	Mugdan
Be-lí-lí	agrig: MAD 5, 88 ——: MAD 5, 70; 86	Mugdan
Qí-nu-mu-pí	dub-sar: MAD 5, 69 énsi: BIN 8, 144; AIA 8	Mugdan
[x]-sag	dub-sar: TLAT 73	Mugdan

TABLE 18

Scribes of Sargonic Ešnunna

NAME	TEXTS
Be-lí	dub-sar: UCP 9/2, 89 ———: MAD 1, 80; 86
Da-ti	dub-sar: MAD 1, 319 šagina: MAD 1, 150 ———: MAD 1, 23; 102; 273; 284; 293
Dab$_4$-si-ga	dub-sar: MAD 1, 321; UCP 9/2, 83
I-da-pi$_5$-ì-li	ụm-mi-a: MAD 1, 336 ———: MAD 1, 72
I-sa-ru-um	dub-sar: MAD 1, 322 ———: MAD 1, 126; 332; 334; TLAT 51
Ìl-sù-GAR	dub-sar: NBC 10920
Lú-sa$_6$	dub-sar: NBC 10920
Pù-su-GI	dub-sar: MAD 1, 322 ———: MAD 1, 326; 334
Su-ru-ús-GI	dub-sar é-DINGIR: NBC 10920 ———: MAD 1, 149
Šu-ì-lí	dub-sar: Or 51, p. 362
Šu-Ma-ma	dub-sar tigi$_x$-di: NBC 10920 ———: MAD 1, 282; 290; 298
[ ]-ì-šum	dub-sar: NBC 10920

TABLE 19

Scribes in the Tell el-Suleimaḫ Archive

NAME	TEXTS
En-na-núm	dub-sar: A 1 ———: A 6
Im$_4$-ta-lik	dub-sar: A 1; A 7 ———: A 8; A 35
Pù-pù	dub-sar: A 33 ———: A 9; 35
Šu-ni-um	dub-sar: A 1; A 7
⌜x⌝-SAG/KA$^?$-a-ni	dub-sar: A 36

TABLE 20

Scribes of Sargonic Gasur

NAME	TEXTS
Da-ti	dub-sar: HSS 10, 160 ———: HSS 10, 55; 65; 107$^?$; 108; 155; 175
Ì-lí	dub-sar: HSS 10, 45; 47; 142 ———: HSS 10, 5; 6; 7; 10; 11; 15; 92; 93; 120; 144; 153; 154; 155
Ìl-su-dan	dub-sar-šabra-é: HSS 10, 205 ———: HSS 10, 71 (written *ilu-dan*)
Šu-ì-lí-su	dub-sar: HSS 10, 160 ———: HSS 10, 31; 35; 68; 104; 154; 155; 169; 173; 179; 193; 203
Ur-zu	dub-sar: HSS 10, 109 ———: HSS 10, 150

TABLE 21

Scribes Outside Any Archivial Context

NAME	TEXTS	PROVENIENCE	PERIOD
A-ḫu-GIŠ.ERÍN	su SU.ù.SAL dub-sar-aša$_5$: ELTS 41	Sippar (Sippar Stone)	Early$^?$ Sargonic
Á-zi	dub-sar: Collon, 1982, p. 100, n. 211	Ur (seal)	Sargonic
Amar-^{d}Sàman	dub-sar: TLAT 21	Girsu	Fara
Aš-tár-dan	dub-sar dumu Lugal-zi: *AfO* 22, p. 14, 14.2	unknown (sealing)	Sargonic
Be-lí	dumu KA-su ḫar-tu ^{d}Tišpak d[ub]-sar: *AfO* 22, p. 14, 14.1	unknown (sealing) (Ešnunna or Mugdan$^?$)	Sargonic
Be-lí-[x]-x	dub-sar: *AfO* 22, p. 14, 13.3	unknown (sealing)	Sargonic
Be-lí-ba-ni	agrig Da-ba$_4$-iš-da-gal: ELTS 40 C	Sippar$^?$ (Maništusu Obelisk)	Maništusu
Bu-na-um	dub-sar: *AfO* 22, p. 14, 13.4	unknown (sealing)	Sargonic
Da-da	I-ti-a-bum šabra-é Da-da dub-sar ìr-sú: Buch. 1981, 430	unknown (sealing)	Sargonic
Da-da	dub-sar Tar$^?$-iš-dan ir$_{11}$-sú: Collon 1982, p. 62, n. 112	unknown (seal)	Sargonic
Da-da-LUM	dub-sar: ELTS 40 A	Sippar$^?$ (Maništusu Obelisk)	Maništusu
Dingir-pa-è	dub-sar: BIN 8, 26	unknown	Lugalzagesi
Du-ba-ba	dub-sar: *AfO* 22, p. 14, 14.4	unknown (sealing)	Sargonic
Du-du	dub-sar: *AfO* 22, p. 14, 13.7	unknown (sealing)	Sargonic

TABLE 21

DUMU-ú-a	dub-sar dumu x.x: *AfO* 22, p. 14, 14.7	unknown (sealing)	Sargonic
En-ki-en-DU	dub-sar: *AfO* 22, p. 14, 13.8	unknown (sealing)	Sargonic
⌜ENGUR$^{?}$.AN$^{?}$. AN$^{?}$⌝	dub-sar ME: Buch. 1966, p. 224, n. 206	Kiš (sealing)	Early Sargonic
Gír-nun-né	dub-sar dumu NÌGIN: *AfO* 22, p. 14, 14.3	unknown (sealing)	Sargonic
Gìri-né	dub-sar: Collon, 1982, p. 55, n. 81	Babylon (seal)	Sargonic
Ḫu-bí-a	dub-sar-aša$_5$: ELTS 41	Sippar (Sippar Stone)	Early$^{?}$ Sargonic
I-bí-ì-lum	su MES.BAR^{ki} dub-sar: ELTS 40 B	Sippar$^{?}$ (Maništusu Obelisk)	Maništusu
I-ti-DINGIR dumu DINGIR.GÀR	dub-sar: ELTS 40 D	Sippar$^{?}$ (Maništusu Obelisk)	Maništusu
Ì-la-ak-nu-id	dub-sar dumu Iš-má-ilum: *AfO* 22, p. 14, 14.6	unknown (sealing) (Ešnunna$^{?}$)	Sargonic
Ì-la-la	dub-sar: TLAT 56	unknown	Sargonic
Ì-lí-aš-tár	dub-sar: *AfO* 22, p. 14, 13.9	unknown (sealing)	Sargonic
Ib-lu-DINGIR dumu NU-gal	dub-sar: ELTS 40 C	Sippar$^{?}$ (Maništusu Obelisk)	Maništusu
Ib-ni-DINGIR	dub-sar: RIM 2, p. 205, n. 2010	unknown (sealing)	Šar-kali-šarrī
Ib-ni-DINGIR	dub-sar dumu La-e-pum$_x$ *AfO* 22, p. 14, 14.5	unknown (sealing)	Sargonic
⌜Il⌝-gu-KU	dub-sar ganun: Buch. 1966, p. 223, n. 137	Kiš (sealing)	ED III
Il-ÙR.MA	agrig ganun-[zí]z: Buch. 1966, p. 223, n. 135	Kiš (sealing)	ED III

TABLE 21

Íl-su-dan	dub-sar dumu x.x: *AfO* 22, p. 14, 14.7	unknown (sealing)	Sargonic
Ilu-ṭāb	dub-sar: *AfO* 22, p. 14, 13.10	unknown (sealing)	Sargonic
Im$_4$-tá-lik dumu I-bí-ì-lum	su MES.BAR^{ki} dub-sar: ELTS 40 B	Sippar$^?$ (Maništusu Obelisk)	Maništusu
Iš-má-DINGIR dumu DINGIR.GÀR	dub-sar: ELTS 40 D	Sippar$^?$ (Maništusu Obelisk)	Maništusu
Ka-ba-ni-maḫ	um-mi-a: Mesopotamia 8, pp. 68ff.	Adab	Pre-Sargonic
Ka-kù	dub-sar: *AfO* 22, p. 14, 13.11	unknown (sealing)	Sargonic
Kal-ki	U-bil-aš-tár Šeš-lugal KAL.DI dub-sar ir$_{11}$-sú Collon, 1982, p. 73, n. 141	unknown (sealing)	Sargonic
Ku-ru-ub-^{d}Ašgi	dub-sar Um-mi-sí-ra-[bi] dam-sú: Collon, 1982, p. 69, n. 129	unknown (sealing) (Diyala region)	Sargonic
La-mu-sa	si agrig: ELTS 40 A	Sippar$^?$ (Maništusu Obelisk)	Maništusu
Lú-dingir-ra	Lú-dingir-ra-na sanga In^{ki} Lú-dingir-ra dub-sar ìr-[da]-ni Buch.1981, n. 423	Isin (sealing)	Sargonic
Lugal-an-né	dub-sar: *AfO* 22, p. 14, 13.12	unknown (sealing)	Sargonic
Lugal-gu$_4$	dub-sar: BIN 8, 26	unknown	Lugalzagesi
Lugal-ḫé-gál-sù	dub-sar-maḫ: ELTS 23	Girsu (Lummatur tablet)	Pre-Sargonic (Eannatum$^?$)
Lugal-kal-⌜a⌝	dub-sar: Collon, 1982, p. 66, n. 112	unknown (sealing)	Sargonic
Lugal-nam-mu-šub-bé	dub-sar lú-aša$_5$-[gíd-da]: ELTS 23	Girsu (Lummatur tablet)	Pre-Sargonic (Eannatum$^?$)

Lugal-sud-ág	dub-sar: *AfO* 22, p. 14, 13.15	unknown (sealing)	Sargonic
Lugal-šùd	dub-sar: *AfO* 22, p. 14, 13.16	unknown (sealing)	Sargonic
Lugal-šùd	Mad 4, 150	unknown	Narām-Sîn
Lugal-uru	dub-sar: Nik I, 318	Girsu	Entemena
Me-ba-šà$^{?}$-sù$^{?}$	dub-sar: Buch.1981, 418	Adab$^{?}$ (sealing)	Sargonic
MES$^{?}$.DUM.LUM	Puzur$_4$-^{d}UTU sanga BÀD^{ki} MES.DUM.LUM dub-sar ir$_{11}$-sú *AfO* 22, p. 16, 24.17	unknown (sealing)	Sargonic
Mes-zi	um-mi-a dub-sar: ELTS 40 A	Sippar$^{?}$ (Maništusu Obelisk)	Maništusu
Nì-gur$_{11}$-ra-ni	dub-sar: *AfO* 22, p. 14, 13.18	unknown (sealing)	Sargonic
NUN.KA	dub-sar: Buch.1981, 426	unknown (sealing)	Sargonic
PA$_4$-la-ḫi	dub-sar: *AfO* 22, p. 14, 13.19	unknown (sealing)	Sargonic
Puzur$_4$-è-a	dub-sar: CT 50, 72	Sippar$^{?}$ (Quradum Archive)	Classical Sargonic
Puzur$_4$-ì-<lí>	dub-sar: *AfO* 22, p. 14, 13.20	unknown (sealing)	Sargonic
Puzur$_4$-ru-um	dub-sar: *AfO* p. 17, 3.3	unknown (sealing)	Sargonic
Sag-gul-lum	dub-sar: Collon ed. Catologue, n. 114	BÀD^{ki}	Sargonic
Sipa-an-né	dub-sar: *AfO* 22, p. 14, 13.21	unknown (sealing)	Sargonic
Šà-TAR	dub-sar lú-aša$_5$[-gíd-da]: ELTS 23	Girsu (Lummatur tablet)	Pre-Sargonic (Eannatum$^{?}$)
Šar-ru-UR.SAG	dub-sar: *AfO* 22, p. 14, 13.22	unknown (sealing)	Sargonic

TABLE 21

⌜Šu⌝-ì-lí	dub-sar x-TAR: *AfO* 22, p. 14, 14.9	unknown (sealing)	Sargonic
Šu-ì-lí-su	dub-sar dumu IB-la-NE: *AfO* 22, p. 14, 14.10	unknown (sealing)	Sargonic
Tú-tá-lik	dub-sar dumu šu-i: *AfO* 22, p. 14, 14.13	unknown	Sargonic
Ù-ma-ni	um-mi-a Nibru^{ki}: *AfO* p. 17, 25.4	unknown (Nippur$^{?}$) (sealing)	Sargonic
Ur-ab-ra dumu Šu-mu-núm	dub-sar: ELTS 40 C	Sippar$^{?}$ (Maništusu Obelisk)	Maništusu
Ur-abzu	dub-sar: Collon, 1982, p. 41, n. 11	unknown (seal)	Sargonic
Úr-bi-šè	dub-sar: *AfO* 22, p. 14, 13.24	unknown (sealing)	Sargonic
Ur-^{d}Bìl-ga-mes	dub-sar dumu Ur-^{d}Sataran: *AfO* 22, p. 14, 14.14	unknown (sealing)	Sargonic
Ur-^{d}En-ki	agrig: ELTS 15	unknown (Isin$^{?}$) (Baltimore Stone)	Fara – Ur-Nanše
Ur-^{d}En-líl	dub-sar: ELTS 40 B	Sippar$^{?}$ (Maništusu Obelisk)	Maništusu
Ur-^{d}Ištaran	TLAT 58	unknown	Sargonic
Ur-^{d}NÁM$^{!}$.NUN	dub-sar: *AfO* 22, p. 14, 13.25	unknown (sealing)	Sargonic
Ur-èn	dub-sar: Buch.1981, 431	unknown (sealing)	Sargonic
Ur-iti-BU	dub-sar: Michail Coll. 29	unknown (Umma$^{?}$)	Sargonic
Ur-l[ú-x]	dub-sar: Buch.1981, 407	unknown (sealing)	Sargonic
Ur-mú	dub-sar: *AfO* 22, p. 14, 13.27	unknown (sealing)	Sargonic
Ur-nab	dub-sar: BIN 8, 26	unknown	Lugalzagesi

Ur-nìgin.GAR (nigar$_x^{gar}$; suggestion Bauer)	dub-sar dumu girì-ni gal$_5$-lá-gal: *AfO* 22, p. 14, 14.15	unknown (sealing)	Sargonic
Ur-nin-mug	dub-sar: Michail Coll. 11	unknown (Umma$^?$)	Sargonic
Ur-sa$_6$	TLAT 61	unknown	Late Sargonic
Ur-sa$_6$	dub-sar: *AfO* 22, p. 14, 13.26	unknown (sealing)	Sargonic
Ur-sa$_6$	Sar-a-dì-qù-bi-si-in dumu-lugal Ur-sa$_6$ dub-sar ir$_{11}$-sú: *AfO* 22, p. 16, 24.18	unknown (sealing)	Sargonic
UTU-il-la-at	dub-sar: Collon ì, 1982, p. 57, n. 90	unknown (seal)	Sargonic
Zà-ga-ni-ta	dub-sar: *AfO* 22, p. 14, 13.29	unknown (sealing)	Sargonic
Zu-zu	dub-sar su kurušda: ELTS 40 A	Sippar$^?$ (Maništusu Obelisk)	Maništusu
Zu-zu	dub-sar: *AfO* 22, p. 14, 13.30	unknown (sealing)	Sargonic
unnamed	dub-sar: Michail Coll. 13	unknown (Umma$^?$)	Sargonic
[x]-AN	dub-sar dumu Ì-lum-NI.TUK.ZU: Collon, 1982, p. 68, n. 126	unknown (seal)	Sargonic
[x]-ki-tuš-DU$_{10}$	[dub-s]ar: RIM 2, p. 39, n. 2005	Ur (sealing)	Sargon

INDEX OF SELECTED TERMS

Akkadian

alākum 104[24]
barû 103[18]
bēlū BAR.E 223
bēlū parsāti 140
buršuma 39, 45, 49
ibissû 149[193]
iškinû 209[466]
kassāru 229[540]
latākum 227
nādinu 30[69]
nisku 180[334]
nukkusu 104[21]
redûm 227
situm 227
ṣāriḫtum, ṣirḫum 221[517]
ṣātum 108
šadādum 219
šadīum 182[338]
šupêltu/ šapûltu 219[509]
tabālum/ wabālum 131
warûm/ tarûm 207[459]
zagāru 208

Sumerian

a-GAR 107[32]
a-tag 184[346]
á-RU 136[137]
ab-gi-né 196[393]
apin-lá-e íb-ur$_4$ 137
aša$_5$ nu-tuku 108
aša$_5$ SU.A/SU.LÁ 91
aša$_5$ SU$_7$/šub-šub-ba 156[226]
aza$_x$ 147, 148
da-bulug^{ninda} 182[339]
DU (opposite of dab$_5$) 155[220]
DU (mu-DU) 160
DU (nu-mu-gub) 138[143]
du-ni 109[43]
dub-sar anše sa$_{12}$-du$_5$ 33
dub-sar <é->giš-kin-ti 200
dub-sar énsi 64
dub-sar-gal 122
dub-sar kurušda 61[168]
dub-sar kuš$_7$ 22
dub-sar-maḫ ^{d}Nin-gír-su 75, 78[243]
dub-sar maškim 25[53]
dub-sar na-gada ^{d}Sùd 37
dub-sar nu-kiri$_6$ 84[267]
dub-sar sagi 114
dub-sar-sanga-GAR 29, 32, 44ff.
dub-sar tigi$_x$-di 31; 221
dub-sar udu 39, 43, 49
dub-ZU:ZU-sar 17[15]
dumu 2[5]
dumu-di$_4$-di$_4$-la-ne 59[157]
dumu énsi 76[232]
dusu é-ad-da 195